Evolutionary and Neo-Schumpeterian Approaches to Economics

Recent Economic Thought Series

Editor:

Warren G. Samuels
Michigan State University
East Lansing, Michigan, U.S.A.

Other books in the series:

Feiwel, G., *Samuelson and neoclassical economics*
Wade, L., *Political Economy: Modern Views*
Jarsulic, M., *Money and Macro Policy*
Samuelson, L., *Microeconomic Theory*
Mirowski, P., *The Reconstruction of Economic Theory*
Lowry, Todd, *Pre-Classical Political Economy*
Officer, L., *International Economics*
Asimakopulos, A., *Theories of Income Distribution*
Earl, P., *Psychological Economics; Development, Tensions, Prospects*
Thweatt, W., *Classical Political Economy*
Peterson, W., *Market Power and the Economy*
DeGregori, T., *Development Economics*
Nowotny, K., *Public Utility Regulation*
Horowitz, I., *Organization and Decision Theory*
Hennings, K. and Samuels, W., *Neoclassical Economic Theory, 1870 to 1930*
Samuels, W., *Economics as Discourse*
Lutz, M., *Social Economics*
Weimer, D., *Policy Analysis and Economics*
Bromley, D. and Segerson, K., *The Social Response to Environmental Risk*
Roberts, B. and Feiner, S., *Radical Economics*
Mercuro, N., *Taking Property and Just Compensation*
de Marchi, N., *Post-Popperian Methodology of Economics*
Gapinski, J., *The Economics of Saving*
Darity, W., *Labor Economics: Problems in Analyzing Labor Markets*
Caldwell, B. and Boehm, S., *Austrian Economics: Tensions and Directions*
Tool, Marc R., *Institutional Economics: Theory, Method, Policy*
Babe, Robert E., *Information and Communication in Economics*
Magnusson, Lars, *Mercantilist Economics*
Garston, Neil, Bureaucracy: *Three Paradigms*
Friedman, James W., *Problems of Coordination in Economic Activity*

Evolutionary and Neo-Schumpeterian Approaches to Economics

edited by
Lars Magnusson
Uppsala University

Kluwer Academic Publishers
Boston / Dordrecht / London

Distributors for North America:
Kluwer Academic Publishers
101 Philip Drive
Assinippi Park
Norwell, Massachusetts 02061 USA

Distributors for all other countries:
Kluwer Academic Publishers Group
Distribution Centre
Post Office Box 322
3300 AH Dordrecht, THE NETHERLANDS

Library of Congress Cataloging-in-Publication Data

Evolutionary and neo-Schumpeterian approaches to economics /
edited by Lars Magnusson.
p. cm.—(Recent economic thought series)
Includes index.
ISBN 0-7923-9385-6
1. Evolutionary economics. 2. Schumpeter, Joseph Alois,
1883–1950—Contributions in economics. I. Magnusson, Lars.
II. Series.
HB97.3.E92 1993 93-5059
330.1—dc20 CIP

Printed on acid-free paper.

Printed in the United States of America

Contents

Evolutionary and Neo-Schumpeterian Approaches to Economics

1 THE NEO-SCHUMPETERIAN AND EVOLUTIONARY APPROACH TO ECONOMICS—AN INTRODUCTION

Lars Magnusson

This volume brings forth attempts to discuss the interrelationships and possible connecting threads between two recent attempts within economic theory to step out of the strait jacket of conventional neoclassical wisdom: evolutionary and neo-Schumpeterian theory. How these approaches should be understood and defined is open to contest, as will become clear for the reader of this volume. Moreover, it is not unusal that these terms are used interchangeably. Thus Richard Nelson and Sidney Winter, in their seminal *An Evolutionary Theory of Economic Change* (1982), which more than any other single work triggered off a modern discussion around these issues, emphasized "Indeed, the term "neo-Schumpeterian" would be as appropriate a designation for our entire approach as evolutionary" (Nelson and Winter, 1982, p. 39).

However, it might, of course, be argued that Joseph Schumpeter might not have accepted being looked upon as an evolutionary theorist. First, in contrast to, for example, Veblen, he was explicitly turned against any reference to Darwinian natural selection as an appropriate tool for understanding economic development and change. Additionally he was not concerned with any discussion of why and for what reason certain firms are more able to innovate than others; that is, to what extent firm-specific "routines" (to use the concept of Nelson and Winter) might be used in this context and perhaps also inherited over time. Moreover, it might be argued that his theory of invention is more revolutionary than evolutionary in spirit. Thus in *Business Cycles* Schumpeter (1939) defined *economic evolution* in a very broad fashion: "The changes in the economic process brought about by innovation together with all their effects, and the response to them by the economic system ..." (Schumpeter, 1939, p. 86).

Whether or not we regard Schumpeter as an evolutionary theorist, in the foregoing short statement we can already grasp the essence of where he departs from the neoclassical approach to economics. Hence the *Schumpeterian approach*, according to Giovanni Dosi (1990), is characterized first by its urge "to look at change" rather than to take equilibrium as the "natural" starting point. Secondly, it takes for granted that "history counts", that is, it stresses the importance of the emergence, change, and death of social institutions in time-space for any kind of economic behavior. Thirdly, it is characterized by a "lower methodological emphasis" on the rational maximizing behavior of the individual. Rather, it stresses what in the tradition of Simon and others has been designated as *bounded rationality*. Thus it tends to put more emphasis on the environmental, institutional, and social restrictions that condition neoclassical rational behavior in real historical time (Dosi, 1990, pp. 335ff).

Schumpeter's theory of economic change pinpointing the role of innovations and the entreprenuer was outlined in *The theory of Economic Development* (1911), and is well known. In stark contrast to the neoclassical tradition, Schumpeter treats innovational activity as an internal factor in economic change. The individuals who carry out innovations are the entreprenuers who are stimulated by the possibility of reaping a temporary surplus profit (the Marshallian quasirent) from being "a first mover"—a profit that "... will vanish in the subsequent process of competition and adaption" (Schumpeter, 1939, p. 105). However, his "pure" analysis of economic dynamics, which pertains to how business cycles are created by clusters of innovational activity, is not carried out in a void. Thus, as has been pointed out several times—most lately by Richard Swedberg—although Schumpeter was highly critical of confounding "economic" theory with "economic history" or "sociolology" his lasting influence on modern scholars is largely due to his focus on social institutions and the role he believed they play in economic development processes (Swedberg, 1991). Most famous in this context is the analysis of growth and stagnation that he carried out in Capitalism, Socialism and Democracy (1942). Most certainly, in this text he did more than just to emphasise that "capitalism is not gentle to the capitalists" (Schumpeter, 1991). Thus, by instead portraying the conflict between entreprenuerial activity and the sociology of the modern state, he came quite close to the analysis carried out by Thorstein Veblen some decades earlier, who emphasized the conflict between progressive technology and the institutions of a contemporary "predatory dynastic State of early modern times, superficially altered by a suffusion of democratic and parliamentary institutions" (Veblen, 1964, p. 398).

Modern neo-Schumpeterian approaches have continued to build on this groundwork provided by their master. During recent years there has been a great upsurge of discussion on technology, innovations, technological regimes, etc. from the dynamic perspective provided by Schumpeter (Dosi, 1984, Rosegger, 1985; Dosi et al., 1988). Thus the search process for (temporal) extra profits has been stressed and has been used for modelling attempts. The wider institutional framework for technological change and innovation activity has also been strongly developed more recently. Hence emphasis has grown in the study of technological and industrial regimes, path dependency, and the network approach, developed recently, that social relationships structure the opportunities and constraints that face firms and agents that, for example, carry out innovations (Snehota, 1990).

Central to Schumpeter's vision of the capitalist economy is the notion of the dynamics of the market process. Thus, he cuvisions the market as something more than a signaling device for the allocation of scarce resources that serve to guarantee a state of equilibrium. Rather, the market is a sphere of radical change that pushes firms and agents to innovate, and the economy to grow and change structurally. Schumpeterian competition is thus the realm of "creative destruction" in which firms grow, survive, or die. Firms that are able to innovate or adapt will grow or survive, while others will be superceded and dethroned. Thus the search for extra profits is metered out in a competetive environment that, at the same time, is an open-ended process of change and transformation.

The view of the role of the competetive process held by Schumpeter and the modern neo-Schumpeterians is shared with economists who explicitly regard themselves as evolutionary. As Nelson and Winter, Langlois, Kirzner, and others have emphasized, this can, to some extent, be regarded as a return to Adam Smith and the classical tradition of political economy (Langlois, 1989, p. 10; Kirzner, 1982). Moreover, this vision is strongly emphasized in the modern Austrian approach developed by Hayek, Mises, Kirzner, and others. According to the Austrians, as well as the group that Littlechild has named the *radical subjectivists* which includes Shackle and Lachman (Littlechild, 1989, p. 29), economic agents are uncertain, ignorant, and indeterminate of future states when they make their (economic) decisions. In this world of parametric as well as structural uncertainty, only those firms that are the fittest, that is, are able to adapt to a changing environment, will survive.

This is also the point of departure for Nelson and Winter's plea for an evolutionary approach to macroeconomic growth theory, which builds on micro growth processes on the individual firm level (Nelson and Winter, 1982). They point out that the economy is dynamic in character, and dynamic processes are, according to them, inherently uncertain with regard to their outcomes. This makes it impossible for a firm to approach decision making with the intention of maximizing some static function. Instead, as is well known, Nelson and Winter depict a firm's "regular and predictable" behavior as "routines" that they see playing the same function for the business enterprise as genes do for the biological organism (Nelson and Winter, 1982, pp. 14ff) Thus decision making on the firm level is, to a large extent, caused by routines that are really the result of learning processes over time. Since such "routines" are used in the daily practice of the business firm, they are apt to undergo change. Nelson and Winter (1982, p. 16) have pointed out that the characteristics of prevailing routines may be understood by reference to the evolutionary process that has moulded them." Also included in their model is the crucial importance of a market process of neo-Austrian stance. Over time firms that are equipped with routines that are most adaptive to market and environmental change survive and grow while others are discareded. In other words, they are able to employ search activities that will make them more profitable. Thus the actual market structure is a two-sided affair. On the one hand, it is created by individual firms that compete in order to gain an extra profit from innovations in a broad sense. On the other hand, it structures the environment in which these firms live and compete.

It is clear that the Schumpeterian and evolutionary theories that we have depicted so far seem to rely on a notion of the survival of the fittest, which stems directly or indirectly from Lamark, Darwin, and Malthus.[1] In Veblen's plea for a biologically informed evolutionary economics, the reference to Darwin is made explicit in his "Why is Economics not an Evolutionary Science" (1898), the same can also be said of Marshall (see Chapter 2). Moreover, in the 1940s and 1950s the survival-of-the-fittest argument was used to defend neoclassicism by Armen Alchian and Milton Friedman as a means of arguing for instrumentalism. The general argument put forward by Alchian and Friedman is well known: We can safely infer that whatever the strategy and motive might be for a singular firm, the competetive process will ensure that "as if" maximizing behavior occur. Only by practicing such behavior is an individual firm able to survive.

During recent years the question of whether or not Alchian's and Friedman's approach is really Darwinian has been discussed at length. Thus Sidney Winter (1964; cf. Hodgson, 1989, pp. 140ff) has argued that procreation and adaptability over time are crucial in any form of biological evolution. In a given population of firms, perhaps the "best" or most fit survive. However, he argued, no mechanism how such "fit" behavior is passed on and inherited by other firms over time is specified by Friedman and Alchian. Furthermore, as Ramstad argues in Chapter 4, to what extent Winter and Nelson really provide us with a theory of the economic change "analogous to the natural selection of genotypes" (Nelson and Winter, 1982, p. 17) is also open to argument. However, their strong insistence on search and selection processes over time, and trial and error, on the individual firm level might, in a *metaphorical* sense, lend itself to evolutionary natural selection theory. However, in the dynamic and fast-changing world, that confronts the search and selection process, the analogy seems closer to the part of Darwin's theory that deals with mutations, or perhaps with Lamarckian theory, instead of the gradual and long-run selection and survival of the fittest. A further problem is understanding how and in what social context "routines" are shaped and the actual mechanisms by which they may give rise to (competitive) best solutions. Lastly, as will be discussed later, the natural selection view of the market process relies on a certain vision of the market process that is not indisputable.

However, as has been emphasized, neo-Schumpeterian and evolutionary approaches to economics imply a challenge to conventional neoclassical orthodoxy. They have already provided new insights into how markets function, how innovations are carried out, how technologies change, and how growth occurs in existing real economies. Thus there are mainly two fields of theory and research in which these approaches have proved to be especially fruitful: the role of innovation in economic change and development, and the theory of the firm. Moreover, the wide range of topics dealt with in this volume provide further proof of the versatility and utility of these approaches. Certainly, the extent to which evolutionary and neo-Schumpeterian economics can be combined is still an open question. More or less explicitly, this theme is dealt with in several of the contributions found in this volume. However, a key element that binds these two strands of thought together is the notion that competetion for resources, such as innovations and "knowledge" (in Arrow's sense), is crucial for an understanding of modern capitalist economy, that agents operate under conditions of "radical," "paradigmatic," and/or "structural" uncertainty; and that an agent's economic behavior is better understood as being part of a learning process over time than as a static function of mere maximization.

As already indicated, the market process is of key importance for both evolutionary and neo Schumpeterian economists. In this volume several authors bring up the crucial issue of how the "market process" should be defined and understood. Further elaboration on this theme is without doubt very important for developing a more viable and dynamic challenge to the neoclassical orthodoxy. Moreover, our understanding of the market and the competetive process has important theoretical and policy implications.

Hence, in the present discussion of evolutionary and neo-Schumpeterian theory, two different views seem to be pertinent: One that closely follows Hayek and von Mises tends to look upon the market process as a realm of "brute force"—to use Ramstad's description in this volume. Agent's face markets as a pure "environment" to which they must adapt or die. In the long run survival of the fittest occurs, and this process of natural selection is really the invisible hand in the vocabulary of Smithian economics. In this struggle for survival, agents are more ignorant than uncertain (Littlechild, 1989, p. 28). Market structure is something that evolves as part of this blind competetive process, rather than the reverse (Langlois, 1989, p. 15).

However, there is another line of thought that instead emphasizes that the market must be regarded as a social institution made up by norms and behaviors that have evolved over time. Thus, according to this institutionalist view, the market structure is a force that actively shapes the competitive process rather than just being a blind outcome of the same process. Morever, the market is the result of social evolution and is materialized both in a judicial systems of property rights, etc. as well as in our cognitive structure. This also means that the institutions of the market, or transactions, can not be separated from value or even moral judgments. Thus the market process is part of a system of social property right that has its own ways of defining cultural and moral institutions such as "trust," "fairness," etc., as well as of defining what is believed to be "external" and "internal" to the market and economic process as such (for example, with regard to the environment, see Chapter 11). In short, the market process cannot be regarded as a "brute environment" standing outside our culturally achieved norms, which are "the lens through which we see the world," as the anthropologist Ruth Benedict once suggested. Hence, by necessity, what happens in the marketplace cannot be understood outside of context, which also involves a conscious evaluation process carried out by purposeful human agents.

The market can thus be regarded as more than brute environment, as an institution made up by social norms, behaviors, judicial procedures, and values. On Chapter 4 Ramstad suggests that John Commons' institutional theory of transaction—according to which a transaction always includes a "fifth" partaker, which might be defined as the collective or society (Commons, 1964, pp. 65ff)—as well as his theory of collective power—might form a point of departure for such an institutional view of the market process. However, the line originating from the anthropologist, economist, and economic historian Karl Polanyi is also of importance in such a context. In his famous study, *The Great Transformation* (1944), Polanyi particularly emphasized how the seemingly free laissez-faire market of the 19th century in reality was a complex social institution created to respond to the social and economic upheavals of the first industrial revolution. To some extent this vision of the market was already acknowledged by Adam Smith. Far from holding to a simplistic Cobdenite position, Smith explicitly made it clear that the "invisible hand" notoriously relied on a virtuous and civic legislator (Winch, 1978; Haakonsen, 1981).

However, most important in this context is acknowledging that such interpretations of the market and the market process imply far reaching consequences, which differ starkly from a Darwinian notion of the survival of the fittest. Ramstad suggests in Chapter 4 one way to dig further into this problem. Certainly, there may also be other ways to proceed. However, it is clear, that further elaboration of a theory of the market process is crucial for the development of evolutionary and neo-Schumpeterian theory in the future. Secondly, we must also acknowledge that the path chosen has serious theoretical as well as political implications, the last certainly being crucial for the future of economics if regarded as a dynamic social science.

Note

1. For interesting new information on the relationship between Malthus and Darwin, see Desmond and Moore (1992, pp. 272ff, etc.).

References

Desmod, A., and Moore, J. 1992. *Darwin*. London: Penguin, 1992.

Dosi, G. 1984. *Technical Change and Industrial Transformation*. London: MacMillan.

Dosi, G. 1990. "Economic Change and its Interpretation, or Is There a "Schumpeterian Approach?" In *Evolving Technology and Market Structure*. A. Heertje, and M. Perlman, eds. Ann Arbor: University of Michigan Press.

Dosi, G., Freeman, C., Nelson, R., Silverberg, G., and Soete, L. eds. 1988. *Technical Change and Economic Theory*. London: Pinter Press.

Haakonsen, K. 1981. *The Science of a Legislator*. Cambridge, UK: Cambridge University Press.

Hodgson, G. 1988. *Economics and Institutions*. Cambridge, UK: Polity Press.

Kirzner, I.M. (ed.). 1982. *Method, Process and Austrian Economics: Essays in Honor of Ludwig von Mises*. Lexington, MA: D.C. Heath.

Langlois, R. 1989. "The New Institutional Economics." In *Economics as a Process*. R. Langlois, ed. New York: Cambridge University Press.

Littlechild, S.C. 1989. "Three Types of Market Process." In *Economics as a Process*. R. Langlois, ed. New York: Cambridge University Press.

Nelson, R., and Winter, S. 1982. *An Evolutionary Theory of Economic Change*. Cambridge: Harvard University Press.

Polanyi, K. 1944. *The Great Transformation*. New York: Henry Holt.

Rosegger, G. 1985. *The Economics of Production and Innovation*. Oxford: Oxford University Press.

Schumpeter, J.A. 1934. The Theory of Economic Development. Cambridge: Harvard University Press.

Schumpeter, J.A. 1939. *Business Cycles*, I. New York: McGraw Hill.

Schumpeter, J.A. 1950. Capitalism, Socialism and Democracy. New York: Harper and Row.

Schumpeter, J.A. 1991. "An Economic Interpretation of Our Time" [1941]. In *The Economics and Sociology of Capitalism*. J.A. Schumpeter, ed. Princeton: Princeton University Press.

Snehota, I. 1990. "Notes on a Theory of Business Enterprise" Dissertation. Uppsala.

Swedberg, R. 1991. "Introduction." In *The Economics and Sociology of Capitalism*. J.A. Schumpeter, ed. Princeton: Princeton University Press.

Veblen, T. 1964 (1924). *Absentee Ownership and Business Enterprise in Recent Times*. New York: Augustus M. Kelley.

Veblen, T. 1966. What Veblen Faught, (ed. W. Mitchell) New York: Augustus M. Kelley.

Winch, D. 1978. *Adam Smith's Politics*. Cambridge, UK: Cambridge University Press.

Winter, S. 1964. "Economic Natural Selection and the Theory of the Firm." Yale Economic Essays, 4.

I EVOLUTIONARY THEORY

2 WHAT IS EVOLUTIONARY ECONOMICS?

Richard N. Langlois
Michael J. Everett

Introduction

All evolution is concerned with the growth of knowledge, a proposition no less true in economic systems (and society in general) than in biological ones. As the philosopher Elliott Sober (1984) notes, evolutionary theory is a theory of forces, that is, a theory of the causes of change, of the processes that produce a certain sequence of events and entities. Hayek (1945, p. 523) proposed that "economic problems arise always and only in consequence of change." This implies that evolutionary theory is one way of studying economic problems. What is the evolutionary explanation in economics? How does it differ from the orthodox, that is, the neoclassical, explanation? The essay is an attempt to answer these questions by looking at the history and present state of evolutionary thinking in economics.

The essence of the evolutionary explanation in economics lies in the variation exhibited by cultural artifacts.[1] That evolution, at least by selection processes, cannot occur without variation seems to be an almost self-evident proposition.[2] In fact, Darwin devotes three of the first five chapters of *The Origin of Species* to the role of variation. Alfred Marshall (1982, p. 295) appropriated this theme to economics, asserting that "the tendency to variation is a chief cause of progress." Variation, however, is not sufficient for evolution by a selection process. The differences that arise among individuals in populations must also heritable.[3] There must exist a mechanism to transmit the variation to offspring. Institutions and routines—which we more broadly call *rules*—perform this function in economic evolution: Rules are "reproduced" as economic actors imitate or borrow knowledge from others. Institutions are, after all, stored knowledge ready and waiting for individuals to adopt.

The History of Evolutionary Economics

The Scottish Enlightenment and Spontaneous Order

Darwin is usually recognized as having proposed natural selection as a novel *kind* of explanation (Sober, 1984b, p. 135), that is, an explanation of the diverse nature of populations by the selection, because of differential fitness, of inheritable variations among individuals. But it was arguably the Scottish moral philosophers of the 18th century who invented such reasoning well before Darwin formulated his ideas.[4] Indeed there is some argument that Darwin borrowed and applied the logic of the Scottish philosophers (and other political economists, such as McCulloch and Malthus) to the biological realm.[5]

Adam Smith and the philosophers of the Scottish Enlightenment accomplished no less a feat than introducing to the world the theory of spontaneous orders.[6] The theory of spontaneous orders explains how complex social patterns arise and function, not because there was any human design, but because of the unintended consequences of many individuals pursuing their own aims. It is as if an invisible hand were coordinating the interaction of many people, devising the rules, and rationally constructing coherent institutions. The chief representatives of the Scottish Enlightenment—David Hume, Adam Smith, Adam Ferguson, Lord Kames, and Thomas Reid—all echoed the same message, whether explaining the origin or continuation of the state, the market, or morals: Coherent, that is, functional, social orders are the results of human action but not of human design.

Invisible-hand explanations have received critical examination in Edna Ullmann-Margalit's (1978) important essay. It is usually thought that invisible-hand explanations are not to be confused with those that explain the "unanticipated consequences of purposive social action."[7] In fact, Ullmann-Margalit distinguishes between two invisible-hand type explanations: the aggregate mold and the functional mold. Aggregate-mold explanations are concerned with the *origins* of complex social patterns understood as the unintended results of individual human action. By contrast, functional-mold explanations are concerned not with the origin but with the function or continued existence of the social pattern. The former asks the question "how?" while the latter asks "why?" The functional explanation (which Ullmann-Margalit identifies with evolutionary explanations) does not attempt to explain causes, which, indeed, can be entirely intentional and conscious or entirely blind, but rather the *maintenance* of the social pattern "as a spontaneously formed order to account for its existence subject to the assumption that there is no outside intervention by any designing agency" (Ullmann-Margalit, 1978, p. 283). Depending on the *explanandum*, we thus have two means of providing an invisible hand explanation.[8]

The Scottish philosophers argued that many institutions fit both the aggregate and the functional molds; in fact, they largely saw them as being necessarily one and the same. David Hume discussed the origin and function of justice and law in his *Treatise on Human Nature*, telling stories of both how and why "the three fundamental laws of nature, that of the stability of possession, of its transference by consent, and of the performance of promises," arise and function (Hume, 1992, p. 526). Hume argued that justice arises and functions, not because of an intelligent being(s) capable of creating and maintaining this complex social pattern, but as the unanticipated consequence of individuals pursuing their own interests. Hume applied an evolutionary theory of the growth of knowledge to individuals in any situation, including the construction of relatively simple objects.

> Were this world ever so perfect a production it must still remain uncertain, whether all the excellencies of the work can justly be ascribed to the workman. If we survey a ship, what an exalted idea must we form of the ingenuity of the carpenter, who framed so complicated, useful, and beautiful a machine? And what surprise must we entertain, when we find him a stupid mechanic, who imitated others, and copied an art, which, through a long succession of ages, after multiplied trials, mistakes, corrections, deliberations, and controversies, had been gradually improving? Many worlds might have been botched and bungled, throughout an eternity, ere this system was struck out: Much labour lost: Many fruitless trials made: And a slow, but continued improvement carried on during infinite ages in the art of world-making. (Hume, 1980, p. 36)

Adam Smith articulated the theory of spontaneous orders in both *The Wealth of Nations* and *The Theory of Moral Sentiments*. In the former, economic phenomena are the more important considerations; in the latter, ethics and jurisprudence; but the works are best considered as a integrated whole enveloping Smith's general philosophical position on social life, what Heilbroner (1986) sneeringly calls "the wonderful world of Adam Smith."

The Austrian Tradition

Neither Marshall nor any of his Scots or English contemporaries extended the Scottish philosophers' notion of spontaneous order. Instead, the heir apparent was an Austrian, Carl Menger. Like Darwin, Menger wished to dismantle the idea that organisms (social ones for Menger) had to be the product of design because they seemed too good, too beneficial, or too intricate to have arisen any other way. "Natural organisms almost without exception exhibit," Menger writes, "when closely observed, a functionality of all parts with respect to the whole, a functionality which is not, however, the result of *human* calculation, but of a *natural* process. Similarly we can observe in numerous social institutions a strikingly apparent functionality with respect to the whole. But with closer consideration they still do not prove to be the result of an *intention aimed at this purpose* . . . They too present themselves to us as 'natural' products (in a certain sense) as *unintended results of historical development*" (Menger, 1963, p. 130). Menger explained that even such institutions as the law arise through individual interaction and not necessarily by overarching human design.

In pursuing the theme of institutions as the unintended results of human action (but not of human design), Menger was following self-consciously in the tradition of Smith. Menger distinguished those institutions arising from human action but not design, which he called *organic*, from those that arise "from the intentions, opinions, and available instrumentalities of human social unions or their rulers" (Menger, 1963, p. 145). He designated institutions arising from the latter process as *pragmatic*. But institutions emanating from the latter process are indeed of slight importance in economics. "Language, religion, law, even the state itself, and to mention a few economic social phenomena, the phenomena of markets, of competition, of money, and numerous other social structures" (p. 149), cannot be satisfactorily explained with reference to the pragmatic origin. Menger proposes that "the most noteworthy problem of the social sciences" is to answer the following question: "*How can it be that institutions which serve the common welfare and are extremely significant for its development come into being [and change] without a common will directed toward establishing them?*" (Menger, 1963, p. 149 emphasis original). The pragmatic approach to social institutions, Menger argues, is simply ahistorical, and a theory of social phenomena must be grounded in history, just as natural historians—Darwin foremost—insisted on examining nature's record.

Money is Menger's exemplar of an organic social institution. Money as a medium of exchange evolved because as traders sought to reduce transaction costs, they eventually came to accept those commodities that were highly valuable and highly marketable. Explaining the origin of money as such does not require an assumption of conscious collective action; rather, an assumption of individualistic pursuits is sufficient. Individuals gradually become aware that certain commodities are better as media of exchange that others. As one or a few come to dominance, individuals recognize that common acceptance establishes the criterion of which commodity they prefer. Consider how money evolved in a prisoner of war camp (Radford, 1945). Cigarettes eventually came to be generally accepted because they were valuable and easily marketable. Even when a restaurant and a food shop at the camp made a conscious effort to establish a paper currency, the value of cigarettes continued to determine the value of the paper currency.

Menger's approach has animated the more recent work of his intellectual descendent F.A. Hayek, whose theory of cultural evolution is even more self-consciously evolutionary. Hayek's theory begins with the conception of rationality, which he prefers to see not as Cartesian conscious deduction from known premises, but as the product of evolution and selection itself. "Mind," says Hayek (1988, p. 21), "is not a guide but a product of evolution, and is based more on imitation than on insight or reason . . . Our reason is as much the result of an evolutionary selection process as is our morality." The mind develops as individuals explore, discover, learn, and imitate rules of behavior and action, thereby acting as the software for the hardware, our brain. Although we are born with a brain, it is largely unfilled, except for the instincts biological natural selection implants in us (Hayek, 1952). This is why Hayek describes the products of cultural evolution as lying between our instinct and our reason. Our skills, capabilities, and routines are learned and accumulated through past generations competing with one another to survive and reproduce. Complex systems, containing many interconnected rules, routines, skills, etc., arise as interactive and diverse individuals compete with one another. They do not result from conscious collective action. Hayek zealously battles the notion, calling it the "fatal conceit," that "man is able to shape the world around him according to his wishes" (Hayek, 1988).

But Hayek's theory departs from narrow methodological individualism when he discusses the unit of selection (Vanberg, 1986). It is not the individual who is selected, but the group of individuals. Groups that adopt the better rules tend to grow relative to other groups. Moreover, the groups that do adopt the better rules and therefore are able to support larger populations will benefit as the population grows because of the increasing specialization of tasks of its members: The system grows more complex (and affluent) when its size increases.[9] This is not to say, however, that because the group is selected there must be conscious actions by the group's members. An example of this would be the adoption of what Hayek calls the "extended order of human cooperation," otherwise known as the market economy. For example, the groups that adopted the rules of the market economy prospered and grew while those that did not—the Soviet Union, for instance—faltered and deteriorated, until, at last, they were forced (at least to start) to imitate the rules of the more successful groups. The idea of group selection is a much-debated topic in both economics and biology,[10] and we return to it below.

Alfred Marshall

Even though Marshall accepted Darwin's theory almost wholesale,[11] he never really developed an evolutionary theory to rival the neoclassical one he had been so instrumental in establishing.[12] That Marshall wished to embrace Darwin's theory comprehensively is clear from the Darwinian motto he adopted as his guiding principle in economics: *Natura non facit saltum.*[13] Although he longed to instill biological concepts into economics, his dream remained largely unfulfilled. In the end, Marshall grappled with the problems of time and irreversibility, but he did so mainly within the neoclassical framework he founded. Time, irreversibility, and gradual, continuous change were the central features of Marshall's biological approach.

Marshall's infatuation with gradualism reflects his philosophical position that knowledge can be accumulated only through a slow, and even imperceptible, process. His theory of development, in sharp contrast to Schumpeter's, is firmly grounded on this belief (Moss, 1982). Marshall viewed the entrepreneurial function as business ability, and associated it with functions within firms. The businessman's purpose is to discover how to recombine or combine the existing activities and methods available (Moss, 1982, p. 6). Natural selection, through the principle of substitution, selects the better firms by selecting the better managers, managers able to draw on an abundance of knowledge already accumulated by the firm.

Schumpeter

Schumpeter, of course, looms large in the evolutionary literature of today; it is for no small reason that this volume devoted to the *neo-Schumpeterian* approach to economics carries a chapter explicitly devoted to evolutionary themes. As Nelson and Winter (1982, p. 39, emphasis in original) observe, "it could reasonably be said that we are evolutionary theorists *for the sake* of being neo-Schumpeterians." What is it that makes Schumpeter the adopted progenitor of the evolutionary proponents of today? The answer, of course, is that Schumpeter's theory of economic development relies firmly on the view that variations induced by entrepreneurs create the essential fuel for natural selection among human artifacts. As we mentioned earlier, the heart of the evolutionary approach lies in the variations exhibited by individuals in a population. And Schumpeter stressed the role in economic development of entrepreneurs who compete not on price alone but primarily in the carrying out of new combinations,[14] that is, who introduce novelty to the economic system.

What was distinctive about Schumpeter was his emphasis on discontinuous rather than continuous change. New combinations represent a sharp break from the past and bear no comprehensible connection to previous achievements. "What has been done already has the sharp-edged reality of all things which we have seen and experienced; the new is only the figment of our imagination. Carrying out a new plan and acting according to a customary one are things as different as making a road and walking along it" (Schumpeter, 1934, p. 85). Schumpeter's famous description of the circular flow of economic life does not portray an absence of change; rather, the changes are continuous ones, "which may in time, by continual adaptation through innumerable small steps [eventually] make a great department store out of a small retail business" (Schumpeter, 1934, p. 62). Thus Marshall's vision of gradual change was for Schumpeter only the backdrop against which to develop what he viewed as the more important process in economic development—entrepreneurship.

Indeed, Schumpeter arguably formulated a theory of what would now be called *punctuated equilibrium*, in which the economy is seen to be in an essentially static equilibrium until it is punctuated by some innovation(s) radically changing the nature of production.[15] In fact, this idea of punc tuated equilibrium formed the basis of his theory of business cycles. His approach is also parallel to that of Kuhn (1970), who saw scientists as working within a particular framework called *normal science* until revolutionary science breaks all tradition and creates a completely new paradigm to guide scientists in a new normal science. As the notion of punctuated equilibrium has only recently come into fashion in biology, it is not surprising that Schumpeter would have associated the idea of natural selection with Marshallian gradualism and thus rejected it,[16] but there is in fact nothing in the theory of evolution by natural selection that says changes must be small or large, slow or rapid.[17]

Who was right about economic change, Marshall or Schumpeter? The answer arguably lies in the realm of emphasis and perspective, and one can hardly dispute Brian Loasby's (1986, p. 56) remark that "we need both Marshall and Schumpeter." Even when the broad framework of action is well known, as in Schumpeter's circular flow, we may still be living in a world of astounding complexity. Because of our cognitive limits, we may still be discovering, inventing, innovating, etc., within a known framework or paradigm.[18] But the problem is best viewed not from an economywide perspective, as Schumpeter seems to see it, but from that of individual firms and industries. Changes in the firm, such as small improvements on products, or in production methods, can be considered as part of normal science or as enhancing the competence of that firm (Tushman and Anderson, 1986). Revolutionary changes, meanwhile, destroy the competencies of firms, and introduce Schumpeterian innovations—something entirely novel. For taxonomic reasons, we think that the problem with knowledge is best broken down into two categories, that arising from complexity within a known framework and that arising from genuine uncertainty, where a new paradigm is created.[19]

Evolution and Marginalism

Almost immediately after Marshall presented his dual programs for normal science, his followers buried his proposal for a bioeconomics, and instead elevated and extended his mechanistic (neoclassical) paradigm. The logic of Pigou, Sraffa, Robinson, and Chamberlin ushered in new rigor—and complications. For one thing, the fundamentally deductive and *a priori* character of the neoclassical approach was at odds with the positive cast of contemporary philosophy of science. Not surprisingly, when neoclassicism met positivism the marginalist assumptions came under attack. Ironically, perhaps, modern evolutionary thinking in economics has its origins in the ensuing defence of marginalism.

The famous marginalist controversy of the 1940s called into question the idea that business people actually calculate on the margin and therefore—or so the critics assumed—the whole of neoclassical microeconomics.

Machlup, the chief defender of marginalism, argued that we can accept the results of marginalism because rational action does not have to be conscious action; it is dictated by a kind of "system constraint" *ex post* (Langlois and Koppl, 1991). But what about the maximization hypothesis embedded in marginalist analysis? Alchian (1950) and Friedman (1953) both take their cues from the controversy and employ in place of the system constraint an explicit natural selection mechanism. Both rightly argue, as did Machlup, that *ex post* success or survival is what counts. They go their separate ways, however, when considering the role of *ex ante* individual maximizing behavior.

Alchian's starting point is to assume "incomplete information and uncertain foresight" as a normal element in a business person's decision making. Under such a scenario, the environment selects the firms whose managers made the better decisions, regardless of how they made the decisions. Since by assumption one cannot predict which decisions will be selected, one cannot predict which firms will be selected. One can, however, explain the consequences of selection by an *ex post facto* analysis.[20] Alchian (1953, pp. 600–601) claims that his "less restrictive axioms do not assert that businessmen try to maximize profits, since, with uncertainty, no definite meaning can be attached to that presciption of behavior. It is true that there is some situation which, if achieved, would, *ex post*, have yielded a larger profit than any other would have . . . [and] to regard [economic analysis] as a theory of individual behavior is fatal." Like biologists, Alchian rightly understands that a natural selection theory only explains events and does not, in general, predict them.[21] He also reminds us (1950, p. 213) that profit maximization *ex ante* is defined only in world of perfect information—"the only way to make 'profit maximization' a specifically meaningful action is to postulate a model containing certainty." Only when we have such information will economists be able to predict individual behavior.

Before moving on to Friedman, let us look first at Penrose's (1952) criticism of Alchian. Penrose charges Alchian with improperly borrowing the concept of natural selection from biologists without paying the price; that is, she thinks his analogy with natural selection unwarranted (and ultimately problematic) as given. Although her criticisms move along several lines, her main thrust concerns reproduction, imitation, heritability, and their relation to the role of purposive behavior. She warns that an assumption of purposive behavior is a must, and "if we abandon this assumption, and particularly if we assume that men act randomly, we cannot explain competition, for there is nothing in the reproductive processes of firms that would ensure that more firms would constantly be created than survive" (1952, p. 812).

How do the firms that survive "reproduce?" Or rather, how do the decision rules employed by the more successful firms become more widespread by a competitive process? Motivation, Penrose (1952, p. 813) asserts, rather ruins the model because economists can no longer know "the conditions of survival." In addition, as Alchian does not specify what he means by environment, selection becomes a meaningless tautology.

Although Penrose's criticisms are legitimate to a certain extent, Alchian was nonetheless on the right track.[22] The real confusion, however, comes from Milton Friedman and Stephen Enke, who argue that natural selection serves to justify marginalism, that is, maximizing behavior. Enke (1951, p. 571) argues that "the greater the intensity of inter-firm rivalry, the more competent is the economist to make long-run predictions of aggregate firm behavior. Perhaps, under certain circumstances, we can predict *as if* firms do in fact maximize profits by consciously equating marginal costs and marginal revenues." It was Friedman's account and not Enke's, however, that made the lasting impression on economists. Friedman liberally applies "as if" reasoning.

> Under a wide range of circumstances individual firms behave *as if* they were seeking rationally to maximize their expected returns and had full knowledge of the data needed in the attempt; *as if*, that is, they knew the relevant cost and demand functions, calculated marginal cost and marginal revenue from all actions open to them, and pushed each line of action to the point at which the relevant marginal cost and marginal revenue were equal . . . Confidence in the maximization-of-returns hypothesis is justified by evidence of a very different character . . . The process of "natural selection" thus helps to validate the hypothesis—or rather, given natural selection, acceptance of the hypothesis can be based largely on the judgment that it summarizes the conditions for survival.

Thus Friedman reverses Alchian's argument: Perfect knowledge comes via the "as if" postulate; thus, we can argue for profit maximization. Friedman resolves Marshall's dualism between the mechanical and the biological by offering natural selection as a brace for marginalism rather than as an alternative paradigm.

Is selection, then, an alternative to marginalism, and, if so, how such is a program to be carried out? Indeed, is it possible? Not until Sidney Winter's 1964 paper was the logic of natural selection fully spelled out. As Penrose noted, what is missing or underemphasized in Alchian's natural selection theory (and more so in Friedman's account) is a mechanism of inheritance. Winter recognized that an indispensable element of natural selection theory is inertia in what's been selected already. Adaptation to one's environment, no less than in biological evolution, requires that selection be cumulative, and this requires that responses to the environment be encoded, retained, and preserved. Contra Friedman, random survival could not possibly explain complex designs like firms. In evolutionary theories, firms are best thought of not as production functions but rather as organizations capable of valuing and storing the results of previous selections. Properly understood, natural selection is a two-step process in which random mutation occurs as the first step and selection proper as the second and determinative step. As Richard Dawkins (1986, p. 317) puts it, "[s]ingle-step selection is just another way of saying pure chance . . . *Cumulative selection*, by slow and gradual degrees, is the explanation, the only workable explanation that has ever been proposed for the existence of life's complex design." Unlike either Alchian or Friedman, Winter postulates the substances needed to bridge the gap in the two-step process.

Nelson and Winter

What is this retained encoding called and how do firms use it? Following Winter (1964), Nelson and Winter (1982) offer the notion of routines as rules of behavior. (We return to this idea later.) On the one hand, Nelson and Winter use this notion to explore the traditional questions of price theory and industrial organization, for example, responses of market price and quantity to exogenous shocks and market concentration, recast in evolutionary terms. Their simulations speak directly to the issues of the marginalist controversy discussed in the previous section. On the other hand, they also use it as a base to erect a more general theory of evolution of social institutions. This more general theory focuses on the nature and meaning of economic capabilities and explores how innovation creates new capabilities.

The work of Nelson and Winter is widely seen as seminal in the modern resurgence of evolutionary thinking in economics. Of course, Nelson and Winter themselves inherited a body of knowledge from previous economists. From Herbert Simon they acquired the notions of bounded rationality and satisficing, which they use to build models of search and selection. From Schumpeter they acquired a workable framework for variation. Adding the essential ingredient of routines, they are able to construct models and theories of evolution. The better routines (introduced first as innovations) are selected by the environment (comprising only the market in most of their analyses) and then propagated by replication (within a firm) and imitation (interfirm), leading to the differential survival (via profitability) of firms. Through the process of competition, the better rules survive. Routines provide the link to Simon and Schumpeter. They function as the coordinative element in a firm, thus providing the continuity of the firm in a sea of change.

Though the search-and-selection models of Nelson and Winter yield broadly the same conclusions one reaches with marginalist theory, that is, firm and industry reaction to changed market conditions, Nelson and Winter suggest that the evolutionary approach offers more explanatory content. This is because some of exogenous variables in orthodox theory become endogenous in evolutionary theory. In evolutionary theory, firms respond to changing market conditions by searching for new routines; by contrast, neoclassical partial-equilibrium comparative statics lacks any theory of adjustment that is consistent with its own behavioral postulates (Arrow, 1959).

Present-day efforts in evolutionary economics almost all take their cues from Nelson and Winter. One body of work picks up the thread of simulation, examining questions of competition and industry structure recast in evolutionary terms, and another strand pursues the ideas of capabilities and routines into the theory of social and economic institutions.

Directions in Evolutionary Economics Today

Industry Structure as a Selection of Routines

Industrial structure and organization, consisting of the rules, that is, the routines and capabilities, of the firms within the industry, is the result of the competitive process of the interacting firms; that is, natural selection operates on firms so that the rules that better fit the environment survive. But a question immediately arises: Is there selection for firms or is there selection for the individual rules of firms? The answer is both. Inasmuch as the organizational routines of firms are part and parcel of a larger system, and are tacitly known only within the firm, with some functioning only in concert to coordinate productive processes, the routines must be considered as part of an interconnected system of rules that defines the organization. Then there will selection for firms or, rather, for a system of interconnected rules. There will, however, also be selection for individual rules within the firms as learning takes place over time, but their fitness will be the average fitness of the firm.

Let us here distinguish between *selection of* and *selection for* certain things. As Sober (1984b, p. 100, emphasis in original) makes clear " 'selection of' pertains to the *effects* of a selection process, whereas 'selection for' describes its causes. . . 'Selection for' is the causal concept *par excellence*." There can be selection of objects but selection for properties of objects. For natural selection to be a causal factor in evolution, two requirements must be met: There must be interaction of something with the environment and there must be replication. David Hull (1989, p. 96) describes a replicator as "an entity that passes on its structure largely intact in successive replications," and an interactor as "an entity that interacts as a cohesive whole with its environment in such a way that this interaction causes replication to be differential." In biological evolution, the phenotype (usually thought of as the organism) interacts with the environment (producing differential reproduction and survival), while heritable genotypic variations (replicating genes) give rise to the phenotype that interacts with the environment. Firms may be considered the objects of selection, that is, we may think of firms as physical entities, composed of ownable assets, capable of surviving.[23] In this regard, firms are the interactors with the environment, while the rules of firms are the replicators.[24] Natural selection then occurs as an interplay between replication and interaction.[25]

This is the approach that a number of writers have implicitly taken in modeling industry structure. Most often, this work takes the form of computer simulations in which firms follow persistent rules of behavior (which are sometimes subject to imitation). The firms interact in a competitive market. Successful rules are replicated not through inheritance, of course, but through the growth in output of the firms following the rules (and sometimes through imitation).

The seminal work here again is Nelson and Winter (1982). See Silverberg (1988) for a recent survey and Silverberg, et al. (1988) for a recent example.

The Evolution of Social Institutions

The evolutionary approach to industry structure uses the idea of rules or routines as replicators, but such rules are of far more general interest. As we have seen, social institutions more broadly involve the following of rules, and the evolutionary explanation of such institutions has a long heritage.

It may seem paradoxical for us now to suggest that the present-day approach to an evolutionary theory of institutions begins with the theory of games. In its pure form, game theory is an equilibrium theory and certainly not a process theory. But there is ultimately no paradox. We will argue that game theory in its simpler manifestations can be a valuable complement to an evolutionary theory of social institutions. Building on the work of philosophers David Lewis (1969) and Edna Ullmann-Margalit (1977), economists like Andrew Schotter (1981, 1986), Jack Hirshleifer (1982), Robert Sugden (1986), and Nicholas Rowe (1989) have looked at social institutions instructively from within the framework of game theory.[26]

In order to simplify the exposition, consider the two most important canonical games that appear in this work. The first of these is the coordination game, of which the automobile example is an instance. If you choose to drive on the left-hand side of the road and an oncoming motorist chooses the right (or vice-versa), the "payoffs" to both of you will likely be negative. If, however, you both choose the same side of the road—either side—you will not incur these penalties. With repeated play of this game, one would expect drivers to keep to one particular side as a matter of convention. Notice that such a convention is self-enforcing: Anyone who consistently drives on the left in the United States will be punished by negative payoffs quite apart from any penalties invoked by the courts. Notice also that, while far superior to discoordination, a convention solution need not be optimal. Suppose, for example, that driving on the right has a higher payoff than driving on the left; perhaps, we might imagine, because automobiles are cheaper when one conforms to the standard that is more popular around the world. But historical accident may lead a region to the opposite standard. Such conventions are path-dependent processes of the sort Paul David (1985) has popularized. (We discuss these issues more fully below.) It is typically costly to alter a convention once established, and it may take some kind of centralized coordination to do so, as when Sweden and Okinawa changed their side-of-the-road driving conventions.

In a coordination game, the incentives of both players are aligned; their common objective is facilitated by the reduction in information costs a convention achieves. By contrast, what characterizes a prisoners' dilemma is a divergence of incentives. The parable commonly attached to the game is as follows. Two suspects are hauled in by the police for a bank robbery. Without a confession, the authorities have insufficient evidence to convict the two, although they could convict them of a lesser crime. The police interrogate the criminals in separate rooms and propose a deal to each: If you turn state's evidence and testify against your cohort, you go free, and we throw the book at him. In this case, each prisoner has a private incentive to confess whereas the "social optimum" is for both to hold firm, in the sense that such steadfastness minimizes the total number of years in prison. Because of the private incentive to confess—both to lower one's own sentence and to insure against confession by one's compatriot—the solution of such a game played once is for both to confess,[27] a result that maximizes total years in prison. If, however, the game is played repeatedly, and neither of the players knows when the game will end, there may emerge a norm of reciprocity, according to which the players refrain from confessing despite the private incentive to do so.

Like a convention, a prisoners'-dilemma norm is an institution with an information function. It substitutes for the costly direct communication and negotiation between the players that might otherwise facilitate agreement on the joint-maximizing solution. Unlike a coordination convention, however, a norm of this sort is not completely self-enforcing. Whenever the players face an end-game, the discipline of repeated play evaporates, and the private incentives loom large. Thus, prisoners'-dilemma situations often call for some sort of external policing mechanism. We should distinguish, however, between privately rational reciprocity enforced by repeated play and the idea of a norm proper. In many situations, people follow norms of behavior—like honesty—even in end-game situations. One often tells the truth, even when lying would be costless and privately beneficial. The reason is that norms of this sort are often internalized to form a part of culture. They are, in effect, instances of tacit rule-following. After repeated play of a prisoners'-dilemma game by many different individuals, the original game situation and the sanctions of repeated play are forgotten. Only the norm remains. In this sense, the norm is itself an enforcement mechanism.

This is not to say that a norm must always emerge or that the mechanism of repeated play must always solve the prisoners' dilemma in a happy fashion. There are far too many examples of social situations in which norms have collapsed or failed to emerge and in which the dilemma of this game is all too real. It is a major task of research in this area to understand the circumstances under which efficiency-enhancing norms will in fact emerge, and we return to these issues below.

By now it should be obvious why a game-theoretic approach is not at all incompatible with a causal-genetic approach. The idea of repeated play of the game implies a process over time. Although formal game theory in its resplendent glory treats repeated games in an equilibrium framework, the theory of social institutions need not. What substitutes for the idea of an equilibrium strategy is the notion of an evolutionarily stable strategy, a concept borrowed from biologists who have adapted game-theoretic models to natural evolution (Maynard Smith, 1982).

Perhaps the best example of evolutionary game-theory modeling is the much-discussed work of Robert Axelrod (1984). Axelrod invited prominent game theorists to submit algorithms for solving the repeated prisoners'-dilemma game. These he tested by a computer tournament in which the algorithms were pitted against one another. The frequent winner was one of the simplest: the tit-for-tat strategy. Under this strategy, a player initially cooperates (does not confess); however, whenever the other player fails to cooperate (confesses) in any period, the first player "punishes" the rival by also failing to cooperate for one period. One can think of this strategy as a kind of norm.

The Evolution of Organizations

The game-theoretic approach to the economics of social institutions concentrates on relatively abstract and fundamental institutions like norms and conventions. But, of course, institutions also take on more concrete and complex forms. For example, organizations of various sorts are also "institutions." This is true not only in ordinary language but also, as we will argue, in theory as well. For simplicity and clarity, we will concentrate on one particular sort of organization: the firm. In principle, however, one could also think of evolutionary theories of other kinds of organizations, including government.

Coase (1937) introduced the notion of the transaction cost in order to explain the existence of alternative organizational modes. Organizations economize on these transaction costs.[28] But what is a transaction cost? Since Coase, two dominant themes have emerged in transaction-cost analysis (Alchian and Woodward, 1988). One we may call the asset-specificity view. Here transaction costs arise because of the possibility that the owner of a specific asset may try to hold up a contracting party in order to extract a larger share of the quasirents of cooperation in production. This possibility arises for two reasons: bounded rationality and opportunism. Bounded rationality means that economic actors are limited in both knowledge and computational capacity. Opportunism, as Williamson (1975) describes it, is self-interest seeking with guile. To the extent that the environment is complex and the contracting parties cannot fully comprehend it, contracts remain incomplete. As a result, contracts cannot include terms *ex ante* to forestall opportunistic behavior *ex post.* Integration of ownership (or perhaps the giving of a hostage) can be an efficient alternative when these transaction costs would otherwise deter productive cooperation or channel that cooperation into less efficient (but less vulnerable) technologies (Williamson, 1985; Klein et al., 1978). The other dominant approach we may call the measurement-cost view. While the asset-specificity view explains organizational structure through the hold-up problem, the measurement-cost view relies on moral hazard. Again, the problem results because of bounded rationality: The parties cooperating in the productive process are unable to measure individual members' contributions to the cooperative effort. Residual claimancy falls to some agent, perhaps the one whose contribution is the most costly to measure, who then must monitor other members, assure performance, and accept the responsibility for assuming these tasks (Barzel, 1987).

Although these approaches explain organizational structures through the use of bounded rationality, they do not consider the roles of learning and adapting over time. If transaction costs are ultimately costs of information and knowledge (Dahlman, 1979), then we would expect to see these costs diminish through the passage of time as firms and individuals learn and adapt to complex relations among transacting parties. Under certain circumstances, for instance, the repeated play of the prisoners'-dilemma game may produce cooperative behavior as the players learn of one another's reaction to reciprocate cooperative actions (Axelrod, 1984). Thus cooperative behavior may emerge in arm's-length arrangements over time, obviating integration. Moreover, business institutions—whether firms or markets or hybrid alternatives—are all capable of learning over time. Understanding how alternative institutions learn is a principal task of a genuinely evolutionary theory of the firm.

The asset-specificity and measurement-cost views both explain integration using the logic of the prisoner's-dilemma situation. But business institutions solve far more types of problems than those that arise from prisoners'-dilemma situations alone. We suggested above that one can think of the firm as a system of rules, routines, and capabilities, a system that coordinates the specialized productive activities among many individuals. Thus, the firm is sort of a vehicle that houses and values the rules possessed by many diverse individuals, that is, rules of coordinative knowledge. Hence, we can understand firms (or other business institutions) as solutions not only to prisoners'-dilemma games but also to coordination games.

The routines of an organization are predictable patterns of more-or-less coordinated behavior. Like individuals, organizations confront bounded rationality and must devise heuristics (routines) for continuously operating in their environments. Like institutions in general, routines within organizations serve the function of economizing on knowledge; that is, by establishing predictable patterns of behavior, routines greatly reduce the cognitive demands on individuals. Thus, in the face of complexity, routines facilitate the interaction of individuals within the organization while serving as storehouses of knowledge.

The firm, then, is a special way to organize knowledge: It links together various kinds of intimate knowledge (capabilities) to coordinate productive activities. Much of the knowledge firms possess is tacit and empirically derived through trial-and-error learning processes. Since these capabilities often come in discrete, lumpy bundles, firms often find themselves with surplus capabilities for performing certain tasks (Penrose, 1959). These firms may then expand their operations and take on additional similar activities (Teece, 1980, 1982). But, as a firm augments its domain, the similarity of the activities diminishes, that is, additional activities become less congruent with the firm's capabilities. This places natural limits on the boundaries of the firm.

As expanding the domain activities increases the complexity of internal organization, why would a firm ever find it prudent to manage anything beyond what is blatantly similar? Why won't it procure all its dissimilar activities through the market? The answer must be that it is sometimes more economical for the firm to develop its own complementary capabilities in house, that is, there must be some sort of a transaction cost impeding market purchase. But when? We already remarked on hold-up and moral hazard problems. But these transaction costs are essentially static in nature: They do not explain fundamental changes in organization arising from changes in productive knowledge; they omit the time-connectedness of learning processes. The organization of industry structure consists in the organization of knowledge, not merely in defensive stratagems to prevent opportunistic behavior.

Since we are taking the evolutionary perspective, we necessarily want to examine what happens to industry structure as knowledge *changes*, that is, we want a dynamic theory of organization of industry. How will new knowledge be organized? The nature of this new knowledge will determine whether the firm or entrepreneur decides to develop the capabilities within its domain or to contract through the market for them. The nature of the new knowledge determines, in other words, what we call dynamic transaction costs. Dynamic transaction costs involve the costs of persuading, negotiating, coordinating with, and teaching outside suppliers (Silver, 1984; Langlois, 1988, 1992). A potential innovation is by definition new, untested knowledge. If the innovation is systemic, introducing this new knowledge will require the simultaneous coordination of a host of complementary capabilities (Teece, 1986). The would-be innovator must then choose whether the cost of coordination is less within the firm or on the market.

Consider the following examples. James Watt's invention of a new, improved steam engine did not meet with instant approval. Many thought his idea simply unmarketable. The costs of persuading the public seemed enormous, until he finally met up with Matthew Boulton, a successful Birmingham manufacturer, whom Watt took on as a partner. The new steam engine required finely made parts. As an expert fine-tool maker, Watt was able to produce the needed parts himself but was unable to buy any of the parts on the market because such delicately made parts were unavailable. Teaching the outside suppliers seems to have been prohibitive, so Watt and Boulton set up factory works at Soho, where Watt struggled to teach his tool makers the sensitive trade of making parts for his steam engine. Silver (1984, p. 15) describes this general situation: "the employer sets up procedures or routines that the employee is told to follow. The key point is that this kind of communication—that is, communication regarding procedure—is less expensive than communication relating to a desired end result (substantive content)."

Henry Ford and his innovation of the moving assembly line also fit this scheme of things (Langlois and Robertson, 1989). Before Henry Ford's innovation, the market's capabilities were sufficient and economical for the auto manufacturers to buy and assemble the parts—no significant in-house manufacturing was necessary. But when Ford developed the moving assembly line, he could not swiftly communicate his new (and still developing) knowledge to the existing suppliers. Thus vertical integration allowed Ford to carry out his new combination, that is, to coordinate the activities of a systemic innovation.

Dynamic transaction costs spring from the introduction of new knowledge. Introducing the new knowledge in the most economical manner depends on the nature of the new knowledge and the existing configuration of capabilities present in the market. The evolution of industry structure *is*, therefore, the evolution of the organization of knowledge and capabilities. Markets learn and adapt; so do firms. This means that, on the one hand, firms become better at what they do, traveling down the learning curve as they specialize in certain activities in which their capabilities are strongest. The nature of their activities become largely routinized. On the other hand, markets learn too as knowledge become routinized, modular, and less dependent on other stages.[29] Knowledge diffuses from firms to the market as other firms imitate and learn the better routines.

Firms are selected on the basis of interaction with the environment, that is, their ability to produce profits. But it is rules and routines that are selected for, becoming, in effect, what is replicated and carried on from one generation of users to the next. The organizational routines (the routines and rules that are firm specific) are also transformed in the process of selection. Here we see a dynamic interplay of selection *for* routines and *of* firms as knowledge unfolds and evolves. This is not to say that at any moment in time selection chooses the fittest or best routines and industry structures; indeed, there may persist for long periods rather inefficient routines and firms. Moreover, depending on the broad institutional framework, the nature of the knowledge, that is, capabilities, and the character of the transaction costs, we may witness any number of industry structures (and organizational forms) equally efficient in some sense. Stated another way, history matters in the evolution of industry structure, where particular past events (indeed, even accidental ones) cast shadows into the present. This is the phenomenon of path dependency, which we discuss in more detail below.

Industry structure, as shaped by transaction costs and changes in knowledge, also has a strong bearing on how knowledge is generated. This is the Schumpeterian hypothesis in another guise. Of course, Schumpeter conjectured that a market structure involving large firms (who wield what neoclassical eyes would see as "monopoly power") is in a better position to carry out new combinations. So not only would it seem that the evolution of market structure is determined by new knowledge, new knowledge flows from market structure. Although we think that market structure plays a vital role in creating and initiating innovation, we do not agree with Schumpeter that innovation will be more likely to be originated in large, powerful firms. Rather, variation (new knowledge) will probably be highest when there are many paths explored and tried. This will occur when there are semi-isolated populations divorced from the established frameworks of action.[30] This has the effect of producing systemwide trial-and-error learning and discovery (Nelson and Winter, 1977).

Consider, for instance, the development of the personal computer at IBM (Langlois, 1990). IBM relied on external capabilities to produce a personal computer production unit, becoming substantially an assembler of bought parts. More than that, though, IBM spun off a semi-isolated unit to carry out this task, since its rigid framework of procedures, corporate structure, and controls (which we may think of as its corporate culture) largely forbade a developmental project of a radically different nature. Consider also Du Pont around the turn of the century. Du Pont recognized the value of separating the research units from the manufacturing concerns (and other operating units) in order to cultivate ideas radically different from those being employed already in the firm. Yet Du Pont also recognized that duplication of effort and equipment might occur and decided that isolation would not be complete; semi-isolation—with the research units communicating and interacting somewhat with the other units—was the happy compromise.

Issues in Evolutionary Theory

The Unit of Selection and Routines as Genes

Biologists remain divided into three camps about what the unit of selection is. The traditional Darwinists insist that natural selection acts most prevalently on individual organisms (where evolution occurs at the population level, and mutations at the genic level).[31] More recently, Wynne-Edwards (1962) inaugurated the controversial idea of group selectionism, which shows up as the predominant mechanism in Hayek's works. Perhaps even more controversial is the view espoused by Williams (1966) and Dawkins (1976, 1982) that the gene is the unit of selection.

Before we can determine what the unit of selection is we need to see what it means to be a unit of selection. This, in and of itself, is a somewhat controversial and ambiguous concept. Mayr (1988, p. 123) thinks that the phrase *unit of selection* is not apt and prefers *the target of selection* as more suitable to the task. The question is, suitable to which task? Here we suppose that the task is to explain the consequences of selection as a systematic causal process. As we noted above, Sober (1984b) offers the distinction between selection *of* and selection *for*, with selection for properties giving us the causal role in the selective process. The distinction, though useful, offers little in the way of establishing what the unit of selection is (Mayr, 1988, p. 123).[32] Sober's *selection for* does, however, offer the most promising avenue of defining the unit of selection, since it is the causal concept in selection. Selection, as a theory of forces, must consider the role of active competition as establishing what the unit of selection is; that is, the proper question is (and we think few would disagree), "what is competing for survival?" Here, we also hold that depending on what we are trying to explain, the unit may change, but not its kind. What we seek is a concept of the unit of selection that offers the greatest explanatory content.[33] In addition, as there must be selection for or against certain properties (actually instructions, as we make clear later), we think that there is one best—least cumbersome and most general—way to represent the selective process.

Let us begin by looking at the traditional Darwinist. He or she holds that "evolution is change in the adaptation *and* in the diversity of populations of organisms" (Mayr, 1988, p. 163), not changes in gene frequencies. As such, the focus is on individual organisms or groups. But Darwin's organisms are selfish individuals competing with one another for life's scarce resources; selection, therefore, acts on individual organisms and not on groups of altruistic individuals. Competition among individual organisms is the typical Darwinist's answer to the unit-of-selection question.[34] Survival and reproductive fitness depend not on one's respective group, but on individual properties. This is, of course, the legacy of Adam Smith and the Scottish moral philosophers, who emphasized the individual pursuit of self-interest as the chief mover behind population growth and variation. The "struggle for existence" is something one must do for oneself.

Group selection usually presents a problem for Darwinian biologists[35] because it usually entails[36] the presence of altruism—individuals acting on the behalf of the group to the neglect of their own interests. A crow caws to the flock warning of approaching danger and thereby draws attention to itself, ultimately resulting in self-sacrificial death, but saving the fleeing flock. Such a group benefits from the presence of sentry crows. Let us follow Sober (1984b, p. 266) and define group selection as existing "exactly when groups vary in fitness, and the fitness of an organism depends on the sort of a group it is in." Group selection without altruism fits into this definition. Without altruistic characteristics as causal factors in explaining group survival and reproduction, one can also reinterpret the instances of group selection in terms of individuals.

The real issue of group selection per se, then, concerns the presence of altruism. This gets at the heart of an issue in economics, individual rationality versus collective rationality. Moreover, the meaning of altruism is usually misconstrued. Consider Hayek's (1988, p. 81) interpretation: "In so far as we can still call his motives altruistic in that they eventually redound to the benefit of others, they will do this not because he aims at or intends to serve the concrete needs of others, but because he observes abstract rules." Thus, for Hayek, behavior can be altruistic because individual actions have (unintended) beneficial social repercussions. Altruism is in his view an externality. But as such, can we really attribute the individual as acting (albeit unintentionally) altruistically? We may as well say that a pig is altruistic when it unintentionally serves as the wolf's evening dinner. Neither is the reciprocation of cooperative behavior in Axelrod's evolutionary theory altruism. Altruism should and must pertain only to situations of self-sacrifice on behalf of others. (The famous tit-for-tat strategy could never have won if it always acted cooperatively; it must sometimes act selfishly and punish others.) Whether altruism exists is clearly an empirical issue, though theory does offer some suggestion that it does not.[37]

Moreover, whatever may be appropriate in biology (Sober, 1984a,b), the view that the gene is the unit of selection seems to lend itself naturally to the social sciences, and it is the position that we, among others, take. The theory's popular expositor, Richard Dawkins, has raised more than a few cries from his colleagues. Some think that genes as the unit of selection is far-fetched because genes do have "direct visibility to natural selection." From this point of view, "selection simply cannot see genes and pick among them directly" (Gould, 1980, p. 90). Dawkins (1982) counters Gould's argument by proposing the *extended phenotype.* In fact, Dawkins argues that there is a kind of nongenetic replicator, which he calls a *meme* and defines as "a unit of information residing in a brain." Like a gene, it has phenotypic effects that play a role in the probability of its being replicated. "Any effect that a meme has on the behavior of a body bearing it may influence that meme's chance of surviving. A meme that made its bodies run over cliffs would have a fate like that of a gene making its bodies run over cliffs. It would tend to be eliminated from the meme-pool" (Dawkins, 1982, p. 109).

> *Of course* genes are not directly visible to selection. *Obviously* they are selected by virtue of their phenotypic effects, and certainly they can be said to *have* phenotypic effects in concert with hundreds of other genes. But it is the thesis of this book that we should not be trapped into assuming that those phenotypic effects are best regarded as being neatly wrapped up in discrete bodies (or other discrete vehicles). The doctrine of the extended phenotype is that the phenotypic effect of a gene (genetic replicator) is best seen as an effect upon the world at large, and only incidentally upon the individual organism—or any other vehicle—in which it happens to sit. (Dawkins, 1982, p. 117)

The point is that memes (rules or routines in our language) also have an extended phenotype. Selection is accomplished through individual interaction, albeit with a result that looks like it was guided by an invisible hand. The better rules become replicated—or, at any rate, propagated—by a competitive process of testing it in the environment of individual interaction.

Frequency Dependence

Another set of issues surround the complex problem of defining fitness. We will not enter into that debate fully, except to highlight one set of phenomena that are perhaps of particular interest to economists. As most biologists recognize, the fitness of an organism (or gene or group, depending on one's perspective) is not an absolute or invariant quantity. Rather, fitness is "context dependent"; that is, fitness depends on the environment, and the environment may change during the course of the selection process. In particular, the very success of some units may change the environment, and therefore the fitness of those units to the environment.

This is not, of course, a problem for evolutionary explanation. It is, however, a difficulty for functionalist explanations, including "maximizing" explanations of the behavior of firms in the manner of Friedman (Winter, 1964) or static transaction-cost explanations of the boundaries of the firm (Langlois, 1984). The problem is this: The "function" one ascribes to the unit one observes to exist corresponds to its fitness in the environment. To the extent, then, that an organized structure faces a range of environments, the "efficient" mode will vary with time. Indeed, we need to be especially careful in judging "efficiency" in terms of the environment we observe at any moment of time, for if that environment is likely to change, an organizational mode adapted to the environment of the moment may well be maladapted in some larger sense. This is, of course, a rather Schumpeterian point.

There may, in fact, be systematic ways in which the very fitness of some units changes the environment so as to make them less fit. One of the best known of these is the idea of frequency dependence.[38] The fitness of units (firms embodying a certain pattern of behavior, let us say) may vary as the number of such units in the population increases. For example, literature in the population approach to organizational sociology (Hannan and Freeman, 1989) models the founding and demise of organizations as density-dependent selection. When the number of organizations of a certain type is small (their density in the population is low), the rate of increase of such organizations will be slow for a number of reasons. As the number increases, however, the rate of growth of this kind of organization will also increase because of complementarities in the nature of what Marshall would have called external economies. As the number of organizations increases further, however, the rate of increase will decline as organizations of this type must compete for resources with a greater number of rivals. The result is a logistic in which the fitness of a particular trait (type of organization) first increases and then decreases as a function of the frequency of that trait in the population.

Path Dependence

Do evolutionary mechanisms assure optimal outcomes and designs in technologies, institutions, etc.?[39] One guise in which this question reaches the attention of economists is that of what the literature today describes as path dependency (Arthur, 1989; David, 1985). Because of increasing returns from such phenomena as network externalities (Katz and Shapiro, 1985) and learning effects, an economy may find itself "locked in" to a particular development path of technology. Because of this path dependence, "important influences upon the eventual outcome can be exerted by temporally remote events, including happenings dominated by chance rather than systematic forces" (David, 1985, p. 332); thus the efficient technology need not result.

David tells the now-familiar story of how the apparently suboptimal typewriter keyboard QWERTY came to dominate all others (including the newer Dvorak keyboard, which David contends is more efficient).[40] Initially QWERTY served a particular purpose, that of preventing the typist from gaining too much speed and thereby causing type-bar clashes. According to David, three factors were responsible for the advent and ultimate dominance of QWERTY: technical interrelatedness, economies of scale, and quasi-irreversibility of investment. These three factors result in increasing returns to adoption. Arthur (1989) showed in a formal model how one of two competing technologies will come to be locked in because of increasing returns to adoption, with path dependency resulting.

These writers argue that history is important in processes displaying these features. Evolutionary processes, in general, however, are prone to path dependency, even without increasing returns to adoption. This fact follows from the nature of evolutionary processes as an unfolding of the knowledge of the environment. History is thus important in any evolutionary process in which time must pass before encoding of the environment takes place.

Functionalism

Unlike biologists, economists have no adequate and ultimately workable conception of adaptation. This is not altogether surprising given the counterpart of adaptation in social theories, functionalism, which is itself a widely misunderstood concept.[41] The basic idea of functionalism is, of course, pervasive: We explain the function of money as that of reducing transaction costs, or we explain the function of antitrust as that of fostering competition, or we explain the function of banks as acting as the intermediary between borrowers and lenders.

The functional explanation does not, as is usually believed, connote the absence of conscious behavior. Larry Wright (1984) has argued quite persuasively that the distinction between conscious and natural functions offers no explanatory content to the matter. "Both natural and conscious functions are functions," he writes (p. 365), "by virtue of their being the reason the thing with the function is there." This follows from his definition of what a function is: "The function of X is Z means (a) X is there because it does Z, (b) Z is a consequence (or result) of X's being there." Contrast this with Elster's (1983, p. 57) criteria of what it means for something to be a function. Elster's criteria are overly restrictive to classes of events that exclude intentional behavior (which he equates with conscious behavior). Whether conscious behavior is present has no bearing on functional explanation. Moreover, behavior itself is often the product of unconscious processes.

At least when not used in the proper context, a functionalist explanation may easily be interpreted as having explained a structure or phenomenon as an optimal solution to some problem. It is, of course, unfortunate that there is nothing in functionalist accounts of things that demands history to be an overriding factor. In biology, natural selection can be invoked to give a causal reason for something's existence. But this does not tell us anything of the history of the thing; all it tells is that the thing has a function because there was selection for the thing to have that function. Again, it is easy to interpret the function as optimal because it was selected for, and therefore represents the end product of natural selection, an adaptation. As Mayr (1988, p. 134) remarks, "the ambiguous meaning of the term adaptation is particularly disturbing. For instance, it is used both for the process of becoming adapted and for the end stage of having achieved adaptedness." Functional explanations almost always neglect the process of becoming adapted and instead favor the end state, which draws attention away from other important factors in the process.

Lewontin (1984) and Gould and Lewontin (1984) harshly criticize an all-too-exclusive focus on the functional aspect of adaptation. The explanation of a trait as having arisen because it solves some problem optimally they christen the adaptationist program.

> Hidden in the adaptive analyses are a number of assumptions that go back to theistic views of nature and a naive Cartesianism. First, it must be assumed that the partitioning of organisms into traits and the partitioning of environment into problems has a real basis and is not simply the reification of intuitive human categories . . . A second hidden assumption is that characters can be isolated in an adaptive analysis and that although there may be interaction among characters, these interactions are secondary and represent constraints on the adaptation of each character separately . . . The entire trend of adaptive evolutionary arguments is toward a Cartesian analysis into separate parts, each with its separate function." (Lewontin, 1984, pp. 241–242)

The Gould and Lewontin attack on the adaptationist program centers on the possibility that the organism as a whole is constrained by the imperatives of architecture. Atomizing an organism into small parts allows one to make broad appeals to optimizing arguments because each trait is not constrained by others. The adaptationist program follows a methodology that always seeks to find the adaptive significance of a trait: When one argument fails, try another—or at worst, admit ignorance—all the while proclaiming the trait to be optimally adaptive. Such a program results in telling "just-so" stories. But as Mayr (1988) points out, this methodology is common to all the natural sciences—when one hypothesis fails try another. Mayr also points out that Gould and Lewontin's charge that most biologists pursue a naive reductionist strategy in their study of adaptation is inaccurate. The adaptationist program, if properly executed, can indeed provide useful knowledge on evolutionary processes. Mayr (1988, p. 155) urges biologists to steer "a middle course . . . between a pseudoexplanatory reductionist atomism and an agnostic nonexplanatory holism."

In the social sciences, what this advice amounts to is an admonition to practice intelligent methodological individualism (Langlois, 1983) or, perhaps more appropriately, intelligent reductionism (Dawkins, 1986).[42] This means that when studying the significance of a certain technology (say QWERTY) or institution, one must explore how the individual aspects (of the system, of the whole) influence or constrain the pathways of evolution. This demands that we look at history. One should not forget to perform some functional analysis as well, especially since, as Gould himself notes, some kind of functional analysis is necessary to save the natural selection argument from tautology (Gould, 1977, p. 42).

Why is it that economists are only just beginning to grapple with the problem of path dependence? The chief reason is the role of rationality as understood in neoclassical theory.[43] Conscious, rational choice means that one always chooses the best among given alternatives, even when optima are constrained so as to produce a second-best outcome. There is no problem with knowledge. Since organisms in biological evolution make no conscious choices among given alternatives (even though they may act as if they did), biologists have a less formidable obstacle impeding their understanding of complex phenomena.

Panglossianism

Many writers view the package of issues we have discussed—frequency and path dependence, the problems of functionalism—as putting the knife to an attitude they broadly describe as Panglossianism.[44] Like Voltaire's Doctor Pangloss, the Panglossian evolutionist thinks that survival implies efficiency, thus what exists is optimal and we live necessarily in the best of all possible worlds. We have already discussed many of the relevant issues, but it is perhaps appropriate here to put these in some perspective.

What gives the question of Panglossianism particular interest, of course, is its political implications. Those who criticize others as Panglossians—and these include biologists as well as economists—do so because they wish to undermine the view that an evolutionary approach supports *laissez-faire* policies or argues against state intervention and central planning. What is little noticed, however, is that there are two different issues involved. To use evolutionary reasoning to justify *laissez-faire* policies—or, indeed, any extant institution or set of institutions one chooses[45]—is indeed some sort of Panglossianism.[46] To argue against the efficacy of certain kinds of administrative intervention is, however, quite a different matter.

What makes many writers eager to attack Panglossianism is the fact that the evolutionary conception of economic, technological, and cultural dynamics surely does commit its adherents to a certain kind of "conservatism." In this view, as we have seen, knowledge—whether biological, cultural, or economic—is the product of systemwide learning over time.[47] It is not the product of design. Moreover, an evolutionary system is necessarily "conservative" in the sense that it must possess a nonvolatile genetic memory. As a consequence, a proponent of evolutionary explanation necessarily sees a complex evolved structure as possessing a wealth of built-up information, and possibly even wisdom. It is on this ground that Hayek criticizes as constructivist rationalism the impulse to synoptic redesign of social order. Such a conception of reason, he says, "gives us a sense of unlimited power to realize our wishes" and "assumes that all social institutions are, and ought to be, the product of deliberate design" (Hayek, 1973, pp. 5, 8).

It is conventional to view Panglossianism and constructivist rationalism as opposites. A fear of constructivism, in this view, commits one to accept whatever exists as optimal. Ironically, however, a true Panglossian *is* a kind of constructivist rationalist. Pangloss reconstructs past designs as optimal. Constructivist rationalists construct hypothetical designs as optimal. In a sense, they are duals—mirror images of one another. Both supply a rationalist interpretation (or reinterpretation) of what is in fact an evolutionary trial-and-error process. The true opposite of the constructivist rationalist is the evolutionary skeptic. Far from seeing what exists as optimal, the evolutionary skeptic sees it a central insight of evolutionary thinking that society is always necessarily an imperfect and unfinished edifice. But the skeptic also understands that improvement is inherently a matter of experiment not synoptic design. Thus the skeptic's proposals for "intervention" will take the form not of a concrete picture of society but of a concern for the abstract structure of society—for its mechanisms for generating and selecting variation; that is, the skeptic is concerned with processes, not directly with outcomes. It is for these reasons that many evolutionary social thinkers, from Smith to Hayek, have favored the background set of institutions so often derided as *laissez faire*.[48] What Smith rather misleadingly called the obvious and simple system of natural liberty is, to many of these thinkers, an "intervention" that recommends itself not for the wonderful *status quo* it produces but for its potential to change and improve society. Evolution means creative destruction, a view with which Schumpeter would no doubt have agreed.

Notes

1. By cultural artifacts we mean not merely technology but institutions in the broadest sense, including culture, norms, conventions, and modes of organization.

2. In fact, variation plays a dual role in the theory of natural selection: It is both *explanans* and *explanandum*. This is so not only because we try to explain the diversity of human artifacts, but also because we do so by explaining how selection causes uniformity in populations. The argument for this assertion is somewhat complicated, and we refer the reader to Sober (1984, Chap. 5), who says that for natural selection "to work at all, there must be variation (in fitness). But once a selection process begins, it gradually destroys the conditions needed for its continued operation. Selection eliminates variation in fitness, and thereby brings itself to a halt" (Sober, 1984b, p. 159).

3. The other well-known condition for natural selection is the principle of differential fitness. All three conditions—variation, heritability, and differential fitness—are necessary and sufficient for a natural selection process to occur (Lewontin, 1984).

4. In his *Dialogues Concerning Natural Religion*, written (though not published) exactly 100 years before *The Origin of Species* appeared, David Hume (1980) clearly articulated the idea of natural selection as a general mode of explanation.

5. There is ample evidence to support this view in light of the examination of Darwin's notebooks by various scholars. Schweber (1977, 1980), in fact, attributes Darwin's concentration on the diversity of individuals in populations to the principle of the division of labor (functional specialization) in market economies. This focus led Darwin to place attention on individual selection, much as in Smith's theory, in which each individual, by pursuing his or her own selfish aims (individual competition), promotes the well-being of society as a whole and creates social order. Darwin's influences here were McCulloch, Smith, and a zoologist, Milne-Edwards, who (unlike Darwin) freely credited his theory to the political economist Jean-Baptiste Say, a follower of Smith. This lack of a directing planner or mind creating social order—the invisible hand—led Darwin to fashion his theory not around a divinity with a certain purpose in mind but around individuals struggling to survive with the environment

favoring those with adaptive characteristics. One biologist, Stephen Jay Gould (1980, p. 66), believes that "the theory of natural selection should be viewed as an extended analogy—whether conscious or unconscious on Darwin's part I do not know—to the laissez faire economics of Adam Smith." One observer of Darwin's notebooks (Gordon, 1989, pp. 456–457), though, believes that "no substantial support can be provided for the thesis that the Darwinian theory of evolution drew significantly upon ideas in contemporary Political Economy." See also Hayek (1988) for more references.

6. Though there were important precursors, such as the Anglo-Dutch pamphleteer Bernard Mandeville, whose chief work was *The Fable of the Bees*, and Giambattista Vico, who presented his ideas in *Scienza Nuova*.

7. Robert K. Merton (1936), quoted in Hamowy (1987).

8. In our view, there is no fundamental difference between evolutionary explanations, notably natural selection, and invisible hand explanations. The distinction Ullmann-Margalit draws is really only one of convenience. Consider the aggregate mold. Once the institution is explained to be the unintended result of human action, then even if we admit that its existence today is predicated on conscious behavior, this does not mean that it hadn't been selected naturally.

9. There is, in fact, good reason to doubt an unqualified version of this assertion. As Eric Jones (1987) suggests, economically successful societies (such as, broadly speaking, Western Europe in comparison with the great Asian civilizations) were the ones that grew not *extensively* through increased population but *intensively* through rising per capita income. The latter process actually involved norms and practices that limited population growth.

10. See, for instance, Hirshleifer (1977, 1982) and Becker (1976) for economists' viewpoints and E.O. Wilson (1975), Dawkins (1976), Maynard Smith (1982), D.S. Wilson (1980), and Sober (1984a, 1984b) for the biologist's perspective.

11. See Marshall's *Principles*, 8th edition reprint (1982), pp. 42, 205–207, 263, 635, and 641 for some his analogies of economics to biology. See also Thomas (1991) for more references. For Marshall's (p. 495) principle of substitution, which he says "is nothing more than a special and limited application of the law of the survival of the fittest," see especially pp. 296–295 and 448. The principle of substitution is actually better thought of as a selection process (Moss, 1982, p. 6).

12. Thomas (1991, pp. 11–12) argues that Marshall "would have to work out within him the foundations of yet another science—economic biology. If that was so, one could hardly blame him for regarding this as a task for his successors not for him."

13. That Marshall incorporated this aspect of Darwin's theory is shown in the introduction to his first edition of the *Principles*. He says (1982, pp. vi, vii): "If this book has any special character of its own, that may perhaps be said to lie in the prominence which it gives to this and other applications to the Principle of Continuity . . . Nature knows no absolute partition of time into long periods and short; but the two shade into one another by imperceptible gradations, and what is a short period for one problem, is a long period for another." By the eighth edition, (1982, p. xii) Marshall asserted that the motto "is specially appropriate to a volume on Economic Foundations."

14. These new combinations, Schumpeter (1934, p. 66) says, cover five broad areas: "(1) The introduction of a new good . . . (2) The new introduction of a new method of production . . . (3) The opening of a new market . . . (4) The conquest of a new source of supply of raw materials or half-manufactured goods . . . (5) The carrying out of the new organization of any industry."

15. The terminology is borrowed from Eldredge and Gould (1972), who used it to describe biological evolution.

16. See Schumpeter (1934, pp. 57–58), who evidently has Marshall in mind when he speaks against Darwinism and evolutionary theory in economics.

17. See Gould (1980) for more. Gould and Eldredge, in fact, believe that "speciation is responsible for almost all evolutionary change" (Gould, 1980, p. 183). This is, of course, similar to Schumpeter's notion that economic change is initiated only by radical innovations.

18. As we mentioned earlier, Marshall was concerned with recombination—finding combinations of existing methods within a known framework. In contrast, Schumpeter's concern was with *new* combinations, those that create new paradigms and destroy older ones—the process of creative destruction.

19. In an earlier paper (Langlois and Everett, 1992), we try to confront this problem and apply it to the economics of organization.

20. Alchian (1950, p. 216) proposes that "if explanation of past results rather than prediction is the task, the economist can diagnose the particular attributes which were critical in facilitating survival, even though individual participants were aware of them."

21. See Scriven (1959).

22. After all, Alchian does consider the role of conscious adaptation, and he suggests that "the economic counterparts of genetic heredity, mutations, and natural selection are imitation, innovation, and positive profits."

23. Here we necessarily leave out the criterion of reproductive success. There is no conceivable way, at least for us, to think of firms as reproducing themselves. They can, however, replicate their routines. Fitness is defined as survivability, or the ability to produce positive profits.

24. Perhaps even better, we may think of firms as the "vehicles in which replicators travel about" (Dawkins, 1982, p. 82). Dawkins (1982, p. 295) defines a vehicle as "any relatively discrete entity, such as an individual organism, which houses replicators and which can be regarded as a machine programmed to preserve and propagate the replicators that ride inside it."

25. We discuss the topic of the unit of selection more fully below.

26. See also Witt (1985, 1989), who takes a more explicitly evolutionary approach.

27. Assuming the so-called Nash conjecture, that is, assuming that, in each iteration, both players will assume that the other will do in the next period what he or she did in that last. There are, of course, many other conjectures, which is the principal problem with the static approach.

28. Or, more correctly, on the sum of transaction and production costs.

29. On the importance of modularity, see Langlois and Robertson (1992).

30. This is similar to the biological theory of Sewall Wright (1931, 1945, 1978), who suggested that a population consisting of N individuals in a closely knit group will produce less variation than N individuals living semi-isolated from each other. The fact that there are isolated populations *is the major cause* for speciation (Dawkins, 1986). Darwin (1975, p. 254), of course, was among the first to notice this fact, writing, "isolation must be eminently favourable for the production of new specific forms." But it's important that isolation be incomplete in some sense, for there must at times be interaction for accumulation of knowledge to occur. Otherwise, every step of the evolutionary process would be random and knowledge would not be stored; moreover, there would be gross duplication of energy with each isolated system starting anew.

31. Darwin himself was unaware of Mendelian biology and therefore had no conception of where mutations originated.

32. Is the unit what there is selection *of* or selection *for*? Apparently, it may be either in Sober's theory.

33. This seems to be the position of Sterelny and Kitcher (1991, p. 601), who propose that "there are alternative, maximally adequate representations of the causal structure of the selection process." But they reject "the idea that natural selection acts on some determinate target, such as the genotype or the phenotype." They are right to assert that selection acts causally on properties and not on entities as such.

34. Darwin, however, did toy with the idea of group selection (Sober, 1984b, p. 216).

35. Though not species selection as a sort of a group selection (Mayr, 1988).

36. Though not necessarily, some assert (Sober, 1984b, pp. 262–263).

37. But see Simon (1990), who argues that genuine altruism may arise in an evolutionary model because of docility and bounded rationality. His argument is that since social learning (docility) contributes to fitness, bounded rationality in combination with such docility may lead to altruistic behavior. He claims that "because of bounded rationality, the docile individual will often be unable to distinguish socially prescribed behavior that contributes to fitness from altruistic behavior" (p. 1667). Rules of behavior then evolve that enforce this type of altruistic behavior, and the individual is committed to following the altruistic rule.

38. See Sober (1984b, pp. 176 ff.) for a biologist's discussion and Witt (1992) for an economist's discussion.

39. We pose the same question below, where we develop the idea more fully. Here we want only to explain path dependency as developed in the literature thus far (and add a more general alternative).

40. But see Liebowitz and Margolis (1990).

41. Adaptation and functionalism are not exact counterparts, however. The functionalist asks "how?" He or she wants to know how a thing works. Adaptation in evolutionary theory evokes a "why?" question. As Mayr (1988, p. 25) puts it, "when the evolutionist asks 'Why?' he or she always has in mind the historical 'How come?' " Adaptation connotes some notion of causality. See also Lewontin (1984).

42. Dawkins argues that the intelligent reductionist is one who practices "hierarchical reductionism," involving just an "honest desire to understand how things work" (Dawkins, 1986, p. 13). Understanding the architecture of complexity demands the examination of the parts in their hierarchical structure and not just "wholes."

43. See Langlois (1986).

44. See especially Hodgson (1991), who explicitly cites many of these issues as invalidating the idea that existence implies efficiency.

45. Charges of Panglossianism are normally leveled at supporters of limited administrative government. In fact, however, there are probably as many writers who, in the modern age of big government, are Panglossians with respect to the institutions of the social-democrat welfare state.

46. This is not to say, of course, that evolutionary considerations are never properly adduced as one set of arguments in favor of one's preferred set of existing institutions. That an institution has passed the test of time is one piece of evidence, even if it is never definitive evidence, in favor of that institution's functionality or desirability.

47. This is true even for the punctuationist, since existing structures are the result of several—possibly innumerable—past episodes of rapid speciation.

48. This is quite clear in Hayek's *The Constitution of Liberty* (1960). A perusal of this volume will disabuse the reader of the idea, which Hodgson (1991) raises in a footnote, that Hayek's conception of constructivist rationalism paradoxically prevents him from arguing in favor of liberal institutions in Eastern Europe.

References

Alchian, A. 1950. "Uncertainty, Evolution and Economic Theory." *Journal of Political Economy* 58:211–222.

Alchian, A. 1953. "Biological Analogies in the Theory of the Firm: Comment." *American Economic Review* 43(4):600–603.

Alchian, A., and Woodward, S. 1988. "The Firm is Dead; Long Live the Firm: A Review of Oliver E. Williamson's *The Economic Institutions of Capitalism.*" *Journal of Economic Literature* 26(1):65–79.

Arrow, K.J. 1959. "Towards a Theory of Price Adjustment." In *The Allocation of Economic Resources*. Moses Abramovitz, ed. Stanford: Stanford University Press, pp. 41–51.

Arthur, W.B. 1989. "Competing Technologies, Increasing Returns, and Lock-in by Historical Small Events." *The Economic Journal* 99:116–131.

Axelrod, R. 1984. *The Evolution of Cooperation.* New York: Basic Books.

Barzel, Y. 1987. "The entrepreneur's Reward for Self-Policing." *Economic Inquiry* 25:103–116.

Becker, G.S. 1976. "Altruism, Egoism and Genetic Fitness: Economics and Sociobiology," *Journal of Economic Literature* 14:817–826.

Coase, R.H. 1937. "The Nature of the Firm." *Economica* (N.S.) 4:386–405.

Dahlman, C. 1979. "The Problem of Externality." *Journal of Law and Economics* 22:141–162.

Darwin, C. 1975. *Charles Darwin's Natural Selection: Being the Second Part of His Big Species Book Written from 1856 to 1858.* R.C. Stauffer, ed. Cambridge, UK: Cambridge University Press.

David, P.A. 1985. "Clio and the Economics of QWERTY." *American Economic Review, Papers and Proceedings* 75:332–337.

Dawkins, R. 1976. *The Selfish Gene.* Oxford: Oxford University Press.

Dawkins, R. 1982. *The Extended Phenotype*. Oxford: W.H. Freeman.

Dawkins, R. 1986. *The Blind Watchmaker*. New York: W.W. Norton.

Eldredge, N., and Gould, S.J. 1972. "Punctuated Equilibria: An Alternative to Phyletic Gradualism." In *Models in Paleobiology*. T.J.M. Schopf, ed. San Francisco: Freeman, Cooper and Co., pp. 82–115.

Enke, S. 1951. "On Maximizing Profits: A Distinction Between Chamberlin and Robinson." *American Economic Review* 41:566–578.

Elster, J. 1983. *Explaining Technical Change.* Cambridge, UK: Cambridge University Press.

Friedman, M. 1953. "The Methodology of Positive Economics." In *Essays in Positive Economics*. Chicago: University of Chicago Press.

Gordon, S. 1989. "Darwin and Political Economy: The Connection Reconsidered." *Journal of the History of Biology* 22(3):437–459.

Gould, S.J. 1977. *Ever Since Darwin.* New York: W.W. Norton and Company.

Gould, S.J. 1986. "The Panda's Thumb of Technology." *Natural History* 96.

Gould, S.J., and Lewontin, R.C. 1984. "The Spandrels of San Marco and the

Panglossian Paradigm: A Critique of the Adaptationist Programme." In *Conceptual Issues in Evolutionary Biology*. E. Sober, ed. Cambridge: MIT Press.
Hamowy, R. 1987. *The Scottish Enlightenment and the Theory of Spontaneous Orders.* Carbondale, IL: Illinois State University Press.
Hannan, M.T., and Freeman, J. 1989. *Organizational Ecology*. Cambridge: Harvard University Press.
Hayek, F.A. 1945. "The Use of Knowledge in Society." *American Economic Review* 35(4):519–530.
Hayek, F.A. 1952. *The Sensory Order: An Inquiry into the Foundations of Theoretical Psychology.* Chicago: University of Chicago Press.
Hayek, F.A. 1960. *The Constitution of Liberty*. Chicago: University of Chicago Press.
Hayek, F.A. 1973. *Law, Legislation and Liberty. Volume I: Rules and Order*. Chicago: University of Chicago Press.
Hayek, F.A. 1979. *The Counter-Revolution of Science,* 2nd edn. Indianapolis, In: Liberty Press.
Hayek, F.A. 1988. *The Fatal Conceit: The Errors of Socialism.* Chicago: University of Chicago Press.
Heilbroner, R. 1986. *The Worldly Philosophers,* 6th ed. New York: Touchstone Books.
Hirshleifer, J. 1977. "Economics from a Biological Viewpoint." *Journal of Law and Economics* 15:1–52.
Hirshleifer, J. 1982. "Evolutionary Models in Economics and Law: Cooperation versus Conflict Strategies." *Research in Law and Economics* 4:1–60.
Hodgson, G.M. 1991. "Economic Evolution: Intervention Contra Pangloss." *Journal of Economic Issues* 25:519–533.
Hull, D.L. 1989. *The Metaphysics of Evolution*. Albany, NY: State University of New York Press.
Hume, D. 1980. *Dialogues Concerning Natural Religion and the Posthumous Essays.* Indianapolis, In: Hackett Publishing.
Hume, D. 1992. *A Treatise of Human Nature*. Buffalo, NY: Prometheus Books.
Jones, E.L. 1987. *The European Miracle: Environments, Economics, and Geopolitics in the History of Europe and Asia*, 2nd ed. Cambridge, UK: Cambridge University Press.
Katz, M., and Shapiro, C. 1985. "Network Externalities, Competition, and Compatibility." *American Economic Review* 75:424–440.
Klein, B., Crawford, R.G., and Alchian, A. 1978. "Vertical Integration, Appropriable Rents, and the Competitive Contracting Process." *Journal of Law and Economics* 21(2):297–326.
Kuhn, T.S. 1970. *The Structure of Scientific Revolutions*, 2nd ed. Chicago: The University of Chicago Press.
Langlois, R.N. 1983. "Systems Theory, Knowledge, and the Social Sciences." In *The Study of Information: Interdisciplinary Messages*. F. Machlup and U. Mansfield, eds. New York: John Wiley, pp. 581–600.
Langlois, R.N. 1984. "Internal Organization in a Dynamic Context: Some Theoretical Considerations." In *Information and Communications in Economics:*

New Perspectives. M. Jussawalla and H. Ebenfield, eds. Amsterdam: North-Holland, pp. 23–49.

Langlois, R.N. 1986. "Rationality, Institutions, and Explanation." In *Economics as a Process: Essays in the New Institutional Economics.* R.N. Langlois, ed. New York: Cambridge University Press, pp. 225–255.

Langlois, R.N. 1988. "Economic Change and the Boundaries of the Firm." *Journal of Institutional and Theoretical Economics* 144:635–657, reprinted in Bo Carlsson, ed., *Industrial Dynamics: Technological, Organizational, and Structural Changes in Industries and Firms.* Dordrecht: Kluwer Academic Publishers, 1989, pp. 85–107.

Langlois, R.N. 1992. "Transaction-cost Economics in Real Time." *Industrial and Corporate Change* 1(1):99–127.

Langlois, R.N. 1993. "Orders and Organizations: Toward an Austrian theory of Social Institutions." In *Austrian Economics: Tensions and New Directions.* B. Caldwell and S. Boehm, eds. Dordrecht: Kluwer Academic Publishers, pp. 165–183.

Langlois, R.N., and Everett, M.J. 1992. "Complexity, Genuine Uncertainty and the Economics of Organization." *Human Systems Management* 11(2):67–75.

Langlois, R.N., and Koppl, R. 1991. "Fritz Machlup and Marginalism: A Reevaluation," *Methodus* 3(2):86–102.

Langlois, R.N., and Robertson, P.L. 1989. "Explaining Vertical Integration: Lessons from the American Automobile Industry." *Journal of Economic History* 49:361–375.

Langlois, R.N., and Robertson, P.L. 1992. "Networks and Innovation in a Modular System: Lessons from the Microcomputer and Stereo Component Industries." *Research Policy* 21(4):297–313.

Lewis, D.K. 1969. *Convention: A Philosophical Study*. Cambridge: Harvard University Press.

Lewontin, R.C. 1974. *The Genetic Basis of Evolutionary Change*. New York: Columbia University Press.

Lewontin, R.C. 1984. "Adaptation." In *Conceptual Issues in Evolutionary Biology*. E. Sober, ed. Cambridge: MIT Press.

Liebowitz, S.J., and Margolis, S.E. 1990. "The Fable of the Keys." *Journal of Law and Economics* 33(1):1–25.

Loasby, B.J. 1986. "Organization, Competition, and the Growth of Knowledge." In *Economics as a Process: Essays in the New Institutional Economics.* R. Langlois, ed. New York: Cambridge University Press, pp. 41–57.

Marshall, A. 1982. *Principles of Economics,* 8th ed. Philadelphia: Porcupine Press.

Maynard Smith, J. 1982. *Evolution and the Theory of Games.* Cambridge, UK: Cambridge University Press.

Mayr, E. 1988. *Toward a New Philosophy of Biology.* Cambridge: The Belknap Press of Harvard University Press.

Menger, C. 1963. *Problems of Economics and Sociology.* Urbana, IL: University of Illinois Press.

Moss, L. 1982. "Biological Theory and Technological Entrepreneurship in Marshall's Writings." *Eastern Economic Journal* 8(1):3–13.

Nelson, R.R., and Winter, S.G. 1977. "In Search of More Useful Theory of Innovation." *Research Policy* 5:36–76.

Nelson, R.R., and Winter, S.G. 1982. *An Evolutionary Theory of Economic Change.* Cambridge: The Belknap Press of Harvard University Press.

Penrose, E.T. 1952. "Biological Analogies in the Theory of the Firm." *American Economic Review* 42:211–240.

Penrose, E.T. 1959. *The Theory of the Growth of the Firm.* New York: John Wiley and Sons.

Radford, R.A. 1945. "The Economic Organization of a P.O.W. Camp." *Economica* 12:189–201.

Rowe, N. 1989. *Rules and Institutions.* Ann Arbor, MI: University of Michigan Press.

Schotter, A. 1981. *The Economic Theory of Social Institutions.* New York: Cambridge University Press.

Schotter, A. 1986. "The Evolution of Rules." In *Economics as a Process: Essays in the New Institutional Economics*. R.N. Langlois, ed. New York: Cambridge University Press, pp. 117–133.

Schumpeter, J. 1934. *The Theory of Economic Development.* Cambridge: Harvard University Press.

Schweber, S.S. 1977. "The Origin of the *Origin* Revisited," *Journal of the History of Biology* 10(2):229–316.

Schweber, S.S. 1980. "Darwin and the Political Economists," *Journal of the History of Biology* 13(2):195–289.

Scriven, M. 1959. "Explanation and Prediction in Evolutionary Theory." *Science* 130:447–482.

Silver, M. 1984. *Enterprise and the Scope of the Firm.* London: Martin Robertson.

Silverberg, G. 1988. "Modelling Economic Dynamics and Technical Change: Mathematical Approaches to Self-Organisation and Evolution." In *Technical Change and Economic Theory.* G. Dosi et al., eds. London: Frances Pinter, pp. 531–559.

Silverberg, G., Dosi, G., and Orsenigo, L., 1988. "Innovation, Diversity and Diffusion: A Self-Organisation Model." *Economic Journal* 98:1032–1054.

Simon, H.A. 1990. "A Mechanism for Social Selection and Successful Altruism." *Science* 250:1665–1668.

Sober, E. ed. 1984a. *Conceptual Issues in Evolutionary Biology*. Cambridge: MIT Press.

Sober, E. 1984b. *The Nature of Selection.* Cambridge: MIT Press.

Sterelny, K., and Kitcher, P. 1991. "The Return of the Gene." In *The Philosophy of Science*. R. Boyd, P. Gasper, and J.D. Trout, eds. Cambridge: MIT Press.

Sugden, R. 1986. *The Economics of Rights, Cooperation, and Welfare*. Oxford: Basil Blackwell.

Teece, D.J. 1980. "Economies of Scope and the Scope of the Enterprise." *Journal of Economic Behavior and Organization* 1(3):223–247.

Teece, D.J. 1982. "Towards an Economic Theory of the Multiproduct Firm." *Journal of Economic Behavior and Organization* 3:3–63.

Teece, D.J. 1986. "Profiting from Technological Innovation: Implications for Integration, Collaboration, Licensing, and Public Policy." *Research Policy* 15:285–305.

Thomas, B. 1991. "Alfred Marshall on Economic Biology." *Review of Political Economy* 3(1):1–14.

Tushman, M.L., and Anderson, P. 1986. "Technological Discontinuities and Organizational Environments." *Administrative Science Quarterly* 31:419–465.

Ullmann-Margalit, E. 1977. *The Emergence of Norms.* Oxford: Clarendon Press.

Ullmann-Margalit, E. 1978. "Invisible Hand Explanations," *Synthese* 39:282–291.

Vanberg, V. 1986. "Spontaneous Market Order and Social Rules: A Critical Examination of F.A. Hayek's Theory of Cultural Evolution." *Economics and Philosophy* 2(1):75–100.

Williams, G.C. 1966. *Adaptation and Natural Selection.* Princeton, NJ: Princeton University Press.

Williamson, O.E. 1975. *Markets and Hierarchies.* New York: The Free Press.

Williamson, O.E. 1985. *The Economic Institutions of Capitalism.* New York: The Free Press.

Wilson, D.S. 1980. *The Natural Selection of Populations and Communities.* Menlo Park, CA: Benjamin/Cummings.

Wilson, E.O. 1975. *Sociobiology.* Cambridge: Harvard University Press.

Winter, S.G. 1964. "Economic 'Natural Selection' and the Theory of the Firm." *Yale Economic Essays* 4:225–272.

Witt, U. 1985. "Coordination of Individual Economic Activities as an Evolving Process of Self-Organization." *Economie Appliquée* 37:569–595.

Witt, U. 1989. "The Evolution of Economic Institutions as a Propagation Process." *Public Choice* 62:155–172.

Witt, U. 1992. "Evolutionary Economics: An Interpretative Survey." Paper presented at the J.A. Schumpeter Society Conference, Kyoto, Japan, August, 1992.

Wright, L. 1984. "Functions," In *Conceptual Issues in Evolutionary Biology.* E. Sober, ed. Cambridge: MIT Press.

Wright, S. 1931. "Evolution in Mendelian Populations." *Genetics* 16:97–159.

Wright, S. 1945. "Tempo and Mode in Evolution: A Critical Review." *Ecology* 26: 415–419.

Wright, S. 1978. *Evolution and the Genetics of Populations, Vol. 4: Variability Within and Among Natural Populations.* Chicago: University of Chicago Press.

Wynne-Edwards, V.C. 1962. *Animal Dispersion in Relation to Social Behavior.* Edinburgh: Oliver & Boyd.

3 THE UNIT THAT EVOLVES: Linking Self-Reproduction and Self-Interest

Michael Hutter

Introduction

It has again become fashionable among economic theorists to model economic development as an evolutionary process. The concept has been used successfully to explain the origin and the development of biological, including human, beings. Although social scientists know that the insights into biological development gained cannot be transferred naively to their subject of observation, the paradigm is too tempting to be left to the colleagues in the natural sciences.

The success of biological evolution theory depended decisively on the conceptualization and subsequent discovery of genes. Since then, the simultaneous continuity and discontinuity characteristic to the development of life forms can be modelled as the simultaneous existence of *genotypes* and *phenotypes*. The phenotypes interact with the environment of the life form and are used up in the process. The genotype maintains the information necessary for a continuous self-reproduction of the life form. But what is it that corresponds to the simultaneous existence of genotype and phenotypes in economic evolutionary theories?

The next section demonstrates that the dominating approaches in the field formulate derivatives of either psychic or physical evolution. The following section explores a theory of self-referential social systems for its application to the evolutionary processes of and within economies. The last section closes by discussing the time frames that characterize alternative approaches in social evolutionary theory.

Leading Approaches

In this section we will discuss three of the leading approaches in the field. We will demonstrate that in every case the actual carriers of evolution remain outside of the economy.

Game Theory

A decision situation involving several actors will lead to predictable outcomes with respect to the strategies chosen by the actors, if alternative strategies and their payoffs are sufficiently well known. If a series of games takes place, then we can observe that the actors' behavior stabilizes into behavior routines or institutions.[1] If changes in the environment of the supergame affect alternatives or payoffs, then routines of behavior will adapt. Schotter (1981) has used this approach to develop a general theory of social institutions; Axelrod (1984) has explored some fundamental behavior routines in empirical detail.

Game-theoretic models have become, without doubt, the most sophisticated technique for modelling cooperative hehavior and its changes. However, the approach is based on demanding information assumptions. Alternative strategies as well as comparable payoffs have to be known. Change occurs on the outside, and the adaptive reactions of rational actors remain always predictable. The choices under discussion are the choices of conscious individuals. What is called *evolution* is actually a process of stimulus-response-adaptation on a psychological level. Even the notion of selection is difficult to integrate, because it would imply the spontaneous invention of new strategies that are tested against traditional alternatives. The continuity of reproduction, therefore, lies either in the rationality of the actors considered or in their biological continuity, but certainly not in the routines that are chosen.[2]

Spontaneous Orders

The approach starts from a question that Boland (1978, p. 240) has aptly called the "Hayek problem": "How can we explain the process of change in economics and remain consistent with the principles of (individual) rational decision-making?" We are now assuming considerably lower information levels than in the game-theoretic approach. Rules and institutions come about by invention or by chance; they are selected and stabilized to form ever more complex systems of behavioral rules.

> "Evolution sehen wir als unbeabsichtigtes Ergebnis des Zusammen-wirkens von Mechanismen der Variation, Selektion und Stabilisierung, welche zur Steigerung der Eigenkomplexität eines Systems führen. Unter anderem zeigt sich die Komplexitätserhöhung in zunehmender Differenzierung der inneren Struktur, der Zunahme der Kontrollfähigkeit und Selbststeuerungskapazität und der damit verbundenen Entwicklung neuer Kommunikationssysteme." (Röpke, 1977, p. 82)

Despite considerable advances in the theory of self-organizing structures,[3] there have been few translations into the theory of spontaneous or self-organizing orders. Hayek, apparently, counted on insights gained through systems theory and cybernetics (1973, p. 37). Röpke (1977) compared in great detail the predetermination of phenotypal characteristics through genetic fixation with the predetermination of economic decisions through behavioral routines. But there seems to have occurred little advance beyond the normative implication that one shouldn't meddle with the Laws of Institutional Change.

The Hayek problem is indeed rather intricate. Institutional evolution alongside individual evolution implies a process of coevolution between "mind" and "spontaneous order," and this relationship remains to be clarified. There are indications in Hayek's work that a genuine autonomous evolution of spontaneous orders is intended. But, faced with the lack of an appropriate logic, only "minds" are acknowledged as having the property of self-reproduction:

> Mind is as much the product of the social environment in which it has grown up and which it has not made as something that has in turn acted upon and altered these institutions. It is the result of man having developed in society and having acquired those habits and practices that increased the chances of persistence of the group in which he lived. The conception of an already fully developed mind designing the institutions which made life in society possible is contrary to all we know about the evolution of man. (1973, p. 17)

The continuity in the development of creative minds, apart from the reproductive continuity of biosystems, seems to be an axiom. Actually, we know very little about the continuity of consciousness. It must be the introspective experience of the modern observer that makes this kind of psychic continuity so much more self-evident and so much less a problem than the process of social continuity.

Biocultural Evolution

This approach has the absolutely lowest information requirements: It thinks in centuries and millenia. It is an attempt to explain the emergence of cultural states as an aspect of biological evolution. We will not discuss the simplistic version, which assumes genes for cooperation and altruism (Dawkins, 1976). A more sophisticated version has been offered recently. Lumsden and Wilson (1981) concentrate on the process of *growth* from genotype code to phenotype specimen. Here, routines take the form of "an array of transmissible behaviors, mentifacts, and artifacts" called *culturgens*. "They are processed through a sequence of *epigenetic rules*, which are the genetically determined procedures that direct the assembly of the mind." (1981, p. 7) This ambitious approach, developed in great formal and empirical detail, goes far to explain basic forms of cultural organization. At no point, however, do the examples approach the degree of detail necessary for, say, the organization of a central bank, or the institution of a patent system. We are still basically talking about biological human evolution, proceeding in 25-year production cycles. The focus of observation is on cultural changes measured in centuries, and if one studies stages in the historical development of an economy, one might indeed opt for such a biocultural approach.

There are some indications that Schumpeter's concept of economic development, for instance, belongs to that category. Schumpeter's innovative leader is a specifically bred human specimen, part of a class that is bound to die out, thus causing the decline of the economic phase, which depends on its creativity. We thus encounter a vision of heightened, refined individuality:

> Auch hier (in der modernen Wirtschaft M.H.) wird der Fortschritt ohne und selbst gegen den Willen der hedonischen Majorität erzwungen. Die Mittel dazu sind hier nicht weniger scharf und wirksam, sondern nur weniger auffallend wie die physische Macht des Sklavenhalters oder die Befehlsgewalt des Feudalherren. . . . Das Prinzip ist also: Der Unternehmer kauft produktive

> Leistungen, entzieht sie so ihren statischen Verwendungen, verwendet sie, ohne ihre Besitzer weiter zu fragen und zwingt so die Volkswirtschaft in neue Bahnen hinein." (1912, pp. 188–89)

Although Schumpeter allows in his later work for a transfer of R + D activities to large corporations, he does not concede a transfer of creativity as well. Other authors have interpreted the original hypothesis in a less elitist fashion by studying the restrictions and incentives for the behavior of average mortals (see especially Witt, 1987). In any case, the source of evolution remains clearly external, either viewed as psychic creativity or physical acculturation.

The Schumpeter hypothesis has also instigated another version of evolutionist modelling. If change is external—be it in the mind of the entrepreneurs or in other systems of the environment—then it can be simulated through random shocks. Economic evolution is then basically a process of adaptation. An additional level of sophistication can be introduced if we assume deliberate search routines within firms, as Nelson and Winter (1982) suggest. Nelson and Winter go as far as labelling the routines within firms as "genes", because they endow them with (stochastic) variation. This thought will be explored in the next section, but in doing so we grant much more autonomy to these processes than Nelson and Winter intended.

We conclude that the approaches under consideration either rely on conscious, rational individuals or on biological genotypes as sources of evolution. In the first case we are restricted to the analysis of short-term choices under high information requirements; in the second case we are restricted to general cultural patterns, independent of specific communication structures. We will now attempt to fill the gap between the two approaches. In doing so we will conserve the basic feature of biological evolution: self-reproduction, but generalize it to social evolution. We will also conserve the basic feature of economic theory: self-interest, but generalize it beyond individual actors.

Institutions and Social Systems

Evolutionary Change in Biological Systems

If the distinction between genotype and phenotype defines the process called *institution*, then this distinction must be maintained in applying the paradigm to the process of social evolution. Already the identification of social phenotypes leads to problems: Is it entire economies; is it individual

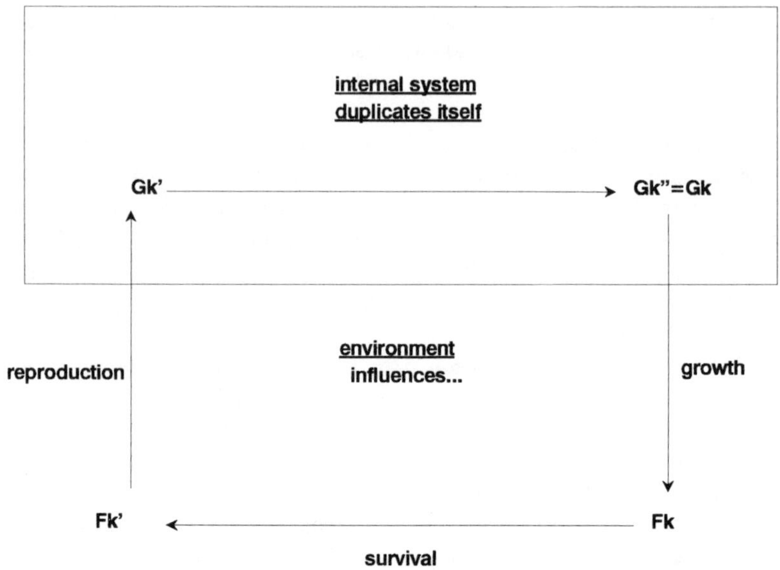

Figure 3.1. The process of evolution.

firms, households and other actors; or is it clusters of institutions that evolve? We will take the position that all of these organizational forms are phenotypes in the social sphere. The internal logic of these phenotypes is quite diverse, however. We will restrict further observations to economies and to firms. Even in these two cases, we encounter great difficulty in our next tasks—the adequate identification of social genotypes. If organizational forms are phenotypes, where are the *units* that maintain the information for self-reproduction?

To enter the argument, it is helpful to recapitulate our present knowledge about evolutionary change. Witt (1987, p. 85) uses a graphical model, which is reproduced in a somewhat altered form in Figure 1. The continuity of the set of instructions for self-reproduction is maintained in a genetic program $G_{K'}$, more exactly, a probability distribution of a genetic program K'. As the set of instructions is reproduced, it can be changed through genetic drift (stochastic variations in recombination), genetic flow (addition of new individuals to the genetic pool), and mutation (copying errors in recombination). The duplicated genetic program $G_{K''}$, recursively redefined as G_K, leads to temporary emanations called phenotypes. The probability distribution of the population of phenotypes K is called F_K. The growth and the survival of F_K depends on the forces of its environment. Finally the population that is able to resist or manipulate its environment reproduces itself, thus reproducing the system's genetic program. The forms of reproduction, in themselves part of the genetic program, vary widely in biological evolution. They determine which part of the surviving population $F_{K'}$ gets a chance to duplicate its genetic program and thus to constitute $G_{K'}$.

Evolution in Social Systems

How can this account of biological evolution be translated into the social sphere? What does $G_{K'}$ look like in firms? We have an explicit statement in the literature as far as that question is concerned.

> Our general term for all regular and predictable behavioral patterns of firms is a routine . . . in our evolutionary theory, these routines play the role that genes play in biological evolutionary theory. (Nelson and Winter, 1982, p. 14)

In Nelson and Winter's theory, routines embody the instructions to search for new solutions or better adaptations. Their further theory development, however, leaves the social and returns to the psychophysical world. Search is assumed to take place in the minds of individuals, just as Schumpeter had suggested. The "real" genes, therefore, are the genes of the individuals involved in the routines. We, however, will stay within the social world. We take the Nelson–Winter routines at face value: They are "predictable behavioral patterns," including technical routines, procedures for hiring and firing, ordering inventory and controlling production levels, policies for investment, R + D, advertising, and strategy.

It is now claimed that this internal language of messages and actions is the source of other messages and actions that are intended to interact with the environment of that firm. Managers come and go, wars break out and end, products and process change, but the set of routines continues. Something called the "identity" of the company, the corporation, or the conglomerate is maintained. At this point, a reduction of firm identity to the identities of participating human life forms is customary. We will not take this step. We will be content with firm identity as the source of self-interest.

Our contentment with the firm as a self-interested actor is based on the contention that self-interest is a property common to all so-called self-referential systems. The class of self-referential systems, however, contains not only humans. It also contains life forms and social organizations. Self-referential systems are a weaker assumption than individuals, yet they are sufficient for the hypothesis of self-interest.

What is self-referentiality?[4] Self-referentiality is the property of a system to constitute its own self. A system is any set of interacting elements. The system is called self-referential if it is able to constitute its *own elements* (interal environment) and its *own distinction* between the self and its surroundings (external environment).

Life forms are obvious examples of self-referential systems because biological organisms produce their own elements in strict autonomy. At the same time, they are able to interact with what they perceive as their environment. Every single biological cell is such a self-referential or "autopoietic" system (Maturana et al., 1974; Varela, 1981).

Mental processes in humans are recognized as being self-referential since, roughly, the 18th century. Apparently, the individual creates its own world through the distinction between its mind and everything outside of it. Since the "enlightenment," the continuity of individual consciousness has become a common experience to modern observers. The self-perception or rationality of individual minds was accepted as the only mode of self-reference. A new social theory, based on the continuity of mind, illuminated the possible stretch of conscious human choice. The restriction to the psychic mode is logically stringent, as Locke already mentioned.[5] Traditional economic theories are still based on this discovery of psychic self-reference. Unfortunately, that has severe consequences: Neither life forms nor social systems are granted autonomy; they are treated as resources in the individuals' environments. For phenomena within brief time spans, the limitation is harmless. But if such theories are used as tools for long-term decisions, then they further the destruction of life forms and social systems.

Throughout the history of economic theory there have also been attempts to base the theory of the social system "economy" on genuine social elements. But historicist biologism (Hutter, 1994a) had as little success as Commons' suggestion of using the transaction as elementary unit. There is no possibility of integrating such a term unless the logical structure of a transaction—as a temporal and, thus, reproducing element in a self-referential social system—is recognized.

The outlines of the proposed model are as follows[6]: Social systems consist exclusively of communication acts or messages. Within their internal communication (conversation), the systems are able to reproduce their own elements (messages). We can observe the continuous sequences of events that constitute an economy or a particular firm. Self-referential systems are able to distinguish themselves from their environments through the use of at least one basic semantic distinction.[7] That defines the system's identity—its unity. The distinctions themselves — and here lies the technical difficulty of theory construction — cannot be reflected by the systems that use them. A code cannot be used to decode itself. Social systems, therefore, are "systems whose descriptions through other social systems lead to undecidable logical contradictions in the observing systems" (Luhmann, 1984, p. 58).[8]

The way social self-reference works is directly experienced in the performance of plays.[9] Whether we are in them or whether we are watching them, we always know the borderline between the unity of the play and its outside world. Every communication act within the play carries an invisible tag that says: "This is play." But the existence of the tag must never be mentioned. Otherwise, the play disappears or becomes part of a larger play. Any play draws that charcoal circle, thus "severing the world into an observing and an observed part" (Spencer-Brown, 1969, p. 105). Some plays are as intricate as in classical theater and opera. They generate reference to a complex and changing outside world. Some plays are as simple as children's plays, generating only reference to the immediate common environment of the interaction.

These remarks were intended to provide a rather intuitive understanding of what is meant by self-referential social systems and to point immediately to the semantic difficulties involved in theory formulation. To make matters even more forbidding, we must keep in mind that the three types of self-referential systems evolve interdependently. Humans, for example, are physical *and* psychic systems. The Fortune 500 companies are mainly combinations of psychic *and* social systems. The self-interested play of the corporate actor coevolves with the self-interested individuals whose minds interact through their play.[10]

The Units of Economies and Firms

Keeping those warnings in mind, we will do our best not to think of physical bodies and human presences. We imagine economies and firms as swarms of events. Our economy presents itself as an ever-growing swarm, merging national economies into a world economy, dominating other forms of social logic. Firms present themselves growing and disappearing. Their basic structural of features have evolved slowly since the incorporations of the 13th and 14th century; greater sizes have become possible, merging and dividing has become commonplace. So these action systems are the phenotypes pursuing self-interest vis-à-vis an outside world. But what are the genotypes of these social forms?

Two questions are to be answered: What are the elementary units of an economy or a firm's identity? How do these units duplicate themselves? Now we are on thin theoretical ice, and every step is a conjecture. Social systems are primitive compared with the age-old life forms. Therefore, we should expect hardly more than a few distinctions to define the unity of an economy or a firm. For economies, the literature provides us with several suggestions: scarcity, value creation, payment, transaction, and property are tried out. In every case, the distinction is something distinct from the action system of the economy. The distinction *constitutes* the economy.

The "measure of value" debate, for instance, has accompanied economic theory since its beginnings. We suggest now that the problem is one of "decoding the code of money." The question, "how is value evaluated?," has only a paradoxical answer (Hutter, 1994b).

For firms, the debate has hardly begun. It is only 50 years ago that Coase planted the idea that teams or contractual relations might be forms of economic organization complementary to markets. Economic theory still assumes a cooperative individual behavior. But in legal science Teubner (1987) assumes the existence of self-interested "corporate actors", and in political science, Coleman (1981) has pointed to the growing relevance of "corporate actors."

As varied as firms, as a form of social organization, may appear, they share one classical feature: Their immediate environment is the action system of an economy. In order to establish identity, a firm must make itself continuously distinct from this environment. In many cases, the distinctions customary in families (a much older social form) are transferred: Leadership and loyalty are unquestionable principles. Where this tradition of distinction is unavailable, another way must be found to distinguish the coordination logic of the economy from the administration logic of internal organization. "Status" distinguishes itself from "contract," and any ritual, sign, or symbol will do if it effectively signifies the difference. Once it succeeds in doing so it is beyond questioning. Sociogenetic elementary units are, because of the blind spot of self-reference, removed from the actors of the economies or firms that they constitute, just as biogenetic codes are carried within phenotypes, but the phenotypes (up to now) have no way of interfering with their own code.

Assuming that there are such primitive sociogenetic codes, how do they reproduce themselves? After all, it is in this process of duplication that variation occurs in the physical world. The logic of self-referentiality has a simple answer: The act of indicating a unity duplicates that unity, and the unity only continues if it is repeated in another event indicating the same unity (Luhmann, 1983). Plays, based on nothing but their self-generated identity, can thus continue themselves endlessly.

The basic process seems to be a continuous comparisons of values. Values are the blind spots in our observations, and we communicate them unobtrusively, since it is their self-evidence that makes them effective (Luhmann, 1987). The message of every play contains information about evaluations that are held within the play. Responses can either *repeat* that evaluation or *negate* it. In either case, a value comparison has taken place that continues the original evaluation, and that can be continued by a future response—a payment, for instance, or an obligation. Since the future "response" complements the past "call," one can fruitfully describe communication acts (including economic and firm transactions) as oscillating relationships (Spencer-Brown, 1969; Teubner, 1987; Hutter, 1989).

In modern economies, these processes are maintained through the price program and through money as an internal medium of value. In firms, similar processes are channelled through the routines of internal decision making. These routines—a subset of the Nelson–Winter routines—process the firm's internal value comparisons. They are the meta-communication (Bateson, 1979, p. 129) that maintains continuity. As money transactions and firm decisions, respectively, continue themselves, they are subjected to variations homologous to the copying process in organic reproduction. We might therefore expect stochastic variations, genetic flow through new, combinable value comparisons, and errors in copying. Copying errors, however, only survive if they fit instantly into the routines of self-reproduction (Roth, 1982). A further exploration of such topics must, however, be based on a more explicit theory than is available today.

Conclusions

It was the primary aim of this paper to demonstrate that social phenotypes, like economies or firms, can be traced to social genotypes. Money transactions and firm decision routines, reproducing themselves and thus the leading distinctions of their plays, form the "unit that evolves." Of course, this approach is only one way to skin the cat called "economic development". If the time span considered is short and if the choices are well delineated, we do well by tracing social decisions to individual preferences and incentives. For secular historical change, we might turn to a study of biocultural evolution. The limitations and capacities of humans are surely the reason for the similarities that we observe in the evolution of civilizations. But for the time span in between, measured in decades, we might do best with the hypothesis of genuine social evolution. We are, to repeat, always implying a coevolutionary process, especially between minds and organizations. We do insist on the reproductive autonomy (not only the self-organization) of both; but we also insist on the continuous competition of psychic and social forms of self-interest. Methodic individualism is not rejected; it is, in fact, taken more seriously, since it is extended to all social persons, not only to those entities one chooses to acknowledge. The extension leads to a multiplication of participating players, but the basic applicability of the method is maintained, albeit without the normative recommendation that social persons should become more individualistic in order to simplify theorizing.

The coevolutionary process includes, last but not least, science's internal conversation.[11] We might, through a theory of self-referential social systems, develop ways of discussing the interaction between an economy and other subsystems of comparable coding, such as science, politics, law, and the arts, and we might develop a way to enter into ecological dialogues, which, in turn, might interfere with the routines of value comparison inside of firms and economies.

Notes

1. We might add the terms *rules*, *right structures*, *incentive structures*, etc. They all grapple with the same type of phenomena.

2. We will not discuss the contractarian or contractual approach in this context. In its traditional Wicksellian version, it implies even more stringent information requirements, permitting unanimity. In its contemporary public choice or transaction cost versions, it is characterized by intentional choices of "autonomous individuals" (Buchanan, 1986; Williamson, 1987). The attempts to unravel what "cost" means leads to the very problems discussed later, but the argument is developed in a somewhat different manner (Hutter, 1989).

3. See Blaseio (1986, ch. 3.2) for a review.

4. Luhmann (1984, p. 58) writes: "Self-reference signifies the unit which an element, a process, a system is "for itself"—that means, independent from the pattern (Zuschnitt) of observation through other." Divergent definitions of self-referentiality are easy to find. The one chosen seemed the simplest. See also von Foerster (1981), Hofstadter (1979), Roth (1982), Blaseio (1986), and Teubner (1986).

5. "Since the mind, in all its thoughts and reasonings, hath no other immediate object but its own ideas, which it alone does or can contemplate, it is evident that our knowledge is only conversant about them" (Essay Concerning Human Understanding, Book IV, caph. i, cited in Russell, 1961, p. 590).

On the career of "individualism," see Luhmann (1986).

6. Luhmann was the first author to present a theory of self-referential social systems (1983, 1984). This theory is still in its developing phase, which accounts for the semantic confusion and the gaps in our present knowledge. Only recently have there been attempts to apply the theory specifically to the economy (Hutter, 1989; Luhmann, 1988; Baecker, 1987).

7. The term goes back to Spencer-Brown's (1969) fundamental study. Luhmann, also referring to the same source, prefers the term *binary code*.

8. The appearance of logical contradiction in the attempt to describe a social system's language is well known in formal logic. The prominent contributions range from Russell's theory of logical types over Gödel's incompleteness proof to Hofstadter's strange loops. See Blaseio (1986).

9. The use of the term *play* enters science through Wittgenstein (1958). We are indeed talking about huge language plays (*Sprachspiele*) when we are considering social systems. For a more thorough elaboration of play as a frame of self-referential social action, see Bateson (1979, p. 154).

10. It is misleading, therefore, to reproach a theory of self-referential social systems for marginalizing individuals, for making them squatters in the house of society. A self-referential theory is based on clear distinctions between internal and external elements, between autonomy and environment, but it leaves always the choice to designate the system of reference. From the point of view of social systems, psychic systems must be part of the environment. From the point of view of psychic systems, social systems must be part of the environment. This approach preserves the autonomy and integrity of both.

11. The observed subjects interact in the same social space as the observing subjects. The genes under investigation are not tiny bits of matter, they are part of all too familiar language routines. We stalk, as it were, through the caverns of our own hereditary code, trying to identify structures and single pieces.

References

Axelrod, R. 1984. *The Evolution of Cooperation*. New York: Basic Books.

Baecker, D. 1987. "Das Gedächtnis der Wirtschaft." In: *Theorie als Passion. Niklas Luhmann zum 60. Geburtstag*. D. Baecker et al., eds. Frankfurt: Suhrkamp, pp. 519–556.

Bateson, G. 1979. *Mind and Nature. A Necessary Unity*. New York: Bantam.

Blaseio, H. 1986. *Das Kognos-Prinzip*. Berlin: Duncker & Humblot.

Boland, L.A. 1978. "Time in Economics vs. Economics in Time: The Hayek Problem." *Canadian Journal of Economics* 240–262.

Buchanan, J. 1987. "The Constitution of Economic Policy." *AER*.

Coleman, J.S. 1981. *The Asymetric Society*.

Dawkins, R. 1976. *The Selfish Gene*. Oxford: Oxford University Press.

v. Foerster, H. 1981. *Observing Systems*. Seaside Intersystems.

v. Hayek, F.A. 1973. *Law, Legislation and Liberty*, Vol. 1; *Rules and Order*. Chicago: University of Chicago Press.

Hofstadter, D. 1979. *Gödel, Escher, Bach: An Eternal Golden Braid*. New York: Basic Books.

Hutter, M. 1994a. "Organism as a Metaphor in German Economic Thought." In *Markets Read in Tooth and Claw*. P. Mirowski, ed. Cambridge: Cambridge University Press, in print.

Hutter, M. 1994b. "Communication in Economic Evolution: The Case of Money." In *Evolutionary Concepts in Contemporary Economics*. R. England, ed. Ann Arbor, Michigan: University Press, in print.

Hutter, M. 1989. *Die Produktion von Recht. Eine selbstreferentielle Theorie und der Fall des Arzneimittelpatentrechts*. Tübingen: Mohr.

Lumsden, C.J., and Wilson, C.O. *Genes, Mind and Culture. The Co-Evolutionary Process*. Cambridge: Harvard University Press.

Luhmann, N. 1983. "Die Wirtschaft der Gesellschaft als autopoietisches System". *Zeitschrift für Soziologie* 13.

Luhmann, N. 1984. *Soziale Systeme. Grundriß einer allgemeinen Theorie*. Frankfurt: Suhrkamp.

Luhmann, N. 1986. "The Individuality of the Individual: Historical Meaning and Contemporary Problems." In *Reconstruction Individualism*. T.C. Heller et al., eds. Stanford: Stanford University Press, pp. 313–354.

Luhmann, N. 1987. "Tautologie und Paradoxie in den Selbstbeschreibungen der modernen Gesellschaft." *Zeitschrift für Sociologie*.

Luhmann, N. 1988. *Die Wirtschaft der Gesellschaft*. Frankfurt: Suhrkamp.

Maturana, H.R. 1981. "Autopoiesis." In *Autopoiesis: A Theory of Living Organization*. M. Zeleny, ed. New York: North-Holland.

Maturana, H., Uribe., R., and Varela, F. 1974. "Autopoiesis, the Organization of Living Systems: Its Characterization and a Model." Biosystems, 5:187–196.

Nelson, R., and Winter, S. 1982. *An Evolutionary Theory of Economic Change*. Cambridge, Belknap Press.

Röpke, J. 1977. *Strategie der Innovation*. Tübingen: Mohr.

Roth, G. 1982. "Conditions of Evolution and Adaptation in Organisms as Autopoietic Systems." In *Environmental Adaptation and Evolution*. D. Mossakowski and G. Roth, eds. Stuttgart: Fischer.

Russell, B. 1961. *History of Western Philosophy*. London: Allen and Unwin.

Schotter, A. 1981. *The Economic Theory of Social Institutions*. Cambridge, UK: Cambridge University Press.

Schumpeter, J.A. 1912. *Theorie der wirtschaftlichen Entwicklung*. Leipzig: Duncker & Humblot.

Spencer-Brown, G. 1969. *The Laws of Form*. London: Allen and Unwin.

Teubner, G. 1987a. "Unitas Multiplex. Probleme einer Konzernverfassung in systemtheoretischer Sicht." Unpublished Manuscript.

Teubner, G. 1987b. *State, Law and Economy as Autopoietic Systems*. Berlin: De Gruyter.

Varela, F.J. 1981. *Principles of Biological Autonomy*. North Holland: New York.

Williamson, O. 1987. "The Contractual Logic of Internal Organization." Unpublished manuscript.

Witt, U. 1987. *Individualistische Grundlagen der Evolutorischen Ökonomik*. Tübingen: Mohr.

Wittgenstein, L. 1971. *Philosophische Untersuchungen* (1958). Frankfurt: Suhrkamp.

4 ON THE NATURE OF ECONOMIC EVOLUTION: John R. Commons and The Metaphor of Artificial Selection

Yngve Ramstad

> But Darwin had two kinds of "selection" among the variabilities: Natural Selection and Artificial Selection. Ours is a theory of artificial selection. John R. Commons. (1934a, p. 657)

In his famous 1898 essay, "Why Is Economics Not An Evolutionary Science?" Thorstein Veblen challenged economists to transform their discipline into an *evolutionary* science. In order to meet that standard, Veblen insisted, economic theory must be recast as "a theory of a cumulative sequence of economic institutions stated in terms of the process itself" (Veblen, 1919, p. 77). Except for the American institutionalists, most of whom self-consciously embraced Veblen's "research program," economists for the most part have ignored Veblen's plea. Trained in a tradition rooted in the "natural law" perspective of Adam Smith, "mainstream" economists[1] have generally conceived of market activity in acultural, ahistorical terms. Indeed, among the major figures in mainstream 20th-century economics, only Joseph Schumpeter has seen a need to incorporate an explicitly evolutionary stance into economic analysis.

In recent years, however, a growing number of economic theorists have come to believe that economic organizations (such as the business firm) and economic institutions (the governing rules of the game) must be accounted for in terms of an evolutionary process.[2] That is, *economic evolution*, if we take that term to mean a process of cumulative change in the way human provisioning (production and distribution) is effected, has become a "legitimate" object of interest for the economic theorist. That this is the case is now evident in such diverse areas as law and economics,[3] industrial organization,[4] and especially the growing literature widely referred to as the *new institutional economics.*[5]

Philip Mirowski has written extensively on the tendency of theories relating to the social realm to evince a conceptual structure mirroring theories originally developed to apprehend the natural world.[6] Applying this insight, he has shown that classical and neoclassical value theories have been based on conceptions borrowed from physics (Mirowski, 1989). Evolution, however, is external to the concerns of the physicist. Hence it is not surprising that in their various attempts to conceptualize economic evolution "in terms of the process itself," economists have frequently turned to the discipline of evolutionary biology for guidance and appropriated the Darwinian theory of natural selection as a metaphor. Jack Hirschleifer (1977) has even gone so far as to assert that sociobiology, which utilizes a strict natural selection framework to explain the social behavior of animal species, and economics are actually subsets of the same general field.[7] According to Hirschleifer, "The fundamental organizing concepts of the dominant analytical structures employed in economics and in sociobiology are strikingly parallel;" indeed, "[T]he social processes studied by economics . . . are not mere analogs but are rather *instances* of sociobiological mechanisms—in the same sense in which chemical reactions have been shown to be a special class of processes following the laws of physics" (Hirschleifer, 1977, pp. 1–2, 17).[8]

While others would perhaps not put it so boldly as Hirschleifer, there is little doubt the natural selection metaphor is widely applied to the phenomenon of economic evolution, even if non-self-consciously—as Alexander Rosenberg (1991, p. 26) has noted, "Darwin's notion of blind variation and natural selection has been one of the most tempting of metaphors in the social sciences." From the natural selection standpoint, the enterprises comprising the present-day economy are presumed to have evolved spontaneously and to have survived because they confer a competitive advantage of some type upon their originators in the struggle to capture real income. Similarly, modern-day economic institutions, which collectively determine the character of the "market mechanism," are presumed to have been "naturally" selected to facilitate ever-greater "efficiency" in the production and allocation of commodities. In other words, it is presumed that movement (economic evolution) has occurred, and will continue to occur, "automatically" or "naturally" under the governance of a brute process. Or to put it somewhat differently, it is presumed that the market system has evolved without conscious human design.[9]

Over the years there have been many who have questioned whether the natural selection metaphor is felicitous in economics.[10] Among the most perceptive of the critics is John R. Commons, who contended that in applying the natural selection metaphor to economic evolution economists had "borrowed" the wrong concept from biology, namely, the wrong selection principle. According to *Chambers Biology Dictionary*, selection is "The process by which some individuals come to contribute more offspring than others to form the next generation in *natural selection* through intrinsic differences in survival and fertility, in *artificial selection* through the choice of parents by the breeder" (Walker, 1989, p. 265). What clearly distinguishes "artificial" from "natural" selection, then, is the substitution of selection via the human *will* for selection via a brute process as the central factor shaping the direction of evolution. This crucial difference was emphasized by Darwin himself, who, without actually using the term in this passage, characterized artificial selection thusly:

> Although man does not cause variability and cannot even prevent it, he can select, preserve, and accumulate the variations given to him by the hand of nature almost in any way which he chooses; and thus he can certainly produce a great result. . . . Man may select and preserve each successive variation, *with the distinct intention of improving and altering a breed, in accordance with a preconceived idea*; and by thus adding up variations, often so slight as to be imperceptible by an uneducated eye, he has effected wonderful changes and improvements. . . . *As the will of man thus comes into play*, we can understand how it is that domesticated breeds show adaptation to his wants and pleasures. We can further understand how it is that domestic races of animals and cultivated races of plants often exhibit an abnormal character, as compared with natural species; for they have been modified not for their own benefit, but for that of man. (Darwin, 1972, pp. 3–4, emphasis added)[11]

As indicated, it was Commons's contention that artificial selection, not natural selection, has governed the actual evolution of the market system and hence provides the metaphor through which economic evolution can best be apprehended (Commons, 1934, pp. 636–637).[12] A failure to correctly perceive the actual principle of selection underlying the historical evolution of the "market mechanism" (economic institutions), Commons argued, has led economists to overlook its volitional derivation and thereby to a mistaken comprehension of its essential character. It was this fundamental misconception that Commons sought to remedy with his "institutional economics" (Ramstad, 1990).

Surprisingly, Commons's critique of the natural selection metaphor has been ignored by subsequent writers. Herein I attempt to redress this failure by showing why Commons's characterization of the selection principle underlying the evolution of economic institutions is both sound and important. I proceed as follows. In the first—and longest—part of the paper, I discuss and assess all manner of attempts to employ the natural selection metaphor in analysis relating to economic evolution. My purpose in so doing is twofold: First, to show how central the natural selection metaphor is to most theories of economic evolution and, second, to spell out some of the profound difficulties that are encountered when it is applied to economic evolution. Commons's alternative understanding of the process through which present-day patterns of economic interaction have actually evolved is outlined in the second part of the paper; it should be understood that my goal is only to indicate why Commons thought Darwin's concept of artificial rather than natural selection is the superior metaphor for economic evolution, not to develop a comprehensive overview of his theoretical standpoint.[13] Finally, in concluding, I briefly explore the practical implications of adopting Commons's standpoint.

Natural Selection in the Economics Literature

The Natural Selection Framework

Darwin developed his theory of natural selection to account for biological diversity and to pinpoint the mechanism through which the traits of organisms undergo qualitative change through time. The basic framework is breathtaking in its simplicity and can be summarized as follows. Nature is filled with living organisms that reproduce and develop according to an identifiable pattern. The ability of an individual organism to survive and reproduce depends on its capacity to provide itself with food; to protect itself from predators and impairments caused by heat, cold, and so on; and to produce viable offspring. Organisms tend to multiply geometrically through successive generations, which eventually produces a situation where, because the aggregate of their needs due to sheer numbers presses up against the carrying capacity of their environment, they must compete with one another in the struggle for survival.[14] There is considerable variation in the traits possessed by individual members of a species of like organisms. This variation is randomly generated rather than elicited by environmental needs. In the struggle for survival, individual organisms possessing traits giving them an advantage over other members of their species in securing food, in protecting themselves against predators and the dangers inherent in the natural environment, or in producing offspring tend to survive disproportionately to those possessing traits that fail to yield such advantages. These advantageous traits, in turn, are passed on through inheritance from possessor to offspring and subsequent descendants in future generations.

Given sufficient time, organisms possessing the most advantageous characteristics will tend to displace those that lack them; or, alternatively, organisms with different adaptive traits come into a sustainable balance. That is, the brute process of natural selection culls out of a species population those individual organisms that are the most "fit" to meet the fundamental challenges of their environment and eventually produces an "adapted" species population consisting overwhelmingly of similarly "fit" descendants. Whenever the relevant environment changes in some important way, variation and diversity within a species along with natural selection function to alter its members' traits so that they better match the requirements of the "niches" of viability afforded by the new environmental circumstances. In other words, as Richard Levins and Richard Lewontin (1985, p. 25) have put it, "The [natural selection] concept of adaptation is that the external world sets certain "problems" for organisms and that evolution consists in 'solving' these problems." It is through the vast number of small changes engendered by the process of adaptive evolution via natural selection, over billions of years, that the countless species of organisms now populating the planet were putatively brought into being.[15]

There are several additional details that should be noted regarding the evolutionary process depicted by the theory of natural selection. First, an organism's traits, such as appearance, function and behavior, are aspects of its *phenotype*. The genes coding those traits constitutes its *genotype*. Phenotypic traits are often coded by the interaction of several genes in combination (Rosenberg, 1985, p. 97). Inheritance is a genotypic phenomenon, whereas survival and reproduction—that is, phenotypic selection—occur at the level of the individual organism; however, inheritance *and environment* work together to shape an organism's phenotypes (Wills, 1989, p. 23). Second, all organisms possess recessive genes coding for traits not evident in the organism; in other words, genes coding for "non-adaptive" traits will be in a species' gene pool and thus will be incorporated into the gene structure inherited by manifestly "fit" members of a species.[16] Third, phenotypic variation can result from either genetic mutation or the recombination of genes accompanying sexual reproduction. Fourth, environmental changes are considered to be exogenous to the process of natural selection itself;[17] more to the point, it lies beyond the *volitional* control of the organisms comprising a species. Fifth, the process of natural selection proceeds without external guidance or design and proceeds toward no goal.[18] Sixth, for adaptive evolution to occur, the environment must remain more or less unaltered over long periods of time (many "generations" see Rosenberg, 1991, pp. 3, 12); natural selection proceeds extremely slowly (Rosenberg, 1991, p. 5). Seventh, what is adaptive for an individual organism, what improves its relative status, might not be adaptive for the species as a group; in such cases *group* adaptation remains imperfect (Hirschleifer, 1982, pp. 11–12).[19] Finally, generally there is no way in any context to predict the specific adaptation that an environmental alternation will induce.[20] This is in no small way a consequence of the fact that it is also impossible, in general, to enumerate in an actual environment exactly of what evolutionary "fitness" consists of (Rosenberg, 1991, p. 6). Moreover, the organism's genetic structure restricts the available paths of change (Gould, 1980, p. 157).

In summary, the biological theory of evolution has four principal constituents: a process for generating variations; a mechanism of inheritance to preserve "favorable" variations; the Malthusian tendency to geometric multiplication, leading sooner or later to "competition for existence" among organisms; and environmental selection (Hirschleifer, 1977, p. 8). Since the meaning of the term *natural selection* cannot be separated from the entire process of biological evolution, it would appear that a strong case cannot be made for the use of natural selection as a metaphor for economic evolution unless there are analogs for each of these four constituents. Indeed, strictly speaking, those analogs should also be consistent with the "additional details" that were enumerated.

As already suggested, several writers have attempted to use the natural selection metaphor in exploring questions of interest to economists. By looking at some of the fundamental problems they have encountered, it will be possible to see that abandonment of *natural selection* in favor of *artificial selection* will not involve a loss of analytical insight. It is to an overview of those problems that I now turn. The reader is forewarned that I make no attempt to provide a comprehensive review of the many uses of natural selection in the economics literature. My purpose is only to illustrate, first, that it is widely employed and, second, that there are sound reasons for questioning whether its use has actually furthered our understanding of processes in which economists are interested. It will be obvious that the brevity of the discussion makes it impossible to do justice to any of the authors whose views are examined.[21]

From Theory to Metaphor

As noted, the present revival of interest among economists in developing an evolutionary framework of analysis stems in the main from the desire to develop a sound theory of institutions and institutional change.[22] In a sense, the Darwinian revolution only reinforced an already well-established interest in the problem of social evolution evident both in British thought (Hayek, 1973, pp. 22–23) and in German Hegelianism. Indeed, Stephen Jay Gould has even gone so far as to assert that Darwin established his theory of natural selection by "grafting Adam Smith upon Nature" (Jones, 1986, p. 1052). All the same, the influence of Darwin is evident in the subsequent demise of the teleological approach to social evolution evident in the perspective that it marches toward the realization of a preexisting design intended by a divine creator, which earlier "evolutionary" thinkers such as Adam Smith had embraced, or toward a knowable destination, as Karl Marx had presumed.

The theory of natural selection itself (a theory of biological change) was originally appropriated by social theorists not in order to analyze economic evolution but to justify *laissez faire* economic policies. Thus Herbert Spencer and the Social Darwinists argued that market success, if it occurs in a context of economic competition, constitutes a selection mechanism comparable to biological natural selection through which the innate "fitness" of individual members of the human race is continually improved. Yet, in the main, Social Darwinism was an "add-on," leaving the conceptual apparatus of "mainstream" economic theory intact. It was not until the Darwinian perspective was appropriated by Thorstein Veblen, who had been a close student of Spencer's ideas (Eff, 1989), that it penetrated the domain of economic theory itself.

In his 1898 essay, "Why Is Economics Not An Evolutionary Science?," Veblen noted that as economic life has been transformed over the eons, "The physical properties of the materials accessible to man [have been] constants: it is the human agent that [has changed]—his insight and his appreciation of what these things can be used for is what [has developed]" (Veblen, 1919, p. 71). Accordingly, he proclaimed, what is needed is "a theory of the development of human nature" (Veblen, 1919, p. 78). A year later, Veblen forwarded such a theory, if in a somewhat scattered manner, in his *The Theory of the Leisure Class* (1889), originally subtitled *An Economic Study of the Evolution of Institutions*. Michael Boyles and Rick Tilman (1992) have shown that the "theory of the development of human nature" advanced in that work was unabashedly cast in a Darwinian natural selection mold. At first glance, Boyles and Tilman's interpretation would appear to fly in the face of the conventional view that Veblen saw human actions in behaviorist terms as the expression of institutions. They argue, however, that what Veblen actually contended was that "certain behaviors may only develop under the proper combination of genetic make-up and environmental conditions, . . . that it is institutional influence ['environmental conditions'] on hereditary make-up [genotype] that determines human behavior [phenotype]" (Boyles and Tilman, 1992, pp. 7, 10).[23] Averring that genetic predispositions lay behind the changing form of "human nature" observed in societies based on successively different modes of securing the material basis of life, and that humans are a hybrid of various original strains, Veblen focused his attention on the manner in which environmental pressures have "selected" from within the possibilities inherent in the human gene pool those whose traits incline them to be the most adaptive to existing conditions (Boyles and Tilman, pp. 3ff).

Unfortunately, or perhaps predictably, Veblen soon abandoned this promising start to the development of an explicitly Darwinian research program. Although he traced the predisposition to a particular line of action (under the right environmental circumstances) to one's genetic makeup, he recognized that the range of conduct to which that predisposition can give expression is extremely broad; that is, Veblen recognized that "genes" explain very little. Thus he changed to the practice of using the term *instinct* to signify, not a fixed inheritable trait, but rather a disposition for which one has an innate capacity yet whose concrete character, as reflected in behavioral traits, is shaped and passed on by cultural experience (Boyles and Tilman, 1992, p. 12).[24] This "mature" view is the one reflected in what may consider to be Veblen's most significant work, *The Instinct of Workmanship and the State of the Industrial Arts* (1914). In that work, Veblen largely ignored "tropisms" (innate reflexes) and concentrated instead on the manner in which *learned* "instincts" and *learned* "habits of thought" (institutions) reveal themselves in the economic choices of individuals and the modern business enterprise. To put it slightly differently, Veblen came to understand that it is the evolution of man as a *social* animal—conceived of as a coherent set of "institutions" ("settled habits of thought")—which must be explained "in terms of the process itself." The evolution of *institutions*, in other words, not the biological (human) organism, is what really matters in explaining the changing form of "human nature." In short, the attempt to cast economic behavior *in* biological theory turned out for Veblen to be a dead end. Metaphorical use of the natural selection framework would have to do.[25]

After Veblen's death in 1929, economists apparently lost interest in developing a "theory of human nature," as it bears on economic conduct, in terms fully compatible with the theory of natural selection. Not until Hirschleifer's recent attempt to synthesize economics and sociobiology, and thereby to work toward a biological interpretation of the goals ("preferences") motivating the economic actions of human beings, do we see a similar undertaking.[26] But even though economists resisted the temptation to attribute economic evolution to changes in the innate characteristics of the human being as a biological entity, many, like Veblen, eventually found biology to provide economics with a useful metaphor.

The Metaphor Misused: Natural Selection and The Business Firm

That natural selection provides an attractive metaphor for economic evolution did not occur only to Veblen. Alfred Marshall, for example, was explicit in stating that "The Mecca of the economist lies in economic biology" (Marshall, 1969, p. xii). This "biological" orientation is quite evident in the approach Marshall took in his *Principles of Economics* in introducing the topic of industrial organization. What he was seeking to do, he declared, was "... to consider the main bearings in economics of the law that the struggle for existence causes those organisms to multiply which are best fitted to derive benefit from the environment" (Marshall, 1969, p. 201). But despite the Darwinian language in this lead-in, Marshall did not in actuality continue on to make the claim that economic evolution proceeds in a manner closely paralleling Darwinian evolution. Indeed, as Margaret Schabas (1991) has pointed out, despite Marshall's avowed adoption of an evolutionary standpoint, the Darwinian revolution in biology actually had little influence on his thinking.[27] Moreover, as Talcott Parsons (1968, pp. 155–161) has shown, Marshall's view of economic evolution was wholly teleological.

In any event, despite his affinity for natural selection as a metaphor for economic evolution, Marshall's economic thought did not turn on evolution, and his analysis was clearly not "evolutionary" in spirit. It was the "real" nonevolutionary Marshall who was emulated by his successors, who uniformly revealed little or no interest in appropriating the biologist's tools to sharpen economic analysis. Thus it was not until the early 1950s that a "mainstream" economist actually attempted to ground an economic argument in the natural selection metaphor. And in yet another example of multiple discovery, the potential of the metphor was simultaneously recognized by two scholars, Armen Alchian (1950) and Milton Friedman (1953), who each employed the natural selection metaphor in order to legitimate continuing use of the conventional theory of the firm as a tool of analysis at a time when it was under severe attack.

The context is important here. During the 1930s and 1940s, conventional economic analysis had been subjected to regular criticism for providing an inadequate image of economic "reality." Seeming to make the case for the critics was a growing body of research findings that established individuals do not, in fact, consciously act to maximize utility, nor do the managers of business firms consciously act to maximize profits. Equally important, this research revealed the extent to which economic actors, rather than possessing "perfect knowledge," experience profound uncertainty regarding even the likely consequences of their own actions, including the manner in which profits will be affected.

Alchian's argument that "profit maximization" can be replaced with the weaker assumption of "positive realized profits" with no loss of predictive content is well known and need not be summarized here. What concerns us is whether or not his appropriation of the natural selection metaphor in order to reach this conclusion was apt. The earlier overview of the theory of biological evolution makes it clear that the "theory of natural selection" delineates an evolutionary process in which: (1) there is an "organism" that evolves by means of "adaptation" to environmental change, (2) there is a process generating "trait" (phenotype) variation among the relevant population of "organisms," (3) there are mechanisms of reproduction and inheritance through which each "organism" passes on its particular "traits" (phenotypes) to "offspring," (4) there is a Malthusian (nonrational) propensity for reproduction inherent in that "organism" that, given sufficient time, inexorably produces "life or death" competition—a "struggle for survival"—between similar "organisms," and (5) there is a brute process through which "organisms" possessing favorable or adaptive "traits" are selected. Accordingly, the obvious starting point in assessing whether or not the natural selection metaphor was felicitous is to ask: What are the "organisms" in whose evolution (adaptation) Alchian was interested? What ensures that such organisms exhibit trait variation? Who (or what) are their "offspring"? What is the mechanism of reproduction through which they expand until they press against the limits inherent in their environment? By what mechanism are "adaptive" traits selected? How are the traits of the "fit" (selected) organisms passed on to their progeny?

The problems inherent in Alchian's use of the natural selection metaphor are well known.[28] For example, even though he did make it clear that the firm is the organism upon which selection operates, Alchian failed to provide an analog for the Malthusian tendency toward overpopulation or to provide for a plausible inheritance mechanism. He also failed to address the issue of whether a market system is, in principle, comparable to a stable environment, which is required in biological theory for natural selection to operate. Even more serious, it is clear that species adaptation can take place within Alchian's conception of evolution without the passing on of "advantageous" traits possessed by a fraction of the original species population to a *different generation* of organisms (firms).[29] All that is needed for species "adaptation" to occur in Alchian's model is the disappearance ("death") of those within the *original* population who possessed "disadvantageous" traits and the concomitant expansion or *growth* (increase in size) of those who survive.[30] Surely, by itself, this is not analogous to *biological* evolution. Indeed, Alchian's conception of "evolution" would appear fully consistent with a situation in which, after a natural disaster, the modal member of an animal species gains weight because the survivors now each have more to eat, and one also, it might be noted, in which the "species" population (number of firms) gradually shrinks over time (toward oligopoly?). Briefly stated, *Alchian's "random choice" model does not refer to an "evolutionary" process even remotely analogous to Darwinian biological evolution.*

Hirschleifer has pointed out that Alchian actually provided a model of an evolutionary process analogous to Lamarckian biological evolution, that it is Lamarckian rather than Darwinian evolution that takes place within the "environment" populated by Alchian's firms. Lamarck maintained, first, that rather than being random, trait variation appears when it is needed and, second, that acquired characteristics (phenotypes) can be inherited directly, as Darwin himself originally believed. In an attempt to provide counterparts for biological mutation and heredity, Alchian appropriated the "Schumpeterian" concepts of purposeful problem solving via *innovation* and *imitation*. It may be granted that "innovation" (which includes failure-induced "imperfect imitation") provides Alchian with a parallel to Lamarckian "trait variation." But since other members of the existing "population" (competing firms) are explicitly allowed to "imitate" a successful innovator, it is difficult to see how Alchian's "imitation" is in actuality the parallel of biological "inheritance." In short, the argument that the model embodies a logic of change analagous to the Lamarckian rather than the Darwinian theory in no way vitiates the criticism being made that the process of "adaptation" postulated by Alchian is fundamentally different from that propelling the process of *biological* evolution.[31]

Edith Penrose (1952) has raised another serious issue. It was Alchian's evident belief that allowing for imitation and innovation as adaptive mechanisms brought his conception of economic evolution into close correspondence to the theory of biological evolution. However, the addition of two postulated "counterparts," in fact, entails a radical alteration of the biological framework and introduces its own logical difficulty. For, to add imitation and innovation is to add the dimension of purpose, a factor that we have noted is explicitly disallowed in the biological theory of natural selection. More important, in the present context, it calls into question the applicability of the adaptation process postulated by Alchian. We shall return to this matter shortly, but let us first turn to Friedman's use of the natural selection metaphor.

Not sharing Alchian's willingness to concede that some aspects of conventional theory—and particularly the assumption of profit maximization—might be dispensed with, Friedman sought to reestablish the legitimacy of what he called "the maximization-of-returns hypothesis" as a tool of analysis.[32] Friedman's use of the natural selection metaphor is well known, but, due to its significance in the subsequent development of economics, nonetheless merits a brief recounting. Friedman's central argument hinged on the proposition that whether a theory's assumptions are "true" or "realistic" is irrelevant to the issue of whether the theory may legitimately be employed. In what is surely one of the most consequential methodological propositions ever forwarded by an economist, Friedman maintained that a theory's "validity" is fundamentally a matter of whether its predictions are on the mark, or at least "close enough." As a result, if, from the vantage point of the theorist, economic agents can reasonably be seen to behave "as if" they are motivated by the desire to "maximize their returns," he is on solid ground in basing his theory—so long as it generates accurate predictions—on the assumption that they actually do so, *irrespective of what their true motives in fact might be.* But this argument leads to the question: Are there indeed plausible grounds upon which business men can reasonably be seen to act *as if* they are rationally seeking to maximize their returns and *as if* they have full knowledge of the data needed to do so? It was in searching for an answer to these (implicit) questions that Friedman recognized the utility of the natural selection metaphor:

> Confidence in the maximization-of-returns hypothesis is justified by evidence of a very different character [than?]. . . . Unless the behavior of businessmen in some way or other approximates behavior consistent with the maximization of returns, it seems unlikely that they would remain in business for long. Let the apparent immediate determinant of business behavior be anything at all—habitual reaction, random chance, or whatnot. Whenever this determinant happens to lead to behavior consistent with rational and informed maximization of returns, the business will prosper and acquire resources with which to expand; whenever it does not, the business will tend to lose resources and can be kept in existence only by the addition of resources from outside. The process of

> "natural selection" thus helps to validate the hypothesis—or, rather, *given natural selection*, acceptance of the hypothesis can be based largely on the judgment that it summarizes appropriately the conditions for survival. (Friedman, 1953, p. 22, emphasis added)[33]

Of particular interest here is Friedman's offhand reference to "natural selection," in which he clearly implied that economic competition among firms for profits is analogous to biological competition among organisms for existence. If one accepts this analogy, it is but a short leap to conclude, with Friedman, that whatever goals the owners of business firms or their agents perceive themselves to be pursuing (the "apparent immediate determinant of business behavior"), competitive pressures will inexorably weed out those that are "unfit," namely, those firms that do not in fact maximize their profits, and replace them with those that are "fit." By this logic he sought to strengthen the plausibility of the "as if" argument he was making and thereby to justify, in the face of extensive and persistent criticism, the continuing use of the conventional theory of firm behavior.

While Friedman's use of the natural selection metaphor was indisputably an effective rhetorical ploy,[34] critics have pointed to numerous problems that call into question the cogency of the argument itself.[35] Like Alchian, Friedman failed to provide for either an analog to the Malthusian principle, that is, a mechanism producing a "surplus" of firms and the consequent necessity of selection, or an analog to genetic inheritance. With respect to the latter, Geoffrey Hodgson has developed an especially interesting point. It is the role of genes in evolutionary theory to program certain types of traits or behaviors into organisms so that they will possess the same capacities and thus, under similar environmental conditions, tend to act in the same way as their parents. Assuming with Friedman that profit maximization is not a conscious goal but that firms failing to maximize profits are nonetheless eliminated through economic competition, if there are no "genes" ensuring that the traits (behaviors) consistent with profit maximization are passed on to ensure continuance of maximizing behavior *as conditions change*, one cannot account for firm survival through time in a rapidly changing economic environment—and is rapid change not a principal feature of the marketplace?—other than "to ressurect the earlier notion that maximizing behavior is deliberative, conscious behavior" (Hodgson, 1988, p. 78). However, as Hodgson points out, this means that criticisms regarding the empirical validity of the maximization assumption itself cannot be disregarded as Friedman sought to do.

Another problem with Friedman's analysis inheres in his presumption that economic competition ("natural selection") ensures that only a "fit"—that is, truly "efficient"—firm will be able to survive through time. Thus, the "as if" argument.[36] However, in a carefully developed mathematical analysis, Katsuhito Iwai has shown that if one allows for the possibility of technological imitation—and recall that Alchian explicitly did so in order to provide adequate analogs in his model for evolutionary theory—"the selective force of market competition is no longer capable of weeding out the less fit even in the long run. Not only the most efficient but also the whole spectrum of firms with diverse efficiencies will survive forever" (Iwai, 1984, p. 347). What this means is that, even if one grants that natural selection is an appropriate metaphor, Friedman's presumption about the consequences of such selection was incorrect in a world in which there is innovation and imitation.

In sum, it would appear that Alchian and Friedman's resort to the natural selection metaphor in order to "save" the conventional theory of the firm was not only fundamentally misguided in its infelicitous analogy between a business enterprise and a biological organism but was also counterproductive. For as we have seen, without specifying a conscious mechanism to guide firm behavior (as implicit in Friedman's "as if" approach), firm survival cannot be accounted for. Yet if "realized positive profits" and the "Schumpeterian" notions of innovation and imitation are introduced into the argument as a substitute for conscious "profit maximization," it cannot be shown that "surviving" firms must by necessity be "fit" in the economic sense of being "efficient" (produce at minimum cost). Only one conclusion is possible: Alchian and Friedman's strategy of treating the business firm as an "organism" subject to "natural selection" *in order to save the conventional theory of the firm* backfired. For it quickly became apparent that "natural selection" as a metaphor for the process through which the modern enterprise has evolved would have to be discarded unless a different conception of the firm than conveyed by conventional economic theory was developed. Richard Nelson and Sidney Winter's *An Evolutionary Theory of Economic Change* (1982) is probably the best known attempt to develop such a conception. While Nelson and Winter's theory is far too complex to recount in detail here, its significance regarding the felicity of the natural selection metaphor merits some probing.

Nelson and Winter (NW) sought in this undertaking to develop "an evolutionary theory of the capabilities and behavior of business firms operating in a market environment" (Nelson and Winter, 1982, p. 3). We have already noted that NW understood this to necessitate a different conceptualization of the business firm from that employed in neoclassical analysis. Thus NW recast the firm as an entity whose observable activities are prefigured in "routines" programming the activities performed, including those relating to problem solving, by individuals associated with the firm. NW further declared that routines in the firm are analogous to genes in the biological organism (Nelson and Winter, 1982, pp. 14, 401). NW therefore perceived themselves to have remedied one of the principal problems evident in Alchian and Friedman's use of the natural selection metaphor.

Nelson and Winter also deviated from mainstream conventions by jettisoning the "maximization hypothesis" and replacing it with the weaker presumption that firms are *motivated* by profit. They further postulated that in the pursuit of profit firms engage in ongoing "search" for new technology and new routines that, if adopted, would likely increase realized profits. Self-consciously employing a "Schumpeterian" conception of competition, NW interpreted search to entail the activities of innovation and imitation, which they deemed to constitute the analog of biological mutation (Nelson and Winter, 1982, p. 18). NW emphasized, significantly, that like all other intrafirm activity, the search process is structured by routines; that is, they considered search to be in actuality nothing other than routine-directed "innovation" and routine-encapsulated "imitation." As a final step, NW proposed that in an environment characterized by "market supply and demand conditions that are exogenous to the firms in question," it is reasonable to presume that firms whose search activity allows them to become relatively more profitable will grow, while firms whose search activity does not will shrink and perhaps even diasappear (Nelson and Winter, 1982, p. 17). This allowed them to declare that economic competition between firms, which operates to relentlessly weed out "unfit" members (less profitable firms) from the "species" population (industry), can appropriately be understood as the analog of natural selection (Nelson and Winter, 1982, p. 9).

Alexander Rosenberg has recently remarked on the puzzling fact that "few books can have had a more disappointing reception [than Nelson and Winter's] in recent economics;" indeed, he opined, it appears to have fallen "still-born from the presses" (Rosenberg, 1991, p. 21). We shall not here explore the many possible reasons for this failure,[37] as our concern is simply to inquire whether the reconceptualization of the firm as a routine-guided "organism" allowed Nelson and Winter to surmount the inherent difficulties we have noted regarding the felicity of the natural selection metaphor. The attentive reader will perhaps have noticed that NW essentially added the concept of routines to the model earlier forwarded by Alchian. Hence it is not surprising to find that here also "adaptation" can be accounted for through the growth or change of *existing* "organisms" (firms). For, according to NW, an existing firm can alter its character through the "new plant decision" (investment decision allowing for a change in its routines; cf. Nelson and Winter, 1982, p. 17). Indeed, NW aver that the new plant decision is analogous to biological "birth" and hence provides their theory with a mechanism through which "inheritance" takes place (Nelson and Winter, 1982, p. 14). Thus it is in the competitive selection of various type of plants, NW aver, that we find a "selection mechanism ... clearly ... analagous to the natural selection of genotypes with differential net reproduction rates in biological evolutionary theory" (Nelson and Winter, 1982, p. 17).

But difficulties remain. It is the firm, not its individual plants, that comprises the "organism" for whose evolution they seek to account (cf. Nelson and Winter, 1982, p. 9). Thus once again we see that differential reproduction success ("birth") spreading "adaptive" traits (profit-producing routines) to successive *generations* of "organisms" (firms) has no *necessary* role in determining the direction of change in the "capabilities and behavior" of business firms (cf. Nelson and Winter, 1982, p. 14). As Mirowski (1983, p. 764) put it, in the NW model of evolution "Nothing is ever the same, yet nothing ever dies either." In short, despite NW's reconceptualization of the firm, their model of evolution also entails a process of change fundamentally unlike that encompassed in the Darwinian conception of biological evolution.

To their credit, Nelson and Winter understood this and were quite clear in asserting that there was a model of evolution more in conformity with the Lamackian than with the Darwinian conception of evolution (Nelson and Winter, 1982, p. 11). However, as Mirowski (1983) has shown, even by Lamarckian logic the NW theory cannot be deemed to encapsulate a process analagous to biological evolution. Just like Darwinian evolution, Lamackian evolution requires a relatively stable species or else "selection" becomes an irrelevant concept; that is, the biological structure of the "selected" entity (for NW, the business firm) must have a general character and must develop traits according to an indentifiable pattern, that tends to persist in the face of environmental change. But the NW theory has no such entity at its core since the "firm" whose evolution NW depicts in their various models is in actuality nothing more than "capital-jello," which by definition has no specific character. It is for this reason, Mirowski points out, that NW's "organisms" are so adept at "undergoing self-initiated transformations in reaction to environmental alternations" (Mirowski, 1983, p. 764). Even on their own "Lamarckian" grounds, then, Nelson and Winter must be judged to have been no more successful than Alchian and Friedman in establishing that firm "capabilities and behavior" have evolved in a manner in any way analagous to the evolution of the characteristics possessed by biological organisms through a process of natural selection.

In sum, the endeavor to treat the business firm explicitly as an economic "organism" whose evolution can be understood through analogies to either Darwinian or Lamarckian biological evolution has proved to be misguided. One can hardly put it better than Edith Penrose did some 40 years ago:

> [Biological analogies] are of no real value and in fact may conceal the essential nature of economic processes.... [They] contribute little ... to the theory of growth and development of firms.... [A]s a metaphor [the biological theory of evolution] is badly chosen.... [I]n seeking the fundamental explanations of economic and social phenomena in human affairs the economist, and the social scientist in general, would be well advised to attack his problems directly and in their own terms rather than indirectly by imposing sweeping biological models upon them. (Penrose, 1952, pp. 804, 819)

If the foregoing analysis is on target, the only possible meaningful similarity between biological evolution of species and the economic evolution of firms is the putative selection of "fit" firms by means of a brute process—economic competition.

Natural Selection and "Schumpeterian" Evolutionary Economics

We have noted that Alchian as well as Nelson and Winter employed a "Schumpeterian" conception of economic evolution by emphasizing the role of innovation and imitation. In actuality there is a distinct movement whose practitioners consider themselves to be developing an evolutionary economics in conformity with the broader framework of analysis forwarded by Joseph Schumpeter. Horst Hanusch has summarized the general standpoint reflected in Schumpeterian evolutionary economics thusly[38]:

> From the point of view of evolutionary economics, Schumpeter copes with one major problem: dynamic growth of the potential aggregate supply ... [T]he driving forces of economic development [in this interpretation] are dynamic entrepreneurs and dynamic competition. It is the role of the entrepreneur to create innovations and to destroy old equilibria by establishing new combinations. Along with this process of "creative destruction," progress in productivity will be achieved. In addition, dynamic competition, forced by innovation, provides the necessary transfer of productivity gains to consumers, resulting in an increase in social welfare. (Hanusch, 1988, p. 1)

It bears noting that Schumpeter's evolutionary theory, as articulated in his *The Theory of Economic Development* (1961), reveals no influences from biology or the theory of biological evolution. In addition, one might wonder how "dynamic growth of the potential aggregate supply" is in any way analogous to biological evolution. Thus it is significant that Burton Klein has made a direct analogy between biological evolution and the Schumpeterian conception of economic evolution:

> What biologists describe as "evolutionary progress" (the adaptation of species to new circumstances), Schumpeter understood as the "process of creative destruction. . . . [B]y "adaptation" biologists mean "that the external world sets certain 'problems' that organisms need to 'solve,' " and that evolution by means of natural selection is the mechanism for creating these solutions . . . "[D]ynamic flexibility"—the capability of firms to make rapid adjustments to new circumstances . . . plays more or less the same role [in the Schumpeterian theory]. (Klein, 1988, p. 96)

If we are to take Klein's resort to biological analogies seriously, we can fairly ask: What is the "organism" that is supposedly "evolving" in this conception of economic evolution? While Klein does not answer this question directly, it is obvious he, like the authors already discussed, considers the business firm to be that entity (cf. Klein, 1988, pp. 96–97). But even though the focus is clearly on "risk-taking" entrepreneurs and the process of innovation, there is no distinct conception of the firm in the Schumpeterian framework, either as genotypes or phenotypes. This being the case, resort to the natural selection metaphor by proponents of Schumpeterian theorists entails even more serious problems than those already noted in reference to the idea of an "evolving" firm. Indeed, it is clear that here, too, the natural selection metaphor is felicitous only to the extent that "dynamic competition," through which "adaptive" firms are selected, is a brute process.

A Neglected Complication

Thus we must conclude that the natural selection metaphor is mostly infelicitous when applied to the evolution of the business firm and in fact entails little more than the proposition that firm selection through time is governed by a brute process—economic "competition." What has not been adequately understood by critics of the natural selection metaphor is that even this limited correspondence with the theory of biological evolution is called into question as soon as one inquires about important matters that Alchian, Friedman, Nelson and Winter, and the Schumpeterians have all taken for granted without meaningful inquiry, namely, the nature of the "environment" facing economic competitors and, even more importantly, the nature of economic "competition" itself.

With respect to the nature of the "environment" facing economic competitors, it will be recalled that in biological theory "natural" selection operates because the environment is presumed to be entirely outside the control of the "organisms" whose numbers are pressing up against its carrying capacity[39]; that is, natural selection operates via *adaptation to a fixed environment.*[40] Now, the concept of the "environment" employed by Alchian, Friedman, Nelson and Winter, and even the Schumpeterians is very murky to say the least, Does it include resources? Knowledge (technology)? Not to mention "rules of the game" such as property rights? Surely it must include the latter. But if so, as Penrose has pointed out, there is no logical basis for presuming that a "nonadapted" firm will limit purposeful action to changing its internal routines (innovation) or imitating those adopted by its competitors. As a logical matter, it is equally possible that it will instead act, singly or collectively with its competitors, to alter, or induce others to alter, the "environment" in which it is operating. In other words, there is no reason for presuming that "nonadapted" firms "will not attempt as much consciously to adapt the environment to their own purposes as to adapt themselves to the environment. . . . [Indeed], one of the chief characteristics of man that distinguishes him from other creatures is the remarkable range of his ability to alter his environment or to become independent of it" (Penrose, 1952, p. 814). But if this is the case, then clearly there is no ground for presuming that the adaptation process of a "firm" is even remotely analogous to species adaptation via the struggle for existence, mutation, and natural selection in the context, from the standpoint of the species, of an unalterable environment.

The significance of this objection to the use of the natural selection metaphor in reference to the process driving economic evolution gains even greater force if one stops to consider what is actually connoted by the term economic *competition*, which is used by Alchian, Friedman, and Nelson and Winter as if it has evident content.[41] What is notable, if not unique, about human provisioning activity is that it is everywhere a *collective* undertaking patterned by "rules of the game" or "institutions"—whether the rules are mores, norms, customs, laws, or convention[42]—enforced on participants through sanctions in the event of noncompliance. It is clear, now that economics has severed itself from the deistic natural law premises embraced by Adam Smith and his followers, that economic "competition" is itself nothing else than a form of "patterned interaction," that is, a rule-structured process of interaction whose character is analytically inseparable from the controlling rules of the game (property rights).[43] What that means, in turn, is that *the character of competition itself* is part of the "environment" that firms might purposefully attempt to alter as they "adapt" to the challenges of "competition." This is a sharp and fundamental departure from the sort of adaptation associated with biological evolution. Indeed, it suggests that evolution of the external (to the firm) rule structure is what actually ought to be studied if one seeks to understand the evolution of the "capabilities and behavior" of the modern business firm—and, indeed, this is precisely the approach that Commons adopted. But to return to the issue at hand, once it is recognized that purposeful action by a firm may not be limited to "adapting to" the competitive challenges posed by its "environment," but may also entail efforts resulting in the alteration of that "environment," the infelicity of natural selection as a metaphor for the process through which the modern business firm has evolved, the inference that the evolution of the modern business firm has been governed by a brute process analogous to biological natural selection, is at once apparent.

Yet, to paraphrase Rosenberg's assertion, natural selection, at least in so far as it connotes the governance of economic evolution by a brute process, *continues* "to be the most tempting of metaphors" for economists. This is evident not only in Hirschleifer's attempt to show that many patterns of economic interaction can be explained through the analytical tools employed by sociobiologists but also *implicitly* in much of the literature of the "new institutional economics." It is to a brief discussion of the centrality of the natural selection metaphor to the new institutional economics that I now turn.

The Natural Selection Metaphor in the New Institutional Economics

As already noted, the attempt to use the logic of biological evolution as the foundation for an "evolutionary" theory of economic institutions dates back at least to Veblen. That "natural selection" was in Veblen's mind central to such a theory would seem to be incontrovertible:

> The life of man in society, just like the life of other species, is a struggle for existence, and therefore it is a process of selective adaptation. The evolution of social structure has been a process of natural selection of institutions. The progress which has been and is being made in human institutions . . . may be set down, broadly, to a natural selection of the fittest habits of thought. . . . (Veblen, 1899, p. 188)

Despite this seemingly direct language and his penchant for Darwinian terms such as "blind drift" and "opaque process," Veblen was frequently less than clear regarding what he perceived to be the actual selection mechanism driving the evolution of the economic institutions he dissected with such brilliance (Tilman, 1992, pp. 41, 58). Hence it remains a legitimate matter of debate the degree to which natural selection was understood by Veblen to provide a useful metaphor for the process through which economic institutions have actually evolved. Still, it does appear that Veblen believed a habit of thought prevalent among members of a social group, which is what he meant by the term *institution*, cannot endure indefinitely if it is inconsistent with the mental proclivities implicit in the production techniques those same members participate in on a daily basis. In this sense, congruence with "technology" served in Veblen's evolutionary theory as a criterion of institutional fitness allowing for the operation, over very long periods of time, of a "brute" selection mechanism analogous to natural selection in biological theory (Tilman, 1992, p. 136).[44] With possibly one important exception,[45] Veblen's successors, while always making evident their affinity for his "Darwinian" orientation,[46] have generally shunned the natural selection metaphor and avoided the temptation to use concepts or logic provided by the biological theory of evolution to articulate their ideas.[47] As a result, biological theory and the natural selection metaphor appear to have played at most an extremely limited role, even implicitly, in the development of neo-Veblenian "evolutionary economics."

However, while it is seldom made explicit,[48] the metaphor *is* central to much of the "new institutional economics." Here I am using this term in its conventional meaning of encompassing all manner of recent attempts, other than those included under the rubric of "economic theory of the law," which will be considered separately, to account for economic institutions from a stance unconnected to or incompatible with the philosophical and methodological predilections of "old-style" institutional economists such as Veblen, Commons, Wesley Mitchell, Clarence Ayres, Karl Polanyi, or John Kenneth Galbraith.[49] Of interest here is the framework of analysis implicit in the new institutional economics with respect to the phenomenon of economic evolution. Hence, in addition to the Nelson and Winter evolutionary framework, which has already been discussed, we are interested in the question of the role of the natural selection metaphor in transaction-cost theories of firm and rule evolution such as those developed by Ronald Coase (1937, 1960), Oliver E. Williamson (1985), and Douglas C. North (1990), in game-theoretic approaches to social institutions such as that developed by Andrew Schotter (1981), and in neo-Austrian theories of economic evolution erected on the foundation provided by Karl Menger

(1963) and Friedrich Hayek (1973).[50] No generalizations about such a diverse literature will ever be entirely accurate with respect to individual cases. Nonetheless, some general features of this literature can be noted.

First, contributors to this broad and diverse "institutional economics" rarely make explicit that they consider economic evolution and biological evolution to be analogous. Yet on occasion the association is made strikingly clear. Schotter, for example, put it this way:

> Economic and social systems evolve the way species do. To ensure their survival and growth, they must solve a whole set of problems that arise as the system evolves. Each problem creates the need for some adaptive feature (Schotter, 1981, pp. 1–2).... Institutions or conventions emerge to help economic agents solve ... [their] problems. The socially adhered to solution to these problems determines regularities in behavior that form the basis of our definition of a social institution (Schotter, 1981, p. 161).... Those societies that create the proper set of social institutions survive and flourish; those that do not, falter and die ... Social institutions are our adaptive tools; we cannot survive without them. (Schotter, 1981, pp. 1–2)

On the other hand, Hayek has been quite explicit in *rejecting* the notion that there is a close correspondence between the logic of biological evolution and cultural evolution (cf. Hayek, 1978, pp. 7–9).

Second, even though there is some disagreement regarding the applicability of the assumption that new institutions arise from textbook-type maximizing behavior (Langlois, 1986b, p. 252), the quest for selfish gain is generally understood to drive the process of economic evolution in most variants of the new institutional economics. This presumption is evident in Schotter's definition of economics as "the study of how individual economic agents pursuing their own selfish ends evolve institutions [including cooperation] as a means to satisfy them" (Schotter, 1981, p. 5; also cf. Schotter, 1986, p. 132). Williamson's framework manifests this supposition in an even stronger form; individuals are presumed not only to pursue their self-interest but also to do so often with guile (cf. Williamson, 1985, p. 2).[51] At the same time, North has explicitly repudiated the self-interest precept as too narrow for a theory of institutions, arguing that there needs to be a greater recognition of additional motivations that underlie economic behavior in many circumstances, including even a sense of fairness (cf. North, 1990, Chap. 3).

Third, the view that economic institutions result from self-interested action leads many of the contributors to the new institutional economics to conclude that economic evolution provides a compelling illustration of the cogency of "invisible-hand explanations" (Langlois, 1986b, pp. 24ff). As Hayek (1973, p. 44) has emphasized, the self-interested actions of the various members of a group will never sum to an orderly whole in the absence of shared "rules of conduct" or, to use Schotter's term, *social institutions.* But it is personal advantage or gain, not "order," that the "innovator(s)" responsible for the appearance of a new practice—and a practice is but the active expression of a rule of conduct—has (have) in mind. The same is true in regard to those who "imitate" the innovator. Thus order is understood to be a "spontaneous," that is, unintended, by-product of the "organic" rules or social institutions resulting from self-seeking individual action.[52] This is not to suggest that Hayek or any other contributor to this literature ignores the reality that there are many "designed" institutions effecting a "made" order, to use Hayek's terms (cf. Hayek, 1973, p. 37). Nonetheless, the presumption is clear that there is in the nature of things a natural or brute process through which social order obtains.

Fourth, the view that economic evolution (new institutions) "naturally" brings about "order" via invisible hand processes generally entails the concomitant presumption that economic evolution proceeds via a process of essentially "voluntaristic" action, that is, social institutions are understood as arrangements to which people in general *freely* consent because it serves their self-interest to do so. This perspective is evident in Hayek's assertion that "Action according to rules—which we do not explicitly know and which have not been designed by reason, but prevail because the manner of acting of those who are successful is imitated" (Hayek, 1978, p. 7). But it is not just in accounting for observed rules and customs that this perspective manifests itself. It is equally evident in Williamson's theoretical explanation of both the genesis of the modern vertically integrated business firm and the various types of contractual relations modern-day firms enter into. To adopt a "voluntarist" stance, it must be understood, is not to suggest that the parties involved cannot freely consent also to have their agreed-upon arrangements enforced by a third party. Schotter's "voluntarist" definition of an institution clearly embodies such an add-on: "A social institution is a regularity in social behavior that is *agreed to by all members of society*, specifies behavior in specific recurrent situations, and is either self-policed or policed by some external authority" (Schotter, 1981, p. 11, emphasis added).

Fifth, to return to the central issue, it is not always clear in this literature upon what "organism" selection operates and what it is that "evolves" as a consequence. Williamson, for example, explores both the evolution of firms as organizations and the evolution of private contractual relations. Presumably, the "firm" is the unit of selection in either case. Schotter, however, in the passage quoted on the previous page, appears to imply that it is social institutions that "evolve," even though it is "societies" and "economies," that is, social aggregations, that must survive and hence that ultimately serve as the locus of selection in the process of economic evolution. Hayek (1978, p. 9) has also suggested that in the case of "cultural evolution" selection (of "fit" rules) occurs at the group level.

It is highly questionable, however, whether a "society" or an "economy," conceptualized as a complex of "rules" or "social institutions," is even remotely similar to a biological "organism" and hence whether its evolution can be understood through biological metaphors, as Schotter clearly implies it can (cf. Schotter, 1981, pp. 3, 164). Fundamentally, "rules" or "social institutions" manifest themselves in action in a "society," which is in actuality an association of individuals, in exactly the same way that "routines" in Nelson and Winter's theory manifest themselves in action in a "firm," which is also an association of individuals. This being the case, when one treats a social abstraction such as an "economy" or "society" as analogous to an evolving biological entity, one encounters all the problems enumerated earlier regarding the evolution of the firm. Those problems have not, to my knowledge, been addressed directly, much less resolved, by those developing the new institutional economics literature.

Lastly, Nelson and Winter being an obvious exception, contributors to the new institutional economics seldom employ the term *natural selection* in reference to the process through which new patterns of economic interaction—new "institutions"—evolve. Yet, with the possible exception of the neo-Austrian analysis of "pragmatic" or "designed" institutions,[53] what governs selection in all these conceptions of economic evolution is a brute process grounded in some notion of "efficiency," that is, the effectiveness with which the "inputs" provided by nature are used in the service of human ends. A few illustrative passages may help. Hayek, for example, averred that "rules" evident in social (provisioning) behavior are the "result of a process of selection, in the course of which groups that achieved a more efficient order displaced (or were imitated by) others [although, reflecting the operation of an invisible-hand process], often without knowing to what their superiority was due" (Hayek, 1978, p. 7). Williamson maintains that private contract and governance structures—the "economic institutions of capitalism"—"have the main purpose and effect of economizing on transaction costs" (Williamson, 1985, p. 1). Similarly, North claims that the development of property rights is "a simple function of changes in economic costs and benefits," although this relationship is sometimes complicated somewhat by problems related to "the efficiency of the political market" in generating tax revenue (cf. North, 1990, pp. 51–52).

Now, Langlois has in effect acknowledged that "efficiency" in the new institutional economics is nothing other than an economic analog for biological "fitness":

> [There are many troubling problems] if we interpret comparative-institutional transaction-cost analysis as providing an explanation of the origin of an institution or organization. If, however, we reinterpret such analysis in a more limited way as instead explaining, as it were, the raison d'être or rationale of the structure in question, then an efficiency analysis . . . is not only justifiable but perhaps logically necessary. In an evolutionary system, for example, *one must ultimately appeal to efficiency arguments to explain why observed structures are able to survive*; to do otherwise would be to risk the sort of tautology Darwinian biology was long, and wrongly, accused of embodying . . . In this sense, the comparative-institutional analysis of Williamson and the organic explanation of institutions in the manner of Menger should be seen as slightly different, but nonetheless complementary, research programs. (Langlois, 1985, p. 21, emphasis added)

What Langlois is obviously proclaiming here is that "Darwinian biology" provides us with the exemplar when it comes to the logic of economic evolution. And what is quite evident in Langlois's inclusive generalization is that greater relative "efficiency" of economic institutions, their serviceability for getting "more" from resources, is the criterion of "fitness" upon which a brute selection process operates; that is, the process of economic evolution reflected in the writings of the new institutional economists proceeds according to a logic paralleling the logic of biological evolution.[54] Thus in the limited sense of signifying that institutional evolution is governed by a brute selection process, the natural selection metaphor, through the code word *efficiency*, lies at the very core of the new institutional economics.

Natural Selection and the Economic Theory of Law

In circumscribing the domain of the "new institutional economics," I explicitly excluded the literature pertaining to the burgeoning "law and economics" literature, some of which[55] deals explicitly with the question of the process underlying the evolution of law. The distinction between a "rule" and "law" is clearly somewhat arbitrary. For the present purpose I have in mind the definition of law provided in *Webster's Third New International Dictionary*, unabridged: "a rule or mode of conduct or action that is prescribed or formally recognized as binding by a supreme controlling authority or is made obligatory by a sanction . . . made, recognized, or enforced by the controlling authority." Accordingly, a "rule" is other than "law" only in those cases where it is not enforced by a controlling authority.

Except for Hirschleifer's seminal article (1982), and subsequent discussions of it, I am unaware of explicit biological analogies of any kind in the economic theory of law literature. Nonetheless, it appears to be the presumption that, at least in so far as primitive societies are concerned, economic evolution is regulated in a manner analogous to that proposed in the new institutional economics—by a brute process in which greater "efficiency" is the selection principle determining which groups survive over the long run (Posner, 1981, p. 205). Similarly, driven by self-interested litigants whose actions generate change in the rules comprising the common law, a brute process is viewed as sufficient to move the common law gradually in a direction allowing for greater "efficiency" in the use of resources (Posner, 1986, pp. 527–528).[56] Judge Posner (1981, pp. 4–5) has summarized the thrust of this analysis as follows: "The hypothesis is not that the judges can or do duplicate the results of competitive markets, but that within the limits set by the costs of administering the legal system . . . , common law adjudication brings the economic system closer to the results that would be produced by effective competition—a free market operating without significant externality, monopoly, or information problems." This, of course, is nothing other than an implicit assertion that common law adjudication is but another example of an invisible hand process.[57]

In sum, while one would hesitate to assert that biological metaphors play a role of any kind in the "economic" theory of law literature, it does appear that this literature reveals an interpretation of the common law that is *not in conflict with* the general propositions at the core of the new institutional economics. It is the heart of that interpretation that economic evolution, in this case the common law, is "naturally" driven by a brute selection process to generate rules allowing for ever greater efficiency in the utilization of economic resources.

Institutions as a Metaphor for Social Man

In my judgment the attempt to apply the natural selection metaphor to economic evolution through biological metaphors involves an inherent difficulty that has not been adequately acknowledged. To illustrate this difficulty, consider Schotter's attempt to establish that the evolution of institutions is a Lamarckian rather than a Darwinian process:

> If we were to pick up the metaphor with which we started this book—an economy evolving and adapting through the creation of social institutions—the best hereditary model to use is not the Mendelian model but the Lamarckian. This is true because in Lamarck's theory it was possible for species to pass on to future generations traits that are presently acquired, and this is precisely what economies do when social institutions emerge in one period and then are passed on from generation to generation." (Schotter, 1981, p. 164)

But, of course, in a literal sense an "economy" cannot have "generations." For, as already noted, a "society" or an "economy" is not itself an entity but an ongoing *association* of ever-changing individuals. While an association *may* have a discernible beginning (birth?) and a decline or disappearance (death?), it has no mechanism for reproducing itself (though it may be imitated by other associations). In other words, as an association a "society's" challenge is not to "replace" itself via "reproduction" but rather to ensure its maintenance, its ongoingness.[58]

The only way to make sense of the foregoing passage is to infer that Schotter, after noting "species . . . pass on to future generations traits that are presently acquired" should have made clear it is not "an economy" but man, now conceptualized as a *social* rather than a biological animal, who "evolves" *within the ambit of a society* through a cultural process of developing new institutions (implicit in new patterns of behavior) and *socially* transmitting them to offspring.[59] Surely this is what Hayek meant when he insisted that "My problem is not genetic evolution of innate qualities, but cultural evolution through learning" (Hayek, 1978, p. 68). In short, the confusion evident in the foregoing passage regarding the "organism" whose evolution is to be accounted for arises out of the fact that it cannot be the rule structure itself—the "economy" or "society"—that evolves in a manner analogous to biological evolution. In would seem that it is the *social* evolution of man—as a complex of socially acquired "habits of thought" or "rules" or "social institutions" rather than as a biologically constituted being—"in terms of the process itself," as Veblen put it, that we must try to explain; that is, the task remains that of working out an adequate evolutionary theory of economic agents as *social* beings.

Where to Turn?

There is one feature of the foregoing theories that has yet to be underscored. Without addressing the issue directly, Hayek has implied that many of the substantive elements of the "new institutional economics" would probably have developed into their present form without Darwin (cf. Hayek, 1978, pp. 67–68). This is quite likely a valid insight. Schotter illustrates rather effectively in the following passage that the new institutional economics is fundamentally an outgrowth of, not a replacement for, mainstream economic analysis:

> Just as Adam Smith's invisible hand can, in a decentralized fashion, lead economic agents to reach a Pareto-optimal competitive equilibrium, it can also lead them to create social institutions that will facilitate their interaction when competitive outcomes are not optimal. Another way to phrase the same problem is to say that "competitive" economics deals with only one institution—the market—which arises organically out of the maximizing behavior of individual agents. However, a host of other institutions, norms, and rules are also created that help to allocate resources in an optimal fashion.[60] (Schotter, 1981, p. 4)

While to one degree or another reflecting the profound influence the Darwinian revolution has had upon the human intellect, all the approaches we have reviewed, save Veblen's, manifest intellectual "habits of thought" already discernible in *pre-Darwinian* classical economics[61]; for example, the hedonistic conception of man (cf. Veblen, 1919; Weisskopf, 1973), the voluntaristic "social harmony" exchange conception of economic activity (cf. Hunt, 1991; Galbraith, 1973), the "invisible hand" conception of economic order discussed above, and so on.[62] Karl Polanyi (1944, 1968) has with great insight shown why those "habits of thought" are seriously defective. He has additionally established beyond question, at least in so far as the case of Great Britain is concerned, that central elements of the market system, such as "self-regulating markets" for the "fictitious commodities" land and labor, simply cannot be accounted for on "voluntarist" grounds. But, writing prior to the resurgence of interest in economic evolution, Polanyi did not address directly the felicity of the natural selection metaphor in theories of economic evolution.[63]

In fact there was no need to do so. Writing even earlier that Polanyi, John R. Commons (1924, 1934) had already addressed this issue directly. As we have seen, whether it is made explicit or not, the natural selection metaphor lies at the root of, or at least is not incompatible with, all manner of recent efforts to account for economic evolution. If one is interested in the rise and fall over the eons of successive independent "societies" or "civilizations," perhaps the natural selection metaphor, rooted as it is in a process in which one organism *replaces* another (its "parent"), offers us some insight into the process of change. But, we have argued, there are profound difficulties in employing it to interpret the course of development occurring within an ongoing association of individuals, that is, to account for the course of change over time *within* a single ongoing "organism" (whether a "society" or a "firm").

In any case, it might still be contended that in actuality the metaphor of natural selection when applied to economic evolution entails little more than the assertion that such evolution is governed by a brute selection process. Significantly, it was just this presumption, that economic evolution is "naturally" directed, that Commons sought to refute. In order to make his point—and it is important to recognize that in so doing he had "Veblenian" as well as "orthodox" economists in mind—Commons made use of a different metaphor. For, as indicated at the outset, it was Commons's view, *and particularly so with respect to the evolution of the modern capitalist market system*, that in appropriating the natural selection metaphor from Darwin economists had borrowed the wrong mental tool. Artificial selection, he insisted, was the proper "Darwinian" metaphor for understanding the process underlying the evolution of the market system. To put it slightly differently, Commons rejected unequivocally the view expressed by Schotter in the passage just cited that the market arose "organically out of the maximizing behavior of individual agents." In actuality, Commons averred, the market has been volitionally constructed through a purpose-driven process of authoritative resolution of disputes. It is to a recapitulation of Commons's theory of economic evolution that we now turn.

Economic Evolution as a Volitional Process[64]

Order

It is next to impossible to go through Commons's major works and find a concise statement of his standpoint.[65] Adopting a stance that Jeff Biddle (1991) has labeled "instrumental presentism," Commons always tended to develop his own concepts through a critique of ideas forwarded by others and, consequently, the exact nature of his own contributions were often obscured. Moreover, Commons's epistemological approach, much closer to what Paul Diesing (1971) has labeled "holism" than the "formalism" implicit if not explicit in the "mainstream" literature of economics, often makes it difficult to discern exactly how he understood various features of economic life to be related (Ramstad, 1986, 1987b).

Despite these difficulties, even a casual reading of Commons's works makes it clear that he never intended his "institutional economics" to be an *alternative to* "mainstream" economics. His goal, as he stated on numerous occasions, was simply to "round out" economic theory by giving collective action its "due place." Upon working through Commons's writings, therefore, one encounters many presuppositions that in no way conflict with established views. For example, Commons began with the "Malthusian" presumption that scarcity is an intrinsic feature of human existence. Indeed, here Commons found an analogy with biology paralleling rather closely Hirschleifer's stance, as discussed earlier. As Commons put it, "[Malthus's presumption of scarcity] was later taken over by Darwin and extended to all living creatures" (Commons, 1934, p. 112). Commons also conformed with established tradition in economics by supposing that human beings are mainly self-interested creatures, that is, can generally be relied upon to desire more for themselves rather than less.

In a number of important regards, however, Commons's presumptions about the inherent nature of social life conflict fundamentally with those embraced by the authors whose works have been reviewed above. For example, Commons found strict methodological individualism to hide from view the more or less "determined" nature of the social man. His conception of human action was also fundamentally different. To be sure, in the chain of "circular causation," Commons did understand purposeful problem solving by individuals to be the motor force of institutional change.[66] But he did not attribute "rationality" to those same individuals. For, as Commons's saw it, human action in general is the product of "stupidity, passion and ignorance." Moreover, he maintained, most of social (economic) life involves not an interactions between equals but between "leaders and followers," "bosses and workers," and so on, in which a psychology of "command and obedience" is revealed in their interaction.

Commons maintained it was in his analysis of the source of order in economic life that the fundamental difference between his "institutional" theory and the mainstream tradition is most sharply drawn. Indeed, all aspects of his theory intertwine to form his unique perspective on that issue. The overriding problem of social theory, Commons maintained, is to explain how order and harmony are brought out of conflicts of interest due to scarcity.[67] Since Adam Smith, economists have presumed that there is a natural ameliorative trend in the course of events that brings the voluntary actions of various individuals into harmony with one another, that is, into a "spontaneous order." This, of course, is the whole thrust of the "invisible hand" thinking that has been central to classical and neoclassical economics as well as to the new institutional economics. Commons, in contrast, rejected unequivocally the view that "organic institutions" allow for the resolution of conflicts of interest and hence, *pari passu*, the view that "spontaneous" order is a "natural" tendency of the social realm. Rather, he believed *conflict* and *disorder* represent the "natural" tendency. In his view, order obtains in social life only if there is in place a coercive structure of rules to which individual members *must* adhere, subject to the sanction of physical violence. In other words, Commons traced social order to "collective action *in control of* individual action," his definition of an "institution," rather than to an "invisible hand process." As he put it, "The only stability we know is that which man himself creates by collective action" (Commons, 1934, p. 213); "[H]armony is not a presupposition of economics—it is a consequence of collective action designed to maintain rules that shall govern conflicts" (Commons, 1934, p. 7). It is the content of the controlling rule structure, in turn, which Commons attributed to "artificial selection," that is, understood to have been *volitionally* constructed through the process of authoritative resolution of disputes by those, or their designated representatives, whose collective will has consecutively controlled the use of superior violence. As he saw it, moreover, the market system itself took form through this process. To return to the present topic, it is to the centrality of this *volitional* process that Commons was calling attention by insisting that "artificial selection" provides economics with its metaphor for the process of economic evolution.

This insight led Commons to adopt a completely different perspective regarding the essential nature of the market system from that reflected in other theories. As his reconceptualization of market activity is not widely known, I now turn to the task of outlining it as a preface to elaborating Commons' understanding of economic evolution in greater detail.

The Economy as a Going Concern[68]

Commons appropriated the term *going concern* to denote an association of individuals who together engage in ongoing coordinated activity directed to ends foreseen in the future. Thus conceived, going concern is clearly an elastic concept, encompassing overlapping groups from the family through the nation. Also included are associations entered into for the purpose of producing needed or wanted things, that is, the business firm. Rather than thinking of participants in economic activities as various individuals, Commons considered them to be "citizens" of the overlapping going concerns of which they are a member. Of great significance is that through the construct of a going concern Commons made the individual analytically subordinate to the group, since it is the general case that the group's existence precedes an individual's membership in it.

In order to be ongoing, an economic concern must successfully coordinate the activities of its "citizens" so that their joint activities result in the production of valued "things" (goods and services). Commons maintained that it is impossible to determine in any objective manner how the various members of the concern contribute to the production of the joint product. Yet, unless the prospective participants are able to anticipate with some reasonable security of expectations what their own efforts will yield them, production cannot take place. To put it slightly differently, before individuals will actually *do* anything, they must negotiate a transfer of the rights to the future ownership of "property." In other words, "ownership" rights in the joint product must be negotiated prior to production.

It was one of Commons' most persistent themes that the exchange of *things* is not the pivotal activity for understanding economic life; rather, he argued, it is legal control that is of foremost importance. Commons coined the term *transaction* to connote the process through which one gains the right to control the use of something currently owned by another. Thus conceived as a "unit of transfer of legal control," Commons perceived that a transaction precedes every economic "exchange" and hence constitutes the "smallest unit" of economic activity. From this point of view, a going concern, as ongoing concerted activity, can be understood as nothing else than a succession of transactions followed by performance.

As noted, Commons understood the basic relationship between individuals to involve a fundamental conflict of interest over how to allocate the burdens and benefits of their joint undertaking. Given his presumption that individuals are inherently self-interested—even selfish—creatures, the reality is that objective conflicts of interest invariably precipitate disputes among the concern's citizens pertaining to their own particular obligations to contribute to, and their "ownership rights" in, the concern's joint product. If the concern is to remain ongoing, it is essential that disputes over such allocations do not undermine the security of expectation upon which all its participants' ongoing activity is premised; that is, the going concern must lay down *working rules* spelling out what individuals can, may, or must do, or not do, within its ambit whenever their transactions entail the conflicts of interest that have precipitated overt disputes.

We have already observed that Commons did not believe order to obtain "naturally." Thus he rejected the presumption that disputes rooted in conflict of interest are "spontaneously" (voluntaristically) resolved by disputants themselves.[69] It was his understanding that every concern must have an "authoritative figure," an individual or group of individuals whose role it is to resolve disputes. This being the case, it is the will of the authoritative figure that is decisive in determining what rule actually is to be followed. Commons similarly rejected the view that individuals "freely" (absent coercion) adhere to the working rules that are adopted. Every concern must therefore have at its disposal sanctions that can be applied against those who transgress the working rules specified by the authoritative figure. Those sanctions may be moral, economic, or physical in character. It is the fear of sanctions, Commons maintained, that underlies the individual's apparently "voluntary" adherance to new working rules. In a word, *coercion* is the fundamental "force" through which the various conflicting proclivities of individuals are transformed into cohesive ongoing interdependent activity.

As the behavior prescribed by a set of working rules is repeated over and over again, the actions of individuals gradually become habitual; that is, even though coercion is always in the background, individuals come "voluntarily" to interact in a harmonious manner as customary modes of behavior are internalized as habits. More importantly, as the patterns inherent in the rules are repeated again and again, they gradually become so familiar that they are perceived as part of the natural order. In other words, customary practices (rules) gradually become widely perceived as "natural" and "right." As this occurs, individuals come to "willingly" acquiesce in, and indeed generally endorse, accustomed patterns. As Commons put it, "[C]ustom is not merely collective action in control of individual action—it is collective opinion in control of individual opinion" (Commons, 1934, p. 698).[70] Commons adopted the term *institutionalized mind* to denote human beings whose concrete behavior and desires can be accounted for in this fashion. Significantly, it was "institutionalized minds" whom he envisioned to populate going concerns.[71] Thus, even though Commons perceived that when a new practice (rule) is first adopted by the concern it must of necessity be "imposed on" many of the concern's citizens, once it becomes "familiar" it generally will be regarded as "right " and "good" by just about all.[72]

Several features of Commons's analysis require emphasis. First of all, it will be noted that "working rules" are equivalent to what we earlier determined to be the substantive meaning of the term *law*.[73] In other words, "law" is indispensable to the "ongoingness" of the going concern. Or, alternatively, in no going concern will activities be harmonized by "social institutions" as distinct from "law." It will also be noted that even at the most fundamental level, order in social life is of the "made" type; that is, order obtains only because there is a "lawgiver" who can *control* the actions of others through the threat or, if necessary, the use of sanctions ("collective action *in control of* individual action"). Also notice that "property rights" are central to the analysis. Commons defined *property* to be "anything that can legally be withheld from others who need or want it" (Commons,

1924, pp. 52ff) and *property rights* as "the working rules enforced by the community upon individuals in their transactions respecting that which is or is expected to be scarce" (Commons, 1934, p. 75). "Legally," of course, means nothing more than "with the permission of the law-giver," and "enforced working rules" similarly means nothing more than rules which the "law-giver" has specified must be followed.

It has been mentioned repeatedly that working rules are enforced through, and acquiesced in a fear of sanctions. Commons distinguished three types of sanctions—the moral sanction of disapproval, the economic sanction of bankruptcy and poverty, and the physical sanction of force. Now, the most powerful of the three sanctions that can be applied against an individual transgressor is the sanction of physical violence, which, if fully and skillfully applied, results in immediate death. Thus the possessor of superior violence is in a position to impose his will on others if he so chooses. As noted, "going concern" is an elastic concept. What is apparent is that most going concerns that for analytical purposes may be treated as independent associations (as, for example, the business firm) are in actuality subordinate to the will of a higher authority; that is, decisions rendered by the "authoritative figure" within subordinate concerns (the "owner") can always be appealed to a superior authoritative figure. Who, then, is the ultimate authority? According to Commons, it is the possessor, individually or collectively, of superior physical power—the *sovereign*. Since all working rules specified by authoritative figures in lesser concerns are ultimately dependent upon the willingness of the sovereign to use its physical force to enforce them, or alternatively, its unwillingness to use force to overturn them, whenever a lesser authority is called upon to specify what a rule shall be it must always do so with an eye to the matter of whether the rule it desires to adopt is compatible with the known "desires" of the sovereign. In other words, whatever rationale may be used to justify it, at the root of every working rule, and thus at the root of property rights, is the sovereign power's "will" to enforce it.

This brings us back to the concept of a transaction. Commons determined there are three fundamentally different types of transactions within the going concern—the bargaining transaction, the managerial transaction, and the rationing transaction—distinguishable on the basis of their function and the status of the participants. *Bargaining transactions* take place between legal equals, that is, between "subjects" of the sovereign who have not been granted the authority ("right") to command the other. In the bargaining transaction, property ownership is transferred and commitments for future actions (performances) are entered into at mutually agreed to terms. Both parties to a bargaining transaction are authorized by the sovereign to use their powers of persuasion and their economic power (to withhold what the other wants) in their negotiations. Of course, *legal* equals can have markedly dissimilar economic power to wait and hence to impose their will on one another. However, as they bargain negotiators must adhere to all restrictions on their actions that have been laid down by (commanded by) the sovereign power, such as the "command" to avoid various improper inducements or the "command" to forbear in the full exercise of one's power to act; similarly, they must adhere to all performances that are "commanded" by the sovereign.[74]

Wealth is produced and delivered by means of *managerial transactions*. These transaction involve the relationship of command and obedience between a legal superior (so determined by the sovereign) and inferior, such as exists between a foreman and a worker or a sheriff and a citizen. In a managerial transaction, the superior gives an order relating to the acquisition, alienation, or use of a thing or faculty (for example, the power to work) and the inferior must obey. The superior, of course, is enjoined to issue commands that do not violate other decrees of the sovereign, that is, established matters of "law."

As noted, a key function of the bargaining transaction is to provide individuals with an inducement for participating in the production of wealth. Put somewhat differently, bargaining transactions prefigure how the "burdens and benefits of collective wealth production" are actually shared. *Rationing transactions*, "the negotiations of reaching an agreement among several participants who have the authority [that is, who are decreed by the sovereign to have such authority] to apportion the benefits and burdens to members of a joint enterprise," also give shape to the actual distribution of real income (wealth). Under the name of "policy," these "authoritative apportionings" of "burdens and benefits" also involve the command and obedience relationship of a legal superior and a legal inferior, as in the case of the state establishing a budget and decreeing a tax or a board of directors establishing a wage or dividend policy.

In Commons's mind these three "units of activity" exhaust all the activities of the "science of economics." As he put it: "Bargaining transactions *transfer ownership* of wealth by voluntary agreement between legal equals. Managerial transactions *create wealth* by commands of legal superiors. Rationing transactions apportion the burdens and benefits of wealth creation by the *dictation* of legal superiors" (Commons, 1934, p. 68). Of the three, rationing transactions are undoubtedly the most strategic, since they place limits on the potential content of bargaining and managerial transactions. All, however, must conform to the will of the sovereign, that is, to existing working rules.

Thus Commons provides us with a dramatically different image of economic processes from that communicated by mainstream theory. Instead of individuals, Commons puts going concerns at center stage. Instead of voluntary action harmonized by the "invisible hand," Commons emphasizes authoritative (managerial and rationing) and authorized (bargaining) transactions in accordance with the working rules of collective action. Instead of economic outcomes synthesizing the various purposes of individuals wills (as implicit in, for example, "consumer sovereignty"), Commons accents the dominant role of the "collective will," that is, the wills of those participating in defining the sovereign's purposes, in determining what takes place.[75] Finally, instead of biological man—an "organism," Commons brings to the fore social man—an "institutionism" (Commons, 1934, p. 639). Thus, as he put it,

> economic society is a changing complexity of personalities, principles, and organizations which are inseparable in fact and are united in the concept of going concern. It is to this complexity within a concern that we give the name politics, in order to distinguish it from the former simplicities of economic theory which are properly named individualism. Instead of assumed equal individuals we have the widely different personalities of leaders and led, bosses and bossed, officers and privates. Instead of the former simple assumption that every equal individual seeks his self-interest, we have widely different and conflicting principles on which unequal individuals seek a common interest. Instead of unregulated individuals, we have hierarchies which regulate them. (Commons, 1934, p. 751)

As indicated earlier, Commons intended only to "round out" established economic theory. The foregoing makes clear, however, that acceptance of his ideas would require a complete recasting of economics. Whatever his intention, in other words, Commons has in actuality provided us with an alternative vision to that lying at the core of mainstream theory (Ramstad, 1992a).

Economic Competition as a Volitionally Instituted Process

The preceding leads one to conclude that—whether it be clan, tribe, or nation—a going concern, so long as it remains free of the will of the possessor of superior force, is free to organize its provisioning process (production and distribution) in accordance with any of its actual possibilities. This means that absent conquest by another "going concern" (clan, tribe, nation) possessing superior command over the means of violence, an economic system (instituted system for carrying out social provisioning) must be understood as the collective choice of those within the history of a society who have consecutively assumed the task of resolving disputes concerning how things are to be done—that is, who have consecutively determined what are to be the governing working rules (Ramstad, 1987b). This standpoint entails a shift in the point of view with respect to economic analysis. If the economist seeks to understand the "essence," the logic reflected in the ongoing transactions, of a nation's economic system, he cannot account for it in terms of universal general "principles" revealed in all provisioning systems.[76] Instead, he must seek that understanding in the distinctive interweaving of bargaining, managerial, and rationing transactions reflected in the ongoing process that is that concern's "economy." In short, he must bring to light the "legal foundations" of which day-to-day economic activity is but the active expression.

This is what Commons attempted in his *Legal Foundations of Capitalism* (1924), in which he traced out the process through which 20th century American capitalism had been volitionally "created" over the course of many centuries through the process of authoritative dispute resolution.[77] Starting with the year 1066, when England became the "property" of William the Conqueror and all its inhabitants were William's "subjects," Commons traced out how the "legal foundations" of the U.S. economy was "created" through the volitional selection of working rules, principally by the courts, as already indicated.[78] In so doing, Commons was able to establish that market "values," by which he meant the product of quantity times price, must be understood as manifestations of authoritative volition rather than as "natural" phenomena arising through the operation of a natural mechanism ("competition"). Indeed, he maintained that what he had worked out in *Legal Foundations* was nothing other than a "volitional theory of value" (Commons, 1924, p. vii).

Economists generally use terms such as *competition*, *supply and demand,* and *the market mechanism* to connote a process of exchange based solely on the motive of self-interest. At the heart of Commons's analysis is the view that these concepts have no intrinsic meaning. Indeed, to repeat, Commons's principal "message" in *Legal Foundations* is that competition is wholly a socially constructed process volitionally crafted out over many centuries by means of authoritative selection of "good" practices (rules, customs). Commons put it this way in criticizing the standpoint evident in the writings of mainstream economists: "[The principles reflected in the operation of markets] were not something innate and natural but were actually constructed out of the good and bad practices of the time" (Commons, 1934, p. 775). Recall that it was Commons's view that working rules specify what individuals can, may or must do, or not do, in their transactions with one another. In the case of the United States, it was first British common law judges and then, after independence, Supreme Court justices—principally by altering the meaning of key terms in the Constitution such as *property* and *due process of law*—who gradually constructed the system of patterned interaction known as the *market mechanism* (*competition*), *pari passu,* as they created a *business law* to regulate transactions.

The details of Commons genetic account of this slow volitional process of creation are far too intricate to recount here. Yet the centrality of that process to economic *competition* is not difficult to fix. For, in determining in the context of specific disputes brought before them what in fact are a transactor's *rights*, the judges defined what individuals *can* do in their transactions with the positive assistance of the state (and its superior power of force) if necessary; by specifying in the same disputes what in fact are the correlative *duties* of other transactors, they defined what individuals *must* and *must not* do, subject to compulsion by the state if necessary; by specifying what is not a duty, that is, by defining what individuals may do without interference from the state, *protected* by the state also keeping other people from interfering if necessary, they created *liberties*; and by simultaneously determining what is therefore not a right, they defined when an individual cannot expect the assistance of the state, that is, created the correlative *exposures*. It was through this process, Commons argued, that property rights, and most notably so the rights to "intangible property," that is, rights to capture exchange values, were established and an authorized domain for the exercise of free choice in determining the terms of transactions—in a word, competition—was created.

It is not generally recognized what a radical view this is. For example, in his insightful analysis of classical economic thought, Warren Samuels (1966) has argued that many of the classical writers used the term *competition* to convey something other than an "invisible hand" process premised on unbridled self-interested action. As actually employed by numerous classical writers, Samuels declared, "competition" signified what *remains* of the pursuit of self-interest after *law-givers* have proscribed pursuit of those alternatives that do not harmonize with the public good (Samuels, 1966, pp. 6–7); that is, competitive outcomes were understood to reflect partly a "spontaneous" order and partly a "made" order. Samuels referred to this conception of economic competition as the "market-plus framework."

Significantly, in order to illustrate what he was getting at, Samuels suggested that Commons's *Legal Foundations of Capitalism* (1924) "is perhaps the classic study evidencing the market-plus framework orientation."[79] I have elsewhere (cf. Ramstad, 1990, n. 74) suggested that this characterization of Commons's standpoint may be slightly misleading. It is quite true that Commons's conception of economic competition was one of "constrained" self-interested action. Yet the foregoing overview of his standpoint makes it clear that he would have taken exception to the view that "competition" or "the market mechanism," that is, the patterned process of interaction based on the motive of self-interest, has any character at all in the absence of affirmative authoritative action (action by "law-givers"). For, authoritative action by "law-givers" has not only imposed limits on self-interested action: By establishing a duty of avoidance on one party to a transaction, and equally by establishing a "no right" (exposure) for one party to a transaction, it *created* liberty for the other. This is why Commons settled on the following as the "derived definition" of an institution: "collective action in restraint, liberation, and expansion of individual action" (Commons, 1934, p. 73). In sum, it is through the authoritative establishment of liberties and exposures that "law-givers" have volitionally *created* the behavioral domain within which self-interested action may "freely" operate. In other words, from the standpoint developed by Commons, in the absence of "plus" (authoritative action) *there cannot be* "the market."

Economic Evolution as a Volitional Process

Let us now return to the matter of Commons's general conception of economic evolution. In the tradition of American Pragmatism, Commons was undeterred by the "infinite regress" problem. It was the evolution of the American system of market capitalism for which Commons sought to account. Thus he accepted as fact that man had developed language, tools, and social organization many millennia ago and began his investigation with the Conquest of 1066; that is, the existence of "going concerns" with previously adopted rules was taken for granted by Commons, as was the existence of the "institutionalized minds" who populated those concerns. It was the restructuring of the working rules patterning transactions within the going concern we refer to as *the American economy* which was of interest to Commons, just as it was the unique details of its evolution that he investigated. Moreover, in so doing, Commons's principal concern was not to spell out the logic of a carefully considered theory of economic evolution but instead to establish that economic theory had developed inadequately, and thereby served to misguide public policy, in ignoring the dominant role in economic behavior of "collective action in control of individual action."

All the same, there *is* a general metatheory of economic evolution whose outlines are evident in Commons's analysis. We have already seen that he conceived of all provisioning activity to take place within groups of "institutionalized minds"—within going concerns. We have also seen that he understood provisioning activity to be analytically reducible to three intertwined types of transactions. In turn, he understood transactions to be "regulated" by authoritatively selected working rules. Despite being selected to effect a future consistent with the purposes of authoritative figures, working rules generally are imprecise and entail a zone of discretionary behavior. As new discoveries are made regarding resources, technology, and so on, and as previously adopted working rules give rise to unanticipated consequences, individuals react by changing their behavior "spontaneously" in a direction consistent with the cultural imperatives imbedded in their "institutionalized minds." In other words, Commons understood new practices to almost always represents an adaptation, extention, or novel application of an existing practice or custom.[80] For example, he accounted for the legal doctrines of *assumpsit* and *quantum meruit* in just such a fashion (cf. Commons, 1934, p. 61).

But rather than ensuring order, the "spontaneous" development of new practices eventually undermines it, as, inevitably, new practices generate conflicts of interest imperfectly regulated by existing working rules and hence precipitate new types of disputes. These disputes invariably pit those who would like to have a longstanding practice (rule) extended to regulate the new conflict of interest against those who would like to have a more recent "innovation" (custom, rule) adopted instead. Alternatively, the dispute may revolve around which of conflicting new ("spontaneous") practices and habits developed in response to the new conditions should be adhered to. If order is to be restored, the authoritative figure—and ultimately this is the sovereign if the dispute is an important one—must *select* which of the "recommended" practices or customs (rules) is to be followed in the future and make adherance to it mandatory (via, ultimately, the sanction of physical force) for all members of the concern.

Put slightly differently, the sovereign, or his designated representative, must determine what constitutes the "best" adjustment of the existing rule structure or "law" in order to restore order, that is, which of the alternative potential governing rules brought before it is the "good" one. Such a determination, Commons maintained, is always forward-looking. In a word, new rules are selected by the sovereign, or its designated representative, with an eye toward their "good" implications regarding the way that "burdens and benefits" will fall upon and be enjoyed by various classes of "citizens" within the going concern in the future.

Commons has thus provided us with an alternative conception of economic evolution from that conveyed through the metaphor of natural selection. Rejecting the view that economic evolution is guided by a brute process, Commons equated economic evolution with volitional institutional adjustment. If one insists on biological analogs, Commons's vision can to some degree accomodate them. He explicitly deemed custom, "the repetition of transactions," to be the analog of heredity (cf. Commons, 1934, p. 638). In addition, in his account of economic evolution it is changing conditions that induce self-interested "innovators" to develop new practices for effecting social provisioning (production and distribution). This is more or less parallell to the Lamarckian conception of biological variation. But, from among the practices (rules) that "innovators" develop, it is *authoritative figures who select* those that are to be adhered to or, alternatively, to be avoided, subject to the sanction of physical force. Commons's insight, then, is that the *direction* of economic evolution is determined not by a brute process but by the purposes of the "breeder"[81]; that is, the purposes of those who consecutively occupy the position of sovereign power, individually or collectively, or his/their designated representatives.

To repeat, the working rules (property rights) that together give modern-day economic competition its character derive from the customs that the sovereign, or its designated representatives, have consecutively selected from among those brought before it (them) and made mandatory for all. It is important to grasp that Commons rejected the view that "the market" or "competition" has an intrinsic character independent of the ends upon which the selected customs were deemed "good." As he put it,

> Competition is not Nature's "struggle for existence" but is an artificial arrangements supported by the moral, economic, and physical sanctions of collective action. The theory of free competition developed by economists is not a natural tendency towards equilibrium of forces but is an ideal of public purpose adopted by the courts, to be attained by restraints upon the natural struggle for existence. (Commons, 1934, p. 713)

This being the case, Commons insisted, economic evolution is not governed by *any* "natural" imperative. Neither is "efficiency" produced "automatically" or "naturally" via a brute process. Instead, he argued, efficiency is a purpose that has been volitionally implanted in "the market" as authoritative figures have consecutively struggled to determine which is the "good" and which is the "bad" practice; that is, Commons contended, efficiency is "not a natural tendency" but "an ideal of public purpose adopted by the courts." But it is crucial to understand that Commons further contended that efficiency was never the *single* "ideal of public purpose" guiding the market mechanism's construction, that is, the single criterion of "good" guiding the selection of customs brought before the courts. Always equally important in the court's mind, Commons determined through his analysis of Anglo-American legal history, has been the goal of ensuring that market processes are *fair*.[82] In Commons' determination, in other words, the anglo-American process of economic competition has been volitionally constructed to allow for greater efficiency *within* contemporary standards of *fairness*.

Going Concern as a Metaphor

As recounted earlier, economic evolution was an important phenomenon in classical economic thought. However, the direction of economic evolution—and hence its revered product, the market system—was therein understood to be controlled by divine will and hence interpreted to represent a gradual movement toward conformity with a knowable "design." Marxism, based as it was on Hegelian philosophy, incorporated a similarly teleological stance toward economic evolution. However, after "Darwin . . . substituted for the will of God a blind mechanism" (Commons, 1934, p. 112),[83] notions such as design and teleological movement were expunged from "scientific" discourse. Economists accordingly adjusted their scheme of thought so as to conform to Darwinian preconceptions about the direction of evolution, but, significantly, they managed to do so without discarding the belief that the central institutions of the market system are inherent in "nature" itself. This "change without change" was made possible, we have seen, by treating "efficiency" as a Darwinian blind selection mechanism (natural selection).

In the main, of course, the shift to a Darwinian view with respect to the logic of evolutionary models has had little practical impact upon the way that economists perceive their subject matter. Newtonian preconceptions have predisposed classical and neoclassical economists alike to adopt mechanical metaphors. Economists in the "mainstream" tradition therefore have generally treated "the market" (the system of voluntary exchange based on the motive of self-interest) as a *mechanism* that organizes the process of capital accumulation (economic growth) as it simultaneously organizes the allocation of scarce resources among competing ends and the distribution of output among potential claimants. As recounted earlier, the few economists whose *theoretical stance* has been influence by the Darwinian revolution have tended to substitute for their mechanical metaphors ones rooted in biology. Accordingly, Veblen and his intellectual descendants[84] being an important exception, economists interested in the problem of economic evolution have tended to conceive of the economy as an *organism* whose characteristics have been naturally selected through a brute process. Yet as we have seen, the metaphor of the economy as an organism cannot come to grips with the fact that it is in actuality an ongoing association of individuals and that "ongoingness" or maintenance of its existence, not "replacement" of itself via a "copy," is its fundamental problem. Recognizing these inherent difficulties, Commons insisted that a different metaphor for the market system was required. In his view, a more adequate metaphor, one that comes to grips with its ongoingness, is the economy as a *going concern*:

> The distinguishing character of a perfected going concern is its capacity to continue with changing personalities and changing principles, not depending upon any particular person or any particular principle. It adapts itself to circumstances, changing its personalities or its principles to fit the changing inclinations, or the conflicting inclinations, of the various groups of people whose allegiance and patronage are needed for the continuance of the concern. (Commons, 1934, pp. 750–751)

This metaphor embodies an entirely different motive force: "The principle of nature's mechanism is blind pressure; the principle of organism is struggle for life; the principle of going concerns is concerted action for ends foreseen in the future . . . [T]he principle of Nature's Mechanism is Energy, that of Organism is Scarcity, that of Going Concerns is Willingness (Commons, 1934, pp. 619–620). In addition, as already indicated, its adoption entails nothing less than a complete shift in one's "gestalt" regarding the "balancing wheel" of economic life—"from mechanical theories of equilibrium to *volitional control of* the forces of nature and *the activities of other people"* (Commons, 1934, p. 621, emphasis added).

Significance of the Artificial Selection Metaphor

As Walter Weisskopt (1973) has argued persuasively, mainstream economic analysis has since Adam Smith been principally an exercise in confirming reason; that is, it has been principally an endeavor to justify extensive noninterference with the "market mechanism." During the second half of the 20th century, the central argument in support of this posture has been the putative efficacy of market processes in promoting allocative "efficiency." As we have shown, "efficiency," now understood to be the analog of selective "fitness," is the common theme also in a wide array of theories relating to the phenomenon of economic evolution generated by practitioners anchored in conventional presuppositions about market processes.

If Commons is correct, all these exercises in confirming reason are fundamentally misguided and, as such, promote what the Marxists refer to as "false consciousness." For example, from the standpoint developed by Commons, rather than having been naturally "selected" due to its greater "efficiency" through the brute force of "competition," the modern corporation, as an ongoing flow of transactions was "constructed" via the authoritative resolution of disputes *pari passu* as "competition" itself was constructed. Each phenomenon, in other words, acquires its "essence" from the *same* set of property rights (working rules of collective action). Accordingly, "competition" *cannot* have been the selection mechanism producing the "evolution" of the modern business firm. Artificial selection according to the purposes guiding the court's resolution of disputes instead accounts for its evolution. That selection ". . . is 'artificial' simply because it is Purpose, Futurity, Planning, injected into and greatly controlling the struggle for life" (Commons, 1934, p. 636). Via that process of "artificial selection," Commons's careful review of legal history convinced him that the human ideals of efficiency and fairness have *both* guided the social "construction" of property rights and hence have "determined" the character of competition *and* the business firm (Ramstad, 1992b). What Commons found objectionable was that the concept of "fairness" the courts have implanted into the market mechanism was one consistent with the point of view of the ruling classes (Commons, 1934, p. 781). It was this "defect" that he sought to remedy with his proposed system of "regulated capitalism" and through his normative construct, Reasonable Value (Ramstad, 1992b).

Now, the foregoing should not be taken as implying that adoption of Commons' standpoint implies a belief that evolutionary theories other than Commons' are uniformly without merit. For example, Commons' conception of economic evolution attributes the *origin* of new working rules to the "spontaneous" actions of self-interested individuals in a manner similar to that postulated by Hayek. And certainly, Commons objected vehemently to the notion that *designed* institutions (working rules), to appropriate Hayek's term, are likely to be efficacious (see Ramstad, 1992b). Good working rules, he insisted on many occasions, must be *found* by the "law-givers" in the customs of the people, not created. Certainly, Commons never meant to argue that "the economy" represents the manifestation of conscious human design. At the same time, however, Commons dismissed Hayek's contention that *order* can also be "spontaneous." Whether or not this entailed a wholesale repudiation of "invisible hand explanations" is more difficult to determine, though, and the matter will not be addressed here (but cf. Commons, 1934, p. 162).

Regardless of the degree to which Commons's theory of economic evolution departs from views articulated by others, the shift in standpoint conveyed by that theory is of enormous practical significance, as it changes entirely the way one conceives of additional encumbrances upon the discretionary action of the modern business firm. Such a shift in standpoint is unmistakable in recent treatises by A. Allan Schmid (1987) and Daniel W. Bromley (1989), each of whom proceeds from a Commons-rooted understanding of competition to mount exceptionally lucid and compelling assaults on the fundamental propositions embraced by proponents of the "economic theory of law." Indeed, in his own way, each reveals that influential intellectual movement to be little more than an apologia for the status quo.[85]

Concluding Thoughts

We have seen that Commons articulated a theory of economic evolution based on purposeful selection rather than blind selection. Ingeniously, Commons recognized that this entailed an image of economic evolution paralleling almost exactly Darwin's theory of evolution by means of artificial selection. Given the power of this Darwinian metaphor in calling attention to the crucial difference between his theory and those articulated by others, Commons appropriated it. It is clear, however, that all of the problems enumerated earlier regarding the lack of correspondence between biological evolution and economic evolution apply equally to Commons' biological metaphor. Thus it is significant that Commons did not actually consider natural processes in general—biological evolution among them—to provide a meaningful frame of reference from which to apprehend volitional economic evolution. In other words, Commons would in all likelihood have concurred completely with the view espoused shortly after his death by Edith Penrose, namely, that since economic evolution can best be understood through concepts rooted in human volition, it would be the wisest course to avoid biological metaphors altogether.

Indeed, it will have been noticed, perhaps, that the term *constructed* has been employed repeatedly in characterizing Commons's account of economic evolution. This was not done by accident, for Commons appears to have regarded the construction of a machine as the appropriate analogy for volitional economic evolution. "Artificial selection," he averred, "bears to Natural selection the relation that Machine bears to Mechanism"

(Commons, 1934, p. 636). What Commons meant by this statement was that while "nature" provides humankind with materials and mechanisms, it is purposeful human action that has converted them into machines useful for the attainment of human ends. Similarly, in his view, it is purposeful human action—"artificial selection"—that has transformed the "struggle for existence" into the wealth-producing "machine" we refer to as the "market system."

Yet despite his seeming rejection of biological metaphors, Commons apparently recognized that biological evolution via artificial selection provided him with an extraordinarily powerful metaphor. As in Darwin's theory, "trait variation" (alternative practices) occurs in Commons's conception of economic evolution through a process outside the control of the "breeder" (authoritative figure). However, it is the "breeder" (authoritative figure) who, by determining which trait is to survive and be nurtured, *determines* the direction of a species' (an economic system's) evolution. As Commons put it: "Natural selection, which is natural survival of the 'fit,' produces wolves, snakes, poisons, destructive microbes; but artificial selection converts wolves into dogs, nature's poisons into medicines . . . A Holstein cow could not survive if left to natural selection—she is a monstrosity created by artificial selection for the sake of the good she can do for man in the future" (Commons, 1934, p. 636). And just as purpose-driven artificial selection has produced a Holstein cow "for the good of man," so has it produced the market system and the patterned process economists refer to as "competition."

Economists have presumed since the time of Malthus and Ricardo that "immutable laws" exercise a "coercive surveillance" over human destiny. Through the natural selection metaphor, this perspective similarly informs much of the resurgent interest in developing an evolutionary economics. As noted at the outset, Veblen long ago set down the requirement: An evolutionary theory must be "a theory of a cumulative sequence of economic institutions stated in terms of the process itself." As we have shown, the theory of natural selection is arguably an extraordinarily infelicitous metaphor for economic evolution. At most it conveys a view that economic evolution is governed by a brute process. Yet as we have also seen, economic evolution, at least that portion of it that has produced the market economy, has in actuality *not* been governed by a brute process.

It was Commons's fundamental insight that economic evolution is guided by human volition. By switching the Darwinian metaphor, by substituting for "natural selection" Darwin's concept of "artificial selection," Commons was able to remain within Darwinian preconceptions without abandoning this central insight. Through this metaphor it becomes evident that, like the Holstein cow, the market system is solely a human artifact, a set of arrangements purposefully selected to advance the well-being of the group (going concern) as a whole. This being the case, Commons insisted, it is properly evaluated *only* in terms of how well it facilitates the attainments of the purposes it was intended to promote. To put it slightly differently, it is nonsensical and illegitimate to oppose further adjustments to "property rights" in "intangible property," such as entailed in the "regulated capitalism" Commons advocated himself,[86] on the grounds that they will result in "distortions" of "natural" phenomena ("efficient" economic outcomes).

This was Commons's most fundamental message—one, alas, that he was never able to communicate effectively to the profession at large. Tragically, we see Commons' "fundamental unit of analysis," the transaction, transmogrified into a theory of "transaction costs" employed by zealots championing a cause antithetical to his own. His liberating message regarding the volitional character of economic competition is ignored completely as the United States submits its arrangements to "natural selection" via "international competitiveness" with potentially disastrous consequences (cf. Ramstad, 1987a). Perhaps if Commons's analysis were taken more seriously by the present generation of economic theorists, economics could, once again, as it was in the hands of Adam Smith, become an instrument in the service of meaningful reform rather than a defense for the vested interests.

Notes

1. I use the term *mainstream economists* to denote those whose writings manifest "neoclassical" philosophical preconceptions and analytical constructs. This classification is admittedly imprecise. Indeed, for a forceful argument that the term *neoclassical economics* is now almost without substantive meaning, see Wiles (1983).

2. *Webster's Third New International Dictionary*, unabridged, provides as its first definition of "evolution": "A series of related changes in a certain direction: process of change; unfolding movement." This is the meaning associated with the term, in its general usage, herein.

3. See, for example, Posner (1981, 1986), Hirschleifer (1982), Priest (1977), and Rubin (1977).

4. For an overview of the contributions that collectively comprise the "new industrial organization," see Eggertsson (1990).

5. It should be noted that economists favoring an "Austrian" approach are also generally included under the rubric of the new institutional economics. On this matter, see Langlois (1986a, p. 1).

6. See, for example, Mirowski (1990). Mirowski emphasizes that the reverse line of influence also is observed in the development of theories relating to the natural realm. This is certainly true with respect to Darwin's theory of evolution.

7. For Hirschliefer's fascinating attempt to demonstrate that the theory of natural selection provides insight into the evolution of law, see Hirschleifer (1982).

8. Interestingly, Mirowski argues that the Darwinian theory of evolution itself reflects the strong influence of the 19th century energetics framework (Mirowski, 1989, pp. 117–119). This may account for the ease with which Hirschleifer sees such close parallels between economics and sociobiology.

9. For a discussion of this point, see Schotter (1986, p. 118).

10. See, for example, Penrose (1952), Winter (1964), Fried (1982), Hodgson (1991), and Rosenberg (1991).

11. It is interesting that

> Darwin's conversion to a hypothesis based on random individual variations was associated closely with his move to investigate the work of animal breeders. Here he found confirmation of his belief that individual differences are inheritable. He also must have become aware that the breeders' success lay in their ability to pick out or select just those variations that happened to suit their purposes. . . . Darwin claimed that this was the key that opened up his search for a natural equivalent to artificial selection. (Bowler, 1984, p. 161)

12. Schabas (1991, p. 9) has noted that at the core of the early neoclassicalists' neglect of evolutionary principles lay a belief that the modern economic order is an "artificial" rather than a "natural" realm; she makes no attempt, however, to extend this insight into a discussion parallelling the subject matter of this paper.

13. For my attempt to do so, see Ramstad (1990). An alternative characterization of Commons's approach can be found in Parsons (1950).

14. Darwin evidently hit upon the idea of the struggle for existence while reading Thomas Malthus' *Essay on the Principle of Population.* On this point, see Bowler (1984, pp. 96–97).

15. For an analysis calling into question crucial elements of the adaptationist conception of evolution, see Gould and Lewontin (1979).

16. A *gene pool* is "The collection of genes held in common by a population or a species, of which each member possesses a more-or-less randomized sample" (Wills, 1989, p. 329).

17. The questionable status of this presumption is discussed at length in Levins and Lewontin (1985).

18. "Nature selects only in the sense that the match or mismatch between the environment and the fortuitously generated variants determine survival and thus reproduction" (Rosenberg, 1991, p. 3).

19. Hirschleifer offers the example of a male peacock's tail to illustrate this situation. Because it is a sign of robustness—the superior strength needed to carry its enormous weight—the possession of a larger tail than its competitors makes a male more attractive to females, thereby increasing its opportunity to produce offspring. But that same weight also makes it more vulnerable to attacks by predators.

20. The lack of predictive power is a significant problem for many economists. See, for example, Fried (1982, p. 62) or Rosenberg (1991, p. 1).

21. One is reminded here of a quip, probably not original with him, once made by Clarence Ayres: "A little distortion saves a lot of explaining!"

22. See, for example, North (1990, p. vii).

23. This is in perfect consonance with the natural selection framework as summarized above.

24. Also see Jensen (1987, pp. 1040–1042).

25. Veblen's theory of institutional development is briefly discussed below.

26. See Hirschleifer (1977, pp. 17ff). Interestingly, Hirschleifer nowhere indicates, to my knowledge, an awareness that he has a precursor of sorts in Veblen.

27. For a contrasting interpretation, see Niman (1991).

28. For a sampling of criticisms, see Enke (1951), Penrose (1952), Winter (1964), and Rosenberg (1991).

29. Recall that Alchian was concerned with the present relevance of the standard theory of the firm. By the 20th century, the firm had become a legal "person" with a "life" independent of its owner(s). It is clear in such a setting that the firm, in principle, need not ever "die." While less obvious, the same is true, in principle, of a "proprietorship" that passes from one family member (owner) to his heir (successor owner).

30. Penrose (1952, p. 807) has pointed out that organisms that reproduce asexually can evolve through processes that do not entail death of the "organism." I am not aware of any attempt to argue that asexual reproduction provides the analog for economic evolution and hence provides content for the natural selection metaphor. This might be an interesting and more fruitful approach, however.

31. It should perhaps be added that the "Lamarckian" hue of Alchian's conception of economic evolution is not aberrant, for as Hirschleifer (1977, p. 15) has observed, "The Lamarckian model . . . seems to be broadly descriptive of *cultural* evolution in general, and of economic responses in particular." Similar views regarding the Lamarckian rather than Darwinian nature of economic evolution have been forwarded by Rosenberg (1991, p. 24) and Schotter (1981, p. 164).

32. One cannot help but suspect that a concern with ideological implications lay at the root of Friedman's reluctance to dispense with the "maximization of returns" hypothesis. For an extremely insightful if unflattering analysis of the relationship between Friedman the economic theorist and Friedman the nation's foremost *laissez-faire* ideologist, see Rayack (1987).

33. Friedman added, surely disingenuously, that compelling support for the maximization-of-returns hypothesis also resides in "the repeated failure of its implications to be contradicted." Not a single specific example was provided to support this remarkable assertion! See Friedman (1953, pp. 22–23).

34. That Freidman's general argument was found compelling by other economists, as evidenced by its strategic legitimating role in practically every subsequent "orthodox" principles textbook, surely provides a compelling item of evidence in support of McCloskey's "rehetorical" reinterpretation of economic "knowledge." See McCloskey (1985).

35. Winter (1964) was first and his analysis has been sharpened or broadened by subsequent critics. Among the latter, see especially Rosenberg (1991) and Langlois (1986b, pp. 243ff).

36. Significantly, Friedman did not explain how one can rationalize the assumption of *individual* or *household* "maximization of returns" on "as if" grounds. It obviously would have been absurd to attempt to do so on the grounds of the natural selection of those who maximize *subjective utility*. Nonetheless, present-day texts typically use the "as if" line of reasoning to justify both the theory of individual behavior and the theory of firm behavior.

37. For a technical critique pointing out the lack of the correspondence between Nelson and Winter's "evolution" and the logic of biological evolution as presently understood, see Rosenberg (1991). For a probing and devastating critique that shows how little Nelson and Winter, in fact, departed from neoclassical methods when translating their general framework into specific models, see Mirowski (1983).

38. Obviously, I disagree completely with Hanusch's contention that Schumpeter "is regarded as the spiritual father [of evolutionary economics]" (Hanusch, 1988, p. 1). Or to put it slightly differently, there is obviously more than one kind of "evolutionary economics" being practiced today. For yet another kind, one not discussed herein, see Boulding (1981).

39. NW state explicitly that they are presuming selection occurs via profitability determined by "market supply and demand conditions that are *exogenous* to the firms in question" (Nelson and Winter, 1982, pp. 18–19, emphasis added). This is clearly a brute process.

40. As noted already, the aptness of this presumption, even in biological theory itself, has been vigorously criticized by Levins and Lewontin (1985).

41. I here am presuming that NW's "market supply and demand conditions" is equivalent to "competition."

42. The classic discussion is provided in Hamilton (1932).

43. It should be apparent that this line of reasoning merely takes the concept of *routine-bound* behavior, to use NW's term, to a more general level of analysis.

44. However, the adjustment of "institutions" to changing "technology" was in Veblen's view always lagging actual conditions and was hence to some degree maladaptive to current conditions (Tilman, 1992, p. 264). *Institutional lag* is the term conventionally employed to indicate this problem.

45. I am here referring to the theoretical standpoint developed by Marc Tool and, perhaps, other proponents of "instrumental value theory." See, in particular, Tool (1986). Recent debate about the meaning of his constructs would suggest that Tool has not yet made it clear to other institutionalists whether or not he presumes that a brute process is ultimately controlling with respect to the issue of the adoption of "instrumentally warranted" rather than "ceremonially warranted" practices.

46. David Hamilton has defined the evolutionary standpoint embraced by Veblen-inspired practitioners thusly: "[T]hose influenced by the Darwinian revolution saw social structure as something arrived at through a process of cumulative change and as something undergoing further change. . . . Darwinian change . . . is a non-teleological process of cumulative change. There is no right and good end towards which things are working out" (Hamilton, 1970, pp. 25, 27).

47. This generalization is based on a review of notes I have taken over the years while working through the writings of economists who have self-consciously embraced the Veblenian perspective with respect to economic analysis.

48. The important exception, to repeat, is Nelson and Winter (1982).

49. For my attempt to summarize these predilections, see Ramstad (1993).

50. See Schearmus (1986) for the connection between Hayek's thought and the "Austrian" standpoint developed by Carl Menger.

51. In fairness, it should be pointed out that Williamson has not attempted to articulate a complete theory of economic evolution but instead only to bring to the forefront a previously neglected element of a comprehensive theory. Cf. Williamson (1985, p. 2).

52. Carl Menger (1963) coined the term *organic institution* in reference to those "arising out of the selfish interaction of a myriad of individual economic agents, each pursuing his own self-interest" (Schotter, 1981, p. 4).

53. I say "possible exception" because in my reading, while he did not to my knowledge explicitly say so, Hayek seems to have assumed that "designed" institutions are also subject to the same selection principle as groups or "societies" prevail over others over very long periods of time. See, for example, Hayek (1978, pp. 7–9; 1984, p. 320).

54. See Gould and Lewontin (1979) for a critique of the "Panglossian" overtones inherent in the "adaptationist" interpretation of biological evolution. See Hodgson (1991) for a parallel critique of the "Panglossian" overtones inherent in the economic "efficiency" interpretation of economic evolution. Hodgson's interpretation of the centrality of efficiency to all variants of the new institutional economics parallels that offered here. Often based on analogies taken from biological evolution, Hodgson shows that the efficiency interpretation of economic evolution is seriously defective on logical grounds. Since all that is of importance

in the present context is that selection via the brute force of "efficiency" is at the heart of the new institutional economics, Hodgson's analysis is not recounted here. Still, it should be noted that his criticisms provide additional grounds for questioning the felicity of the natural selection metaphor in accounting for economic evolution.

55. For example, see Coase (1960), Demsetz (1967), Hirschleifer (1982), Posner (1981, 1986), Rubin (1977), and Priest (1977).

56. See Rubin (1977) and Priest (1977) for the details of the brute process through which this outcome is achieved. It should be noted that Posner does acknowledge that if *stare decisis* (following precedent) matters to the court, the process of change may be a very slow one (Posner, 1986, p. 528).

57. See Ellickson (1989) for a cogent and compelling critique of Posner's theoretical framework.

58. The use of the term *reproduction* in much of the Marxian literature to denote the maintenance of existing patterns of behavior or social structures entails, in my judgment, the same difficulty and is entirely an infelicitous term. Its origins in that literature, however, cannot be traced to Darwin or biology. Rather, it inheres in Marx's appropriation of the "advance-economy" metaphor evident in Physiocratic thought. On the nature of the advance-economy metaphor, see Schumpeter (1954, pp. 564–565).

59. Significantly, for just such an interpretation see Commons (1897).

60. In this passage, Schotter actually is summarizing his understanding of Menger's position with respect to "organic" institutions. However, as the subsequent pages make evident, this is essentially the stance that Schotter himself adopts.

61. For an historical analysis of the evolution of economics as a discipline that shows the close correspondence with respect to preconceptions between "secondary" contributors to the "classical" literature, in particular, Nassau Senior and Frederic Bastiat, and all variants of "neoclassical" and "Austrian" economics, see Hunt (1991).

62. See Hunt (1991) for what is in the present writer's view an exceptionally penetrating critical analysis of the predilections underlying "mainstream" economics. See Jones (1986, p. 1049) for the argument that Darwin's emphasis upon the *individual* in evolution came from his reading of Smith and the other Scottish philosophers who tried to understand "the whole in terms of the individual parts and their interaction."

63. See, though, Polanyi's account (1944, pp. 124ff) of the process through which Darwin's intellectual forerunner, Thomas Malthus, generated his pre-Darwinian theory of population and the significance of this theory to the Poor Law Reform of 1834, through which the labor market in England, as a self-regulating mechanism, was created (1944, pp. 140ff).

64. This section draws heavily on an interpretation of Commons' standpoint developed, with extensive documentation, in Ramstad (1990). In the present account, documentation will be provided only for quotes and when extending that analysis.

65. For his most direct statement of his theory, see Commons (1931).

66. The author's argument that "circular causation" rather than methodological individualism lies at the heart of Commons' theory of social change may be found in Ramstad (1990, pp. 77ff).

67. For Commons, "order" signifies a situation in which there is security of expectations with respect to the behavior of others. Cf. Commons (1934, pp. 57–58).

68. The reader should understand that Commons' analysis is substantially more complex than might be suggested by the summary provided here. For a more comprehensive overview of Commons' "volitional" conception of the market system, and hence one that deals much more satisfactorily with many of the subtle issues involved, see Ramstad (1990).

69. It might be noted that it is unlikely a concern will survive if it waits for its citizens to play a "repetitive game" an infinite number of times in order to discover viable strategies and

thereby to develop a "convention." That is, Commons' conception of authoritative dispute resolution is clearly an alternative to the game-theory approach now in vogue.

70. Commons further elaborated that "collective opinions . . . are the assumptions to which individual opinion must conform if individuals are to work together" (Commons, 1934, p. 698).

71. Thus at the root of Commons' evolutionary conception is an evolving "social man," as discussed earlier. Significantly, it was Commons' explicit view that social psychology provides the constructs most relevant for an understanding of transactional behavior. See Ramstad (1990, p. 67).

72. See Ramstad (1990, pp. 67–69 and 77–82) for qualifications that must be kept in mind before judging Commons to be a strict determinist. In fact, Commons rejected the utility of the distinction between "free will" and "determinism." In order to make sense of Commons' general line of argument with respect to his own normative program, one must infer that he did believe that some dimensions of the human character are independent of human evolution as a "social" being, that is, inhere in human biological character. On this, see Ramstad (1992b).

73. See pp. 89–90 above.

74. Commons understood avoidance, performance, and forbearance (a limit placed on performance) to be the three crucial dimensions of economic behavior.

75. It should perhaps be added that Commons never suggested that "designed" institutions were likely to be willingly aquiesced to by a concern's citizens. As he put it, "Custom . . . may . . . be even more mandatory than the decrees of a dictator" (Commons, 1931, p. 651). Thus it was his view that the sovereign's will is effective in selecting among established customs (practices), not in inventing new ones.

76. For the view that this proposition comprises a core belief of American institutionalists, see Dugger (1989).

77. In actuality, Commons simultaneously developed both his general perspective on economic evolution and his evidence in its support in *Legal Foundations* without at the time doing either self-consciously. Discussion of the significance of the process he therein recounted with respect to the logic that ought to inform "evolutionary" economic theory was deferred until he wrote *Institutional Economics* 10 years later.

78. Property, Commons once declared, "is sovereignty taken collectively from the king by his tenants" (Commons, 1924, p. 221).

79. Certainly, many passages in Commons' works would suggest exactly that interpretation. For example: "The field of authorized liberty is the field where behavior is unrestrained or uncompelled by authority" (Commons, 1924, p. 99).

80. We have here a parallel with biological evolution. Thinking now of "existing practice or custom," like Nelson and Winter's "routines," as the analog of "genes," the potential course of economic evolution cannot go beyond the potentialities inherent in habitual assumptions any more than biological evolution can go beyond the potentialities inherent in existing genes.

81. Cf. the passage from Darwin on p. 67 above.

82. For the analysis underlying this assertion, see Ramstad (1992b).

83. Commons frequently used the term *blind mechanism* for what I have called *brute process*. This is evident in the complete passage: ". . . substituted for the will of God a blind mechanism of heredity, variation, struggle, natural selection and survival."

84. See, for example, Bush (1987).

85. For an insighful analysis showing that Williamson's "institutional economics" serves a similar apologetic function, see Dugger (1983).

86. See Ramstad (1992b) for a general overview of Commons' proposed system of "regulated capitalism."

References

Alchian, A.A. 1950. "Uncertainty, Evolution and Economic Theory." *Journal of Political Economy* 58:211–221.

Biddle, E. 1991. "The Ideas of the Past as Tools for the Present: The Instrumental Presentism of John R. Commons." In *The Estate of Social Knowledge*, edited by Jo Anne Brown and David van Keuren, Baltimore: Johns Hopkins University Press, pp. 84–105.

Bowler, P.J. 1984. *Evolution: The History of an Idea.* Berkeley, CA: University of California Press.

Boulding, K.E. 1981. *Evolutionary Economics.* Beverly Hills, CA: Sage Publications.

Boyles, M., and Tilman, R. 1992. "Thorstein Veblen, Edward O. Wilson and Sociobiology: An Interpretation." Paper presented to the Western Social Science Conference, Denver, Colorado, April, 1992.

Bush, P.D. 1987. "The Theory of Institutional Change." *Journal of Economic Issues* 21:1075–1116.

Coase, R.H. 1937. "The Nature of the Firm. *Economica (N.S.)* 4:386–405.

Coase, R.H. 1960. "The Problem of Social Cost." *Journal of Law and Economics* 3:1–44.

Commons, J.R. 1897. "Natural Selection, Social Selection, and Heredity." *The Arena* 18:90–97.

Commons, J.R. 1924. *Legal Foundations of Capitalism.* New York: Macmillan.

Commons, J.R. 1931. "Institutional Economics." *American Economic Review* 21:648–657.

Commons, J.R. 1934. *Institutional Economics: Its Place in Political Economy.* New York: Macmillan.

Darwin, C. 1972 [1875]. *The Variation of Animals and Plants Under Domestication*, 2nd ed., reprint. New York: AMS Press, Inc.

Demsetz, H. 1967. "Toward a Theory of Property Rights." *American Economic Review, Papers and Proceedings* 57:347–359.

Diesing, P. 1971. *Patterns of Discovery in the Social Sciences.* Chicago: Aldine Atherton.

Dugger, W.M. 1983. "The Transaction Cost Analysis of Oliver E. Williamson: A New Synthesis?" *Journal of Economic Issues* 17:95–114.

Dugger, W.M. 1989. "Radical Institutionalism: Basic Concepts." In *Radical Institutionalism: Contemporary Voices*, W.M. Dugger, ed. Westport, CT: Greenwood Press, pp. 1–20.

Eff, E.A. 1989. "History of Thought as Ceremonial Genealogy: The Neglected Influence of Herbert Spencer on Thorstein Veblen." *Journal of Economic Issues* 23:689–716.

Eggertsson, T. 1990. *Economic Behavior and Institutions*. New York: Cambridge University Press.

Ellickson, R.C. 1989. "Bringing Culture and Human Frailty to Rational Actors: A Critique of Classical Law and Economics." *Chicago-Kent Law Review* 23:23–55.

Enke, S. 1951. "On Maximizing Profits: A Distinction between Chamberlin and Robinson." *American Economic Review* 41:566–578.

Fried, C. 1982. "Comments on Hirshleifer Paper." *Research in Law and Economics*, Vol. 4. Richard O. Zerbe, Jr., ed. Greenwich, CT: JAI Press, pp. 61–65.

Friedman, M. 1953. "The Methodology of Positive Economics." In *Essays in Positive Economics*. Chicago: University of Chicago Press, pp. 3–43.

Galbraith, J.K. 1973. "Power and the Useful Economist." *American Economic Review* 63:1–11.

Gould, S.J. 1980. "Hyena Myths and Realities." In *Hen's Teeth and Horse's Toes: Further Reflections in Natural History*. New York: W.W. Norton & Company, pp. 147–157.

Gould, S.J., and Lewontin, R.C. 1979. "The Spandrels of San Marco and the Panglossian Paradigm: A Critique of the Adaptionist Programme." *Proceedings of the Royal Society of London* B205:581–598.

Hamilton, D. 1970. *Evolutionary Economics: A Study of Change in Economic Thought*. Albuquerque, NM: University of New Mexico Press.

Hamilton, W. 1932. "Institution." In *Encyclopaedia of the Social Sciences*, Vol. VIII. Edwin R.A. Seligman, ed. New York: Macmillan, pp. 84–89.

Hanusch, H. ed. 1988. *Evolutionary Economics: Applications of Schumpeter's Ideas*, with introductory essay. Cambridge: Cambridge University Press, pp. 1–7.

Hayek, F.A. 1973. *Law, Legislation and Liberty: Vol. 1, Rules and Order*. Chicago: University of Chicago Press.

Hayek, F.A. 1978. *New Studies in Philosophy, Politics, Economics and the History of Ideas*. Chicago: University of Chicago Press.

Hayek, F.A. 1984 (1983). "The Origins and Effects of Our Morals: A Problem for Science." In *The Essence of Hayek*, C. Nishiyama and K.R. Leube, eds. Stanford: Hoover Institution Press, pp. 318–330.

Hirschleifer, J. 1977. "Economics From a Biological Viewpoint." *The Journal of Law & Economics* 20:1–52.

Hirschleifer, J. 1982. "Evolutionary Models in Economics and Law." *Research in Law and Economics*, Vol. 4. R.O. Zerbe, Jr., ed. Greenwich, CT: JAI Press, pp. 1–60.

Hodgson, G.M. 1988. *Economics and Institutions: A Manifesto for a Modern Institutional Economics*. Philadelphia: University of Pennsylvania Press.

Hodgson, G.M. 1991. "Economic Evolution: Intervention Contra Pangloss." *Journal of Economic Issues* 25:519–533.

Hunt, E.K. 1991. *History of Economic Thought: A Critical Perspective*, 2nd ed. New York: HarperCollins.

Iwai, K. 1984. "Schumpeterian Dynamics: An Evolutionary Model of Innovation and Imitation." *Journal of Economic Behavior and Organization* 5:321–351.

Jensen, H. 1987. "The [Institutionalist] Theory of Human Nature." *Journal of Economic Issues* 21:1039–1073.

Jones, L.B. 1986. "The Institutionalists and *On the Origin of Species*: A Case of Mistaken Identity." *Southern Economic Journal* 52:1043–1055.

Klein, B.H. 1988. "Luck, Necessity, and Dynamic Flexibility." In *Evolutionary Economics: Applications of Schumpeter's Ideas*. Horst Hanusch, ed. Cambridge, UK: Cambridge University Press, pp. 95–127.

Langlois, R.N. 1986a. "The New Institutional Economics: An Introductory Essay." In *Economics as a Process: Essays in the New Institutional Economics*. R.N. Langlois, ed. New York: Cambridge University Press, pp. 1–25.

Langlois, R.N. 1986b. "Rationality, Institutions, and Explanation." In *Economics as a Process: Essays in the New Institutional Economics*. R.N. Langlois, ed. New York: Cambridge University Press, pp. 225–255.

Levins, R., and Lewontin, R. 1985. *The Dialectical Biologist*. Cambridge: Harvard University Press.

Marshall, A. 1969 (1920). *Principles of Economics*, 8th ed. London: Macmillan.

McCloskey, D.N. 1985. *The Rhetoric of Economics*. Madison, WI: University of Wisconsin Press.

Menger, C. 1963 (1883). *Problems of Economics and Sociology*. Trans. F.J. Nock. Urbana, IL: University of Illinois Press.

Mirowski, P. 1983. "*An Evolutionary Theory of Economic Change*: A Review Article." *Journal of Economic Issues* 17:757–768.

Mirowski, P. 1989. *More Heat Than Light: Economics as Social Physics, Physics as Nature's Economics*. New York: Cambridge University Press.

Mirowski, P. 1990. "Learning the Meaning of a Dollar: Conservation Principles and the Social Theory of Value in Economic Theory." *Social Research* 57:689–717.

Nelson, R.R., and Winter, S.G. 1982. *An Evolutionary Theory of Economic Change*. Cambridge: Harvard University Press, 1982.

Niman, N.B. 1991. "Biological Analogies in Marshall's Work." *Journal of the History of Economic Thought* 13:19–36.

North, D.C. 1990. *Institutions, Institutional Change and Economic Performance*. New York: Cambridge University Press.

Parsons, K.H. 1950 (1942). "John R. Commons' Point of View." In *The Economics of Collective Action*. J.R. Commons. New York: Macmillan, pp. 341–375.

Parsons, T. 1968 (1937). *The Structure of Social Action*, Vol. 1. New York: The Free Press.

Penrose, E.T. 1952. "Biological Analogies in the Theory of the Firm." *American Economic Review* 42:804–819.

Polanyi, K. 1944. *The Great Transformation: The Political and Economic Origins of Our Times*. New York: Rinehart.

Polanyi, K. 1968 (1947). "Our Obsolete Market Mentality." In *Primitive, Archaic and Modern Economies: Essays of Karl Polanyi*. G. Dalton, ed. Boston: Beacon Press, pp. 59–77.

Posner, R.A. 1981. *The Economics of Justice*. Cambridge: Harvard University Press.

Posner, R.A. 1986. *Economic Analysis of Law*, 3rd ed. Cambridge: Harvard University Press.

Priest, G.L. 1977. "The Common Law Process and the Selection of Efficient Rules." *Journal of Legal Studies* 6:65–83.

Ramstad, Y. 1986. "A Pragmatist's Quest for Holistic Knowledge: The Scientific Methodology of John R. Commons." *Journal of Economic Issues* 20:1067–1105.

Ramstad, Y. 1987a. "Free Trade Versus Fair Trade: Import Barriers as a Problem of Reasonable Value." *Journal of Economic Issues* 21:5–32.

Ramstad, Y. 1987b. "Institutional Existentialism: More on Why John R. Commons Has So Few Followers." *Journal of Economic Issues* 21:661–671.

Ramstad, Y. 1990. "The Institutionalism of John R. Commons: Theoretical Foundations of a Volitional Economics." *Research in the History of Economic Thought and Methodology*, Vol. 8. W.J. Samuels, ed. Greenwich, CT: JAI Press, pp. 53–104.

Ramstad, Y. 1992a. "A Wolf in Sheep's Clothing: John R. Commons and the Question of Social Order." Paper presented to the Association for Evolutionary Economics, New Orleans, January, 1992.

Ramstad, Y. 1992b. "Towards an Economics of the Just Price: John R. Commons and Reasonable Value." Paper presented to the Kress Society, Boston, Massachusetts, February, 1992.

Ramstad, Y. 1993. "Institutional Economics and the Dual Labor Market Theory." In *Institutional Economics*, Marc Tool, ed. Boston: Kluwer-Nijhoff Publishing, pp. 173–233.

Rayack, E. 1987. *Not So Free to Choose: The Political Economy of Milton Friedman & Ronald Reagan*. New York: Praeger.

Rosenberg, A. 1985. *The Structure of Biological Science*. New York: Cambridge University Press.

Rosenberg, A. 1991. "Does Evolutionary Theory Give Comfort or Inspiration to Economics?" Paper presented to the Conference on Natural Images in Economics, University of Notre Dame, October, 1991.

Rubin, P.H. 1977. "Why Is the Common Law Efficient?" *Journal of Legal Studies* 6:51–63.

Samuels, W.J. 1966. *The Classical Theory of Economic Policy*. New York: World Publishing.

Schabas, M. 1991. "The Greyhound and the Mastiff: Darwinian Themes in Mill and Marshall." Paper presented to the Conference on Natural Images in Economics, University of Notre Dame, October, 1991.

Schearmus, J. 1986. "The Austrian Connection: Hayek's Liberalism and the Thought of Carl Menger." In *Austrian Economics: Historical and Philosophical Background*. W. Grassl and B. Smith, eds. New York: New York University Press, pp. 210–224.

Schotter, A. 1981. *The Economic Theory of Social Institutions*. New York: Cambridge University Press.

Schotter, A. 1986. "The Evolution of Rules." In *Economics as a Process: Essays in the New Institutional Economics*. R.N. Langlois, ed. New York: Cambridge University Press, pp. 117–133.

Schumpeter, J.A. 1954. *History of Economic Analysis*, edited from manuscript by Elizabeth Boody Schumpeter. New York: Oxford University Press.

Schumpeter, J.A. 1961 (1934). *The Theory of Economic Development*. New York: Oxford University Press.

Tilman, R. 1992. *Thorstein Veblen and His Critics: 1891–1963*. Princeton, NJ: Princeton University Press.

Tool, M.R. 1986. *Essays in Social Value Theory: A Neoinstitutionalist Contribution*. Armonk, NY: M.E. Sharpe.

Veblen, T. 1899. *The Theory of the Leisure Class: An Economic Study of the Evolution of Institutions*. New York: B.W. Huebsch.

Veblen, T. 1914. *The Instinct of Workmanship and the State or the Industrial Arts*'. New York: B.W. Huebsch.

Veblen, T. 1919 (1898). "Why Is Economics Not An Evolutionary Science?" In *The Place of Science in Modern Civilization and Other Essays*. New York: B.W. Huebsch, pp. 56–81.

Walker, P.M.B., ed. 1989. *Chambers Biology Dictionary*. Cambridge, UK: W & R Chambers Ltd and Cambridge University Press.

Weisskopf, W.A. 1973. "The Image of Man in Economics." *Social Research* 40:547–563.

Wiles, P. 1983. "Ideology, Methodology, and Neoclassical Economics." In *Why Economics is not yet a Science*. A.S. Eichner, ed. Armonk, NY: M.E. Sharpe, pp. 61–89.

Williamson, O.E. 1985. *The Economic Institutions of Capitalism: Firms, Markets, Relational Contracting*. New York: The Free Press.

Wills, C. 1989. *The Wisdom of the Genes: New Pathways in Evolution*. New York: Basic Books.

Winter, S.G. 1964. "Economic 'Natural Selection' and the Theory of the Firm." *Yale Economic Essays* 4:225–272.

Winter, S.G. 1971. "Satisficing, Selection and the Innovating Remnant." *Quarterly Journal of Economics* 85:237–261.

II NEO-SCHUMPETERIAN DYNAMICS

5 THE PHENOMENON OF ECONOMIC CHANGE: Neoclassical vs. Schumpeterian Approaches

Kurt Dopfer

The Issue

This study addresses an issue that few economists have pioneered like Schumpeter: economic change. The prominence he achieved in this field reflects, however, not only his intellectual stature, but also an apparent reluctance of economists to deal with this issue. This analysis starts with a brief reflection on the neoclassical notion of change. It is increasingly recognized that neoclassical economics takes as exogenous exactly those variables that would represent the very core of a theory of economic change. The theoretical deficiency is viewed to consist not only in the static nature of the equilibrium concept, but also in the choice-theoretic scheme of relative allocation that ignores the issue of "energy for change." The analysis proceeds with an account of Austrian endeavors to overcome the neoclassical limitations by introducing a cognitively alert agent who searches actively for economic opportunities. This approach allows one to endogenize essential aspects of change relating to adjustment and equilibrium converging processes. It is argued in a next step that a global theory of economic change must put forth propositions that refer to the evolutionary dynamics—highlighting change from one local economic regime to another.

In this perspective, the issue of the generation of innovative potentials that provide a continuous flow of economic opportunities receives primary attention. Schumpeter is seen to have made the crucial step from an analysis that deals with activities under conditions of given opportunities to one in which these opportunities as well as the conditions on which they rely are continuously generated by innovative agents. It is shown that the "young" and the "old" Schumpeter have conceived the role of the thus defined entrepreneur in the evolutionary dynamics of economic change very differently, leaving scope for controversy and various developments of the Schumpeterian research program. The analysis concludes with reflections on the future role of the entrepreneur under the conditions of the emerging "technological paradigm".

The Concept of Change in Neoclassical Economics

Modern neoclassical economics has its roots in the so-called marginal revolution that occurred at the end of the last century. Its founders, such as L. Walras, H.H. Gossen, V. Pareto, W.S. Jevons, and C. Menger, believed firmly in the laws of classical mechanics they frequently made analogies between mechanics and economics. Their ontic perspective has not only profoundly influenced the nature of economics as a science; it has also influenced the direction of theoretical efforts by determining what questions economists qua theoreticians were allowed to ask and what they were not. The *mechanistic* background model of neoclassical economics explains why the issue of *economic change disappeared* from the research agenda and, where it survived, received a peculiar *reductionist* expression.

Some essential aspects of the *neoclassical* notion of *change* can be highlighted on the basis of a figure that suggested V. Pareto. He starts off with the explicit recognition that economic phenomena resemble mechanical ones, and that we should "take advantage of that peculiarity" (Pareto, 1919, p. 1309; transl. K.D.). In Figure 1, the horizontal axis *t* denotes time, where *ab, bc, cd, de,* . . . stand for equal time intervals, and the vertical axis *q* denotes quantities of goods exchanged or transacted. Discussing the dynamics of economic phenomena, Pareto relies faithfully on Newton's *Laws of Motions*. The first law states that every body will continue in a state of rest or of uniform motion unless it is compelled by some external force to change that state. Pareto denotes the state of rest or of uniform motion by *X*, and says ". . . that the state *X* is a state such that if it is subjected to a change that is different from the one it undergoes normally, a reaction takes place instantaneously, tending to restore it to its normal

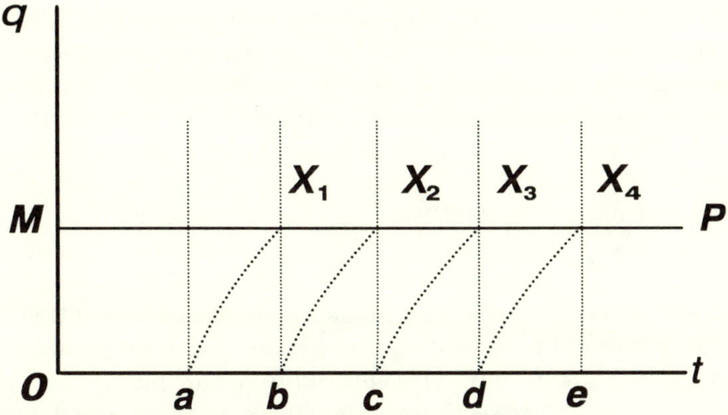

Figure 5.1. Pareto's equilibrium trajectories.
Source: Pareto 1919, p. 1310

state." (Pareto, 1919, p. 1309; transl. K.D.). The analytical unit constitutes a *trajectory* that may be subdivided into *three phases*: an initial phase where the equilibrium is disturbed, a subsequent adjustment phase, and a terminal phase where the equilibrium is restored. The mechanical trajectory represents a differential equation of the form

$$\frac{dx}{dt} = f(x, y, t),$$

where x represents a vector of endogenous, and y of exogenous, variables. Pareto mentions the example of an economic agent who has a preference for wine. The agent starts with no wine at a and has traded at the end of the time interval ab, for instance, at the end of a day, the quantity of wine bX_1. The disturbance at a may represent a metabolic flow-disequilibrium; economically, it represents an opportunity to improve welfare through trading. In the third phase, the transaction is completed and equilibrium restored. Pareto argues that the dynamics of the adjustment process, defined by the second phase, is theoretically uninteresting, since the trajectory of the system is determined completely by the initial conditions and laws of motion. He represents the second phase by an index function (Pareto, 1927, p. 659):

$$R_i(x_i, y_i, \ldots), \quad i = 1, 2, 3 \ldots,$$

where "x_1 is considered to represent one of the independent variables" (Pareto, 1927, p. 659). The property of the index function is such that whenever x_i changes in a certain direction (decrease, increase), R_i changes in the same direction. An index function denotes an "inherent tendency" of the system to restore equilibrium after a disturbance. "No movement will take place, if the increase (or decrease, K.D.) is zero." (Pareto, 1927, p. 660). Thus we have for equilibrium (third phase):

$$\left(\frac{\delta R_i}{\delta x_i}\right)^0 = 0, \left(\frac{\delta R_i}{\delta y_i}\right)^0 = 0, \ldots, \quad i = 1, 2, 3, \ldots$$

Major propositions of classical mechanics support the contention that the equilibrium position of the system provides *all information* about its dynamics. First, the law of motion is *deterministic. All past and all future is known*—echoing Laplace—if knowledge of the position and velocity of x at a single instant of time is available. If we take a single trajectory line, say from a to X_1, we do not have to discuss it "in all its details" (Pareto, 1919, p. 1309) since we may get all information from computations on the basis of the trajectory law. The second proposition of mechanics refers to the *global* application of the thus defined (local) trajectory. An economic agent can *repeat* the transactions every day; the law of motion will apply in *all time-space* contexts. *Repeatability* and *time symmetry* are constituent features of mechanistic trajectory laws. The global path of an economic system can therefore be described as a *succession* of equilibria X_1, X_2, $X_3, \ldots$, or by the *P-line* of Figure 1 that "is called the line of equilibrium and that, generally, is the line determined by the equations of pure economics." (Pareto, 1927, p. 1310). In contradistinction, the succession of exogenous disturbances a, b, $c, \ldots$, represents a *historical* dynamics that is dealt with as an *arbitrary, theoretically inaccessible* succession of disturbances.

The question is how *change* can be accounted for in the present trajectory model. Newton propounded a universal law where the gravitational force stands in a quadratic relationship to the distance of two bodies. His theory allows us to describe the equilibrium pace of planetary motions, but does not provide a theory of cosmic origins and evolution from the original to the present state. The "historical" dynamics of the universe is *exogenous* to Newton's model; the laws of motion make statements about the *consequences*, not about the *origin* of cause. In the neoclassical economic model, the causes of change are analogously exogenous to the system. Pareto distinguishes between a set of exogenous variables that refers to "tastes" and one that refers to "obstacles" (Pareto, 1927, pp. 248–284, 285–342). The latter variable set encompasses institutions and organizations in which the agent's decisionmaking occurs. Schumpeter has endorsed the exogenous treatment of these variables by praising Pareto's merits to have lifted up "... the logical core of the economic process above the ground of the institutional garb in which it is given to observation" (Schumpeter, 1952, p. 125). The economic agents are analogously supplied with preferences: *De gustibus non est disputandum*. A change may be explained as resulting from "historical" occurrences that relate to tastes or to obstacles. However, change may also occur as a process of (dis-)equilibrium adjustments under *given* tastes and obstacles—methodologically accommodated by the *ceteris paribus* clause. We must therefore distinguish between change that refers to what we may call a *constellation*—defined at this juncture as a composite of *exogenous* variables—and a *situation* in which the constellation variables are kept *constant*. Situational change can therefore not be explained by constellation change, and vice versa. The question then is how neoclassical theory accounts for *situational change* that occurs under conditions of a *given* constellation. Various approaches are conceivable. In Pareto's analysis, the question is merely whether an individual has a preference for a good *A* or *B*. This addresses the issue of relative allocation, but it leaves in limbo that of *change*. In its *dynamic* interpretation, taste may be conceived as addressing *a need that calls for satisfaction*. A need, for instance, for wine, constitutes an *energy for change*. It is not the structure of preferences that explains situational change, but the *energetic potential of the needs that call for satisfaction*. The trajectory of the neoclassical model relies on the causality principle of need satisfaction.

The causality principle thus conceived would still fail to provide support for the invariance and time symmetry of the trajectory. Pareto obtains the *determinism* of the law of motion by introducing the concept of *homo oeconomicus* who behaves—a priori, thus invariantly—perfectly "logically" (Pareto, 1971, pp. 29–101). Given a disequilibrium, the rational response leads to a *unique equilibrium*.

In a *choice-theoretic* framework a theoretical account of *change* relies either on assumptions about a change in the historical variables of a constellation or about local disturbances of a situational equilibrium. Rationality is neither a necessary nor sufficient condition for change; rather it is a specific *mode of responding to change*. If we accept a *behavioral* core of economic theory, change depends on *active* (rather than passive) human behavior. A choice-theoretic scheme that views the economic agent as a mere decider in the context of given alternatives emphasizes—from the point of view of economic change—the *passive* aspect of economic behavior. The argument may be clarified with a scheme whose structure is inspired by behaviorism:

$$\begin{matrix} S_y(S_x) & \rightarrow & \{(R_b) & \rightarrow & R_r\} \\ (a) & & (f) & & (X_I) \end{matrix}$$

S stands for a stimulus released from an exogenous disturbance y, or an endogenous disturbance x (first equation). If, for instance, the *ceteris paribus* clause is applied to S_y, the stimulus originates from situational disturbances, such as market opportunities. The trajectory is represented by R, and can be defined in terms of a behavioral or a resources trajectory. R_b stands for behavioral response, and R_r for the respective resources change. The trajectory law f has choice-theoretic underpinnings, and is hence assumed to represent a behavioral invariancy. S^j evokes a unique response R_b^i. The behavioral response is linked to a respective resources outcome. Methodologically, resources are empirically readily accessible—they can be observed, counted, and measured—while cognitive-psychic and behavioral variables appear as empirically intangible. Pareto and modern neoclassical economists have emphasized the need to free economics, not only from its "institutional garb," but also from its behavioral-psychological premises. To make economics scientific, it should be explained by the *laws of resources motions* alone. The reduced situational neoclassical model attains thus the form $S_x \rightarrow R_r$. Substituting the behavioristic terms by a_j and X_j (Fig. 1), economics becomes a science whose laws resemble, indeed, as the founders of marginalism have conjectured, those of classical mechanics.

The Neo-Austrian Escape: Search for Opportunities

The neo-Austrian economists have critized the notion of an economic agent who is reduced to adaptive features. In their view economic agents do not operate in a world of given opportunities, but rather in one where opportunities must *continuously be searched for*. Decision making is thus an element of an *ongoing process of human action* (e.g., Kirzner, 1982; v. Mises, 1962; coincidentally, this has long been recognized by Institutional Economists). For instance, a consumer who likes wine will not be content with given information, but will look for further information about that commodity. Depending on the behavioral capacities to search for and to process information, the terminal equilibrium may attain—even in a simple choice-theoretic model—multiple positions.

Figure 2 provides a scheme that allows us to discuss various theoretical positions. The range of *search* behaviors is expressed by the index bB^* that represents *various situational* behaviors. Reference point b denotes a

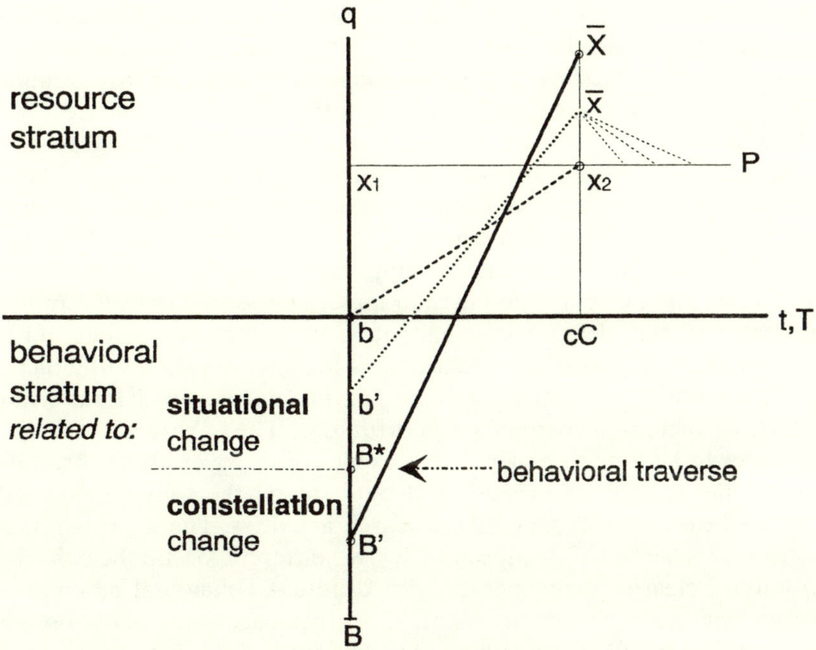

Figure 5.2. Behavior and resources: an integration

$\overline{qb}$ = Resource domain
$\overline{bB}$ = Behavioral continuum
$\overline{tT}$ = Time related to situation and constellation respectively
. . . = Situation
— = Constellation

Behavioral stratum:
b = Situational behavior; passive in terms of constellation change
B = Constellational 'Schumpeterian' behavior, active in terms of constellation change
B* = Behavioral traverse

Resources stratum:
$\underline{C}$ = Time of availability of novel potential
$\overline{X}$ = New profit constellation
x_1, x_2 = Situational equilibria
$\overline{x}$ = Situational disequilibrium, profit as distance from P
P = Competitive zero-profit equilibrium

situation where a *passive* agent has perfect information. The behavioral continuum *bB**, in turn, accomodates those behaviors that involve *active search*. A distinction is further introduced between a *behavioral* and a *resources* stratum. Changes in the information search process are assumed to covary with changes in the resources domain. A theoretical link is suggested between cognitive alertness and active entrepreneurial search for opportunities and the additional resources that accrue from those activities. The range of surplus values (resource stratum) is related to the index values of active behavior. For instance, behavior b' yields a surplus $\bar{x}$. This raises the question: how can active entrepreneurs improve economic performance if they have—as neoclassical theory assumes—perfect information at b. A theoretical clarification of this issue reveals the basic difference between the neoclassical and Austrian approaches. The neoclassical agent is supplied with a *given* set of opportunities; the Austrian searches for information not only with regard to superior alternatives within a given set of opportunities, but is concentrating also on *new opportunities* that are not given at the outset of the decision making process. Locus b represents (perfectly rational) decision making that occurs within the confines of given opportunities. The Austrian agent makes profits not (mainly) by increasing the rationality of actions, but by moving on the behavioral stratum towards an increased search for opportunities. The behavioral continuum bB relates to a scope of newly discoverable (or discovered) opportunities. The surplus variable is viewed as dependent on the thus defined index of active behavior and opportunity-search activities. The neoclassical and Austrian approaches are represented by two different loci on the behavioral continuum; clearly, they operate with different behavioral assumptions. Various degrees of rationality—stated, for instance, in terms of "bounded rationality" (Simon, 1959) or "selective rationality" (Leibenstein, 1987)—can be applied to the continuum of behaviors bB^*. The outcome of an economic action appears thus to be determined by a composite of both search alertness and the rationality degree applied.

The further theoretical question is how entrepreneurs respond to *given profit opportunities*. The neoclassical entrepreneur—in contrast to the Austrian—does not generate those opportunities; profits fall right into his lap due to an exogenous disturbance. The question is, what happens in a *neoclassical* context to this profit. Cournot has provided an early insightful answer to this question. He has argued that the "survival capacity" of profits depends on the market structure defined by the number of agents. Being interested in the duopoly problem, he started with a few agents (Schmidt, 1992). Basically, there are two ideal types of market structures—one with a single agent and one with an infinite number of agents. In the monopoly case, the welfare-suboptimal maximum profit defined by the intersection of marginal returns from demand and marginal production costs remains unchallenged by competitors. Rational decision making in a static context pays forever. Under a competitive regime profits disappear instantaneously; in fact, assuming rational expectations of all agents, there is no need to attempt to take advantage of any profit opportunity in the first place. In Figure 2, the relationship between various market structures and equilibrium-converging profits is indicated by the dashed lines, $\bar{x}P$ (where P represents the competitive minimum costs supply curve).

Austrian economics differs also with regard to the interpretation of the adjustment process. In the neoclassical approach, structure determines behavior. In the Austrian, various behavioral alternatives occur in a market structure. At this stage of the ongoing research, it would seem to be difficult to demonstrate that the Austrian approach sheds much light upon the theoretical issue of how economic behavior relates to market structure. The "Neo-Austrian synthesis" that marries market structure analysis with a behavioral approach is still wanting. Meanwhile, the rapidly booming game theory fills the gap—much in the tradition of neoclassical economics.

We have seen that Austrian economics highlights the entrepreneur's search for and discovery of economic opportunities. This line of theoretical argument has been introduced more generally by Hayek in his early contribution on the search for market information and the limits to knowledge (Hayek, 1945). The scope of this analysis is well captured by his remark that adaptation rather than initiation of change represents the core of the economic problem:

> [E]conomic problems arise always and only in consequence of change . . . [T]he economic problem of society is mainly one of adaptation in the particular circumstances of time and place. (Hayek, 1945, pp. 523–524)

The crucial question from an evolutionary point of view is: where do all the economic opportunities to which the economic agents adapt come from? Evidently, there must be some agency that generates inventions, new products, new production processes and organizations. It is still a peculiar feature of contemporary Austrian economics that it attempts to gain theoretical profile by contending that Schumpeter has overemphasized the process of the generation of opportunities and that he has overlooked the processes of search and selective adoption. This leaves the behavioral and process approach of Austrian economics close to the tradition of equilibrium analysis, with the phenomenon of economic change falling by the wayside.

Economic Change as Resource "Traverse"

We have conceived an economic constellation as a composite of situations. Two theoretical interpretations of the general notion are possible. One refers to resources; another to economic behavior. The issue is one of demonstrating how an economy changes from one constellation to another. We turn first to an approach that suggests an interpretation on the basis of resources motions. Emphasizing the discrete aspect of constellation change, we are interested in economic change as a *discontinuous* process. An elaborate statement along this line of research has been provided by J.R. Hicks.

The analytical problem in his "Capital and Time: A Neo-Austrian Theory" is to trace out the *economic path* that results from an *exogenous disturbance* under the familiar assumptions of rational decision making. In pursuing this, Hicks proposes

> ... to consider the problem as one of "Traverse." We begin with an economy which is in a steady state, under an "old" technique; then, at time 0, there is an "invention," the introduction of what, in some respects at least, is a new technology. Among the new techniques which thus become available, there is one which, at the initial rate of wages, is the most profitable, so, for processes started at time 0 (or immediately after time 0) it is adopted. The new technique is adopted for new processes, but the old processes are continued, so long as it is profitable for them to be continued. (Hicks, 1973, p. 81)

The first analytical phase expounds the conceptual features of the Pareto model. An invention constitutes an exogenous disturbance that provides an opportunity for a new, potentially efficiency-superior production function. The "traverse" from invention to innovation is discussed in a choice-theoretic framework. Stated in resources terms, the distance $\bar{x}P$ (Fig. 2) represents a rent (or quasirent in Marshall's sense). The second analytical phase is conceived as a "traverse" process from an old to a new equilibrium (Hicks, 1973, p. 102). In Figure 3, *B/A* denotes the "path of productivity" marked in the figure as Hicks-neutral. (The schedule recalls a figure that has been additionally applied by Pareto where the linear *P-equilibrium* line is replaced by an "erratic" one that allows for multiple terminal equilibria; Pareto, 1919, p. 1311). Hicks' analysis provides an explicit theoretical account of the *second* phase: the *convergence* from a (disturbed) old to a new equilibrium.

Hicks' analysis provides *micro*economic foundations. Since macro-economic analysis is conceived as a logical extension of micro theory on the basis of the principles of aggregation and factor equilibration, the conclusions can be extended straightforwardly to the macro domain (Hicks, 1973, pp. 47ff). However, the aggregation of micro decisions is possible only on the basis of restricting assumptions that diminish the explanatory power of the model. The earlier mentioned Cournot argument that the number of agents or a macro structure determines the values of perfect

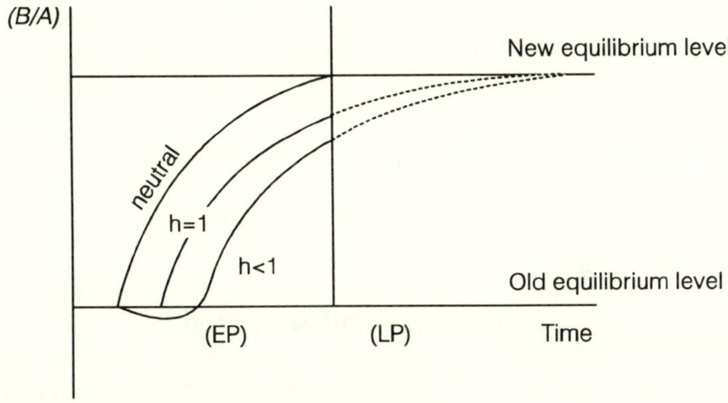

Figure 5.3. Hick's equilibrium trajectories.
Source: Hicks 1973, p. 102
(EP = Early Phase, LP = Late Phase)

profit realization and elimination provides a first clue to the limitations of the approach. Hicks operates, for instance, with homogenous products, which rules out any opportunity for monopolistic distortions (Hicks, 1973, p. 178). The lack of statements about the constellation processes and emerging market structures appear from an evolutionary perspective only as a specific instance of a more general conceptual deficiency. Hicks' approach represents a resources dynamics that is based on laws of motions that find their economic rationale in restrictive behavioral choice-theoretic assumptions under conditions of exogenously provided opportunities. The approach fails in a fundamental sense, however, to account for the problem of why the curve converges macroscopically from $\overline{X}$ to equilibrium (Fig. 2). Hicks' steady-state path analysis appears as an attempt to specify the deterministic mechanism of the second phase that Pareto considered redundant (Fig. 1, dashed lines). Underlying Hicks' analytical intention is the *Neo-Austrian hope* nourished by *Böhm-Bawerk's capital theory* that the uncertainty of future events can be reduced to a discounting procedure, which would yield a theory about economic processes "in time." From an evolutionary perspective, both choice-theoretic micro- and macroeconomics are flawed. *Evolutionary microeconomics* has to deal with behavior under uncertainty, the search for opportunities and the generation of innovative potentials. *Evolutionary macroeconomics* has to highlight the macroscopic consequences of a micro potential, its multiple, path-dependent economic actualizations, competitive adoption, and selective retention.[1] Any behavioral approach is—in an integrated evolutionary explanatory scheme —supplemented by evolutionary macro principles.

The Generation of Novelty: Schumpeter's Challenge

Schumpeter's approach starts where the Austrians stop. As we have seen, Austrian economics—in the behavioral process tradition (not in Hicks' sense)—highlights theoretically the search for opportunities, and this itself has a disequilibrating effect, whose time scope and level depend on the availability of opportunities. The adjustment process converges to equilibrium if economic opportunities are exhausted and entrepreneurial action fails to counter that tendency. It is at this juncture that Schumpeter's ideas about the entrepreneur as an innovator—a generator of novel opportunities —becomes relevant if an explanation of the sustained dynamics of a capitalistic market system is intended.

We turn again to Figure 2 in order to demonstrate the difference to the previous approaches. *In nuce*, Schumpeter's entrepreneur *crosses the "behavioral traverse" B** that sets apart situational from *constellational* behaviors. Economic agents not only search for, but also *generate* economic opportunities. The crossing of the traverse represents an entirely new type of behavior

> . . . it is not only more difficult to do new things, but this involves also something essentially different. The difficulties that one has to surmount are not only marginally different from those that one has to tackle in routine situations, but they represent altogether a different type of difficulties. We meet obstacles that within the old familiar ways of doing things are entirely or to a large extent absent. (Schumpeter, 1912, p. 121; all transl. of 1912 edition by K.D.)[2]

The theoretical problems that arise when applying conventional concepts of the phenomena of novelty can be demonstrated by referring to an important concept of modern economics: *learning by doing.* Arrows' (1962) original concept has been specified by Rosenberg (1982), who applies it to the use of technology. Though generally useful, the concept fails to contribute to an understanding of human behavior that relates to novelty. A Schumpeterian entrepreneur is incapable of improving his or her performance by learning by doing or using. The case may be demonstrated by the metaphor of two gladiators in combat. Both will learn during the fight. But the victor will be released to freedom, and the loser will die. In both cases, learning by doing does not improve future performance. The victor will have a new "occupation," which corresponds to entrepreneurial tasks that relate to new opportunities. The loser is equally robbed of the fruits of his recognition of what in the fight was obviously the wrong strategy or hold; the case corresponds to bankruptcy. The essential point that obtains in both cases is *knowledge specificity*. It constitutes the very nature of novelty that it deviates from old knowledge, and learning by doing that occurred in the past is necessarily bound to fail to serve as a basis for dealing with novelty. What characterizes the Schumpeterian entrepreneur is thus a behavioral attribute that represents something like *unlearning by doing.* Old cognitive and behavioral dispositions must be "erased"—in a process of *mental traversing*—in order to serve as a base for innovative cognition and behavior.

Schumpeter has linked the capability of innovative cognition and behavior to a specific *personality type.* (Schumpeter, 1913, p. 128f.) He compares entrepreneurial creativity with that of an artist: the vision of the entrepreneur as a *Gestalt-maker*. The entrepreneur differs also from the passive-hedonistic type of neoclassical homo oeconomicus; he/she represents an energetic-active agent—a distinction that had been introduced earlier by Veblen (1898). The personality type required for the generation of novelty combines the genius of *creative discovery* with the courage of "*creative destruction*". Above all, Schumpeter's entrepreneurs are wholehearted fellows ("ganze Kerle," Schumpeter, 1912, p. 137), who receive joy from success and victory over others. Schumpeter's entrepreneur may in certain historical contexts also be a "Führer" who has the capacity to lift himself above the masses (Schumpeter, 1912, p. 184f). Schumpeter relaxed this behavioral characteristic in his later work when dealing with the modern industrial large-scale firm, though he made still some favorable remarks in his diary about certain organizational forms of National Socialism (W. Stolper, personal communication).

The next theoretical step is to specify how Schumpeterian behavior influences the "resources motions." Referring to Figure 2, the answer is straightforward: the Schumpeterian entrepreneur's innovative behavior generates a profit $\overline{X}x_2$. The innovative entrepreneur obtains here larger profits than he or she who only searches. But this may be accidental. The crucial point is that there is a distinct *difference* between an *economic opportunity* and *an innovative potential*. It seems essential for an evolutionary interpretation of economic change to grasp this difference. Conceptually, *a potential is an idea*. As such, it is timeless and spaceless. An idea becomes a potential if it can be *actualized in time and space*. For instance, ideas underlie a plan to construct a building, a blueprint to organize production, or an algorithm for decision making. Ideas are *singularities*. It would be nonsensical, for instance, to talk about a "doubling" of an idea. Evolutionary mutation is always substantively unique. We will address the practical implications of this ontic peculiarity when discussing aspects of an evolutionary interpretation of economic change. *Actualizations*, in contrast, do not constitute singularities. Their very nature refers to *multiplicity*. A novel technology is a singular idea that can be actualized in various historical contexts and in *large numbers*. Actualizations represent economic opportunities (or vice versa). Ideas are never consumed; only their actualization in time and space is. We see that a theoretical discussion about the adoption of new technology in a macroscopic context addresses theoretical issues that are different from those that have to do with the generation of potentials. Large numbers, statistical mass, sample, and measurement are analytical categories designed to tackle actualization processes. Actualization refers to the multiple representation of an idea in matter-energy and addresses issues of feasibility in terms of known physical laws as well as historical adaptability.

The analytical clarification allows us to comprehend what is a new *opportunity* and what is a new *potential*. Basically, *novelty refers only to a potential*, that is, constitutes (new) information about an idea. There are no new novel opportunities, but only *undiscovered opportunities*. Opportunities result—as possible actualizations—from an innovative potential. As actualizations in time and space they can be exhausted; an innovative potential *qua* idea is inexhaustible. At this juncture, it becomes clear that an entrepreneur who faces an environment with exhaustible opportunities cannot make more profits by looking for more opportunities, but must generate innovative potentials, that is, cross the "behavioral traverse". Discontinuous economic change is inconceivable in the situational context of opportunities.

Evolutionary Principles

Discussing the "circular flow," Schumpeter has emphasized that it is "not the constancy of the parameters but the mode of the economic process that defines what is static" (Schumpeter, 1912, p. 446). We can conclude from this that it is analogously the *mode and the quality* of an innovative potential rather than its mere "size" that defines its very essence. An innovative potential thus represents not only a potential "super-profit" (in Fig. 2, a superimposed Cournot line), but rather a *generating source for new economic opportunities* that await actualization by entrepreneurs. Schumpeter—at least when young—was interested in explanations, not only in detecting regularities of the developmental dynamics. Having restated the first phase in evolutionary terms, the *second and third* phases call for an analogous *reinterpretation.* Evolutionary adjustment processes and equilibria cannot be stated in terms of conventional concepts of equilibrium convergence and static market structures.

In the following, an evolutionary core model that highlights the dynamics of an economic constellation is suggested. Three analytical phases of the evolutionary dynamics are distinguished. They represent a specification of the general potential-actualization scheme. Underlying the analytical distinction is the view of an economic process that has a beginning and an end. In its analytical exposition it thus resembles the neoclassical trajectory that is composed analogously of three analytical phases. The evolutionary phases are

1. *Novelty generation*: Generation of potentials, creative discovery process; "micro selection," as entrepreneurial (re-)cognition process; "pioneer actualization" of innovating entrepreneur.
2. *Selective adoption*: Macroscopic adoption by "imitators" on basis of time-space specific actualizations; initially macroscopic bifurcation(s), unpredictable—chaotic—consequences; cumulative adoption of "winning" potential, path-dependency, selective environment, interplay of path-dependency and competition in adoption process.
3. *Retention*: Path-dependent process terminates, repetitive behavior sets in, constant parameters feeding "circular flow", perfectly predictable behavior leads (endogenously) to pressure to overcome "stagnation equilibrium": *link to first phase*; actions depend c.p. on institutions and behavioral dispositions of entrepreneurs in concrete historical setting.

It is possible to contrast Schumpeter's work with the evolutionary scheme suggested, and ask questions such as, "Was Schumpeter an evolutionary economist?", or "What did Schumpeter say about the evolutionary issues stated?". We take up the second issue briefly in the following. There are outstanding studies in the field of the history of economic thought that address the various issues (e.g., Shionoya, 1990; Swedberg, 1992). The key question is whether Schumpeter was basically a devotee of the neoclassical equilibrium concept or whether he was ultimately a heretic of that doctrine. Schumpeter has given a hard time to scholars working in the field of the history of economic doctrines since his writings allow one to gather ample evidence that he belonged to both intellectual camps. The theoretical issue can be reduced to the question: *Does the economic system converge to an equilibrium or does it not*? Does, for instance, the system in

Figure 2 move from X towards the (equilibrium) P-line? And if it does, how long is it likely to stay there? Or, does the system escape an equilibrium convergence? Is there a probability pattern in the exogenous disturbances, or is there an inherent disequilibrating tendency in the economic system itself (e.g., endogenously generated "pressure to overcome" stagnation equilibrium of phase 3)?

Schumpeter has divided economics into a *static* and *dynamic* branch. *Situations* apply to the former, *constellations* to the latter. He has applied his dynamics to two major fields of economic theory: *business cycles* and *development theory*. The analyses conducted in the two fields surprisingly demonstrate much conceptual and methodological homogeneity. In both theoretical approaches the conceptual scheme of the generation and actualization of innovative potentials is applied. In the case of business cycle theory, the innovative potentials are comparatively "small"; in that of development theory they constitute—to mention merely Schumpeter's historical master example of the railways in the first half of the 19th century—epochal breakthroughs propelling the historical dynamics of the system for decades. The shorter the time horizon of the phenomena analyzed, the closer is Schumpeter's theory to Walras' equilibrium model. In his business cycle theory, a boom is (sometimes) defined as a departure from equilibrium, and a recession accordingly as an equilibrium state. (Schumpeter, 1939). As Schumpeter moves away from "situational analysis," the evolutionary concept of generation and actualization of innovative potentials receives prominence.

The litmus test lies with the *theory of economic development*. Conceptually, the essential question is whether the equilibrium concept is instrumental for the theoretical representation of developmental change. Theoretically, the issue is whether there is a *long-run tendency* towards an *equilibrium*, and, if there is, whether there is an inherent tendency to *keep* the system in a long-run equilibrium position. Relatedly, the issue is whether short-run market transactions and business cycle equilibria are embedded in the overall dynamics of a continuous or a discontinuous development. Faithful to the heritage, Schumpeter states the second and third phases in terms of the *equilibrium* approach. Accordingly, he conceives the first phase as a *disturbance* of equilibrium. However, Schumpeter's approach differs radically from the static in terms of what he has to say about the dynamics of systemic disturbances. Essentially, *disturbances* originate "*from within*" the economic system. They do not merely represent a heuristic device for defining the mechanics of automatic equilibrium adjustments. Rather, Schumpeterian disturbances constitute the *endogenous core of a dynamic theory* of which equilibrating processes and equilibria are a part. He considers the continuous generation of innovative potentials by the entrepreneur to constitute the very nature of the capitalistic process. The entrepreneur initiates a process that

> ... incessantly revolutionizes the economic structure *from within*, incessantly destroying the old one, incessantly creating a new one. This process of Creative Destruction is the essential fact about capitalism." (Schumpeter, 1943, p. 83; emphasis in original)

Schumpeter gives a dual specification to the *equilibrium* concept applied to an economic *constellation*. First, he conceives the third phase in terms of a *classical gravitation center*, where the market price converges to the cost price constituting a "natural" equilibrium. He argues in this context that "all complex movements" of an economy can be "generally summarized and comprehended as a tendency towards restoring a disturbed equilibrium or respectively as one towards a new equilibrium" (Schumpeter, 1912, p. 439). He calls this the "process of statization" (*Statisierung*; Schumpeter, 1912, p. 440). He evokes the determinism of the classical gravitation center when contending that "a process of statization occurs necessarily and always as a consequence of development" (Schumpeter, 1912, p. 447).

Second, Schumpeter applies the equilibrium concept when discussing the "*circular flow*." Again, the spirit is classical. The classical issue was whether industrial capitalism was trapped in the long run in a "stagnation-equilibrium" or could succeed in maintaining its developmental dynamics. Schumpeter does not ponder much over the classical question, but his theoretical exposition relies on a set of variables that are "classical". The analysis has an *interdisciplinary* scope encompassing both economic and *non-economic* variables. His description of the developmental "circular flow" is a masterpiece in "stylized history." The question arises at this point of why Schumpeter portrays the "stagnation equilibrium" so carefully. After all, the scientific objective is a theory of development. Indeed, the script of the drama is designed to lead to the "*focal question*", of how a historical equilibrium—where all factors reinforce the constancy of the parameters—*can conceivably ever change*. It appears that equilibrium analysis here mainly follows the purpose of piling up developmental obstacles, resistances, and constraints in order to demonstrate the extraordinary impetus of the forces required to overcome it and in order to sharpen the profile of the personality required to perform the task. To the extent that the societal equilibrium locks in the ordinary human, the entrepreneur gains both a historical and theoretical profile.

Schumpeter's Causal Scheme

A more comprehensive interpretation of Schumpeter's work will be attempted in the following on the basis of a conceptual background model that is inspired by his *own* epistemological viewpoints. Econometrics (n.b. Schumpeter was the founder of the Econometrics Society) starts with the choice of variables that "typically" represent reality, and follows with a set of "causal" propositions furnished by economic theory. This presumes that the scope of variables is adequate and that the epistemological basis of the theory on which the propositions are put forth is valid. If these presumptions are not accepted, the procedure must be reversed. This raises two questions. First, which causality principle can be considered to be ontologically valid? Secondly, based on this preassessment, what range of variables can be included in a theory that suggests propositions on the basis of the causality principle chosen? It can be shown that Schumpeter's predilection for the *linear causality principle* has determined his decisions on whether to treat various theoretical variables as *endogenous* or as *exogenous*, and that this predilection has had a decisive influence on the *theoretical scope of his work*.

Figure 4 helps to develop the argument departing from Schumpeter's concept of the entrepreneur.[3] An economic subject S_b, or respectively the "behavioral continuum" beyond the "behavioral traverse" (Fig. 2), constitutes the center of the causal scheme. It provides an intuitive understanding of Schumpeter's proposition that change originates "*from within*". Or put on its head: change must *not* be assumed to come "*from outside*". The methodological implication of this premise represents the *essential* aspect of Schumpeter's causality principle: change must be conceived as *autonomous*, that is, as "*un-caused.*" Cause A has an effect B; A itself must not be caused by either another variable, say C, nor—as propounded by the concept of *circular causation*—by B. The first restriction refers to the autonomy of the human subject. The entrepreneur initiates change autonomously *qua subject*. The second restriction of the causality principle refers to the "causative feedback" from B to A. If we specify A to represent subjective-behavioral and B objective-environmental, say, organizational or institutional variables, then the causal proposition implies *contingency-independence of human action*. Schumpeter supports this view by specifying the causality principle explicitly:

> We speak of cause and effect only in the case of a non-reversal causal relationship. . . . In contrast, we do not speak of cause and effect in those instances where we have a reciprocal relationship between two facts, . . . We consider as a cause of an economic phenomenon only its explanatory principle

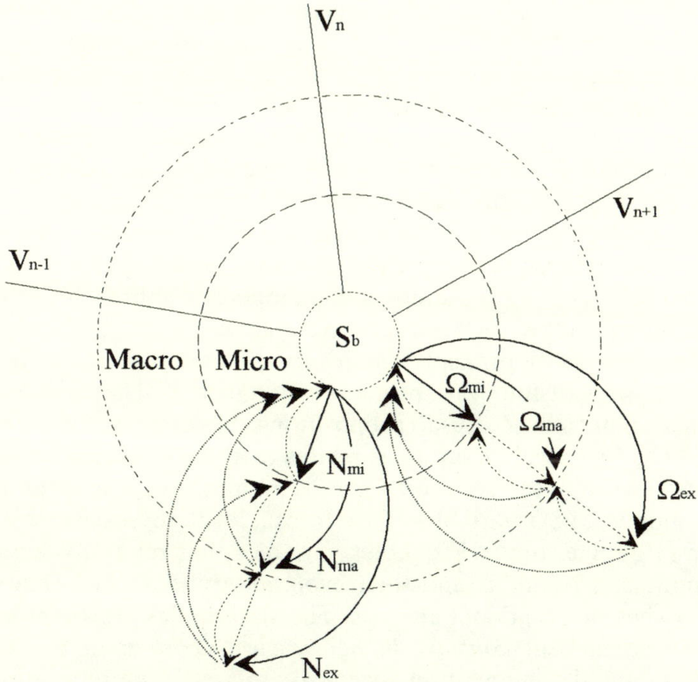

➤ = Links based on Schumpeterian "linear causality"
Sb = Subject(s), entrepreneurial behavior
V_j = V- variable j
N, Ω = Organization, Institution (V-variables analysed)
mi = Micro
ma = Macro
ex = Exogenous

Figure 5.4. Subjective core: entrepreneurial origins of micro and macro change

(Erklärungsprinzip), that is to say, that aspect that allows us to comprehend the nature (Wesen) of the cause. (Schumpeter, 1912)

The application of the principle of *linear causality* allowed Schumpeter, on conceptual grounds, to reject any dynamic theory that would propound that each analytical regime produces conditions of such a nature that a regime of the subsequent period is completely determined by them. Schumpeter has rejected the causality principle of mechanics. Not only Schumpeter's subjectivist core, but, methodologically, also the *causative discontinuity* (it implies) set Schumpeter's approach apart from one inspired by classical mechanics. Mechanical models cannot generate endogenously discontinuous change. A relative change (second derivative) is due to an exogenous disturbance. A second implication is that Schumpeter's principle of linear causality has excluded *circular causality*, which allows one to address, for instance, the important interrelatedness between micro and macro variables. While the linear causality principle has allowed Schumpeter to escape from the determinism of laws of motion, it has also imposed conceptual restrictions on his approach. It will be shown that shortcomings inherent in Schumpeter's approach, result from his reluctance to allow for "*causative feedbacks.*"

The linear causality principle applies to all variables chosen. In Figure 4, the composites of four variables are distinguished. They are related to each other in terms of causal propositions, yielding various *orders of causality*. The first level of variables relates to entrepreneurial action—the subjective core (S_b); the second to microeconomic (V_{mi}), and the third to macroeconomic (V_{ma}) variables. The fourth level represents exogenous variables (V_{ex}). The prefix V denotes variables that relate to the analysis of economic *constellations* and their *evolutionary dynamics*; they do not relate to issues of situational analysis. The V-variables represent basically all the variables kept *constant in neoclassical economics*, for instance, population, capital accumulation, technical progress, preference formation, organizations, and institutions. J.B. Clark shared with Schumpeter the theoretical intention to develop a dynamic economic theory that would include the mentioned variables. Unlike Schumpeter, he did not succeed, but got stuck in his first volume on statics. His work, however, offers an authoritative statement about the set of those mentioned variables that are kept constant in neoclassical theory (Clark, 1899). In Figure 4, the theoretical scheme is composed of $n + 1$ V-variables. For simplicity, a full statement of all causal relationships is provided only for the variables of organization (N) and institution (Ω).

A principal distinction may help us to reduce the complexity. We have, on the one hand, a causality that relates to *systemic* entities, and, on the other one that is stated in terms of a *relationship between subjective and objective* entities. The systemic causality is indicated in Figure 4 by the dashed lines. We distinguish in both cases between *linear* and *circular* (non-Schumpeterian) causality. If Schumpeter's subjectivist core is accepted as representing a valid interpretation, systemic causality must be ruled out as an adequate explanatory tool. Schumpeter has strongly objected to any systemic causality deploring the metaphysical nature of Comte's positivism and of Marxist objectivism (Schumpeter, 1912, p. 468). He has suggested instead linking the "subjective" entrepreneur with all three levels of objective variables. First, he viewed the entrepreneur as the key figure of the firm. In fact, firm and entrepreneur appear as basically identical. The entrepreneur shapes a firm's organization and institution, and not vice versa. The arrows from N_{mi} and Ω_{mi} to S_b are "inactive." The *second* causal link is from the micro (*mi*) to the macro (*ma*) level. Applying our distinction between subject-object related and systemic causality, the macro domain is influenced by entrepreneurial action either by a direct link from S_b to V_{ma}, or, indirectly, via the micro level of the firm from V_{mi} to V_{ma} (dashed lines). In an economic system in which personality-ruled entrepreneurial firms predominate, the first link will be significant; in one in which large-scale industrial business organizations predominate, S_b will disappear, leaving only a systemic micro-macro link. The Schumpeterian model provides scope for theoretical interpretations that rely on either of the two causal subschemes. Our contention is that an analysis that fails to account for *circular* causality between entrepreneurial actions and firm-related V-variables is bound to be flawed. Even if the relationship from micro to macro is specified, its substantive theoretical value will depend on a further specification of the micro domain.

A further direct link is from the composite variable levels discussed to the level of *exogenous* variables. The link is of particular importance with regard to *technology*. The topic that interests us at present is how Schumpeter has interpreted the *theoretical status* of this key variable. Our premise has been that Schumpeter employs a subjective-linear causality principle, and that, accordingly, we must expect a causal statement that suggests that technology is basically generated by the entrepreneur. Schumpeter's theory of economic development provides various indications that he saw a direct link between the entrepreneur and the generation of technology. It is not only the *application* of inventions (innovations)—as is generally recognized—but also the *generation of* inventions that Schumpeter considered to lie in the domain of the entrepreneur. Inventions are basically an *effect*, not a cause of economic development. The capitalistic system is not technology driven, but the technological dynamics results from entrepreneurial ingenuity and action:

> . . . inventions, to the extent they are of practical relevance for the economy, do not give rise to economic development, but are rather their result. Inventions occur if the entrepreneur requires them, and if the personality of an entrepreneur who is capable of making use of new inventions is lacking, they will never be of any practical relevance. . . It is not inventions which have made capitalism, but capitalism which has brought forth its necessary inventions. (Schumpeter, 1912, p. 479)

Capitalism is interpreted as a *specific historical expression of human action*. Schumpeter rejects explicitly the principle of *systemic causality*, where a social or economic system generates technology, or vice-versa; in Figure 4 represented by dashed arrows that link V_{ma}- to V_{ex}-variables.

> The view exists that there is an autonomous element in the technological and organizational progress that carries in itself a law of development and that rests essentially on the advances in the accumulation of our knowledge. In this view, the combination that is best with regard to the state of our knowledge constitutes some sort of gravitation center around which the various combinations are clustered, and to which, once it is reached, a more or less automatic tendency prevails, similar to the one that we have in an equilibrium of a static economy in our sense. This view is incorrect. No automatic progress exists, and where it does exist, it does so only to a very limited extent. (Schumpeter, 1912, p. 480)

Schumpeter recognizes the fact that scientific and technical development is to some extent autonomous. Thus he considers the notion of a static economy to be consistent with technological progress. However, it would always be the entrepreneur who has to step in to actualize the dormant scientific and technological potential. We may conclude that the principle of linear causality gives the theoretical propositions at all levels indicated its specific Schumpeterian brand mark. The general direction of causality is "from within" the economy leading to the "outer" levels.

Petrifaction of Schumpeter's Subjective Core: Hayek's Criticism

The picture of Schumpeter as a "subjectivist" calls for a reconsideration when turning to his later work. The "old" Schumpeter has conjectured—particularly in his "Capitalism, Socialism and Democracy"—that modern large-scale production renders entrepreneurial functions obsolete. The theoretical reference point is still the entrepreneur, but the *direction of causality is reversed*: technical progress determines the industrial organization of the modern business enterprise, which, in turn, determines the role of the entrepreneur. In Figure 4, the respective link is from N_{ex} to N_{mi}, and from N_{mi} to S_b. This drastic theoretical reversal has its methodological corollary in Schumpeter's later work on the conceptual-epistemological foundations of economic science. In an article entitled, "The Meaning of Rationality in the Social Sciences," he takes up explicitly the issue of the role of behavioral variables that support hypotheses concerning entrepreneurial action and resources variables that may be stated theoretically in terms of law-like empirical regularities. Though Schumpeter still argues that all that he is saying about theoretical and empirical regularities in the resources dynamics still "would inevitably lead to acting man" (Schumpeter, 1984, p. 579), his conclusion that "acting man" becomes eventually superfluous appears as straightforward:

> But all these do not seem to me to be relevant to the question of principle involved. In particular, if we find a certain relation between price level and total production, it is for this kind of research completely immaterial whether or not this relation can be reduced to reactions of firms that appear to us rational or not . . . Wherever we have entities that can be quantitatively expressed and display regular relations to other such entities, we can get some "laws" out of them in much the same way in which the physicist does and, again, the epistemological problems that may arise do not seem to differ from those inherent in scientific procedure in general. (Schumpeter, 1984, p. 579)

This statement sets Schumpeter apart from his original "Austrian" position that is intrinsically related to a subjectivistic view. F.V. Hayek in "The Use of Knowledge in Society" has strongly objected to Schumpeter's view for what he considered to be a peculiar form of positivism:

> A recent statement by Professor Joseph Schumpeter in his *Capitalism, Socialism and Democracy* provides a clear illustration of one of the methodological differences which I have in mind. Its author is preeminent among those economists who approach economic phenomena in the light of a certain branch of positivism. To him these phenomena accordingly appear as objectively given quantities of commodities impinging directly upon each other, almost, it would seem, without any intervention of human minds. (Hayek, 1945, p. 529)

It is difficult to escape the conclusion that Schumpeter is entangled in *methodological contradictions*.[4] The principal question which arises is how the *subjectivist* Schumpeter could ever be cast in the mold of *methodological and theoretical positivism*. The answer is closely linked to his principle of linear causality. Subjectivism has many varieties and applications. A possible variant is to link it to linear causality, that is, to a unidirectional causality, for instance, of the type $S_b \rightarrow V_{mi} \rightarrow V_{ma} \rightarrow V_{ex}$ or $S_b \rightarrow V_{mi}$, $S_b \rightarrow V_{ma}$, $S_b \rightarrow V_{ex}$. It is easy to see that this causative line may lead to an interpretation in terms of a *subjectivist determinism*. When Schumpeter turned to the empirical study of the modern industrial large-scale enterprise, he seemed to have applied an analogous principle of linear causality. The starting point was now *modern technology*, and the causal chain stated was *reversed*. The methodological consequence has been *objective determinism*. This conclusion confirms the findings of students of the history of economic doctrines, who suggest that Schumpeter's esteem for Marx's works was growing during his lifetime (Rosenberg, 1992). Schumpeter's methodological contradiction lies not in the application of the two counterpositions of subjectivism and objectivism, but in the application of linear causality and the consequent failure to combine the two ontic domains. *Circular causation is at the very base of an evolutionary approach.* Human action is embedded in an environment. It shapes that environment, and it is simultaneously and continuously shaped by it.

Micro- and Macroeconomics Reconsidered: New Schumpeterian Vistas

The following analysis will take up some issues that relate to the circular causation between the *V-variables* stated. We place technology in center stage. Schumpeter has demonstrated that the phenomenon of technology can be approached from various angles. Two major lines of inquiry result from an inspection of his work. First, there is technology as an engine of change. Along this line technology represents an *exogenous driving force* that produces *regular long-run economic waves*. Schumpeter's idea of Kontratief cycles has inspired a substantial body of research discussing theoretically and empirically the mechanism of the "Schumpeter Clock" (e.g., Mensch, et al., 1989; Reati, 1991; Tylecote, 1992; Metz, 1993). However, our earlier analysis of Schumpeter's work suggests that Schumpeter saw the law-like regularities as also disturbed by the *subjective* forces of the entrepreneur. If the entrepreneur is assumed to represent the ultimate promoter of technological progress, and not only a passive executor of an objective technological dynamics, then Kontratief cycles lose *a priori* much of their historical objectivity and of their predictive promise.

The analysis of the characteristics of the *contemporary* "Kontratief cycle" has thus far provided more insights than the search for historical laws. A "tour d'horizon" of the terms used to capture the *problematique* may suffice here to provide an idea of the scope of this branch of Neo-Schumpeterian research: "Technological Paradigm" (Dosi, 1988, p. 224 ff.), "techno-economic paradigm" (Freeman and Perez, 1986), "focusing devices" (Rosenberg, 1976), "Technological guideposts" (Sahal, 1985), "general natural trajectories (Nelson and Winter, 1982), "Technological Trajectory" (Nelson and Winter, 1977), "general purpose technology" (Bresnahan and Trajtenberg, 1992), "technological system" (Carlsson, 1992), or "regimes of accumulation" (Boyer, 1992). The following passage demonstrates that "technological paradigms" (and the like) constitute a specific (technological) application of our conceptional notion of *potential*:

> A technological paradigm defines contextually the needs that are meant to be fulfilled, the scientific principles utilized for the task, the material technology to be used. In other words, a technological paradigm can be defined as a "pattern" for solution of selected techno-economic problems based on highly selected principles derived from the natural sciences. A technological paradigm is both a set of exemplars—basic artefacts which are not to be developed and improved (a car—of the type we know—an integrated circuit, a lathe, etc., with their particular techno-economic characteristics) and a set of heuristics—"Where do we go from here?", "Where should we search?", "On what sort of knowledge should we draw?", etc. . . . for example, general search rules of the kind: 'strive for an increasing miniaturization of the circuit", . . . putting it another way, technological paradigms define the technological opportunities for further innovations and some basic procedures on how to exploit them. (Dosi, 1988, pp. 224–225)

The *empirical message* is that the new information technology—its hardware and software applications—will profoundly change the base, structure, and operations of economic activities. Information can be processed, stored, transmitted, and transformed at a much higher speed compared to the analogue principle. Given the all-pervasive nature of information in the economic process, profound changes in information technology are bound to affect the latter in a significant way.

We suggest the following hypothesis with regard to the impact of the contemporary technological paradigm on the evolution of the economic system: the new technological paradigm will change not only the *recombination of production factors*, but also—and above all—the *organizational-institutional base* of the economic micro and macro domains. Specifically, there will be a *long-run shift* in the innovative dynamics from market-transactions to *firm-specific or network-related* economic activities. Ambitious approaches may call here for a more "operational" or consistent body of hypotheses for the purpose of prediction. We are choosing a more modest route, attempting to provide a tentative analytical framework that allows us to view the relevant empirical issues more clearly and to state some major theoretical propositions.

We apply our analytical distinction between potential and actualizations, and our scheme of the three evolutionary phases. Further theoretical specification requires that we define micro and macro processes. We propose that the evolutionary phases apply to both micro and macro domains. Generally, the evolutionary phases apply to all conceivable levels of human and social systems. Hence, the evolutionary principles apply to the four levels mentioned.

Singularity and Fractals

This proposition can be expressed on the basis of *fractal theory*. Fractal theory propounds that there is an entity that is composed of *self-similar* parts. It proposes that each part of the whole is itself a whole that is constituted of parts that have the same structure as the initial whole, of which the latter whole constitutes a part. There are thus *fractal dimensions* (scales). A whole is defined by a fractal unit and the number of fractal dimensions (see e.g. Peitgen, et al., 1992). Figure 5a represents a fractal unit. The numbers *1*, *2*, *3* denote the three evolutionary phases. Stated in terms of Figure 2, *1* represents the $C(x_2\, \overline{X})$-line, *2* an "actualization-line" converging from $\overline{X}$ to *P-line*, and *3* the evolutionary equilibrium, P-line. Figure 5a represents a fractal of *one* dimension. Figure 5b represents a fractal of *two* dimensions. The crucial point is that the initial phase of the *generation* is a locus where *all fractals meet.*

For instance, a new idea results from brain activities defined by a cognitive-neuronal theory based on the evolutionary principles stated. In a next fractal dimension of the micro context of a firm, the potential thus generated is actualized again on the basis of the evolutionary principles stated. The important point is that we are dealing theoretically in both cases with the same potential, but with different actualizations. Analogously, the same potential may attain a third dimension and enter the market context. The potential, for instance, a new technology, becomes a *seed* (a term sometimes used in chaos theory for an initial parameter value of a discrete iterated nonlinear function) that is now adopted in the macroscopic context of the market. The actualization process, as described by the second and third phases, applies in the former case to the micro, in the latter to the macro, context. Still, in all three cases we are talking about the same potential. We see that the fractal theory in the present interpretation expresses the logic of *singularity* of the potentials. The fractal dimensions represent various *dimensions of deepening* of the actualization process. Our earlier proposition can now be restated in terms of fractal theory. There will be a *shift from the evolutionary fractal of the third (macro) to the second (micro) dimension* (taking S_b as first fractal dimension).

At this juncture, we can combine the previous proposition that a potential has multiple actualizations with that made for fractal dimensions. In Figure 5c, the singularity of a potential is expressed by a circle. The "dimensions" of an idea are uniquely defined as are those of a circle with a given radius *r*. Each potential, however, is the source of a possibly large number of matter-energy actualizations, the actual number of which will depend on actual historical time-space conditions. We have thus two types

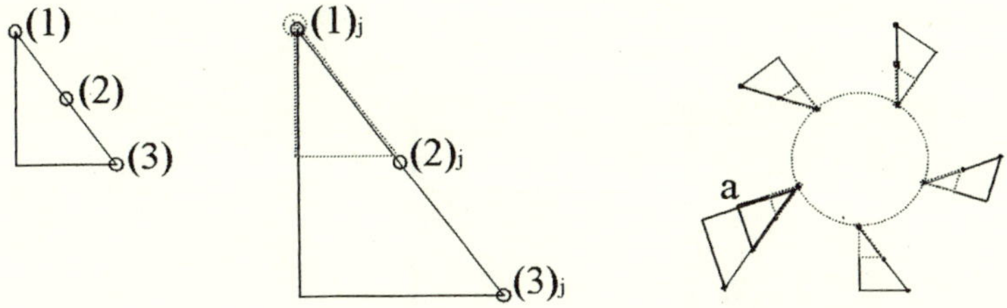

(a) Fractal unit (b) Fractal dimension j (c) Potential actualized in j fractal dimensions

(1), (2), (3) = Evolutionary phases, specific evolutionary principles apply (represented in Figure 2 by set of dashed lines xP)

Applications:

(a) = Firm, "embedded" evolutionary principles, e.g. improvement without transactions

(b) = Markets, conventional application of evolutionary principles, e.g. innovation generated by firm (phase 1), in market adopted (phase 2), and retained (phase 3)

(c) = Singular potential ( ) and actualizations in j dimensions ( )

Figure 5.5. Fractal dimensions of change

of actualizations of a potential. One refers to the dimension of deepening, and thus to a single fractal and its multiple dimensions; the second refers to the number of actualizations on the basis of a potential. As fractal *a* in Figure 5c indicates, the fractals need not necessarily have dimensional unity. The population of actualizations does not necessarily have to be composed of homogenous fractals. An *economic structure* may be expressed on the basis of a scheme that accommodates a *potential with multiple actualizations specified according to their fractal dimensions*. While for a comparative-static theory, aggregation may suffice, modelling evolutionary complexity, that is, novelty generation and macroscopic adoption, suggests that the application of more intricate—such as fractal-theoretic—approaches is necessary.

We now turn to a theoretical specification of the general evolutionary fractal unit. It is by no means self-evident what an "*elementary*" *economic unit* is. We may refer for its specification to the prevailing activities, such as consumption and production. This, however, is a specification that presumes that we know already what we specify. We conceive an economic unit as a *living system*, and distinguish accordingly between *structure* and *process*. The structure allows processes, as processes maintain structure.

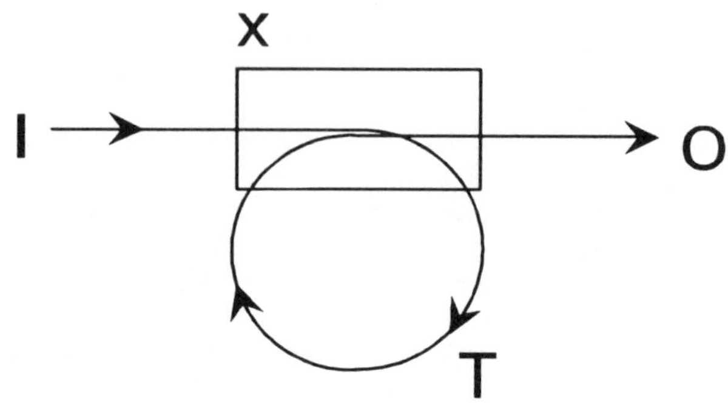

Figure 5.6. Living system
I, O = Inputs, outputs
T = Transformation activities, firm specific interconnectivities
x = Firm

Thus, the theoretical task is to specify structure and process of an economic unit. In so doing, we confine our discussion to production, that is, the firm. Figure 6 provides a bird's eye view of the *firm*. A basic distinction is between a firm's structure—its *organizational-institutional framework*—and the ongoing *productive processes or transformations*. The structural base is denoted by the rectangle *x*, the ongoing productive processes by the circle *T*. The link between a systemic structure and its environment is denoted by the *I-O* (input-output) arrow. The link represents activities that cross a firm's systemic boundaries. We call activities that relate to a firms boundaries *interactions or transactions*. In contrast, there is a set of activities that is boundary independent. We call these *interconnectivities*, which may occur either internal or external to the firm. We call a composite of (boundary-independent) interconnectivities a *network*. A *firm* appears thus as a *network with systemic boundaries*.[5]

The notion of boundary is essential for grasping the characteristics of a systemic unit. Any living system maintains its functions and evolves on the basis of self-organization. There is no escape from this major organizational task for a firm operating in a market context (without a central planning agency performing that function). We conceive a constituency that performs boundary-setting self-organization as an *integrator*. Applied to the firm, we distinguish between two types of integrators: *organization* and *institution*. They constitute a subset of *V-variables*, and are denoted as *integrator* or *K-variables* (leaving scope for further specification of the respective V-variable).

An *organization* is a scheme that apportions decision making and productive activities designed to serve the purpose of a whole, for instance, a firm's goals. Division of labor, differentiation, and specialization all lead to vertical disintegration, and the basic task of an organization is thus to *reintegrate* the partial functions of a dissected whole. In cultural systems (as distinct from biological), organizations are usually *constructed*, deliberately planned, and in their operational rationality permanently reflected. The organizational task may be performed by distributing decisionmaking authority in a *centralized* or *decentralized* way.[6] Any organization, however, is *always hierarchical* since the basic task is to integrate operations, which requires *authority of the integrator* and submission of the parts. (There is thus hierarchy also in selforganization.)

Institutions, in turn, are defined (following a widely shared practice) as correlated behaviors that recur under same or similar conditions. The *repetition* of behavior is decisive, not its direction. An institution is not an organization, and vice versa; but there is a close nexus between them. For instance, the relationship $A \rightarrow B$ may become an institution, that is, *routinized behavior*, if it is repeated with sufficient frequency. The actual organization of a firm is thus "*institutionalized.*" *The actual firm is an institutionalized system whose boundaries are defined by an organization* (for further discussion, see Dopfer, 1992). In (only) this sense, a firm is an institution. Since the branch of New Institutional Economics excludes the institutionalization process, the firm is stated in terms of a (noninstitutionalized) organization.

Figure 7 conveys an idea of the systemic integrators. The circles denote the boundaries of the organizations and institutions, A, B, C. K represents both an *organizational decision-distribution (centralization, decentralization) parameter (N)* and an *institutional order parameter* (Ω). The feedback arrows arriving at K indicate that the integrator requires "support" from its parts. In the case of organization, this will be messages to the upper levels of a hierarchy. In the case of institution, K is not constructed, but represents a "correlator" (Ω) that emerges spontaneously from collective behavior. As individual behaviors converge, they may parameterize—represented by the concept of cumulative and circular causation—individual behaviors.

The analytical picture looks different when we deal with *nonsystemic* structures. Generally, a network represents a *composite of loosely interconnected members.* Network analysis has been used in other scientific disciplines, for example, anthropology, sociology, and (particularly interesting from a conceptual viewpoint) neurophysiology (Dorffner, 1991; Rumelhart, 1986). The distinctive difference from a systemic unit is its lack

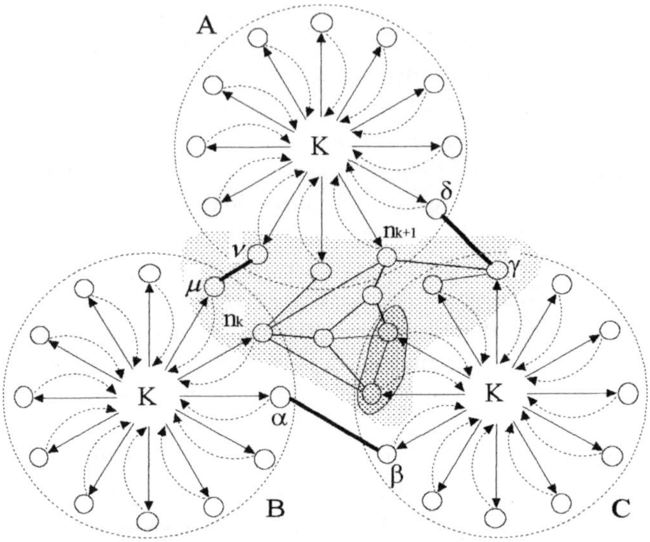

K = Systemic integrators = {N, Ω}
N = Organisation, (de-)centralisation
Ω = Institutions, behavioral order parameter
= Systemic boundaries determined by K
= (intra-)systemic interactions determining integration
= network interconnectivities
= systemic interactions (boundary crossing)
= internal network
= external network, interconnectivities among network units of different systems (boundary crossing)

Figure 5.7. Systemic interactions and network interconnectivities

of (systemic) boundaries. A network has no systemic purpose, no goal, and thus no integration rule. A network is useful, increases efficiency and systemic performance but is *altruistic* in the sense of "systemic interests." Since boundaries are nonconstituent for networks, they may represent boundary-*internal* or boundary-crossing *external* networks. A network context is shown in Figure 8. The lightly dashed area represents the total network context, and the darkly dashed a network within a network. The latter may be conceived as representing a network that is allocated within systemic boundaries, for instance, as a department within a firm. *A* stands

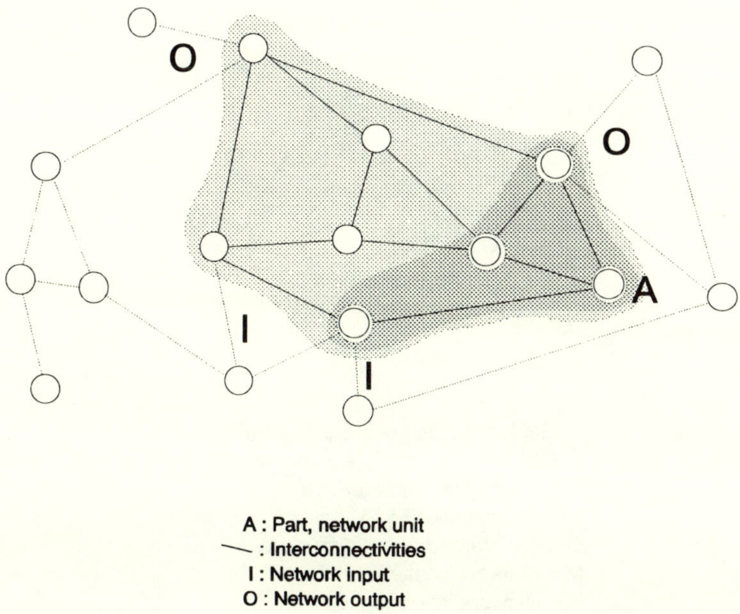

Figure 5.8. Network units and interconnectivities

for an agent or network unit. The circles outside the dashed area represent a social environment in which the network is embedded; the links can be conceived as network inputs and outputs (I, O).

An essential aspect of networks is their *historicity*. Scope and structure of the knowledge base depend exclusively on the historical dynamics of the interconnectivities. Networks are not institutions. The behavior of network units may be influenced by institutional parameters, but the emergent knowledge base of the network is basically *open* with regard to the *future*. It is *historical* with regard to *both its past and its future*. Recognizing a firm as a network allows us to capture an additional analytical feature that an organization-institution oriented approach (with its emphasis on K-integrators) is bound to understate. The compelling conclusion is that any changes in the network structures will have implications on the scope of boundary and the type of integration of future firms.

The following discussion *combines* the concepts of systemic integration and network interconnectivity. By doing so, we may specify the theoretical

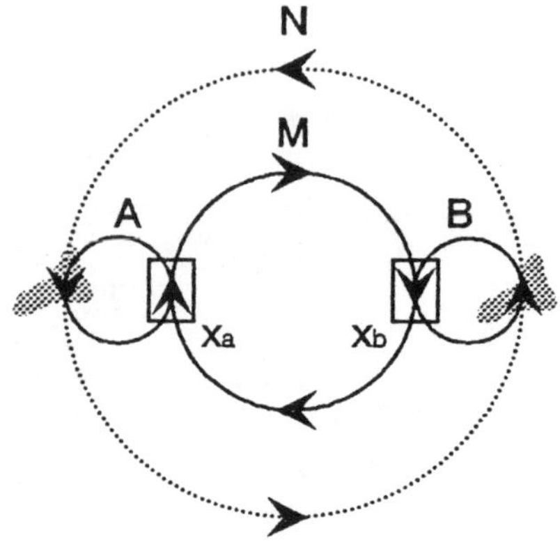

A, B = Economic units, i.e. firms (Fig. 6)
□ = X_a, X_b; systemic boundaries,
unity by K-integrators (Fig. 7)
= Network (Fig.8)
$E_{M,N}$ = Environment of economic units
M = Market transactions
N = Network interconnectivities,
boundary crossing, non-market

Figure 5.9. The environment of the firm: markets and networks

issues that relate to our proposition that there will be a historical shift from systemic interactions to network-specific interconnectivities. Figure 9 combines the analytical domains of systemic integration and network interconnectivity. *M* denotes transactions, *N* interconnectivities between firms *A* and *B*. We have two *macro environments* of the micro (*A*, *B*) units: *market-transaction* and *non-market-network* environments. Transactions and interconnectivities occur within and across the firms. Conventionally, the issue of micro economics is to optimize decisionmaking with regard to firm-specific and market transactions. The intrafirm activities are defined by the systemic boundaries of the firm. Economic calculus calls for a minimization of costs that occur within those systemic boundaries. More generally, the management chooses along a continuum of transaction costs (or decisional options) that include parameters of both firm-internal and market transactions. This choice continuum makes the systemic micro and macro boundaries "permeable." The question is how a management can decide rationally if—as in the case of boundary-neutral networks—the systemic boundaries of the firm become blurred. In this case the management will not be in a position to influence economic activities by exercising control over systemic integrators. The choice-theoretic paradigm becomes ineffective, since in such a context efficiency does not depend only on the optimal choice between transactions Y and Z, but mainly also on the dynamic knowledge base and interconnectivities of the network. It adds to decision making complexity if a firm's network crosses the boundaries interconnecting with external networks.

Figure 7, introduced earlier, allows us to highlight some of the intricacies of the interrelatedness between systemic transactions and network-interconnectivities. The critical "matching" is represented by the *structural Venn-diagram*. There is the simple case of transactions, for instance, between firm B and C, denoted by transaction $\alpha\beta$. There is complete discretion of the management over these (market) transactions. The case is different when firm C interacts with firm A using the link $\gamma\delta$. C's agent γ is also a member of an external network that has established interconnectivities within and across the firm's boundaries. The historically grown knowledge base of the network will in some way or other influence the decision of γ. There will be an asymmetry between the firms A and C with regard to the type of knowledge base and the type of actual management control. The case is again different if the agents involved in transactions all belong to networks. A case is denoted by the (bold) transaction link between the agents ν and μ of the firms A and B. The agents ν and μ represent their respective firms and are both members of a common network. There will be a symmetry of the knowledge base and in the type of hierarchical subordination to the management. The historical dynamics of the network will, as in the previous case, again influence decisions that concern a firm's transactions. The consequences will be felt most severely in a centralized organization where agents are expected to execute received orders. Generally, the "noise" factor of a network will decrease with the delegation of decision making powers to the lower levels of the systemic hierarchy. If the evolution of network structures is considered to be a characteristic of the future economy, a continuous pressure towards decentralizing economic organizations—in the micro as well as the macro domains—must be expected. Of further relevance are the "*pure*" network interconnectivities. All network interconnectivities delineated in Figure 7 by the dashed area that are not indicated by systemic (bold) interactions are of this type. For instance, the agents n_k and n_{k+1} are network members without involvement in systemic interactions.

Propositions about Contemporary Historical Dynamics

The following five propositions summarize some of the essential features of the historical dynamics sketched. The first two propositions refer to a *recombination* of production factors in the original Schumpeterian sense, the subsequent three to the structural base, the *reintegration of K-variables*, *shifting systemic boundaries*, and *emergent network knowledge base*. The propositions are, respectively:

1. The new technological trajectory allows *flexible manufacturing*; there will be an increase in *product variety* independent of user-specificity (proposition 2). Fordist large-scale production will become efficiency and cost inferior to *production-specific solutions*.
2. *Producer-user-relationships* will become more important and deeper on the basis of new and extended network interconnectivities. *Demand and supply* will obtain a *specificity* that resembles that of the medieval guild system—with the difference of a distinctively higher transaction speed in terms of both volume and novelty of consumer goods transacted.
3. The new technological paradigm will change the firms' *organizations*. There will be a gradual shift from centralization to decentralization in actual information acquisition and processing, and hence, eventually in the decision making authority. The traditional organizational paradigm, pioneered by Frederick Taylor, where knowledge, competence, and expertise reside with the "scientific management," will be undermined by the growing "tacit knowledge" and competence base of the emerging networks.
4. The novel technological paradigm will induce *institutional* changes within the firm, and as such influence institutionalization processes in the economy at large. Network cultures will compete with firm cultures; network identity with corporate identity. The specificity with regard to path dependency and adoption applies also to "behavioral seeds," implying that there will be a larger variety of institutionally parameterized behaviors. Asset, product, and production specificity will interrelate with *institutional specificity*.
5. The novel technological developments will lead to "*boundary flexibility*." Given shifts in 3 and 4, repercussions on the firm size and scope of production and transaction activities seem necessary in terms of efficiency considerations and unavoidable in terms of the social forces underlying this development. Schumpeter's prime

mover—the *entrepreneur*—will change his/her role, as the organizational-institutional foundations of the firm will be subject to the trends described.

Concluding Remarks

Various theoretical approaches dealing with economic change—the neoclassical, capital-theoretic traverse, neo-Austrian behavioral, and Schumpeterian approach—have been introduced. The objective of our analysis was not to "prove" the scientific superiority of any of these approaches, but merely to demonstrate that a climbing up of the "cognitive ladder" to the Schumpeterian approach has been a necessary condition for dealing with the phenomenon of economic change. We have suggested focusing on the empirical issues of the contemporary technological paradigm and its far-reaching implications for the evolutionary dynamics of economic change. When Schumpeter analyzed the dynamics of the industrial economies half a century ago, he brought into focus issues such as the relationship between firm size, or monopoly and volume of R and D, and registered patents. These "old" questions of the neo-Schumpeterian research program are still a source for fruitful research. However, as the historical conditions themselves have been changing, a different set of questions has been arising—constituting a *"new" branch of neo-Schumpeterian research.* For instance, a relevant line of future research will not only address the issue of the type of correlation between firm size and innovation performance but highlight the dynamics of the techno-economic forces underlying this relationship. The contemporary technological paradigm generates novelty, uncertainty, and surprise in an unprecedented way. It suggests that we formulate our theories and empirical findings with great caution and modesty. Schumpeter has in a way anticipated this contention when alluding in the foreword to his *Theory of Economic Development* to the tentative nature of his *own* research:

> The structure of thoughts that I will present here are certainly not, and much less so in detail, without any mistakes. However, they would well serve their purpose if only the reader would feel stimulated by them and would be led to the conclusion that there is "something true in them." Economic theory cannot simply ignore the facts and arguments that have been presented here on the basis of careful study and in consideration of the state of arts of our discipline. Having said this, I should wish that this work becomes outdated and forgotten as soon as possible. (Schumpeter, 1912, p. VIII)

Acknowledgments

I acknowledge gratefully suggestions by Bernard Michael Gilroy, Annegret Irrgang, Karin Minder, Markus Schwaninger, Wolfgang Stolper, and Ulrich Witt, as well as editorial help by André Palitzsch and Olivier Cardinaux.

Notes

1. *Macroeconomics* relevant for evolutionary economics is defined throughout the paper not in the neoclassical-Keynesian tradition referring to aggregate magnitudes; it is rather conceived as that branch of economics that deals with a *macroscopic environment* in which economic agents—*coevolutionary* interconnected—are *micro-units*.

Elements of a Dialogue

2. I have used throughout the original 1912 edition of the "Theorie." This was not without risk. I am glad to admit that I was much relieved when Wolfgang Stolper, from whose comments I benefitted much, endorsed that I was on the right track, quoting the original edition: "incidentally, I was fascinated that you keep quoting the 1912 edition of the Theorie, not the substantially revised and substantially shortened second edition of 1926 and later, or the future revised and shortened English edition of 1934" (letter from Wolfgang Stolper to author, February 3, 1993).

3. Ulrich Witt has suggested that I mention that the causal scheme of Figure 4 is "the author's own scheme and not that of Schumpeter." Witt's interesting viewpoint is that Schumpeter fails to acknowledge appropriately the subjectivist nature of all economic processes. Indeed, the scheme is general enough to accommodate not only Schumpeter's views discussed subsequently but numerous other combinations of causal interconnectivities and ontological viewpoints. The fact that the subject (Sb) constitutes the center of the scheme does not necessarily imply that the subject is also the primary causal agency "moving" all other variables. The emphasis on the "subjectivistic core" of Schumpeter's early theoretical model represents a specific case of a possible interpretation of causal links. As is evident from our subsequent text, Schumpeter has turned around the causal direction in his later work, emphasizing the "objective" organizational factors and leaving the subject deprived of *gestalting* power (letter from Ulrich Witt to the author, February 12, 1993).

4. Wolfgang Stolper has strongly objected to Hayek's interpretation of Schumpeter's view stating that Schumpeter has well recognized the fact that all important economic phenomena or events are "evolutionary in character." The reader may appreciate Stolper's interesting line of argument: "That Mises . . . makes absurd statements hardly astonishes me. But Hayek really ought to know better than accusing Schumpeter in 1945, 'To him these phenomena accordingly appear as objectively given quantities of commodities impinging directly upon each other, almost it would seem, without any intervention of human minds.' "

Stolper continues:

> This is a thorough misunderstanding of Schumpeter. In a stationary situation, which included changes coming from outside the system, it makes little difference what people

> think they are doing. Even a saint wishing to do only altruistic good surely wants to make the best with limited resources. Schumpeter's point really is that all the important facts and the theory to be applied to them are evolutionary in character, and that this very much involves the "intervention of human minds." For Schumpeter the problem is less whether an equilibrium exists—there is no dynamic equilibrium—but that traditional equilibrium theory involves the analysis of adaptive processes. It took the neo-Austrians 40 years to come to a similar conclusion as Schumpeter did essentially in 1908, certainly by 1912. (Stolper letter, p. 2)

Stolper's interpretation and line of argument is in my view essentially sound. The counterpositions may be partly reconciled by recalling our distinction between causality that refers to systemic magnitudes (reminiscent of Keynesian economic aggregates) and causality that refers to the subject-object or agency-structure relationships. Hayek's interpretation of Schumpeter's approach may be considered to be incorrect to the extent that he criticizes Schumpeter as conceiving the economy as composed of "objectively given quantities of commodities impinging directly upon each other." As stated earlier, "Schumpeter has strongly objected to any systemic causality deploring the metaphysical nature of Comte's positivism and of Marxist objectivism" (p. 145). Hayek's criticism is less unwarranted if conceived as applying to the "direction of causation" between "system" and "human mind." Schumpeter has argued that the industrial system "impinges" on the "human mind." Hayek's fallacy is that he generalized what Schumpeter considered to be a specific historical feature in capitalist development.

Stolper's further point is highly revealing: "Schumpeter does consider the development of the industrial system itself a major innovation. His is a very institutional as well as truly historical theory" (p. 3). While Schumpeter's developmental approach may indeed be considered as belonging to the branch of "historical economics," the reason that this is so because Schumpeter considered "the development of the industrial system itself a major innovation" is not entirely convincing. May we recall here Schumpeter's explicit rejection of any systemic causality in general, and of systemic causality relating to "technological and organizational progress" in particular. My objection against Stolper's interpretation, however, may again be reconciled by recalling his insight that all Schumpeterian economics is "evolutionary in character"; thus, the statement that the industrial system is itself a major innovation must necessarily refer to the "subjectivist" side of the relationship, that is, to the "intervention of human minds".

5. The distinction between a firm's structural base and ongoing productive operations allows us to make an analytical clarification with regard to the *production function*. Schumpeter conceives production as a *combination* of productive factors:

> Technically, as economically, producing means to combine things and forces (Kräfte) that are within our command. Each production method represents a specific combination. Various production methods may be distinguished according to the way they carry out combinations, either as combination of resources or as a specific relationship between quantities. (Schumpeter, 1912, p. 21)

Accordingly, a change in production means *recombination* of production factors. The process of combination of production factors corresponds in Figure 6 to *T*. It does not relate to the systemic unit as a whole (rectangle), on the basis of which *T* is performed. Schumpeterian (process) innovations refer to a recombination of production factors. He has recognized that economic progress does not take place as a movement on the isoquante of a given production function but is characterized by a continuous shift of the curve itself. A homogeneously smooth twice differentiable production function contributes to a theoretical specification of Pareto satisfactoriness, but is meaningless in representing the evolutionary dynamics of the economic process. In Schumpeter's model the recombination of production factors is closely linked to entrepreneurial decisions; the recombination process occurs at the T-level and does not necessarily call for a change in the firm's systemic organizational-institutional base. A recombination of production factors, for instance, the application of new production methods or the opening up of new markets, is possible on the basis of a *given* systemic organizational-institutional framework. There is, consequently, a second dimension of economic evolution that relates to a change of a firm's systemic base itself. As we have seen, a conceptual limitation is likely to preclude here an appropriate analysis within a Schumpeterian framework: *linear causality*. It does not allow us to analyze the *reciprocal* relationships between entrepreneurial agency and the firm as a productive systemic unit. A discussion of major structural shifts in the economic micro and macro domains brought about by the dynamics of the contemporary technological paradigm requires that we correct this conceptual deficiency.

6. Hayek (1945) has emphasized that true decentralization consists of delegating decisions to those who process the most relevant information:

> The problem is precisely how to extend the span of our utilization of resources beyond the span of the control of any one mind. (Hayek, 1945, p. 527)

References

Acs, Z.J., and Audretsch, D.B. 1991. *Innovation and Technological Change: An International Comparison*, New York: Harvester Wheatsheaf.

Albert, H. 1990. "Methodologischer Individualismus und historische Analyse." In K. Acham and W. Schulze (eds.). *Theorie der Geschichte, Bd. 6: Teil und Ganzes*. Mūnchen, pp. 219–239.

Allen, P.M. 1988. "Evolution, Innovation and Economics." In G. Dosi, et al., eds. *Technical Change and Economic Theory*. London: Pinter, pp. 95–119.

Andersen, E.S. 1992. "The Difficult Jump From Walrasian to Schumpeterian Analysis or Characterising Schumpeter's Analysis: Dynamics, Development or Economic Evolution?". Paper presented at Kyoto Conference of the International Joseph A. Schumpeter Society, August 19–22, 1992.

Antonelli, C. (ed.). 1992. *The Economics of Information Networks*, London: Elsevier.

Aoki, M. 1986. "Horizontal vs. Vertical Information Structure of the Firm." *American Economic Review* 76(5), pp. 971–983.

Arndt, H. 1992. *Die Evolutorische Wirtschaftstheorie in ihrer Bedeutung für die Wirtschafts und Finanzpolitik: Lehrbuch der ōkonomischen Entwicklungstheorie*. Berlin: Duncker & Humblot.

Arrow, K.J. 1962. "The Economic Implication of Learning by Doing." *Review of Economic Studies*, 29 June, pp. 155–173.

Arthur, W.B. 1985. "Competing Technologies and Lock-In by Historical Small Events: The Dynamics of Choice under Increasing Returns." CEPR Paper 43, Palo Alto, CA: CEPR.

Audretsch, D.B., and Acs, Z.J. 1992. "Entrepreneurial Activity, Innovation, and Macroeconomic Fluctuations." Paper presented at Kyoto Conference of the International Joseph A. Schumpeter Society, August 19–22, 1992.

Bauer, L., and Matis, H. (eds.). 1989. *Evolution—Organisation—Management, Zur Entwicklung und Selbststeuerung komplexer Systeme*. Berlin: Duncker & Humblot.

Best, M. 1990. *The New Competition: Institutions of Industrial Restructuring*. Cambridge: Polity Press.

Bombach, G. 1991. "Konjunkturtheorie einst und heute." Basel: Unpublished manuscript.

Bresnahan, T.F., and Trajtenberg, M.F. 1992. "General Purpose Technologies: Engines of Growth?". Paper presented at Kyoto Conference of the International Joseph A. Schumpeter Society, August 19–22, 1992.

Brunner, H.J. 1991. "Ascom—Lösungen für heterogene Netzwerke." Referat Bufa-Fachseminar, October 1–5, 1991, Basel: Unpublished manuscript.

Carlsson B. (ed.). 1989. *Industrial Dynamics: Technological, Organizational, and Structural Changes in Industries and Firms*. Boston: Kluwer.

Carlsson, B., and Stankiewicz, R. 1991. "On the Nature, Function and Composition of Technological Systems." *Journal of Evolutionary Economics* 1, pp. 93–118.

Carlsson, B. 1992. "Technological Sytems and Economic Development Potential: Four Swedish Case Studies". Paper presented at Kyoto Conference of the International Joseph A. Schumpeter Society, August 19–22, 1992.

Casson, M. (ed.). 1990. *Entrepreneurship*. Aldershot: Elgar.

Casson, M. 1992. *The Economics of Business Culture; Game Theory, Transaction Costs, and Economic Performance*. Oxford: Clarendon Press.

Chaloupek, G. 1992. "Long Term Perspectives Compared: Joseph Schumpeter and Werner Sombart." Paper presented at Kyoto Conference of the International Joseph A. Schumpeter Society, August 19–22, 1992.

Cheah, H.B., and Robertson, P.L. 1992. "The Entrepreneurial Process and Innovation in the Product Life Cycle." Paper presented at Kyoto Conference of the International Joseph A. Schumpeter Society, August 19–22, 1992.

Clark, J.B. 1899. *The Distribution of Wealth: A Theory of Wages, Interests and Profits*. New York: Macmillan.

Clark, N., and Juma, C. 1987. *Long-Run Economics: An Evolutionary Approach to Economic Growth*. London: Pinter.

Cohen, W.M., and Klepper, S. 1992. "Firm Size and the Nature of Innovation within Industries: The Case of Process and Product R&D." Paper presented at Kyoto Conference of the International Joseph A. Schumpeter Society, August 19–22, 1992.

Colemont, P., Groholt, P., Rickards, T., and Smeekes, H. (eds.). 1988. *Creativity and Innovation: Towards a European Network*. Dordrecht Kluwer Academic Publishers.

Corsi, M. 1991. "Stochastic Models of Division of Labour." Presented at 6th Congress of the European Economic Association, Cambridge, Aug. 31–Sept. 2.

Dahmén, E. 1989. *Development Blocks in Industrial Economics*. In Carlsson, B. ed. *Industrial Dynamics: Technological, Organizational, and Structural Changes in Industries and Firms*. Boston: Kluwer, pp. 109–122.

De Bresson, C. 1987. "The Evolutionary Paradigm and the Economics of Technological Change." *Journal of Economic Issues* 21, pp. 751–762.

Dopfer, K. 1991. "The Complexity of Economic Phenomena: Reply to Tinbergen and Beyond." *Journal of Economic Issues* 25, pp. 39–76.

Dopfer, K. 1992. "The Institutional Entrepreneur: Innovative Origins of Economic Institutions." Paper presented at Kyoto Conference of the International Joseph A. Schumpeter Society, August 19–22, 1992.

Dorffner, G. 1991. *Konnektionismus: Von neuronalen Netzwerken zu einer "natürlichen" KI*. Stuttgart: Teubner.

Dosi, G. 1988. "The Nature of the Innovative Process." G. Dosi et al., eds. *Technical Change and Economic Theory*. London: Pinter, pp. 221–238.

Dosi, G., Freeman, C., Nelson, R.R., Silverberg, G., and Soete, L. (eds.). 1988. *Technical Change and Economic Theory*. London: Pinter.

Eliasson, G. 1988a. "Schumpeterian Innovation, Market Structure, and the Stability of Industrial Development." In H. Hanusch (ed.) *Evolutionary Economics: Applications of Schumpeter's Ideas*. New York: Cambridge University Press, pp. 151–198.

Eliasson, G. 1988b. *The Knowledge Base of an Industrial Economy*. Stockholm: IUI.

Elliott, J.E. 1980. "Marx and Schumpeter on Capitalism's Creative Destruction: A Comparative Restatement." In *The Quarterty Journal of Economics*, 95, August, pp. 45–68.

Fontalea, E. 1987. "Innovation et structure du marché." In *Schw. Zeitschrift für Volkswirtschaft und Statistik*. 123, 3, pp. 275–288.

Freeman, C. 1990a. Schumpeters Business Cycles Revisited, in Heertje, A., et al., (eds.) 17–38.

Freeman, C. (ed.). 1990b. *The Economics of Innovation*. Aldershot: Elgar.

Freeman, C., and Perez, C. 1986. "The Diffusion of Technical Innovation and Changes of Technoeconomic Paradigm." Paper presented at Venice Conference on Innovation Diffusion, March 17–21, 1986.

Goodwin, R.M. 1990. "Walras and Schumpeter: The Vision Reaffirmed." In Heertje, A., et al. (eds.) *Evolving Technology and Market Structure: Studies in Schumpeterian Economics*, Michigan: University of Michigan Press, pp. 39–50.

Gowdy, J.M. 1992. "Higher Selection Processes in Evolutionary Economic Change." In Journal of Evolutionary Economics 2, 1, pp. 1–16.

Gunning, J.P. 1991. "The Use of the Method of Imaginary Constructions to Elucidate Entrepreneurship." National Tsing Hua Univ. Taiwan. Unpublished manuscript.

Gustafsson, B. 1991. *Power and Economic Institutions: Reinterpretations in Economic History*. Aldershot: Elgar.

Hagemann, H. 1991. "The Structural Theory of Economic Growth." In Baranzini, M., Scazzieri, R. (eds.), *The Economic Theory of Structure and Change*. Cambridge: Cambridge Univ. Press, 144–171.

Hanusch, H. (ed.). 1988. *Evolutionary Economics: Applications of Schumpeter's Ideas*. New York: Cambridge Univ. Press.

Harabi, N.M. 1992. "Appropriability, Technological Opportunity, Market Demand, and Technical Change—Empirical Evidence from Switzerland." Paper presented at Kyoto Conference of the International Joseph A. Schumpeter Society, August 19–22.

Hayashi, K. 1992. "From Network Externalities to Interconnection: The Changing Nature of Networks and Economy." In Antonelli, C. (ed.), *The Economics of Information Networks*. London: Elsevier, pp. 195–215.

Hayek, F.A. 1945. "The Use of Knowledge in Society." In *The American Economic Review*, Vol. 35, Sept. 45, pp. 519–530.

Heertje, A. 1988. "Schumpeter and Technical Change." In Hanusch, H. (ed.), *Evolutionary Economics: Applications of Schumpeter's Ideas*, pp. 71–89.

Heertje, A., and Perlman, M. (eds.) 1990. *Evolving Technology and Market Structure: Studies in Schumpeterian Economics*. Michigan: University of Michigan Press.

Herrmann-Pillath, C. 1991. "A Darwinian Framework for the Economic Analysis of Institutional Change in History." In *Journal of Social and Biological Structures*, Vol. 14, No. 2, pp. 127–148.

Herrmann-Pillath, C. 1993. "*Macht und Ordnung: Grundzüge einer evolutionstheoretischen Neubegründung der Ordnungstheorie*," book manuscript, Bergisch Gladbach.

Hicks, J.R. 1973. *Capital and Time: A Neo-Austrian Theory*. Oxford: Clarendon Press.

Hippel, E.U. 1988. *The Sources of Innovation*. Oxford: Oxford Univ. Press.

Hodgson, G.M. 1992. "Is There Still a Place for Neoclassical Theory?" In *Journal of Economic Issues* 26, 3, pp. 749–767.

Hodgson, G.M. 1993. *Economics and Evolution: Bringing Back Life into Economics*. Cambridge: Polity Press, forthcoming.

Imai, K. 1990. "Patterns of Innovation and Entrepreneurship in Japan." In Heertje, A., et al. (eds.), *Evolving Technology and Market Structure: Studies in Schumpeterian Economics*, Michigan: University of Michigan Press, pp. 187–201.

Imai, K., and Yamazaki, A. 1992. "Dynamics of Japanese Industrial System from a Schumpeterian Perspective." Paper presented at Kyoto Conference of the International Joseph A. Schumpeter Society, August 19–22.

Ireland, T.R. 1990. "The Formation of Organizations, Networks and Markets." In *The Journal of Behavioral Economics* 19, 1, pp. 103–124.

Jay, E.J. 1964. "The Concepts of 'Field' and Network". In *Anthropological Research* in *Man*, 64, 177, pp. 137–139.

Johanson, J., and Mattson, L.G. 1987. "Interorganizational Relations in Industrial Systems: A Network Approach compared with a Transaction-Cost Approach." In *International Studies of Management and Organisation* 17, pp. 34–48.

Kalmbach, P., and Kurz, H.D. 1986. "Economic Dynamics and Innovation: Ricardo, Marx and Schumpeter on Technical Change and Unemployment." In Wagener, H.J., et al. (eds.). *The Economic Law of Motion of Modern Society—a Marx-Keynes-Schumpeter Centennial*. London: Cambridge Univ. Press, pp. 71–92.

Kaplinsky, R. 1983. "Firm Size and Technical Change in a Dynamic Context." In *The Journal of Industrial Economics* XXXII (September) pp. 39–59.

Kerber, W. 1992. "Rights, Innovations, and Evolution: The Distributional Effects of Different Rights to Innovate." Paper, presented at 19th Annual Meeting of the History of Economics Society, Fairfax, May 30–June 2.

Kessler, U. 1992. *Unternehmensgrösse, Innovation und Wertschöpfungswachstum: Eine empirische Untersuchung im Lichte der Schumpeterschen Innovationsdiskussion*. Frankfurt: Lang.

Kindleberger, C.P. 1990. *Historical Economics: Art or Science*?, New York: Harvester Wheatsheaf.

Kingston, W. 1992. "Institutional Change and Long Cycles." Paper presented at Kyoto Conference of the International Joseph A. Schumpeter Society, August 19–22.

Kirzner, I.M. (ed.). 1982. *Method, Process, and Austrian Economics: Essays in Honor of Ludwig von Mises*. Lexington, MA: Lexington Books, D.G. Heath and Company.

Klein, B.H. 1988. "Luck, Necessity, and Dynamic Flexibility." In Hanusch, H. (ed.), *Evolutionary Economics: Applications of Schumpeter's Ideas*, New York: Cambridge Univ. Press, pp. 95–120.

Klepper, S. 1992. "Entry, Exit, and Innovation over the Product Life Cycle: The Dynamics of First Mover Advantages, Declining Product Innovation, and Market Failure." Paper presented at Kyoto Conference of the International Joseph A. Schumpeter Society, August 19–22.

Kogut, B., and Kulatilaka, N. 1992. "What is Critical Capability?" Paper presented at Kyoto Conference of the International Joseph A. Schumpeter Society, August 19–22.

Kregel, J.A. 1986. "Laws of the Market and Laws of Motion." In Wagener, H.J., et al. (eds.), *The Economic Law of Motion of Modern Society—a Marx-Keynes-Schumpeter Centennial*, London: Cambridge Univ. Press, pp. 31–48.

Langlois, R.N. 1989. "Economic Change and the Boundaries of the Firm" in Carlsson, B. (ed.), *Industrial Dynamics: Technological, Organizational, and Structural Changes in Industries and Firms*, Boston: Kluwer, pp. 85–108.

Langlois, R.N., and Robertson, P.L. 1989. "Explaining Vertical Integration: Lessons from the American Automobile Industry." In *The Journal of Economic History* XLIX, 2, pp. 361–375.

Lazonick, W. 1990. "Organizational Integration in Three Industrial Revolutions"; Commentary by Y. Shionoya, in Heertje, A., et al. (eds.), *Evolving Technology and Market Structure: Studies in Schumpeterian Economics*. Michigan: University of Michigan Press, pp. 77–103.

Leibenstein, H. 1987. *Inside the Firm: The Inefficiencies of Hierarchy*, Cambridge MA: Harvard Univ. Press.

Loasby, B.J. 1991. "Change and Continuity in the Process of Innovation". Paper presented at European Economic Association, Cambridge, 30 August–2 September.

Lundvall, B.A. 1988. "Innovation as an Interactive Process: From User-Producer to the National System of Innovation". In Dosi, G., et al. (eds.) Technical Change and Economic Theory. London: Pinter, pp. 349–379.

Maclean Johns, C. 1992. *Technology, Culture, and Creativity: Factors Connecting Invention and Scientific Discovery*, St. Gallen: Diss.

Mäki, U. 1990. "Practical Syllogism, Entrepreneurship and The Invisible Hand: A Critique of the Analytic Hermeneutics of G.H. von Wright". In Lavoie, D., *Economics and Hermeneutics*. London: Routledge, pp. 149–176.

Magnusson, L. 1991. "From Verlag to Factory: The Contest For Efficient Property Rights" In Gustafsson, B. (ed.), Power and Economic Institutions: Reinterpretations in Economic History, Aldershot: Elgar, pp. 195–222.

Malerba, F. 1992. "Learning by Firms and Incremental Technical Change". In *The Economic Journal*, Vol. 102, (July), pp. 845–859.

Mansfield, E. 1985. "How rapidly does New Industrial Technology Leak Out?", In *The Journal of Industrial Economics*, Vol. XXXIV, (December), pp. 217–223.

Marengo, L. 1992. "Structure, Competence and Learning in an Adaptive Model of the Firm" In ESGEE, Papers on Economics & Evolution, No. 9203, Freiburg.

Matthews, R.C.O. 1984. "Darwinism and Economic Change", in Collard, D.A., Helm, D.R., Scott, M.F., Sen, A.K. (eds.), *Economic Theory and Hicksian Themes*, Oxford Economic Papers, Supplement, 36, Oxford: Clarendon, pp. 91–117.

Mensch, G., Haag, G., Weidlich, W. 1989. "The Schumpeter Clock. A Micro-Macro Model of Economic Change: Applied to United States and West German Data", paper: Paris, OECD-Seminar, June 5–8, 1989.

Metcalfe, J.S. 1989. "Evolution and Economic Change", in Silberston, A. (ed.), *Technology and Economic Progress*. London: Macmillan.

Metz, R. 1993. *Langfristige Konjunktur- und Wachstumsschwankungen: Zur theoretischen Konzeption, empirischen Evidenz und historischen Bedeutung langfristiger ökonomischer Prozesse*. Köln: forthcoming.

Mises, L. von. 1962. *The Ultimate Foundation of Economic Science: An Essay on Method*. Kansas City: Sheed Andrews and McMeel, Inc.

Monge, P.R. 1987. "The Network Level of Analysis". In Berger, C.R., Chaffee, S.H. (eds.), *Handbook of Communication Science*. London: Sage, pp. 239–270.

Nelson, R.R. 1981. "Research on Productivity Growth and Productivity Differences: Dead Ends and New Departures". In *Journal of Economic Literature* 19, 3, pp. 1029–1064.

Nelson, R.R., and Winter, S.G. 1982. *An Evolutionary Theory of Economic Change*, Cambridge, MA: Harvard Univ. Press.

Nelson, R.R. 1989. "Capitalism as an Engine of Progress", in Carlsson, B. (ed.), *Industrial Dynamics: Technological, Organizational, and Structural Changes in Industries and Firms*. Boston: Kluwer, pp. 177–192.

Nooteboom, B., and Vossen, R.W. 1992. "R&D Spending and Efficiency in Relation to Firm Size". Paper presented at Kyoto Conference of the International Joseph A. Schumpeter Society, 19–22 August.

Nooteboom, B. 1992. "Schumpeterian and Austrian Entrepreneurship: A Unified Process of Adjustment and Change", Groningen: unpublished manuscript.

Oakley, A. 1990. *Schumpeter's Theory of Capitalist Motion: A Critical Exposition and Reassessment*. Aldershot: Elgar.

Ōtsch, W. 1991. "Gibt es eine Grundlagenkrise der neoklassischen Theorie?". In *Jahrbücher für Nationalökonomie und Statistik*, Bd. 208/6, pp. 642–656.

Ōtsch, W. 1991. *Kreativität und Logik im ōkonomischen Handlungsmodell.* Linz. Unpublished paper.

Pareto, V. 1919. *Traité de Sociologie Générale (Vol. II)*. Lausanne: Payot.

Pareto, V. 1927. *Manuel d'Economie Politique*, Paris: Giard.

Pasinetti, L.L. 1981. *Structural Change and Economic Growth: A Theoretical Essay on the Dynamics of the Wealth of Nations*. Cambridge: Cambridge Univ. Press.

Pavitt, K. 1986. "Chips and 'Trajectories': How Will the Semiconductor Influence the Sources and Directions of Technical Change?" in Macleod, R. (ed.), *Technology and Human Prospect*. London: Pinter.

Peitgen, H.O., Jürgens, H., and Saupe, D. 1992. *Fractals for the Classroom*. New York: Springer.

Pelikan, P. 1988. "Can the Imperfect Innovation Systems of Capitalism be Outperformed?" In Dosi, G., et al. (eds.). *Technical Change and Economic Theory*, London: Pinter, pp. 370–398.

Pelikan, P. 1992. "The Dynamics of Economic systems, or How To Transform a Failed Socialist Economy". In *Journal of Evolutionary Economics*, Vol. 2, No. 1, pp. 39–63.

Perez, C. 1985. "Microelectronics, Long Waves and World Structural Change: New Perspectives for Developing Countries", in *World Development*, Vol. 13, No. 3, pp. 441–463.

Perlman, M. 1988. "On the Coming Senescence of American Manufacturing Competence". In Hanusch, H. (ed.), *Evolutionary Economics: Applications of Schumpeter's Ideas*. New York: Cambridge Univ. Press, pp. 343–382.

Rahmeyer, F. 1991. "Evolutorische Ökonomik, technischer Wandel und sektorales Produktivitätswachstum, in Beitrag 52, Univ. Augsburg, Institut für Volkswirtschaftslehre.

Reati, A. 1991. "Are We at the Beginning of a New Long Term Expansion Induced by Technological Change?". Paper presented at Economic Papers, Directorate-General of Economic and Financial Affairs, Commission of the European Communities, No. 85, Brussels.

Renault, M. 1991. *Du Temps Newtonien Au Temps De L'Evolution Dans L'Analyse Economique*, Rennes: Thèse de Doctorat.

Richardson, G.B. 1972. "The Organisation of Industry". In *Economic Journal*, 82, pp. 883–896.

Roepke, J. 1977. *Die Strategie der Innovation: Eine systemtheoretische Untersuchung der Interpretation von Individuum, Organisation und Markt im Neuerungsprozess*. Tübingen: Mohr.

Rosegger, G. 1991. "Advances in Information Technology and the Innovative Strategies of Firms". In CIRCIT Working Paper 1991/1, Melbourne.

Rosenberg, N. 1982. *Inside the Black Box: Technology and Economics*, Cambridge: Cambridge Univ. Press.

Rosenberg, N. 1992. "Joseph Schumpeter: Radical Economist, paper". Paper presented at Kyoto Conference of the International Joseph A. Schumpeter Society, August 19–22.

Rothschild, K.W. 1986. "Capitalists and Entrepreneurs: Prototypes and Roles". In Wagener, H.J., et al. (eds.), pp. 186–196.

Ruggles, M. 1992. "The Value of Tacit Communicative Competences in Telecommunication Networks". In CIRCIT Newsletter, Vol. 4, No. 9 (November), pp. 3–4.

Rumelhart, D.E., and McClelland, J.L. 1986. *Parallel Distributed Processing: Explorations in the Microstructure of Cognition*, Vol. 1, Foundations, Cambridge, MA: MIT Press.

Schefold, B. 1986. "Schumpeter as a Walrasian Austrian and Keynes as a Marshallian". In Wagener, H.-J., et al. (eds.), pp. 93–111.

Scherer, F.M. 1992. "Schumpeter and Plausible Capitalism". Paper presented at Kyoto Conference of the International Joseph A. Schumpeter Society, 19–22 August.

Schmidt, C. 1992. "Concurrence, Concours Des Producteurs Et Modes D'Organisation De La Production Chez Antoine Augustin Cournot". In *Economies et Sociétés, Série Oeconomica*, PE no. 16, pp. 71–99.

Schumpeter, J.A. 1912. *Theorie der wirtschaftlichen Entwicklung*. Leipzig: Duncker & Humblot.

Schumpeter, J.A. 1939. *Business Cycles: A Theoretical, Historical and Statistical Analysis of the Capitalist Process*. New York: McGraw-Hill.

Schumpeter, J.A. 1943. *Capitalism, Socialism, and Democracy*. London: Allen & Unwin.

Schumpeter, J.A. 1952. *Ten Great Economists: From Marx to Keynes*. London: Allen & Unwin.

Schumpeter, J.A. 1954. *History of Economic Analysis*. New York: Oxford University Press.

Schumpeter, J.A. 1984. "The Meaning of Rationality in the Social Sciences." In *Journal of Institutional and Theoretical Economics* 140, 4. (December), pp. 577–593.

Shackle, G.L.S. 1990. *Time, Expectations and Uncertainty in Economics: Selected Essays of G.L.S. Shackle*. Aldershot: Elgar.

Shionoya, Y. 1990. "The Origin of the Schumpeterian Research Program: A Chapter Omitted from Schumpeters Theory of Economic Development", in *Journal of Institutional and Theoretical Economics*, Vol. 146, No. 2, June, pp. 314–327.

Simon, H.A. 1978. "Rationality as Process and as Product of Thought". In *The American Economic Review*, Vol. 68, pp. 1–6.

Simonetti, R., Archibugi, D., and Evangelista, R. 1992. "Product and Process Innovations: How are They Defined? How are They Quantified?" Paper presented at Kyoto Conference of the International Joseph A. Schumpeter Society, August 19–22.

Stankiewicz, R. 1990. "Basic Technologies and the Innovation Process". In Sigurdsson, J. (ed.), *Measuring the Dynamics of Technological Change*, London: Pinter.

Stiglitz, J.E. 1992. "Endogenous Growth and Cycles". Paper presented at Kyoto Conference of the International Joseph A. Schumpeter Society, August 19–22.

Stolper, W.F. 1988. "Development: Theory and Empirical Evidence". In Hanusch, H. (ed.), pp. 9–22.

Stolper, W.F. 1991. "The Theoretical Bases of Economic Policy: The Schumpeterian Perspective". In *Journal of Evolutionary Economics* 1, 3, pp. 189–206.

Streissler, E.W. 1992. "The Influence of German and Austrian Economics on Joseph A. Schumpeter". Paper presented at Kyoto Conference of the International Joseph A. Schumpeter Society, August 19–22.

Swedberg, R. 1992. "Schumpeter's Early Work". In *Journal of Evolutionary Economics* 2, 1, pp. 65–82.

Sydow, J. 1992. *Strategische Netzwerke: Evolution und Organization*, Berlin: Gabler Verlag.

Teece, D.J. (ed.). 1987. *The Competitive Challenge: Strategies for Industrial Innovation and Renewal*. Cambridge MA: Ballinger.

Torre, A. 1992. "Untraded and Technological Interdependencies: Some New Developments and Conclusions". Paper presented at Kyoto Conference of the International Joseph A. Schumpeter Society, August 19–22.

Tushman, M.L., and Nelson, R.R. 1990. "Introduction: Technology, Organizations and Innovation". In *Administrative Science Quarterly* 35, pp. 1–8.

Tylecote, A. 1992. *The Long Wave in the World Economy: The Present Crisis in Historical Perspective*. London: Routledge.

Utterback, J.M., and Abernathy, W.J. 1975. "A Dynamic Model of Process and Product Innovation." In *OMEGA* 3, 2, pp. 639–656.

Valentino, R. 1990. "Schumpeter and Walras in Latin America: A Dualistic Structure of Innovation the Market versus the State". In Heertje, A., et al. (eds.), *Evolving Technology and Market Structure: Studies in Schumpeterian Economics*. Michigan: University of Michigan Press, pp. 103–120.

Veblen, T. 1898. "Why is Economics not an Evolutionary Science?" In *The Quarterly Journal of Economics*, 12 (July), pp. 373–397. Reprint in Veblen, T. (1990) *The Place of Science in Modern Civilisation and Other Essays*. New Brunswick: Transaction, pp. 56–81.

Wagener, H.J., and Drukker, W. (eds.). 1985. *The Economic Law of Motion of Modern Society—a Marx-Keynes-Schumpeter Centennial*. London: Cambridge Univ. Press.

Wagner, A. 1989. *Mikroökonomik*. Stuttgart: Gustav Fischer.

Weinel, I., and Crossland, P.D. 1989. "The Scientific Foundations of Technological Progress". In *Journal of Economic Issues*, 23, 3 (September), pp. 795–808.

Williamson, O.E. 1990. "A Comparison of Alternative Approaches to Economic Organization." In *Journal of Institutional and Theoretical Economics* 146, 1 (March), pp. 61–71.

Winter, S.G. 1984. "Schumpeterian Competition in Alternative Technological Regimes". In *Journal of Economic Behavior and Organisation* 5, 3–4, pp. 287–320.

Winter, S.G. 1987. "Knowledge and Competence as Strategic Assets", in Teece, D.J. (ed.), *The Competitive Challenge: Strategies for Industrial Innovation and Renewal.* Cambridge, MA: Ballinger, pp. 159–184.

Witt, U. 1986. "Firms' Market Behavior Under Imperfect Information and Economic Natural Selection". In *Journal of Economic Behavior and Organization* 7, pp. 265–290.

Witt, U. 1992. "Evolutionary Economics: An Interpretative Survey". In ESGEE, Papers on Economics & Evolution, No. 9104, Freiburg.

Witt, U. 1993. *Individualistic Foundations of Evolutionary Economics*, Cambridge: Cambridge Univ. Press.

6 THE THEORY OF THE FIRM AND THE THEORY OF ECONOMIC GROWTH

An Essay on the Economics of Institutions, Competition, and the Capacity of the Political System to Cope with Unexpected Change

Gunnar Eliasson[1]

Introduction and Summary

The nature of the firm, as we understand it, is totally conditioned by the market environment in which the firm is operating. This is true for the real as well as for the theoretical firm. In attempting to link the behavior of the firm to the growth process of a national economy, it thus becomes important to present a theoretical firm that is as close as possible to a real firm of a capitalistically organized market economy. As we will see, this will force us also to discuss economic growth in terms of a realistic model representation of the dynamics of firm behavior in markets, in fact, making aggregation endogenous and explicit.

What I have just said may sound trivial to some. But anyone familiar with the logic of mainstream neoclassical theory will understand that we are touching on a deep intellectual problem. Standard neoclassical theory has no place for the entity called a firm. The problem lies in its focus on static equilibrium modeling and its failure to redefine the equilibrium such that the dynamics of a profoundly imperfect competition process can be captured. Some notion of equilibrium or self-coordination is, of course, necessary in a relevant theory of a dynamic economy. But the same theory also has to allow playroom for its most important actors, the business firms. I will attempt here to move theory in this direction, and perhaps not surprisingly, the result will be fundamentally different from the classical model.

The existence of a firm, based on its *competence* to generate organizational synergies needed to earn a rent above production and financing costs is central to this theoretical economy. Competence is local and defined as the ability of the firm to commercially exploit internationally available technology. To explain *how* this firm captures its rent, both a theory of the firm and a theory of the market environment in which the firm is supposed to operate are required. The deep problem in economics is that the characteristics of the market needed to explain firm behavior is dependent of the dynamics of all business agents. Mainstream economic theory offers very little in the form of a useful theory of dynamic markets to accommodate the dynamics of firm behavior. Micro-macro theory is needed, embodying an explicit representation of competition as a dynamic process. This process does not necessarily converge to an equilibrium determined outside the economic system. The direction of change of the macro economy depends on the path micro structures take along the way, and on how competing agents react to and change it. This is the theory of the market.

The *intensity of competition* depends on the spread in the capacities of business organizations to generate synergies, scale economies, rents, or productivity. A ranking of such capacities, sometimes called Salter (1960) curves (Fig. 1), is made up not only of existing firms, but also of what every firm expects existing firms to be capable of doing, such as the consequences for market competition of investment, of exit and of not yet existing firms, that may come into existence (entry). The combined "carrots and whips" of markets make up the incentives and the dynamics of the macro economy.

This paper will be about how the performance of the macroeconomy depends on how firms build and exploit their organizational competence. This is not an analytical piece, but a story about ongoing self-coordinated economic activities, moved by live agents. My story will be about micro firm behavior, with particular attention being paid to how firms stay in business in a competitive landscape that they themselves create and change.

Figure 6.1. Salter curve structures illustrating the dynamics of the Swedish Micro-to-Macro model.

(a) Excess rates of return (= ε) distributions 1983 and 1990.

(b) Actual and potential labor productivity distributions 1983 and 1990 (shaded areas denote unused labor capacity (labor hoarding)).

Source: Eliasson (1991c)

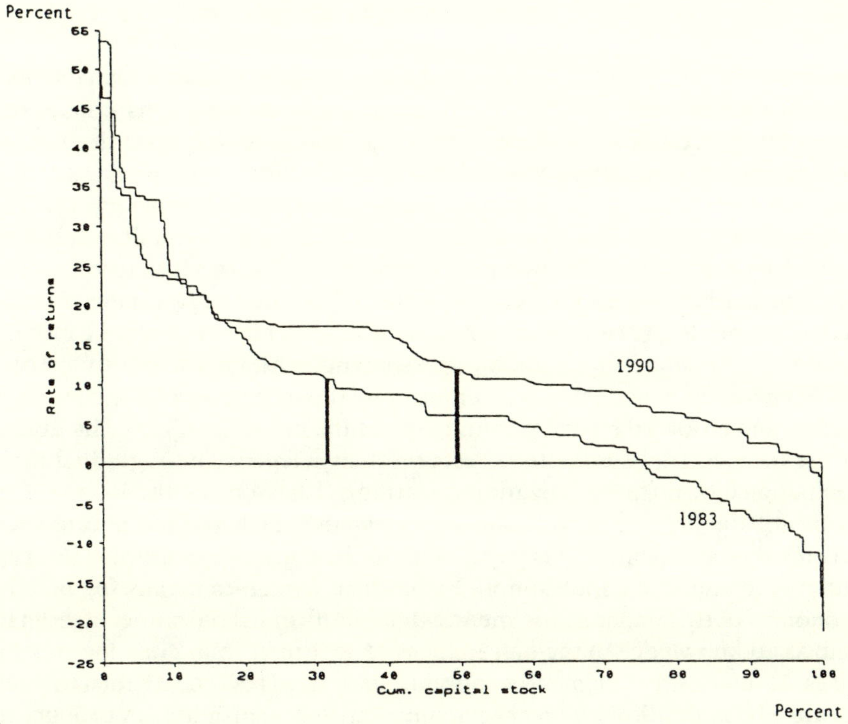
Percent
Rate of returns
1990
1983
Cum. capital stock
Percent

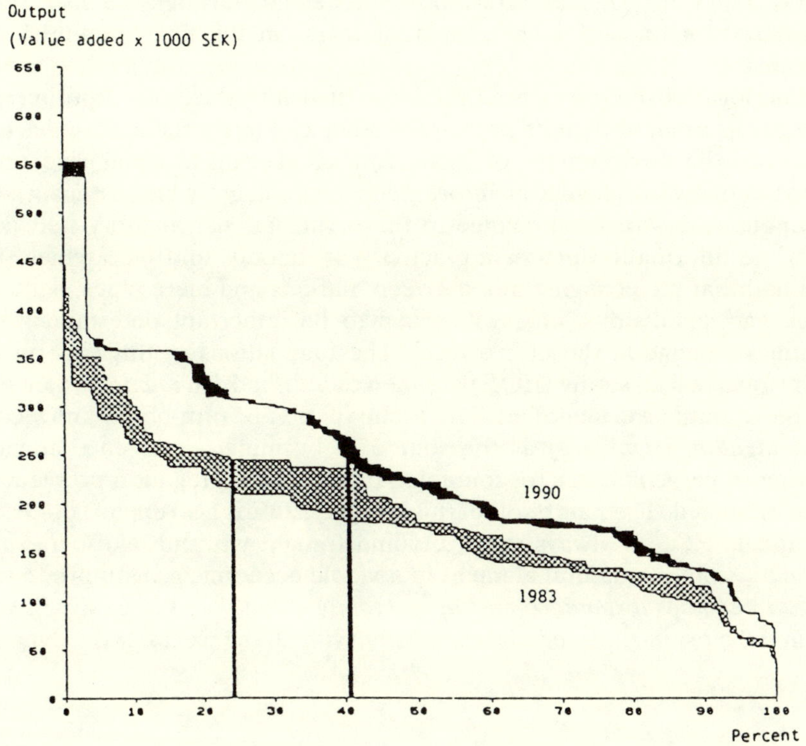
Output
(Value added x 1000 SEK)
1990
1983
Percent

My notion (1987, 1990b,c, 1991c) of the *experimentally organized economy* (EOE) will be fundamental for my explanation of how firms create and maintain the competence they need to do that. It determines the nature of firm behavior as "experimental learning machines" that operate in the imperfect intersection of the product, labor, and financial markets, making up a *path-dependent* economic system. In order to understand firm behavior guided by competence in dynamic markets, I need this "picture" of the dynamic market organization of an economy as an alternative to the classical economic model. It can be obtained by a few seemingly innocent modifications of the standard economic model. The constant competitive struggle of agents to beat each other, induced by the incentives of the economic system and enforced by competition, moves the macroeconomy. The ability of the firms to stay competitive rests on their efficiency in upgrading their competence through organizational learning (Eliasson, 1990a, 1992a). The theory of the firm, to be relevant for my analysis, has to incorporate such organizational learning. This paper is about how this competence is learned and put to use in competition and what firm dynamics means for macroeconomic performance. This means that the firm organization of human embodied knowledge in the hierarchies of the firm becomes one theoretical focus of this essay on macroeconomic growth. The second focus is the nature of competition among such competence organizations in product of markets and the possible diffusion of competence through the dissolution and recombination of such competent teams in the financial and labor markets.

The logic of the paper is as follows. I first introduce the experimental nature of economic activity among the advanced industrial economies that make up the environment of modern firms. Technical change becomes synonymous with change in information technology, which is again synonymous with structural change in the organizational memory that controls the information processing activity of markets and hierarchies. We will find that the changing mix between markets and hierarchies, between large and small firms, etc., will prove to be important determinants of technical change at the macro level. The foundations of this experimentally organized economy (EOE) are then established. The *nature of the firm* in the EOE is next identified. The accumulation of firm-based knowledge (*organizational learning*) as the source of business competence and the driving force behind macroeconomic growth (the aggregation problem) is then discussed. The nature of learning in the EOE is also explored. Learning in the EOE is always imperfect and fraught with mistakes. *Business failure* becomes a natural element in a viable economic growth process; in fact, it becomes *a standard cost of economic growth*, and success will turn up in the most unexpected places. Finally, with all the pieces of the dynamic market process put together, I will address the problem of radical *economic reorganization* of an economy and the ability of firms to learn and of the economy to self-coordinate under such circumstances. There are, in fact, quite a few cases of such fundamental reorganization forced by rent-generating technological change, the most well-researched case being the industrial revolution and a very imminent example being the current restructuring of the Eastern European economies.

Human competence dominates economic performance at all levels. Its hallmark is heterogeneity to the extent that in each agent certain dimensions of it are unique and not (directly) imitable or communicable. Each of us walks through life with strong opinions of what is the best, whether it be our views about how to run a firm, which economic theory to use, or how to organize family life.

We all need a theory to be able to make decisions and to feel reasonably comfortable (Eliasson, 1992a), and whether good or bad, we have to believe in the theory we have chosen to use. We need a theory to restrict our vision to make it possible to organize the facts we think we know and our thoughts, to get a coherent picture of the whole, without getting lost in the complexities of our entire economic environment. *Theory* is just another name for the "bounded rationality" of Simon (1955) and others. There are many possible "theories" to guide firm behavior, which means that although some of them will be right, most of them will be more or less wrong. This is the essence of what I call the *experimentally organized economy* (Eliasson, 1987, 1991c).

The Experimental Nature of Economic Activity

Adam Smith (1776) laid down the principal design of a decentralized market economy in which division of labor made economies of scale "in the small" possible and the realization of large macro productivity effects feasible. This benefit, however, came at a significant cost, a fact that "modern" mathematical representations of the "invisible hand" have missed. The organization of the division of labor is an instance of innovative behavior. It evolved gradually in the market. Once realized, economic activity had to be *coordinated* physically (transports) and through communication.

Once an innovative design, whether technical, organizational, or commercial, has been accomplished, competitors will be "on your doorstep" to learn (imitate). If your organization is large enough you will want to diffuse the new knowledge throughout your organization. You may also want to sell your knowledge at a profit (consulting). *Learning*, hence, becomes a general and resource, using economic activity.

Even very simple and tiny tasks (you soon learn) can normally be solved in a large number of ways. The higher up, the more complex the decision problem and the larger the number of possible solutions. Some of these solutions are better than others. The problem, however, is that *you will never know until you have tried them. This is the essence of the experimentally organized economy*. The number of solutions defines the large *business opportunity set* that faces each agent who has to search his way into the opportunity set by trial and error, being directed by a limited vision (theory) of all possibilities (bounded rationality). Since each agent has his or her particular vision as guidance, there will be strong limitations on communication because of limited and differently composed *receiver competence* (Eliasson, 1990a, p. 17; 1990b). The result will be, at each point in time, a heterogeneous structure of competence, defined by the organization of people in the economy.

Much of the knowledge put to use in a firm, especially high level knowledge, vested in the top competent team of a firm is difficult or impossible to communicate in coded form as information. It is *tacit*. Tacit knowledge is acquired through on-the-job learning and filters through the economy (selection) through the acquisition of the whole, or parts of, firms in the M&A market or through the mobility of people or teams of people with competence in the labor market (Eliasson, 1991e).

I have now introduced four general, knowledge-based information activities: coordination, innovation, learning, and selection (see Table 1, and Eliasson, 1990a). Together they can be defined to cover all economic activity[2] representing the intellectual superstructure (the memory) of economic activity that controls all other activities.

A reasonable modification of the traditional economic measurement system is sufficient to demonstrate the economic importance of knowledge-based information activities. We can establish that most of what we call technical change, as observed through macro production function analysis, really is composed of changes in the technology of economic information processing, which in turn originates in *innovative organizational change*, including innovative change in the organization of learning to accumulate new competence (Eliasson, 1992a). This observation demands a very broadly based definition of innovation. Innovation is not restricted to hardware equipment in factories. Innovation occurs throughout business organizations. It is particularly important at the level of the top competent team in the form of *innovative organizational change* exercising strong leverage effects on the entire firm (Eliasson, 1990c). Innovative organizational change is also associated with the organization of the entire economic system and its capacity to efficiently coordinate economic activities. Particularly important is the balancing of the reliance on coordination through free

Table 1. Four basic economic activities in the knowledge-based information economy

1. Coordination (organizational structure)	The invisible and visible hands at work • competition (in markets, Smith, 1776) • management (of hierarchies, Chandler, 1977)
2. Innovation (exploring state space)	Creation and exploitation of new business opportunities (Schumpeter, 1912) • innovation • entrepreneurship • technical development
3. Selection (organizational change)	Incentives for change • entry • exit • mobility
4. Learning	Knowledge transfer (Mill, 1848) • education • imitation • diffusion

Source: *The Knowledge Based Information Economy*, IUI, Stockholm, 1990, p. 73.

markets, on the one hand, and through the central regulation by government on the other. Another equally important problem is the tradeoff between the short and the long run.

On this score we can learn three important things from research carried out by Bo Carlsson. First, in an early IUI study, Carlsson (Carlsson et al., 1979, p. 34; Carlsson, 1980) demonstrated that when stripped down to the level of a division, or an establishment, more than 50 percent of total factor productivity change at the manufacturing industry level originated in structural adjustment between existing establishments, most of which was due to the exit of low performing units and the transfer of resources to high performance units. Second, Carlsson (1989) reports that technological change in manufacturing is generally making smaller scale production more economically viable than earlier, which is reflected in a general reduction in the average size of both plants and firms among the industrialized countries. This observation is strengthened by the relatively faster advance of private service production observed above. Carlsson notes that

Sweden was the only important exception to this development during the 1980s, but that also this deviant trend among Swedish manufacturing firms appears to have slowed towards the end of the 1980s (Carlsson, 1992). Smaller scale, service-oriented, and competence-intensive production will increase the importance for macro performance of structural adjustment at the plant and establishment levels. It is also interesting, in this context, to recall Pratten's (1976) results from an analysis of comparable Swedish and U.K. manufacturing firms. While the U.K. firms were generally larger (by a financial definition) than their Swedish counterparts, the Swedish production plants were generally much larger and much more productive than the corresponding U.K. units. The predominant concern with process cost efficiency in Swedish firms was also obvious from a comparison between Swedish and U.S. budgeting practices in the early 1970s (Eliasson, 1976, p. 227). Apparently the Swedes have continued to enjoy increasing such economies of scale through the 1980s, in contrast to a contrary development in the rest of the world. This time, however, the base for such economies has been broadened to include also financial (group) size, meaning that R&D, product development, and global marketing have come into play in a relatively more important way (Eliasson, 1985b).

Third, Carlsson (1991) observes that in a 20-year perspective total factor productivity growth is almost all a matter of reallocation of resources within and between existing plants. This tallies nicely with my own results on entry and exit (Eliasson, 1991a). Beyond the 20-year horizon, the introduction of new technology through entry and through new investment begins to exhibit sizable macroeconomic effects. I will return to this conclusion below.

The deviant pattern of development in Swedish industry structure during the 1980s raises a number of interesting and worrying questions. A particular instance of high level organizational knowledge is the competence to build, to operate efficiently, and to reorganize large business firms on which many advanced economies, which cannot fall back on generous raw material sources, base their economic wealth. The Swedish economy currently very much bases its economic prosperity on a small number of giant international firms (Table 2), which in turn base their performance on the organization of metal manufacturing around a collection of machine tools originally developed during the industrial revolution. The critical question for the future has a competence and a policy side. The competence question is to what extent mature industrial countries like Sweden, in order to stay ahead, can continue to base their economic wealth on this manufacturing technology as the rest of the advancing industrialized world learns to do the same thing, and maybe better, while the frontier industrial nations or

Table 2. Dominance of the 10 largest Swedish corporations

	1965	*1970*	*1978*	*1986*	*1990*
Swedish goods export	19	25	31	37	34
Foreign Swedish employment	78	73	69	75	85
Manufacturing employment in Sweden	16	19	24	31	27
including indirect employment with subcontractors	—	—	ca 31	—	—
Total manufacturing	42	—	44	74	72

Source: Eliasson (1988b).

regions rapidly move into a new type of smaller scale, competence-intensive production, to a large extent based in the private service sector. Another equally pertinent question (the policy question) is whether a particular high-wage nation, like Sweden, will be able to enjoy the presence in Sweden of the highly mobile international firms operating in global markets. There is a critical competence problem at the top national level. How much of promised economic growth is the political system capable of delivering? We can observe that while policymakers all over the world are concerned with promoting (industrial policy) new techniques in industries based on old technologies (robots, factory automation), new technologies are learned and introduced through competition with the best actors in markets.

An Open Economic System Bounded by Local Competence

Having come this far we can conclude that the engine of the macroeconomic growth machinery has to be sought out in the individual, rent-seeking behavior of firms that are more or less competent in organizing themselves to exploit the vast number of commercial and technological opportunities of the global business opportunity set. The question is how such dynamic competition occurs in the experimentally organized economy and to what extent particular industry structures mean better preparedness than others for the future.

Karl Marx, observing the impressive economic performance of the industrial revolution, did what economists have always done: He extrapolated what he saw and, hence, saw no end to the production potential of the "modern" industrial (factory) organization of work. The problem was that his mind, like the minds of economists in general, was shaped in terms of the firm as a factory, producing increasing tonnage of a homogeneous product (steel). Marx, then, of course had to explain why production was not unlimited, and, hence, borrowed an old idea from Adam Smith, again restated by Stigler in 1951, about the market as the limiting factor. What Marx and Stigler missed was the *quality dimension* of output. Quality removed the market restriction to economic growth. There may be a limit to how much quantity (steel) you can consume, but not to how much quality you *can* consume (French village wine vs. Chateau Margaux), only a *competence limit* to how much you can enjoy the quality. This revised notion of output changes the unlimited productivity potential of Marx into, for all practical purposes, an *unlimited set of business opportunities*, where unlimited quality differentiation constitutes the important expansionary element.

The Smithian market limit is now replaced (Eliasson, 1988a, 1990b) by a *local, competence limit on the supply side*, namely, the local competence of the firm

- to create new qualities, including new technology (*innovation*) and
- to receive and implement new technology (*learning*).

Also this competence is characterized by extreme heterogeneity, making its quality dimension virtually incommunicable in coded form, that is, as *marketable information* (type instruction books).[3] This introduction of competence, rather than the market as the limiting factor is more compatible with facts. It allows me to keep an open economic system very much as the premarginalist economists did (see Loasby, 1991), but still bounding the economy by local competence and known technology.[4]

Having come this far we can summarize the fundamental assumptions of the experimentally organized economy as follows (Eliasson, 1991c):

1. *State space*, or the (international) opportunity set, is for all practical purposes unlimited.[5]
2. *Behavior* of agents is characterized by
   - bounded rationality
   - tacit knowledge

   add to this (remember my introduction)
3. *Free access* to state space or the set of business opportunities (free competitive entry),

and the model of the experimentally organized economy emerges. The free entry clause is imperative. It allows anyone who feels competitive to enter the market and take on incumbents. This *deregulation* of markets was exactly what happened in Europe just about the time the industrial revolution started, and this happened only in those economies where the lid was taken off (Eliasson, 1991a). This deregulation is currently being enacted in the previously planned economies of Eastern Europe. It is currently also being reluctantly enacted in some financially more or less defunct welfare economies of Western Europe in an attempt to create new incentives for economic growth. The problems are the same in principle but different in scope.

In the experimentally organized economy, a large number of *locally competent* firms search into (or compete their way into) a vast space of opportunities. The individual outcome of such *technological competition* depends on their initial competence endowment and *how* they search.

The competitive situation is such that the firms are always more or less mistaken, *business mistakes* being the important cost to society to make room for business successes ("creative destruction"), which is needed to achieve economic growth. In addition, mistakes are part of the on-the-job (economic) learning process of firms, and of society contributing to the updating of the *organizational memory* of firms and the economy at large. In this competitive market environment no firm, no (small) economy, not even IBM, is safe.

The experimentally organized economy is born out by statistics. Jagrén (1988) demonstrates how even the largest firms, when observed over a sufficiently long time, disappear from the Fortune 500 list, and even altogether as independent firms. He selected a random sample of 150 Swedish firms from a register in the 1920s and followed them into the 1980s. By the mid-1980s only 21 independent firms remained and most of them (19) had not grown very much in terms of employment during the period. Despite this, total employment of the remaining firms each year had grown faster than aggregate manufacturing employment (and output). The reason, of course, is that two firms that Jagrén had selected by chance—Electrolux and Bofors—had grown extremely quickly. We would, however, on the basis of the theory of the experimentally organized economy (EOE), expect total employment or output of a randomly selected sample of 100–500 firms 50–100 years ago to grow somewhat more slowly than the corresponding total of all manufacturing, the difference being accounted for by entry. The theory of the EOE, however, predicts that most of the incumbents at the time of the random selection 50–100 years ago would no longer remain as independent firms. Some would have been shut down, and some would have been acquired by other firms. The bulk of output would be accounted for by new firms and by a small group of remaining firms (Eliasson, 1991a). In addition, the growth of the total industry aggregate is not independent of the business mistakes that occur along the way (Eliasson, 1991c, 1992a).

The point of the argument is that no individual firm can feel comfortable and safe in the creative destruction process of the experimentally organized economy. An economy in which the majority of firms remains after a 50- to 100-year period is not a viable growth economy. The ultimate aim of policymaking has to be to organize the economy such that no agent can escape the competitive pressure of the EOE and to design a commercially minded culture that makes people capable of coping with its dynamic environment. This is the exact opposite of the classical, static model of economics and its materialization in the form of a centrally planned command economy.

The Firm in the Experimentally Organized Economy

The managing director of each firm would prefer to look forward to a long and successful business life, without the hazards of the EOE. Even though his horizon is considerably shorter than the life already realized by STORA (see Fig. 2, the world's oldest joint stock company), survival and growth (forever) as a portfolio of wealth is, and has to be, the goal of a firm. Management, however, prefers a pace of competition that is comfortable and not unduly risky. Hence, management does not feel at ease in a viable, experimentally organized economy. In the classical model firms can plan (in principle) to achieve the state of full information, and this theoretical possibility of the classical economic model exerted significant influence on the business administration literature of the 1960s and early 1970s, which abounded with treatises on "business planning" (see Eliasson, 1976), until reality struck back in the form of the series of macroeconomic crises of the 1970s. This literature, and its promotion of formal, long-range business planning, is now gone.

In the experimentally organized economy, and in reality, each firm has to reckon with the presence of many competitors aiming for its market niche through technological product competition (Eliasson, 1987). The set of business opportunities is huge and mostly nontransparent to the individual firm. A firm that wants to survive cannot wait to compute its fully informed plan of what to do. Such a plan is unfeasible by definition (in the experimentally organized economy). More to the point, however, if the firm does not act prematurely on a very incomplete information base, it can be sure that one of its many competitors will score a success, because it happened to approach the opportunity set from the right angle.

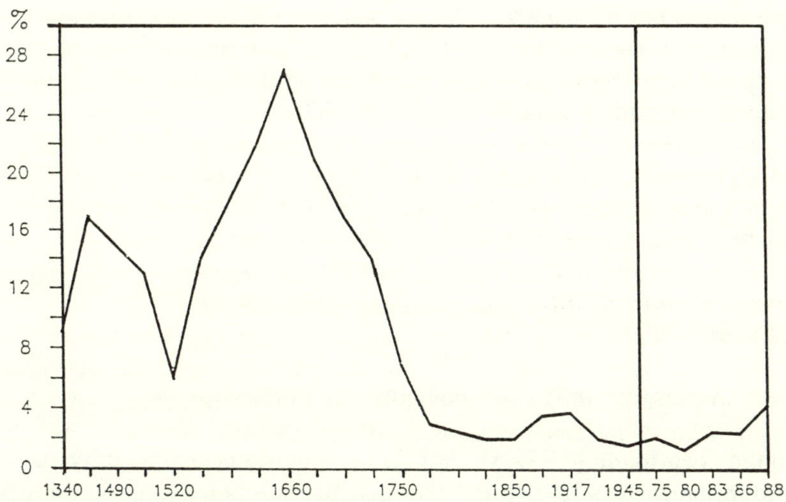

Figure 6.2. Share of total Swedish manufacturing of STORA 1340–1988. Company output in percent of total manufacturing and mining production.

Source: See Introduction by Gunnar Eliasson to Day-Eliasson-Wihlborg (eds.), *The Markets for Innovation, Ownership and Control*, IUI and North-Holland, 1993.

Thus top firm management had better be equipped with a good *sense of direction*, which is the first, dominant competence requisite for success (see items in Table 2). If it does not, it will fail anyway. Hence, a firm will have to demonstrate itself to outsiders as a gambler, taking on seemingly large risks. With a good sense of direction, however, the true risk exposure to the insider management is very much smaller. It should, in fact, be normal to define the competence of the firm in terms of its ability to transfer uncertainty, in Knight's (1921) sense, into (for its own management) computable risks.

There are nevertheless learnable, administrative techniques to minimize the costs of mistakes. Techniques can be developed that make it possible to take on (reduce the risk of taking on) large risks, that is, a technique to manage in situations when the first competitive requisite (intuition) has failed. This management technique consists of two elements: *identifying* mistakes early and *correcting* mistakes immediately (Eliasson, 1990b,c). Once these tests (elements 3 and 4) have been passed and the firm can set out to sea, another and quite different element of competence has to be clicked on: the ability to *operate* the firm *efficiently* on a day-to-day basis and to feed experience back to the top (*learning*). Different groups of people are normally responsible for managing these different tasks. This orientation of administrative techniques is apparent from an ongoing study of business information systems in practice (Eliasson, 1990c). This organizational technique dominates when firms have found themselves in the right market for a long time and in high volume activities. The large Swedish multinationals have been very successful in this field in the 1980s. The problem is that too much success in routine volume management is normally detrimental to the earlier "innovative" tasks, and even very large firms are at peril in the EOE.

Market Dynamics and Macroeconomic Performance

We have been made to believe that "perfect markets" or the fully informed "competitive market" represent the invisible hand of the market economy (see, for instance, the motivation for giving the Nobel prize in economics to Debreu in 1983). This is wrong. The competitive market of mainstream economic theory is nothing but a set of conditions describing the resting point of, the equilibrium of, or the solution to an equation system, representing an economy with exogenously given structures in which no innovative behavior occurs. This is not Adam Smith's idea of the invisible hand, but it has gradually become the idea of the invisible hand among economists after Walras. Even Schumpeter embraced the market representation of Walras. He liked to start his analysis with a disturbance (by the entrepreneur) of a Walrasian equilibrium. His worried conclusion was the nonsurvival of a competitive market economy because of the ever increasing concentration that would come out of its successful performance. This dismal prediction has so far been refuted by reality. With the notion of the experimentally organized economy (EOE) in the background, it can be safely concluded that Schumpeter's notion of forever successful, routinized, or planned innovation is not of this world.

Market rivalry à la Smith (1776) and Schumpeter (1942) through innovative product development, that is, through innovative *entry*, contrasts clearly with the classical Ricardian idea of markets, where prices are set at the margin where the worst performer earns no profit. In the experimentally organized economy, the best performers raise product quality through innovation or lower prices such that the worst performers have to leave the market. Since this is an ongoing process and innovations cannot be predicted by definition, there is no well-defined equilibrium in the EOE. I will use the Swedish micro-to-macro model to illustrate the incentive and competitive push mechanisms that keep a sufficient number of agents on their toes all the time, competing for improved wealth positions in markets, and to explain why they cannot lay back and relax, or in short, to explain the process of economic growth (Eliasson, 1991c).

A Generalized Salter Curve Analysis of Innovative Learning and Competition

A market, or the entire economy, can at each point in time be represented by a distribution of potential performance characteristics, like the rates of return over the interest rate ($\bar{\varepsilon}$) in Figure 1A. These types of distributions—especially if presented as productivity rankings of establishments (Fig. 1B)—are often referred to as Salter (1960) curves. Each firm is represented in this curve by a ranking on the vertical axis (the columns in Fig. 1), the width of the column measuring the size of the firm in percent of all other firms. Figure 1A shows that even though the firm in the model has increased its rate of return between 1983 and 1990, it has lost in ranking. Figure 1B shows the same firms' labor productivity and wage cost positions. Finally, each firm is operating under its productivity frontier to position itself on the productivity and rate of return rankings (see Eliasson, 1991c, Fig. 1). This is still actual *ex post* performance 1983 and (simulated) 1990. The dynamics of markets, on the other hand, are controlled by the potential *ex ante* set of distributions that capture the planned action of all other firms, including new entry.

There is a third set of Salter curves that tell how *each firm sees itself positioned relative to other firms*. The real world of the experimentally organized economy, as well as its model approximation, the Swedish micro-to-macro model, shows large divergences between actual and perceived positions.

The *ex ante* distributions tell the potential for the firm to outbid all other firms in wages, or in paying a higher interest rate.

Learning about one's competitive situation—in reality or in theory—occurs in different dimensions. Prices offered in the market tell something about how other firms—notably the best firms—view their competitive situation. Competition, production, hiring, etc. can also be directly observed. The firm, finally, learns directly itself, when it enters the market. The critical learning experience to observe in this context occurs when firms observe that competitors can do better. Firm management then knows that this *can be done* and that it had better improve in order not to be pushed down, right along the Salter distribution, and, perhaps, out.

Similarly, when the firm finds itself at the top, or close to the top, it knows that a whole lot of "closely inferior" firms feel threatened and are taking action to better their positions through innovation or imitative learning.

The conclusion is that if potential Salter distributions are sufficiently steep and if all firms know it, firms—and especially the top left-hand group —will feel sufficiently threatened to actively aim for improving their positions on the Salter curve through innovation. If such innovative activity, notably through innovative entry in markets, is freely allowed, necessary conditions for maintaining sufficiently steep Salter distributions to move the entire economy through a self-perpetuated competitive process have been established (Eliasson, 1985a, 1991a,c). These conditions become both necessary and sufficient if the opportunity set (Eliasson, 1987) is sufficiently large. This also establishes the link between dynamic competition through the Schumpeterian (1912) entrepreneur and innovative entry, argued by Smith (1776) to be the critical mover of macroeconomic growth that perpetuates the disequilibrium economic process type of Wicksell (1898). A sufficiently large and heterogeneous state space, boundedly rational behavior on the part of agents, and sufficiently free innovative entry are the small modifications of the classical model that create the experimentally organized economy.

The Swedish micro-to-macro (M-M) model exhibits these features. Dynamic competition as described above determines entry and exit, and hence the selective process that creates a path-dependent evolution, and the nonstationary behavior that prevents classical learning (see Lindh, 1993. This is the case even though the M-M model, for all practical purposes, is deterministic). If you have the code of the M-M model, you can of course predict through a deterministic simulation. The question was, however, whether you would be able to learn the structure of the model (to perform that prediction), without access to this code, from observing the output from a large number of simulations, and with such precision that it would predict over a chosen future period, barring a predetermined and limited stochastic error. This question reduces to the problems of (1) finding an acceptable, estimable approximation of the M-M model and (2) obtaining unbiased estimates of the parameters of that approximate model. If (3) the error terms between the M-M simulation ("reality") and the corresponding computed model values do not pass a test for randomness over any chosen simulation period, classical learning is not feasible and the particular behavioral characteristics of the firm of the EOE should exhibit themselves. The seemingly erratic behavior exhibited by the model economy, like major macro collapses that occur out of the blue (Eliasson, 1983, 1984, 1991c), all originate in the endogenous changes of the Salter distributions, characteristics that are impossible to reproduce in a predictable way by known estimable modeling techniques. This is sufficient to rule out classical learning in the experimental setting of the M-M model (I could also add the amusing experience we have had over the many years of modeling work. If you sit down at the computer and attempt to correct unexpected, disruptive, and "socially undesirable macro behavior" by using its almost full assortment of traditional policy parameters you tend to create more and stronger disruptive macro behavior of the same kind at some later period (Eliasson, 1985a, pp. 78 ff; Eliasson and Taymaz, 1992)).

The M-M model is an approximate dynamical systems representation of the real market economy. Even though individual mechanisms are traditional and can be understood partially, the dynamics of the evolving system prevents classical learning. Reality, of course, requires that much more complexity be coped with.

Innovative Entry and Creative Destruction Is the Key to Macro Dynamics

The critical understanding of markets, hence, comes with understanding the nature of competitive, innovative entry and the dynamic market process that innovative entry keeps in motion. This understanding requires a broad definition of entry, from the launching of a new product, via the establishment of a new company, to the merger of two large companies, with the purpose of improving long-term profit performance. Experience would suggest that small firms are superior to large firms as innovators, even though the consensus is not 100 percent (cf. Holmström, 1989; Granstrand and Sjölander, 1990). The large firms, however, together spend significantly more on R&D than do small firms. New entry is not always in the form of new firm entry. It can occur through the establishment of a new business activity within a large firm or through the introduction of a new product. As I said, the merger of two large firms exercises market effects similar to that of new entry (Eliasson, 1991a).

The role of small firms and new entry should be seen in the context of the following three observations:

1. The direct macroeconomic effects will be very slow in coming (Eliasson, 1991c). Empirical evidence shows very small effects within a 10-year period. Simulations on the Swedish micro-to-macro model show a significant direct macroeconomic influence only after some 20 years.

2. New innovative entry in a broad sense, however, serves as a competitive force to shake up incumbents and move the market from Ricardian to Schumpeterian-type competition. This influence on the macro economy is immediate, when incumbents realize the long-term competitive threat.
3. New entry preserves structural diversity, making faster growth feasible (Eliasson, 1984, 1991a). Even if entrants are on average no better than incumbents, the spread in performance among them is larger. Since only the best survive in the long run, viable entry and exit preserve the diversity of structure.

Hence, understanding competition requires understanding the forces that drive new entry, how this entry affects industry structure (the Salter curves), and potential competition as well as actual competition. This is not easy. First, the economic importance of exit as a consequence of competitive entry (creative destruction) has to be understood. If bad firms are not forced to leave the market, scarce factors will be locked up in the wrong production units, raising the level of factor costs. Simulation experiments on the Swedish micro-to-macro model (Eliasson and Lindberg, 1981) demonstrate that the macroeconomy could relatively easy cope with sizable investment mistakes, as long as the mistaken investments were forced, through competition, to be closed down quickly. The socially most costly thing to do was to carry on production in plants that did not, and could not, produce positive economic values above what the same factors would have created elsewhere in more profitable firms. The main reason for the negative growth effects in the macroeconomy was the increase in factor costs (notably wages) caused by the large locking-in effects in large and inefficient firms, due to the distorted rent perception associated with the corporate income tax system.

The extreme subsidy program in the 1970s to save the high-wage Swedish shipyards and mines from immediate bankruptcy and shutdown had even larger, negative macro effects on the Swedish economy (Carlsson et al., 1981; Carlsson, 1983a,b). Devaluation of the currency to "save jobs" will have the same negative long-term effects through saving badly managed firms and temporarily creating more unemployment in the long run. This observation on locking-in effects generalizes nicely to the entry and exit phenomenon. With the average new entrant being somewhat inferior to the average incumbent—if performance is measured by labor productivity or the rate of return (Granstrand, 1986)—but, the spread in performance being much wider, most new entrants will soon fail and exit. Good macroeconomic performance requires that they are allowed to fail and are even pushed to exit faster. The Swedish micro-to-macro model (Eliasson,

1977, 1978, 1990c) embodies this competition through new entry and exit typical of competition in the EOE. It occurs in the "broad-based Salter (1960) landscape of firms" described above, depicting the distribution of productivities or rates of return over the firm population. Entering firms are represented by a "smaller such Salter distribution" with a much wider spread, disrupting the balance on the margin in the tail end of incumbent firms, where the marginally worst producer just covers wage costs. Marginal incumbents exit and new product and factor prices are established at levels where most of the new entrants will soon perish and exit.

Many large incumbents will, however, be shaken by the remaining supreme entrants and be forced to shape up their competitive performance in order not to lose market shares, which presumably correspond to the size of their invested capacity to produce. In the very long run the remaining, superior "new" entrants will begin to exercise a direct influence at the macro level. Performance characteristics after a 30-year simulation show the upper left, "supreme" corner of the Salter distribution to be occupied by the new, now old entrants (Eliasson, 1991a). As most analytical results, this one is, however, obvious from the assumptions made. The critical issue is to understand *why* firms enter the market in large numbers, despite being inferior, and do it repeatedly.

Such phenomena cannot be explained within the static, full information general equilibrium model, and not within an asymmetric information version of the efficient market theory that is so popular in financial economics. It fits nicely, however, into the EOE. Under the assumptions of the EOE the entrants perform an experiment whose outcome cannot be assessed until it has been tested. There has to be a sufficiently large number of such potentially competent and optimistic entrants willing to perform business experiments for growth to occur.

At first sight it is tempting to approach this problem as a lottery with known or exogenously given odds. This is the standard procedure in R&D rivalry games that address similarly formulated problems. This is unacceptable for two reasons. First, the inclination of actors to play the lottery has to be explained. Second, the business lottery is a game in which you can learn to improve your odds, and this learning will affect the willingness to participate in the game. The standard lottery of economics (R&D rivalry and efficient market theory) has no learning of that kind. It is a stationary process that is unaffected by the ongoing business. Third, if the (market) economy is well organized (see below), the odds will be strongly tilted in favor of the competent actors. Once learning to improve your competence to participate in business is introduced, a path-dependent, nonstationary process emerges. Hence, competitive entry in the experimentally organized economy can only be explained if the theory clearly distinguishes between

Table 3. Competence specification of the experimentally organized firm

1. Sense of direction (intuition)
2. Willing to take risks
3. Efficient identification of mistakes
4. Effective correction of mistakes
5. Efficient coordination
6. Efficient learning feedback to (1)

Source: Eliasson (1990a).

ex ante and *ex post*. The new entrant exhibits strong risk willingness to the outsider based on a strong belief in its own competence (Table 3, item 1). The *ex ante/ex post* realization process (competition) filters out those entrants that were really good (Eliasson, 1991a). Hence, the *ex post* outcomes are also influenced by the competitive filter, which cannot, as we have shown, be characterized as a stationary process. What matters, however, besides this filter, is the entrepreneurial mentality, the culture that breeds these optimistic and bold entrants.

Third, and importantly, innovations are not well-defined events. Much of the ongoing upgrading of the capacities of an economic system can only be seen at very high levels of resolution, partly through piecemeal improvements of existing economic activities and partly through the introduction of new solutions and the phasing out of old solutions. The large, very visible (*ex post*) inventions of the steam engine, or more subtle generic electronics technologies, have been generating waves of higher and lower frequencies of innovations through increasing the immediately available business opportunity set, but the actual moving of the economy takes place on a small scale at the implementation level.

Once this empirical fact has been recognized, it follows that one also has to recognize the conditions, institutions, and organizational circumstances that allow the structural change process to occur. Economic growth or productivity change is a matter of institutional and organizational change. Hence sustained economic growth can only be understood when studied over a sufficiently long historic period to allow also the economic organization of the economy to change.

The Institutions of Economic Growth—The Case of Industrial Revolutions

The analyses of the previous sections can now be generalized to include not only the incentives moving rent-seeking innovators and entrepreneurs, but also their influence on economic structures and on the organization of the institutions of the economy that determine the distribution of rents. Apparently, and this is something we are relearning from the East European deregulation experience (Eliasson, 1991d, 1992c), as long as the problem is to introduce new technology into existing distribution schemes, we have only small political problems to cope with. But when new technology involves the renegotiation of existing distributional principles, the political process becomes immensely complex and slows down [cf. Block's (1966, pp. 124ff) interesting discussion of medieval crop rotation]. Among the many reasons for this are the risk-averse people who have no way of assessing the final outcome of the total adjustment, a circumstance that effectively blocks the reorganization of mature welfare economies towards something that has a chance for survival (Eliasson, 1986a). We can thus distinguish between four different layers of analysis: (1) *macro* economics with no recognition of institutions; (2) *given institutions* as in the static general equilibrium model, recognized by fixed parameters; (3) *exogenously changing institutions*, such as the rewriting of law, and (4) *endogenously changing institutions*. As we have finally learned the fourth case is critically important for economic growth to occur. It goes beyond the simple investment growth idea and multimarket interaction among given actors. It captures the slow-moving dynamic mechanisms associated with the exit and entry processes and feed backs when the economic process breaks down regulations, makes them redundant, or forces the rewriting of law.

Property Rights Made an Efficient Market Economy Possible

In their well-recognized book, North and Thomas (1973) observed that by the end of the 18th century the necessary institutions for the organization of a functioning market economy were in place in Great Britain and North America, notably the property rights system. The property rights system made it possible to define the rights to manage, to access the value of, and to trade in goods and land. Such trade is the essence of a market economy. The introduction of the property rights institution fundamentally changed the principles of income distribution. Economic growth rapidly changed speed in England and the United States.

The property rights system includes not only the legal possibilities of defining the goods to be traded but also the right to do so and the unrestricted right to enter into competition with existing producers. Hence, the property right system is instrumental in defining the firm of a viable market economy and its existence as a tradable entity in financial markets (Eliasson,

1992c). One could therefore say that the *institutional foundation of the industrial revolution gave the modern firm a role to play in the dynamic markets of the experimentally organized economy, releasing an enormous growth potential.*

Few restrictions on entry existed in England and North America at the time. In other countries the craft system restricted access to markets, and the industrial revolution did not begin until these restrictions had been taken off (Eliasson, 1991a). In those countries where the lid was not taken off, the industrial revolution did not occur, and they remained in a relatively nonindustrial state.

Four Scenarios of Fundamental Institutional Change

The industrial revolution brought a dramatic change in the economic organization of the country, forced by a new technology that both radically altered the production potential of the nation and also the principles for distributing its rents. Such dramatic changes are rare but merit very close study. In fact, three dramatic scenarios of similar consequences are currently, but slowly evolving around us. In addition to (a) the *industrial revolution* of the 19th century, three similar and currently ongoing dramatic reorganizations of the production and distribution systems of nations; (b) the new, gradually emerging *small-scale, competence-intensive production technology*; (c) the forced *dismantling of the welfare* system of some mature industrial nations; and (d) the economic *reorganization of Eastern Europe* will be briefly discussed.

The Industrial Revolution. The industrial revolution forced a dramatic economic reorganization from a handicraft-oriented industry and an economy dominated by agriculture to an industrial organization based on specialization around the machine tools of mechanical engineering industries. The growth potential of this reorganization was immense, but so also were the disruptive social consequences. Countries that were late to reorganize around those industrial technologies or could not cope with the social and political consequences never made it into the industrial age. Those who were early were those nations who gave up protection of the craft system early or had no protection of the crafts to begin with. An interesting observation to make is that the mature industrial nations are still, to a large extent, basing their industrial performance on the same organization around the same set of (now only more sophisticated) machine tools. One wonders what this means for the future.

The New, Small-Scale, Competence-Intensive Industries. The world is facing several similar situations of potentially dramatic reorganization right now. Mechanical engineering industries and other mature industries are no longer the potential growth generators. The future may be shaped by some other, smaller scale but much more competence-intensive production technology with dramatically different consequences for distribution (Eliasson, 1986b, pp. 18ff, pp. 72ff; 1990a, pp. 41–44, pp. 55ff). We can observe that some countries, regions, and firms are rapidly pushing themselves into this new organization around potentially very rewarding technologies. If they catch on rapidly, these changes may be socially and politically very disruptive; however, this will probably not be the case for innovative firms and industries but for the old firms and economies based on the old industrial organization, being unable to change.

Western European industry and North American industry are based on the same principal organization of production around a collection of machine tools developed during the industrial revolution. That industrial technology is rapidly being learned by other, less advanced nations, forcing change on the high-wage European and North American industries. It is instructive to observe that the competence that still keeps western firms ahead in the race is organizational, and not based on the actual manufacturing of goods (Eliasson, 1985b, 1990a). The giant multinationals that dominate western markets base their competitive performance on product development, global marketing, and manufacturing in combination, and the actual making of the goods may largely take place outside the mature industrial economies. The distress of automotive manufacturing is a case in point. What is interesting to consider is to what extent the mature industrial countries will be able to enter successfully the new production organization of the service-based, highly competence-intensive production structures now evolving around new information technology and science-based production (pharmaceuticals, fine chemicals, etc.). The entrepreneurial competence and incentives needed may not be around, and the political system may not be willing to accommodate to the necessary social adjustment.

The socioeconomic situation of the industrial revolution, that is, radical change of the organization of an economy and the difficulties in coping with it politically, is not all that unusual. During the industrial revolution the modern democratic form of government was unknown and organizational change was reasonably slow. Political power could not be mobilized to stop the process. Currently such radical reorganization processes, forcing drastic change on people, can be countered and slowed through the political process (Eliasson, 1986a).

Dismantling the Welfare State. A similar problem is associated with the dismantling of the state-operated welfare economies all over Europe, but in particular, its most extreme versions in Scandinavia. There are several sides to this dismantling. Costs for maintaining the redistributional transfer systems are outrunning economic growth, and politicians are slowly recognizing that incentives and economic growth have been affected negatively. Governments are also realizing that large parts of so-called public services can be produced more efficiently privately, with government restricting its responsibilities to the financing of some of this service production. Thus, even education and health care are being privatized. This deregulation of formerly protected public production activities, amounting in some countries to significantly more than half of GNP, is similar in principle to the deregulation of the relatively much smaller manufacturing production during the industrial revolution and to the deregulation of Eastern European economies. The serious problem with deregulating the welfare states is that the consequences are very complex to figure out and affect the voters directly. Such changes are thus politically resisted, even though most would benefit (Eliasson, 1986a). Hence, in the long run the welfare states might not make the transition and may be overcome by some East European nations that succeed in reorganizing their manufacturing sectors.

From Plan to Markets. The big difference to the welfare state is that the formerly planned economies have destroyed their manufacturing sectors as well as other production sectors. With the engine room of the economy in a mess, the crisis of the formerly planned economies is immensely larger than that of the mismanaged welfare economies. On the other hand, the potential for growth in the long run is much larger in the East European economies, if they can make it. There is no "soft" way of fixing leaking pipes and collapsing mounts. The whole machine has to be replaced, including its staffing. The conflicts between distributional principles and rent-creating capacity are, however, manifest. Their solutions hinge on the time dimension of the adjustment process and the uncertainties associated with the transformation. The long-run potential outcome of transforming a planned economy into a market economy is clearly very much superior to the initial, current situation. But the distributional consequences along the transition process are very negative and impossible, both to comprehend and to control. Politicians have a very reduced role to play in that process and hence tend to slow it down rather than to promote it. The time dimension pushes the fruits of the transformation outside reach for the older part of the population. The transformation, furthermore, moves previously privileged persons down the relative welfare scales. Above all, whether justified or not, people fear the unknown consequences. Thus, the political counteraction operates on the adjustment of the institutions that control the distributional consequences. Hence, the privatization process that should have come first (Eliasson, 1991d) is slowed down.

Can an Orderly Transition from Plan to Market be Planned?

The rents created in the new, open organization are, however, so large that new activities are, nevertheless, created all the time, but not on the scale needed to rapidly exploit the potential. The Eastern European nations are thus facing a difficult dilemma.

Can they wait for prosperity as long as it takes for newly entering firms and entrepreneurs to become large enough to move the macroeconomy, and just let the old actors slowly die, that is, wait a generation or so? Or is the presence of obsolete production structures from the past an obstacle to new innovative entry?

The question arises: Can an orderly transition from plan to market be planned? Is it possible, for instance, to speed up transformation significantly without disrupting the country socially through inviting foreign investment? Is it necessary—in order to get economic growth moving—to reorganize or dismantle the old production structures with all the social turmoil that would follow.

The answer is both no and yes. Firstly, a planned transition from plan to market is a contradiction. The transition requires a fundamental reorganization of the entire economy towards an experimental organization, the best outcome of which only the market can determine. Significant unexpected adjustments at the micro level will be necessary. There exists no competent political process to engineer that transition.

However, the efficiency of the micro transition depends on the existing institutions, to a large extent embodied in the political system. This is the case in both the welfare and planned economies. These institutions are, in large measure, detrimental, both to the transition process itself and to the functioning of the market economy (Eliasson, 1986a, 1992c). Labor market law, and the existing politically supported and dominant labor union organization of Europe, based on an 100-year old work organization, is the perhaps most serious obstacle to necessary changes in the industrial nations. Hence, the task of the political system is to reorganize itself such that the institutional impediments it has itself created are changed or removed! In both the welfare and the formerly planned economies, the desired outcome is to relieve the productive powers of agents in the markets (firms and individuals) of the institutional restrictions imposed from above. Hence, creative destruction, to use Schumpeter's theory, is needed not only to reallocate resources for growth where they are most productively employed and at factor prices that do not discourage growth through new investment and new entry, but also creative destruction is as important among the institutions that control the rent-creating and reallocation processes. This political change process, paradoxically, appears to be even more difficult than the reorganization of physical production structures. Perhaps this difficulty reflects the fact (Eliasson, 1990b, p. 285, footnote) that political institutions are not organized for effective corrective action. Their guiding principle is to make the right decisions from the beginning. Since this is in general not possible in the experimentally organized economy, such behavior is irrational. It should be taken as evidence that the political element in economic decisions should be minimized.

Notes

1. This paper summarizes the results of a number of my recent studies, notably Eliasson (1987, 1988a, 1990a,b,c, 1991a,c).
2. See Eliasson (1990a, p. 57) on automation of factory production.
3. Please note that this is the only type of knowledge recognized by classical theory, including so-called efficient market theory.
4. This is also the design of the Swedish micro-to-macro model, on which much of my reasoning is based (Eliasson, 1991c). The reader should note that with the marginalists since the late 19th century, the business opportunity set has been defined such that local agents operate on its frontiers (fully informed agents). This takes all dynamics out of the economy, except the exogenous shifting of the opportunity set, or the production frontier.
5. For a discussion, see Eliasson (1987, 1988a, 1990b, 1991c).

References

Block, M. 1966. *Land and Work in Medieval Europe*. London: Routledge and Kegan Paul.

Carlsson, B. 1980. "The Content of Productivity Growth in Swedish Manufacturing." In *The Firms in the Market Economy, 40 years 1939–1979*. Stockholm: IUI.

Carlsson, B. 1983a. "Industrial Subsidies in Sweden: Macro-Economic Effects and an International Comparison. "*Journal of Industrial Economics* 32(1):1–23.

Carlsson, B. 1983b. "Industrial Subsidies in Sweden: Simulations on a Micro-to-Macro Model." In *Microeconometrics, IUI Yearbook 1982–1983*. Stockholm: IUI.

Carlsson, B. 1989. "The Evolution of Manufacturing Technology and Its Impact on Industrial Structure: An International Study." *Small Business Economy* 1(1):21–37.

Carlsson, B. 1991. "Productivity Analysis: A Micro-to-Macro Perspective." In *Technology and Investment—Crucial Issues for the 1990s*. E. Deiaco, E. Hörnell, and G. Vickery, eds. London: Pinter.

Carlsson, B. 1992. "Industrial Dynamics and the Role of Small Plants in Swedish Manufacturing Industry 1968–1988." Paper presented at the conference on Management of Technology, Grenoble, October 13–14, 1992, IUI Working Paper No. 348, Stockholm: IUI.

Carlsson, B., Dahmén, E., Grufman, A., Josefsson, M., and Örtengren, J. 1979. *Teknik och industristruktur—70-talets ekonomiska kris i historisk belysning* (Swedish Technology and Industrial Structure—the Crisis of the Seventies in Historic Perspective). Stockholm: IUI and IVA.

Carlsson, B., Bergholm, F., and Lindberg, T. 1981. *Industristödspolitiken och dess inverkan på samhällsekonomin* (*Industry Subsidy Policy and its Macroeconomic Impact*). Stockholm: IUI.

Chandler, A.D. 1977. *The Visible Hand: The Managerial Revolution in American Business*. Cambridge: Harvard University Press.

Day, R.H., Eliasson, G., and Wihlborg, C. (eds.). 1993. *The Markets for Innovation, Ownership and Control*. Amsterdam: North-Holland and Stockholm: IUI.

Eliasson, G. 1976. *Business Economic Planning—Theory, Practice and Comparison*. London: John Wiley & Sons.

Eliasson, G. 1977. "Competition and Market Processes in a Simulation Model of the Swedish Economy." *American Economic Review* 67(1):277–281.

Eliasson, G. 1978. *A Micro-to-Macro Model of the Swedish Economy*. IUI Conference Reports 1978:1. Stockholm: IUI, p. 1.

Eliasson, G. 1983. "On the Optimal Rate of Structural Adjustment." In *Policy Making in a Disorderly World Economy*. G. Eliasson, M. Sharefkin and B.-C. Ysander, eds. IUI Conference Reports 1983:1. Stockholm: IUI, p. 1.

Eliasson, G. 1984. "Micro Heterogeneity of Firms and the Stability of Industrial Growth." *Journal of Economic Behavior and Organization* 5:249–274.

Eliasson, G. 1985a. *The Firm and Financial Markets in the Swedish Micro-to-Macro Model—Theory, Model and Verification*. Stockholm: IUI.

Eliasson, G. 1985b. "De svenska storföretagen—en studie av internationaliseringens konsekvenser för den svenska ekonomin." In *De svenska storföretagen* (The Giant Swedish Industrials). G. Eliasson et al. Stockholm: IUI, pp. 7–70.

Eliasson, G. 1986a. "On the Stability of Economic Organizational Forms and the Importance of Human Capital: A Proposition about the Endogenous, Market Induced Disintegration of the Non-Market Sector." In *The Dynamics of Market Economies*. R.H. Day, and G. Eliasson, eds. Amsterdam: North-Holland and Stockholm: IUI, pp. 454–467.

Eliasson, G. 1986b. "Kompetens, kommunikation och kunskapsuppbyggnad—sammanfattning och arbetshypotes för industripolitiken." In *Kunskap, information och tjänster* (The Manufacturing Firm as an Information Processer and Service Producer). G. Eliasson, B. Carlsson, E. Deiaco, T. Lindberg, and T. Pousette, eds. Stockholm: IUI, pp. 9–38.

Eliasson, G. 1987. "Technological Competition and Trade in the Experimentally Organized Economy," IUI Research Report No. 32. Stockholm: IUI.

Eliasson, G. 1988a. "Schumpeterian Innovation, Market Structure and the Stability of Industrial Development." In *Evolutionary Economics, Applications of Schumpeter's Ideas*. H. Hanusch, ed. Cambridge, UK: Cambridge University Press, pp. 151–199.

Eliasson, G. 1988b. "The International Firm: A Vehicle for Overcoming Barriers to Trade and a Global Intelligence Organization Diffusing the Notion of a Nation." IUI Booklet No. 295. Stockholm: IUI.

Eliasson, G. 1990a. *The Knowledge Based Information Economy*. In Eliasson, G. et al. The Knowledge Based Information Economy. Stockholm: IUI.

Eliasson, G. 1990b. "The Firm as a Competent Team." *Journal of Economic Behavior and Organization* 13(3):275–298.

Eliasson, G. 1990c. "The Firm, its Objectives, its Controls and its Organization." IUI Working Paper No. 266. Stockholm: IUI.

Eliasson, G. 1991a. "Deregulation, Innovative Entry and Structural Diversity as a Source of Stable and Rapid Economic Growth." *Journal of Evolutionary Economics* (1):49–63.

Eliasson, G. 1991c. "Modeling the Experimentally Organized Economy; Complex Dynamics in an Empirical Micro-Macro Model of Endogenous Economic Growth." *Journal of Economic Behavior and Organization* 16(1–2):153–182.

Eliasson, G. 1991d. "The Micro Frustrations of Privatizing Eastern Europe." IUI Working Paper No. 306. Stockholm: IUI.

Eliasson, G. 1991e. "Financial Institutions in a European Market for Executive Competence". In C. Wihlborg, M. Fratianni and T.D. Willetts, eds. *Financial Regulation and Monetary Arrangements after 1992*. Amsterdam: Elsevier Science B.V., pp. 149–166.

Eliasson, G. 1992a. "Business Competence, Organizational Learning and Economic Growth—Establishing the Smith–Schumpeter–Wicksell (SSW) Connection." In *Entrepreneurship, Technological Innovation, and Economic Growth. Studies in the Schumpeterian Tradition*. F.M. Scherer and M. Perlman, eds. Ann Arbor: The University of Michigan Press.

Eliasson, G. 1992c. "A Note: On Privatization, Contract Technology and Economic Growth." IUI Working Paper No. 339, Stockholm. To appear in R.H. Day, G. Eliasson and C. Wihlborg, eds. (1993).

Eliasson, G., and Lindberg, T. 1981. "Allocation and Growth Effects of Corporate Income Taxes." In *Business Taxation, Finance and Firm Behavior*. G. Eliasson and J. Södersten, eds. IUI Conference Reports 1981:1, Stockholm: IUI, pp. 381–435.

Eliasson, G., and Taymaz, E. 1992. "The Limits of Policy Making: An Analysis of the Consequences of Boundedly Rational Government using the Swedish Micro-to-Macro model (MOSES)." IUI Working Paper No. 333. Stockholm: IUI.

Granstrand, O. 1986. "On Measuring and Modelling Innovative New Entry in Swedish Industry." In *The Dynamics of Market Economies*. R.H. Day and G. Eliasson, eds. Amsterdam: North-Holland and Stockholm: IUI, pp. 295–310.

Granstrand, O., and Sjölander, S. 1990. "The Acquisition of Technology and Small Firms by Large Firms." *Journal of Economic Behavior and Organization* 13(3):367–386.

Holmström, B. 1989. "Agency Costs and Innovation." *Journal of Economic Behavior and Organization* 12(3):305–327.

Jagrén, L. 1988. "Företagens tillväxt i ett historiskt perspektiv." In *Expansion, avveckling och företagsvärdering i svensk industri.* J. Örtengren et al. Stockholm: IUI.

Knight, F. 1921. *Risk, Uncertainty and Profit.* Boston: Houghton-Mifflin.

Lindh, T. 1993. "*Lessons from Learning About Rational Expectations.*" In R.H. Day, G. Eliasson and C. Wihlborg, eds. (1993), pp. 81–115.

Loasby, B.J. 1991. "Alfred Marshall's Connecting Principles of Firms and Markets." Paper presented to the RES Annual Conference, University of Warwick, April 8, 1991.

Mill, J.S. 1848. *Principles of Political Economy with Some of Their Applications to Social Philosophy*. London.

North, D., and Thomas, P. 1973. The Rise of the Western World. Cambridge: Cambridge University Press.

Pratten, C. 1976. *A Comparison of the Performance of Sweden and UK Companies.* Cambridge, UK: Cambridge University Press.

Salter, W.E.G. 1960. *Productivity and Technical Change.* Cambridge, UK: Cambridge University Press.

Schumpeter, J.A. 1912. (English edition 1934). *The Theory of Economic Development*, Harvard Economic Studies, Vol. XLVI. Cambridge: Harvard University Press.

Schumpeter, J.A. 1942. *Capitalism, Socialism and Democracy.* New York: Harper & Row.

Simon, H.A. 1955. "A Behavioral Model of Rational Choice." *Quarterly Journal of Economics* 69:99–118.

Smith, A. 1776. *An Inquiry into the Nature and Causes of the Wealth of Nations.* New York: Modern Library, 1973.

Stigler, G.J. 1951. "The Division of Labor is Limited by the Extent of the Market." *Journal of Political Economy* 59:185–193.

Wicksell, K. 1898. *Geldzins und Güterpreise* (*Interest and Prices*). New York: AMK Bookseller, 1965.

7 EVOLUTIONARY REGIMES AND INDUSTRIAL DYNAMICS

Giovanni Dosi
Franco Malerba
Luigi Orsenigo

Introduction

This paper concerns the relationship between the observed patterns of evolution of industry structures and the underlying microeconomic processes that might account for them. It should certainly come as no surprise that the forms of organization of industries differ significantly across sectors. In fact, this observation has been at the origin of decades of research in industrial economics, attempting to account for such differences by looking at structural variables that characterize any individual industry (such as economies of scale, size of the market, etc.). More recently, emphasis has shifted to the relevance of the strategic behavior of firms as the major determinant of industrial organization.

Early contributions to industrial economics—such as Mason or Bain—emphasized the importance of some relatively invariant features of production technologies as ultimate determinants of observed structures and performances under an implicit assumption that microeconomic behaviors would be shaped—at least in a first approximation—by these deeper technological constraints. In the late 1950s, Sylos Labini (1958), building on this *structuralist* setup, added a notion of *path dependency*: any observed industrial structure is the result of a specific history of growth/decline of particular size frequencies, which in turn are associated with different technologies.[1] On the behavioral side, the model involves what are generally called *boundedly rational* behaviors (e.g., mark-up pricing, etc.). However, in most of the discipline, the interpretative focus has been increasingly placed on the motives and the rational decision procedures of individual agents, and, symmetrically, structural constraints on microbehaviors have been treated in a rather casual manner (the "New Industrial Organization" is a good case in point).

Still, if one takes the two opposite archetypes, namely structuralist theories of the 1950s and contemporary—for example, game-theoretic—models, one easily finds in both a strong static and equilibrium flavour. In the former, the burden of the interpretation of empirical regularities is pushed upon unexplained features of sectoral production functions. In the latter, the core of the exercise is an *ex post* generalization showing that whatever is observed can also be interpreted as the equilibrium outcome of some (rather sophisticated) strategic interactions.

Central to any Schumpeterian or evolutionary perspective is, on the contrary, the emphasis on diversity and change. Market structure, in this perspective, is analyzed as endogenously emerging out of evolutionary processes of discovery and adaptation in environments characterized by a variety in behaviors and uncertainty. Economic analysis of industrial evolution should therefore focus on understanding the nature of the *learning and selection processes* that generate industrial structures.

The evolutionary approach, in our view, tries to identify relatively invariant (1) *sources* of innovative opportunities, (2) industrial *characteristics*, (3) *processes* of innovative explorations, and (4) *mechanisms* of interfirm *interactions*.

In a very loose biological analogy, the industrial characteristics belong to the same level of analysis as Linnean taxonomies of species, families, etc.; the sources relate to the notional domain of opportunities upon which innovation draws, *processes* clearly relate to the mutation dynamics; and *mechanisms of interaction* underlie selection processes.

It may be surprising to realize how little we know about how industries evolve over time. The life-cycle hypothesis is possibly one of the few generalizations produced by empirical analysis, and still it is not sufficiently robust. The stability of the firm size distribution is another important result, but no undisputed (and empirically corroborated) theoretical explanation has yet been produced. Recently, however, some interesting empirical research has concentrated on the analysis of the patterns of industrial change, reconsidering older results and presenting novel evidence and puzzles.

In particular, one may observe a puzzling coexistence between variety, stability, and change. One may start from the naive observation of high degrees of diversity in firms' technological capabilities, organization, strategies, and ultimately efficiency, both across industries and within industries. Together with this diversity, one also observes significant changes. Technological progress is a major engine of change and is ubiquitous. Many firms enter a sector in any given period of time and many other exit it. The rankings of the largest (or more profitable) companies change significantly over time. Similarly, industries as a whole emerge, grow, stabilize, and eventually decline. Growth, stagnation, and decline of firms and industries, and more generally turbulence, appear to be a fundamental feature of industrial evolution.

Coexisting with variety and change, however, industrial evolution seems to be characterized also by remarkable degrees of persistence. This is particularly evident in the case of investments in innovative efforts and innovative performances. In addition, profitability differentials among firms tend to persist over time. At the same time, some aggregate regularities, such as relatively invariant skewed distributions of firm sizes, may be observed.

Finally, large and significant intersectoral differences in the degrees of variety, persistence, and change are seen. In some sectors diversity is more pronounced, whilst in others firms are relatively more similar to one another. Technological change derives in some industries from the activities of a few large companies that innovate systematically over time, whilst in others new small companies play a significant role in the generation of technical progress. The degree of market share volatility, the persistence of profitability above the norm, and the relative role of small firms also differ widely across industries.

In general, a satisfactory theory of industrial evolution should therefore start from and try to account for (a) the existence of significant and persistent variety within and across sectors in firm behavior and organization; (b) the existence of sectoral specificities in the patterns of industrial dynamics, and (c) the existence of regularities and "order" in the patterns of industrial dynamics, despite such variability at the micro level.

In what follows we present an interpretation of the available evidence based on an "evolutionary" analysis of industrial dynamics. We try to provide some substance to the fundamental contention that market structures are endogenous to the processes of industry evolution and have to be explained as the emergent outcome of evolutionary processes of learning and selection. In particular, we claim that both the "stylized facts" mentioned above and the sectoral variety can be explained as the outcome of different learning and selection regimes that are implied by the nature of technology. Moreover, we conjecture that these stylized regularities are to be analyzed as *emergent properties* of processes of complex disequilibrium dynamics. Since the economics of innovation has been the origin and the main subject of interest of evolutionary economics, the following discussion will be concerned mainly with technological innovation. Other phenomena, however, concerning various aspects of firm behavior and industrial dynamics, will also be examined.

The paper is organized as follows. First some empirical evidence on the patterns of innovation and industrial dynamics is discussed. Next the concept of *technological regime* is introduced and it is argued that this can be used fruitfully at the empirical level to provide a framework for analyzing different phenomena as firms' innovative strategies and organization, sectoral patterns of innovative activities, and some crucial aspects of industrial dynamics. Finally, some preliminary theoretical exercises meant to "explain" the evidence on technological regimes and the dynamics of industrial structures are presented.

Patterns of Innovation and Industrial Dynamics: An Emerging Empirical Evidence

One of the major results of empirical studies on the sources and patterns of innovation is that technological change proceeds differently across technologies, industries, and over time. Such diversity concerns the sources of innovation, the organization of innovative activities, the set of competences involved in the innovation process, and the type as well as the rates of technical change. However, important regularities in the sectoral patterns of technological change are also found.

Sectoral Patterns of Innovative Activities

A first attempt to put some order in this diversity is Pavitt's taxonomy (Pavitt, 1984) of the patterns of organization of innovative activities and features of technological change. According to Pavitt, four basic sectoral patterns of innnovative activities can be identified:

- *Science-based industries*, in which R&D and learning by searching are key elements in firms' innovative activities. The structure of the industry is characterized by large oligopolistic firms with advanced and often diversified competences (the *core* of the industries), and in several cases also by small new Schumpeterian firms (the *fringe*). Major as well as incremental innovations are frequent. Technological trajectories may involve increases in performance and physical properties of products, as well as improvements in process yields.

- *Scale-intensive industries*, in which scale economies and productive features play a relevant role in competition among firms and in shaping the structure of the industry. Learning by doing and by using, as well as R&D, play a major role in the innovative activities of firms. The structure of the industry is characterized by large firms, usually upstream vertically integrated, with long-term relationships with equipment suppliers. High barriers to entry are present. Production and engineering competences play a major role in affecting competition among firms. Both process and product innovations are important. At the process level, technological trajectories are focused on the improvements of process yields, increases in the scale of production processes, and automation.
- *Specialized supplier industries*, in which firm competencies in development, engineering, and design, and the ability to adapt and tailor products to user needs, are highly idiosyncratic and mostly tacit. They generate products aimed at specific applications, market segments, or single users. Interactions with users are relevant in the innovative process and give a relatively high appropriability of product innovations. The structure of the industry in often made of small- and medium-size firms that are highly specialized (or at most, diversified in correlated applications or market segments). Product innovations, mostly of the incremental type, are common. Technological trajectories relate to improvements in the performance and reliability of products.
- *Supplier dominated*, in which innovative activity is rather limited (mainly of a learning by using and by doing type), centered on incremental improvements and adaptation of new capital equipment, which have been developed and produced by upstream suppliers. The rapidity in adopting new technologies, rather than the generation of new process and products, becomes a key element in the competitive process. This implies that the speed of diffusion, rather than technological innovation itself, becomes crucial in industrial dynamics. Firms in the industry are of small and medium size. Technological trajectories are aimed at improvements in process yields.

Schumpeterian Patterns of Innovation

At a different level of analysis, another taxonomy concerns the patterns of innovative activity according to some typical learning patterns of firms over time. It is convenient to classify them on the grounds of the two extreme Schumpeterian models of innovation: *Schumpeter Mark I* (Schumpeter, 1939; characterized by technological ease of entry in an industry and by a major role played by new firms in innovative activities) and *Schumpeter Mark II* (Schumpeter, 1950; characterized by the prevalence of large, established firms in innovative activities and by relevant barriers to entry for new innovators). Schumpeter Mark I and II patterns of innovations could also be labelled *widening* and *deepening*. A widening pattern of innovative activities is related to an innovative base that is continuously enlarged by the permanent entry of new innovators and the continuous erosion of the competitive and technological advantages of the established firms in the industry. A deepening pattern of innovation, on the contrary, is related to the dominance of a few firms that are continuously innovative through the accumulation over time of technological capabilities.

Malerba and Orsenigo (1992) have developed an empirical analysis of the patterns of innovation in four countries, Germany (Federal Republic), France, the United Kingdom, and Italy. Patterns have been identified according to several dimensions: concentration of innovative activities and asymmetries among innovators, size of innovating firms, change over time in the hierarchy of innovators, and relevance of new innovators compared to established ones. A few remarkable results emerge from this analysis.

First, a significant similarity is observed in the sectoral patterns of technological change across countries. Second, not only are large firms responsible for the largest share of patenting activities, but innovative activities are also characterized by high degrees of concentration and stability in the hierarchy of major innovators. These results would seem to provide preliminary support to the Schumpeter Mark II model in the explanation of the patterns of innovation in contemporary advanced industrial economies. However, various indicators of the patterns of innovative activities differ consistently across technological classes in each country. For example, as far as the concentration of innovative activities is concerned, technological classes, such as agricultural chemicals, mineral oils, dyeing, nuclear reactors, aircraft, semiconductors, and photography, show very high degrees of concentration in all four countries, while nonmetallic minerals, metallurgical processes, chemical apparati, nonelectrical industrial equipment, and metal products have low degrees of concentration.

This lends support to the hypothesis that innovative activities do not conform simply and in general to any one of the two Schumpeterian models; rather, they appear to display different combinations between the two archetypes. More specifically, empirical investigation suggests that systematic differences in the patterns of innovative activities can be found in the three main technological families: chemicals, electronics, and mechanics. Chemicals and electronics seem to have the characteristics of the Schumpeter II model, whilst mechanical industries seem to show a Schumpeter I model.

Finally, an important property of stability of innovative activities emerges, especially in relation to technological performance. A significant correlation emerges between international technological performance and the various indicators of stability. Econometric analysis shows that technological performance is significantly and positively affected by, for example, limited change in the hierarchy of leading innovators, both in the deepening and widening technological classes. This means that the international technological performance of a country in a specific technological class is closely associated with the presence of a rather stable group of leading innovators, who innovate consistently and continuously over time. It also implies that what matters most for the successful technological performance of a country is not the mere presence of large firms or high concentration rates (the traditional variables used in empirical analyses of the relationship between market structure and innovation). Rather, the processes of *creative accumulation* of technological competencies and the cumulative technological advancements generated by a stable core of innovators appear to be relevant factors in the explanation of the international technological performance of countries.

Industries' Evolution and Life Cycles

Ideally, a satisfactory evolutionary analysis would require both a comprehensive taxonomy of the sectoral patterns of innovation and a full dynamic story of the life cycle of each industry. Neither is currently available. However, some basic properties have been identified by empirical analysis.

- The rates and directions of technological innovation within an industry change over time. Whilst the history of different industries does not allow any sweeping generalization, in several cases firms appear to focus first on product innovations and on a dominant design and, subsequently, on process innovations and incremental product improvements (once a dominant product design has emerged;

Abernathy and Utterback, 1978).

- Entry of new firms may differ along the life cycle. In the early days of an industry, when technology is rapidly changing and the uncertainty of future developments is high, rates of entry of new firms are also high (Gort and Klepper, 1982; Gort and Konakayama, 1982) because public information about technologies is still widespread and incumbents do not have major advantages over entrants in terms of accumulated capabilities. Later on, rates of entry decrease and new firms grow and become large. Specific technological trajectories become established, and sometimes opportunity conditions decline during the development of the industry. In general, the empirical evidence drawn from several industries points to a decline in opportunity conditions from new to established industries.
- Other case studies of high-technology industries highlight how the organization of firms and industries evolve over time. Dosi (1984) and Malerba (1985), for instance, show in the case of the semiconductor industry how the knowledge sources of innovation and, relatedly, the relevant competences of firms have changed in the course of the history of the industry, moving from science in the early days to applied research, design, and engineering and, in general, to firms' internal tacit skills. Relatedly, the industry dynamics has been characterized by competition among and within two types of firms: vertically integrated electronics producers and merchant firms. Waves of new entrants have been associated with technological discontinuities, such as the transistor, the integrated circuit, and the microprocessor. Finally, the change in the nature of the knowledge base for application-specific integrated circuits added recently the possibility of a division of labor between firms that design circuits and those that produce the integrated circuits with a design received from design houses. In general, industry structure has evolved from an oligopoly based solely on differentials in innovative capabilities towards an oligopolistic structure based also on scale economies and on the control of specific market niches.

In the case of biotechnology, Orsenigo (1989) emphasizes the division of labor between new companies—specialized in R&D activities in the new technologies, but lacking competences and organizational structures in manufacturing and marketing—and large established corporations, which need to have access to the new technologies. This has led to the development of complex organizational arrangements, centered upon the establishment of linkages of various sorts (involving, at the same time, cooperation and competition, hierarchical and market-based relationships) between the new and the established companies. As the technology developed, however, pressures towards increasing degrees of vertical integration became stronger, although collaboration remains a crucial feature of the industry.

Patterns of Industrial Dynamics

Together with the patterns of innovation, a growing body of empirical studies highlights some important stylized facts about industrial dynamics.

Entry, Exit, Market "Turbulence". A first set of "stylized facts" concerns the rates of entry and exit. It appears that most industries are characterized by significant degrees of *turbulence* (Acs and Audretsch, 1990; Beesley and Hamilton, 1984). Thus, the firms composing a given industry are constantly changing through processes of entry and exit.

In particular, *gross entry* is a pervasive phenomenon in manufacturing (and more so in service industries). Birth rates are quite high in most industries, even in those characterized by high degrees of capital intensity (Acs and Audretsch, 1989, 1991). Most entrants are small firms, far below any measure of minimum efficient scale, and a large percentage of new entrants exit the industry within a few years after entry. However, an important source of entry stems from incumbent firms operating in other industries or countries that diversify into other sectors. In this case, entry often occurs via acquisition of existing plants. The role of this second type of entry is limited in terms of the number of firms, but is much more important in terms of their share of output or employment.

It must be noticed also that we know very little about the degree of turbulence in the "core" of the industry among large firms. Older studies (Kaplan, 1964; Collins and Preston, 1961; Mermelstein, 1969; Bond, 1975) suggested a relative stability in the hierarchy of large firms: rates of turnover among the largest corporations appeared to be small and declining over time. Acs and Audretsch (1991) confirm that turbulence among small firms is higher than among large firms by an estimate of 35% in the 247 manufacturing industries included in their sample.

Mortality is, however, high too, so that *net entry* is much smaller than gross entry and significant turbulence characterizes industrial evolution. Moreover, the probability of survival increases or at least variation in performance stabilizes with size and age (Aldrich and Auster, 1987; Acs and Audretsch, 1991, 1992).

These results would seem to suggest that turbulence is primarily a characteristic of the fringe of the industry. This is confirmed by the observation that substitution of "old" firms with "new" firms occurs to a much larger extent among small, young firms that are relatively similar to each other. In other words, entrants in the fringe often are not more efficient than the incumbents. Turbulence is much lower in the core if the industry and among larger firms. The latter appear to be relatively sheltered from selective pressures.

Turbulence differs drastically across sectors, however. Econometric literature investigating the determinants of birth rates is now burgeoning, and it is now possible to draw some consistent results.

1. Turbulence tends to be comparatively lower in industries characterized by high rates of innovation and advertising, high capital intensity, low concentration, low growth (Acs and Audretsch, 1991). However, one has to distinguish between the determinants of gross entry, net entry, and exit, and between large and small firms.

2. In particular, advertising appears to constitute a greater barrier than capital intensity to both gross and net entry, irrespective of firm size. Concentration seems to inhibit the entry of small firms but not of large companies. Similarly, high rates of innovation do not necessarily deter small firms from entry. In certain industries in which small firms account for a significant share of total innovative activities, birth rates are rather high.

Evidence is less clear about the role played by variables such as industry growth and profitability. The latter variable does not seem to have any significant effect in attracting entry, whilst mixed results are obtained for industry growth. Similarly, the growth of GNP (but also unemployment) appears to trigger new firm formation. In any case, there appears to be no robust evidence on the cyclic behavior of birth and death rates. Some studies report a strong correlation between indicators of favorable macroeconomic conditions, birth rates (positive), and death rates (negative). Other studies, however, find an absence of correlation or even an inverse correlation (as in the models of self-employment).

3. The probability of exiting the industry increases for small and young companies (Acs and Audretsch, 1990; Evans (1987a,b); Dunne et al. (1989); Aldrich and Auster, 1987).[2] Moreover, the probability of survival of new, small firms appears to be lower in capital-intensive industries and in sectors characterized by high rates of innovation and high economies of scale. However, further distinctions need to be made. Concentration, scale economies, and capital intensity actually seem to facilitate survival in the short run, but not in the long run. Indicators of innovativeness do not affect survival in the short run, but only in the long run. Moreover, survival is also easier in those industries in which small firms are important sources of innovation.

Finally, it must be noted that surviving firms have either a higher initial size or higher growth rates. Bigger initial size implies lower growth, but higher survival. Surviving new firms tend to grow faster in innovative industries. Scale economies and capital intensity have a positive effect on growth in the short run: surviving firms tend to grow faster in the early periods, but afterwards those disadvantages do not matter.

In sum, capital intensity does not affect entry but rather survival, and thus turbulence. Surviving firms appear to grow faster as a function of the gap between minimum efficient scale (MES) of output and firm size. At the same time, however, the likelihood of survival decreases as a function of that gap. The same happens in terms of innovation rates. Thus, factors promoting growth reduce survival and vice-versa. An exception is the industry growth rate, which has a positive effect on both growth and survival.

Interfirm Asymmetries. A second set of stylized facts concerns the existence and persistence of significant differentials in productivity (Nelson and Winter, 1982) and profitability across firms and (at least in the United States) across industries (Mueller, 1990). Firms enjoying higher (lower) profits tend to earn higher (lower) profits in the future. Profits, thus, do not converge on a common rate of return, but some firms earn above normal rates of return for a statistically unspecified "long time."

The observed persistence of profitability differentials reflects both the existence of permanent differentials in "efficiency" among firms, which are not eroded away by the competitive process, and the sluggishness of the competitive process that should generate convergence to "long run equilibrium." However, the evidence seems to indicate that the adjustment of profits to "permanent" values is relatively quick, although high variability is observed in across-country comparisons.

Persistence of profits appears to depend both on industry-specific characteristics and on firm-specific characteristics. In particular, industry-specific features, such as the intensity of advertising and R&D, appear to be robust explanatory variables of the persistence of profits above the norm. The significance of firm-specific variables, on the other hand, varies across sectors. Firm effects are important *within* any one industry. Thus, for instance, market share is positively related to profitability in the presence of high advertising and patent intensity.

Empirical evidence is rather fuzzy, as it concerns the effects of industry- and firm-specific variables of the speed of adjustment. Important differences among countries and industries emerge in both the extent to which profit differentials permanently persist and in the speed of adjustment to "equilibrium." In general, however, firm-specific variables are more important in explaining the long-run "equilibrium" levels of company profits, whilst industry-specific variables are more important in the explanation of the adjustment process to those long-run equilibrium values. In the United States, excess returns appear to erode more slowly in highly concentrated industries, experiencing rapid demand growth, and are characterized by significant economies of scale, large absolute capital requirements, large sunk outlays, and high advertising expenditures (Kessides, 1990). (Other studies, however, challenge these results, cf. Odagiri and Yamawaki, 1990).

Size Distributions. The last set of stylized facts concerns the remarkable stability of a skewed distribution of firm and plant size, approximately a Pareto distribution, with the highest frequency found with small companies. This phenomenon has been conventionally accounted for by some version of Gibrat's Law of proportionate growth, that is, independence of growth rates from size. However, empirical evidence in this respect is rather inconclusive, the results depending on the particular specification and on the sample used. Considering only the more recent studies, Hall (1987) and Evans (1987a,b) found that both the firm growth rates and their variation decrease with size (and age, in Evans' studies). Conversely, Acs and Audretsch (1991) find confirmation for Gibrat's Law by including in the sample firms exiting the industry. Indeed, as has been documented by several studies (Evans, 1987a,b; Hall, 1987), that small (and young) firms tend to exit with greater frequency than large companies. Thus, consideration of exit offsets, to some extent, the higher growth rates of small firms.

Results are even fuzzier at the industry level. Acs and Audretsch (1990), for instance, found that growth rates are significantly different across firm-size classes in about 40 percent of the industries considered in their sample. Sectors in which Gibrat's Law is not confirmed include petroleum, rubber and plastics, paper, and leather. Conversely, Gibrat's Law appears to hold in furniture, printing, chemicals, fabricated metals, transportation equipment, and instruments.

Technological Regimes, Patterns of Innovation and Industrial Dynamics

Technological Regimes

This evidence provides an extensive array of problems to be explained. As such, each of the stylized facts mentioned previously constitutes somewhat of a puzzle, the more so, if these facts are considered simultaneously. For instance, the evidence on the sectoral specificities in the patterns of innovation and turbulence and on the persistence of differential innovative performance and profitability over time clearly contrasts with an explanation of the stability of firm-size distribution based on some version of Gibrat's Law, whereby independence of the variance of growth from initial size is assumed. Similarly this last assumption is clearly at odds with the reported evidence on the relationship beween size and age, on the one hand, and growth and survival, on the other.

In general, evidence seems to suggest the existence of (a) strong firm and sector specificities in the patterns of innovation and industrial dynamics; (b) rather permanent factors at the firm level that generate the persistence of innovative and economic performance over time, and (c) discontinuities and shocks, which may radically change the competitive advantages/disadvantages of individual firms and the patterns of industrial dynamics from time to time.

Empirical research provides some further indication of a preliminary interpretation of these phenomena. In particular, the economics of innovation suggests a few useful concepts in this respect. First, innovation studies have started to disentangle the plausible idea that innovative activities are to be analyzed as a complex learning process. Such processes are inherently *cumulative* and generate *specific competences* that define what a firm can do (and what it cannot do) and where a firm can search when trying to improve its technological and economic performance. In this perspective, firms are defined by their competencies. Their ability to change is heavily constrained by the level and nature of their competences (Teece et al., 1990). On these grounds, one would expect to observe high degrees of diversity and variety in firms' competencies, as well as relatively high degrees of persistence in their activities and performance. Thus, firms appear to be able to build up over time specific capabilities and assets that shelter them from selection and make them persistently "better" (or worse) than competitors.

Second, and relatedly, it has been suggested that technologies differ drastically and that their development retains a strong autonomous internal logic. The notions of technological paradigms and trajectories try to capture this insight (Dosi, 1982, 1988). It must be noted that paradigm shifts imply radical changes in the relevant competencies, in the directions and procedures of technological change, and—as a consequence—also significant changes in the relative innovative capabilities and "efficiency" of firms.

Third, activities in an industry are heavily affected by the nature of what has been termed *technological regimes*. The notion of technological regime dates back to Nelson and Winter (1982), and provides a description of the technological environment in which firms operate. More generally, Malerba and Orsenigo (1990, 1993) have proposed that a technological regime is a particular combination of opportunity and appropriability conditions, degrees of cumulativeness of technological knowledge, and characteristics of the relevant knowledge base.

Opportunity conditions reflect the easiness of innovating for any given amount of money invested in the search. High opportunities represent a powerful incentive to the undertaking of innovative activities.[3] In addition, opportunity conditions may or may not be highly pervasive. Highly pervasive opportunities may mean that the generation of new knowledge may be applied to a variety of products and markets. On the contrary, low pervasiveness means that the generation of new knowledge concerns only a limited and specific set of products and processes.

Appropriability conditions summarize the possibilities of protecting innovations from imitation and of extracting profits from innovative activities.[4]

Cumulativeness captures the properties that innovations and innovative activities of today form the starting point for innovations of tomorrow and that innovative firms of today are more likely to innovate in the future in specific technologies and along specific trajectories than noninnovative firms.[5]

Technologies also differ in terms of the characteristics of their knowledge base. The knowledge base can be primarily tacit, local, and firm specific or rather codified and "universal," and thus relatively more easy to get access to. Similarly, the relevant knowledge base may show varying degrees of complexity because innovations may require the integration of different scientific disciplines and technologies, and because innovative activities may be fed by the contribution of a variety of competencies concerning the production process, the nature of markets, the features of demand, and so on. Some of these competencies may be external to the firms in the industry and may derive from, for example, suppliers of materials, equipment producers, users, universities, and government laboratories.[6]

The notion of technological regime has indeed proved to be useful in providing a framework for interpreting a substantial body of empirical evidence on firms' organization and strategies, and on the sectoral patterns of technical change and industrial dynamics.

Technological Regimes, Firms Strategies, and Organization

Notice first that the notion of technological regimes can provide the basis of an explanation of some aspects of the dynamics of firms' organization and strategies. The nature of the specific technological regime, in fact, identifies some problem-solving tasks that are common to all the firms active in a particular industry.

For instance, Dosi et al. (1989) use some features of learning activities to explain the coherence and patterns of diversification of business firms. In a similar vein, Malerba and Orsenigo (1993) provide a discussion and some evidence based on case studies on the relationships between firms' innovative strategies (defined very roughly as radical, incremental, and imitative) and technological regimes.

Notice, first, that high-opportunity conditions tend to make the pursuit of strategies of radical search and exploration of new innovative opportunities relatively more attractive (March, 1990). Moreover, in so far as technological progress is rapid and innovations are generated from every quarter, high opportunities also imply that companies have to establish windows and channels of communication with the external environment (e.g. scientific institutions) in order to keep pace with progress. In terms of organizational structures, this entails that a company be prepared to jump rapidly and continuously on the new opportunities, changing and adapting its research organization quickly. High cumulativeness conversely implies a strategic bias in favor of incremental search and of the exploitation of existing technologies and capabilities. Moreover, it implies a tendency towards increasing specialization of innovative activities along specific directions.

Low appropriability conditions imply that imitative strategies are viable for followers and that innovative firms have to view the protection of innovations as a key strategic dimension in their innovative activity, possibly also via the development of complementary assets (Teece, 1986).

The combination of these conditions, therefore, identifies some general strategic trade-offs that firms have to cope with and sets of "viable strategies". In different technological regimes, firms face different strategic imperatives and options. Let us consider some examples.

Think of a combination of high opportunity and high cumulativeness: this determines a major tradeoff between the continuous exploitation of existing technologies and the continuous exploration of new technologies. Sole exploration may imply too high a cost of finding radical innovations without being able to fully profit from them later on. Sole exploitation may imply the risk that firms may end up being locked-in in existing technologies, without moving rapidly and forcefully to the new ones.

In the case of high opportunity and high appropriability, but low cumulativeness, firms may be induced to follow mainly strategies of exploration of new technologies. For example, this is the case in biotechnology, where established firms have to monitor what is going on in the technological frontier and develop an extensive network of collaboration between new specialized biotechnology companies, pharmaceutical firms, and universities. On the contrary, in case of high cumulativeness and high appropriability, but low opportunity, strategies of exploitation of existing technologies are the only viable strategies. This is the case with firms involved in the production of very large-scale integration semiconductor memories.

However, in conditions of high opportunity, high cumulativeness, and high appropriability, firms may follow either strategies of exploration of new technologies, or exploit existing technologies or some combination of the two, like strategies of exploration of new technologies followed by exploitation of these technologies. Semiconductor firms' strategies based on a combination of the introduction of major innovations, rapid movements down the learning curve in existing products, and continuous improvement of established components within a broad product family are a case in point.

In general, high opportunity, high cumulativeness, and low appropriability imply more complex strategic tasks, but also higher degrees of strategic freedom, that is, the number of viable strategies is likely to be bigger. High opportunity allows *exploration strategies,* high cumulativeness allows *exploitation strategies*, while low appropriability also allows follower firms to pursue imitation strategies. Conversely, when regimes are characterized by low opportunity, the menu of viable strategies becomes narrower.

Two further dimensions that affect the set of viable strategies relate to the pervasiveness of opportunities and the complexity of knowledge. Pervasiveness implies opportunities for diversification through the application of the core technological knowledge to a variety of products and markets. Conversely, lack of pervasiveness (i.e., specific opportunities), particularly if coupled with high degrees of cumulativeness, entail a tendency towards product and market specialization. Thus, diversified companies will tend to emerge in regimes characterized by pervasive opportunities and low cumulativeness, whilst specialist companies are more likely to emerge in highly cumulative and nonpervasive technologies.

The properties of the knowledge base identify some further tradeoffs and imperatives. The more the knowledge base is tacit, the stronger the need to develop internal codes and channels of communication, and the weaker the ability and possibility to transfer it to other firms and institutions. The more the knowledge base is complex, the stronger the need for firms to develop mechanisms for the integration of its various components.

If appropriability is high and knowledge is codifiable, complexity may allow firms to specialize in specific innovative activities generating only part of the relevant know-how. These specialized companies may coexist and establish complementary relationships with "system integrators," which then may make use and put together knowledge produced externally. This is the case in the software industry, which is rich with specialist firms and system integrators.

On the contrary, low appropriability conditions and high degrees of tacitness of the knowledge base favor strategies and organizational solutions directed towards full integration through the control and the integration of various innovative activities, and the development of complementary assets and strong internal codes of communication (Von Hippel, 1988; Teece, 1986; Mowery, 1983).

Finally, in the case of high appropriability and tacitness of the knowledge base, firms may be induced to develop strategic alliances. This is because knowledge cannot be easily exchanged nor replicated; hence, the incentive for firms to join in long-term agreements concerning common innovative activities.

In general, high complexity of the knowledge base and high opportunity conditions make it more likely that firms develop external networks. Even a company such as IBM, which was for a long time fully vertically integrated, has since the early 1980s begun to form cooperative agreements and strategic alliances with software firms, users, and component producers.

Finally, it the case of high pervasiveness and high complexity, a major organizational trade-off concerning centralization and decentralization may emerge, particularly when knowledge is tacit. Without entering into this issue in great detail, let us mention that the need to develop full integration through a centralized organizational structure in order to coordinate and exploit a complex core capability may clash with the need to decentralize the organizational structure for the exploitation of opportunities for diversification (Pavitt, 1990; Marengo, 1991).

Technological Regimes and the Sectoral Patterns of Technical Change

The notion of technological regime also provides the basis for an explanation of the variety in the patterns of innovation across sectors (and/or technologies). The introduction of even rough proxies of opportunity and appropriability conditions significantly improves the performance of econometric tests on the relationships between market structure (e.g., firm size and degrees of concentration) and innovation (Cohen and Levin, 1989).

Malerba and Orsenigo (1990) showed in the case of Italy that the nature of technological regimes highly affect the specific patterns of innovative activities at the sectoral level. In particular, a high concentration of innovative activities is related to high opportunity, appropriability, and cumulativeness conditions, while high stability in the hierarchy of leading innovators is related to high appropriability and cumulativeness conditions. Finally the easy of entry of new innovators in an industry is related to high opportunity and low cumulativeness conditions. Thus, Schumpeter Mark I sectors are characterized by high opportunity and low appropriability conditions, which favor the continuous entry of new innovators into the industry, and by low cumulativeness conditions, which do not allow the persistence of monopolistic advantages in the industry by any one innovator. Schumpeter Mark II patterns are determined by high opportunity, high appropriability, and high cumulativeness conditions, which allow innovators to incrementally accumulate technological knowledge and capabilities and to build up innovative advantages over non-innovators and potential entrants. The remarkable similarity in the sectoral patterns of innovative activities across countries provides some further indirect evidence of the relevance of technological regimes in determining some sectoral invariances in the patterns of technological change (Malerba and Orsenigo, 1993).

Technological Regimes and Industrial Dynamics

The notion of technological regime can also be employed to account for the size distribution of firms at the industry level as well as for differential patterns of turbulence. Indeed, in so far as innovation is a primary force of firm growth and industrial change, there ought to be a direct link between technological regimes and the patterns of industrial evolution. For instance, following Gort and Klepper (1982), Winter (1984), Acs and Audretsch (1991) argue that sectoral differences in the patterns of entry and exit, and in the relationships between size, age, growth, and survival—and therefore, firm size distribution—are to be accounted for by the nature of the relevant technology, defined in terms of accessibility of technological knowledge by firms external to the industry as opposed to incumbents. Acs and Audretsch, indeed, find econometric evidence that turbulence is higher and survival rates of young firms are lower in industries characterized by an "entrepreneurial" as opposed to a "routinized" technological regime. The latter is defined as a technological environment characterized by high degrees of cumulativeness, appropriability, and tacitness of the knowledge base.

Towards a Theoretical Explanation

The empirical evidence reviewed so far strongly supports the suggestion that the patterns of innovation and industrial dynamics follow sector- and technology-specific paths: they are a function of some structural characteristics of the technology and, more generally, of some specific features of learning processes.

However, these empirical findings still need to be thoroughly backed and "explained" by theoretical models, which should make explicit the links between technological regimes and patterns of change. That is, a theory of industrial dynamics ought to be able to show that different functional representations of the mechanisms of access to innovation, and different parametrizations of variables, such as opportunity appropriability, cumulativeness, etc., can be mapped into different aggregate descriptions of industrial structures and industrial change (cf. the "stylized facts" taxonomized above). Moreover, an "evolutionary" approach would claim that different technological regimes affect primarily the *processes* of learning and market selection, and that it would be misleading to simply project these intersectoral differences into some given, possibly sector-specific, "production function" to which agents try optimally to adjust.

Permanent opportunities of innovation imply that industry evolution occurs within an environment that is not functionally defined by scarcity, but in which technological discovery (and, in general, the creation of something new) is always possible. Highly imperfect appropriability mechanisms also imply the widespread existence of externalities and spillovers. Cumulativeness implies that increasing returns are a structural feature of industrial dynamics.

From this perspective, we suggest that the observed regularities and variety in the patterns of industrial dynamics can be accounted for by the consideration of the specific properties of learning (as proxied by technological regimes) and selection in any one industry. Admittedly, theoretical results in this respect are still less compelling compared to empirical analysis. However, a growing body of theoretical exercises lends strong support to this claim.

Some models have tried to account for the observed patterns on the grounds of microfoundations resting on heterogeneous agents, imperfect learning, and non-instantaneous market selection. Others have attempted to explain some industrial regularities (e.g., firm size distributions and patterns of entry and exit) as an equilibrium outcome of a stochastic process of convergence to optimal techniques by rational agents under imperfect information. In particular, Jovanovic (1982) assumes that new firms are continuously entering the industry that are unsure of their own productive efficiency. By producing they acquire noisy information about their productivity. Those firms that discover their efficiency exceeds their expectations expand their scale of output, while those that receive unfavorable signals contract or even exit. Thus, industry evolution is driven by noisy selection, which fosters the growth of efficient firms and the decline of inefficient ones. Pakes and Ericson have extended this model to consider the possibility that firms can affect their productivity by investing in learning (e.g., R&D) activities, the outcome of which, however, is random. In the same vein, other models (Lambson, 1991) examine industry evolution and try to account for some of the stylized facts discussed above as the result of changing exogenous market conditions.

In the evolutionary tradition, the seminal models by Nelson and Winter provided some basic reference for subsequent efforts. As known, Nelson and Winter's model was based on heterogeneous firms, characterized by different strategies of innovation and imitation and by different propensities to invest in innovative activities. Simulation exercises examined two different technological regimes: a "science-based" regime and a "cumulative" one. The models were actually able to generate different patterns of innovative activities and industry structures, yielding different measures of concentration and firm-size distributions.

Developing on these lines, Silverberg (1987) and Silverberg et al. (1988) provide further support to the idea that disequilibrium evolutionary models can generate ordered patterns of change, wherein certain key variables representing firm- and industry-specific learning regimes give rise to quite different patterns of evolution.

The basic structure of the latter models (and of more recent developments, reviewed below) builds on some firm-specific learning dynamics and on a replicator equation governing market selection and, thus, linking underlying regimes to the evolution of industrial structures. Consider the dynamics of market shares as expressed by

$$\dot{f}_{it} = A[E_{it} - \overline{E}_t]f_{it},$$

where f_{it} is the market share of the ith firm at time t; $E_{it} = G[m_{it}]$ is the competitiveness of firm i, which in turn is a function of some vector of its technological and organizational characteristics m_{it}. $\overline{E}_t$ is the average competitiveness of the industry, and the dots stand for rates of change. The composition of the vector m, its changes over time, and the G (fi) function depend, in principle, on the learning regimes of each industry. In stochastic versions, the learning mechanisms specific to each technological regime govern the transition probabilities in m_{it}.

In Silverberg et al. (1988), firms have to choose when to acquire a new production technology, the efficiency of which improves with use for the users. Part of these gains in efficiency, linked to phenomena such as learning-by-using, etc., remain "private," meaning that they can be reaped only by those firms that actually use the new technology. Part of that knowledge, however, can become public, that is, spills over to new adopters. Firms have therefore to decide the date of acquisition of the new technology, facing basically the trade-off between early acquisition (with the possibility of gaining irreversible advantages vis-à-vis competitors, but also facing high degrees of uncertainty) and late acquisition (which might allow for lower uncertainty and exploitation of part of the experience of early adopters, but possibly accumulating too large a gap in efficiency).[7]

In this model, therefore, the technological regime is described by the opportunity conditions (the potential superiority of the new technology), appropriability conditions (the degree to which experience in the use of the new technology becomes public), and cumulativeness conditions (the degree to which the new technology improves with use). Simulations of the model actually yield not only "ordered" patterns of diffusion, that is, a sigmoid diffusion curve, as observed in the empirical analyses, but also a different speed of diffusion and differential rates of success between early and late adopters as a function of the two parameters expressing the "private" and the "public" rate of learning (i.e., cumulativeness and appropriability conditions).

In Dosi and Salvatore (1991), industrial dynamics is explicitly examined, considering entry and exit as well as the growth of firms. The model contrasts two extreme types of learning regimes. In the first one, the Schumpeter Mark II model, learning is cumulative. Thus, one assumes that (1) the probabilities of exit decrease with the age of the firm (e.g., firms accumulate competencies and competiveness over time); (2) the probability of exit decreases with size (e.g., economies of scale in production, R&D, etc. are assumed); (3) the variance of growth rates decreases with age (e.g., older firms are relatively more stable in the competences they incorporate and the market niches they occupy); (4) birth rates are proportional to the number of incumbents (as empirically suggested by Dunne et al., 1989). The opposite occurs in the other extreme regime (the Schumpeter Mark I model), where no learning occurs, frequent discontinuities render the skills of incumbents obsolete, diseconomies of scale characterize production and R&D, etc.

In between these two extreme regimes, the model experiments with other intermediate conditions and studies firm-size distributions that emerge over time in each of the archetypical "industries." The results indicate that indeed that sectoral distributions so generated depart significantly from a Pareto distribution. Clearly, this corroborates the conjecture that industry evolution is strongly influenced by the industry-specific regimes of learning and selection. However, a Pareto distribution is obtained as a result of a random aggregation over these different industrial archetypes, each characterized by different "technological regimes," and therefore different evolutionary processes. Such a distribution tends to remain stable as long as, on average, the learning (and selection) conditions do not dramatically change, such as, for instance, in the case of a generalized "technological shock" (a change in some dominant technological paradigm) that devalues older competences and introduces a negative influence of age on growth.

Dosi et al. (1992) try to generalize the previous results, examining explicitly the processes through which firms accumulate competences. The model starts with n firms, identical in size and efficiency (m). The latter grows over time via a learning dynamic, which is different in various regimes. In the first model (the Schumpeter Mark I), incumbents do not learn. Evolution relies entirely on the entry of new innovators, the efficiency of which is given by

$$m_{i,t+1} = \overline{m}_t[1 + e_1], \tag{1}$$

where $\overline{m}_t$ is the average efficiency of incumbents and e_1 is a random variable drawn from a Poisson distribution with mean l (whose value captures the notional levels of innovative opportunities).

In the Schumpeter Mark II model, the learning regime is cumulative; that is, the dynamics of $m_{i,t}$ for incumbents is a Markov process:

$$m_{j,t+1} = m_{j,t}[1 + e_I], \tag{2}$$

where the stochastic variable e_I is, again, drawn from a Poisson distribution specific to incumbents.

Learning by entrants is given by

$$m_{i,t+1} = \overline{m}_t[1 + e_E].$$

The birth of new firms is proportional to the number of incumbents, h:

$$b_{t+1} = n_t(h + k),$$

where k is a random variable uniformly distributed on some finite support.

Market shares, f_i, grow according to

$$\dot{f}_{i,t+1} = A[m_{i,t+1}/\overline{m}_{t+1} - 1]\, f_i. \tag{4}$$

Finally, exit occurs whenever the firm's efficiency or market share falls under a certain threshold.

A crucial heuristic task of this type of simulation models (and in a sense their "validation") concerns their ability to generate some emergent aggregate properties and to allow some mapping of the latter into identifiable distributions of system parameters and micro characteristics. In fact, a rich set of properties, consistent with the evidence, appears.

First, some sort of life cycle, similar to those described by Gort and Klepper (1982), emerges at the level of "microsectors." Second, whenever such microsectors are aggregated in "industries," corresponding to particular industrial regimes, the expected relationships between age, size, and growth emerge. For instance, in the Schumpeter I industry, regressions of firms' growth rates on age and size have a negative sign. Third, the nature of technological regimes exerts a primary influence on the average degrees of industrial concentration. Fourth, overall stochastic aggregation over "industries" (and "regimes") produces Pareto-type size distributions, which, however, hide a much greater underlying heterogeneity in the processes of corporate growth.

Conclusions

In this paper we have argued that the nature of technological (and organizational) learning, interacting with the processes of market selection, define specific regimes of industrial evolution, which in turn generate empirically observable regularities, such as differentiated modes of corporate organization and strategies; different patterns of innovation; specific industrial dynamics, as revealed by varying degrees of turbulence; persistence of differentials in innovative performance and profitability.

We have also argued that some empirical invariances at a broader level of observation, for example, the relative stability of particular distributions in firm sizes over the whole population of manufacturing enterprises, might be simply the outcome of aggregation. While still admittedly in their beginning stages, "evolutionary" interpretations of industrial dynamics hold the promise of accounting for a rather wide set of "stylized facts." They try to do this by identifying robust correspondences between distinctive features of observable industrial dynamics, on the one hand, and underlying characteristics of the microeconomic processes of learning and market selection, on the other.

Stating this as a biological metaphor, this research perspective suggests that explanations of industrial dynamics can be found in links between taxonomies on "species," mutation processes, and selection criteria. We have still rather incomplete and rough evidence on all three sets of phenomena.

In addition, the theory joining them has yet to undergo stringent tests for robustness, but significant progress has been made over the last decade or two: more systematic evidence has been collected; the growing field of the economics of innovation has provided rich insights into micro learning processes; business economics has increasingly focused on the nature of problem-solving activities of firms and their related competences; and theoretical exercises on the properties of evolutionary processes are (slowly) spreading.

Notes

1. We owe this interpretation of Sylos Labini's model to discussions with Marco Lippi.

2. The literature on population ecology provides further important empirical evidence on these points. See Hannan and Freeman (1990) among the others.

3. Science is certainly a major source of opportunities. Yet the sources of opportunities differ among industries and technologies. As Rosenberg (1982) and Nelson (1992) have shown, in some industries opportunity conditions are related to advancements in science; in others, research equipment and instrumentation or external sources of knowledge, such as suppliers and users, may play a major role.

4. As known, firms utilize a variety of means in order to protect innovations, ranging from patents, to secrecy, to continuous innovation, to the control of complementary assets (Levin et al., 1987; Teece, 1986).

5. These definitions identify two levels of cumulativeness, related to technology (cumulativeness may be linked to the specific features of technologies and the cognitive nature of learning processes or to the amount of resources needed for innovation needed for innovation) and organizational forms (cumulativeness may be related to the organization of the various learning activities). Note that high indivisibilities imply also high appropriability of innovations.

6. Other dimensions of the knowledge base refer to the various sources of technological knowledge. Some of these sources may be internal to firms, such as R&D, production, and marketing; while others may be external, such as suppliers, users, universities, and public R&D laboratories.

7. In the model, firms' decisions concerning investment are governed by a desired payback period rule. Expectations with regard to the efficiency of the new technology are expressed by an "anticipation bonus," which is different among firms.

References

Abernathy, W.J., and Utterback, J.M. 1978. "A Dynamic Model of Product and Process Innovation." *Omega* 3(6):639–656.

Acs, Z., and Audretsch, D.B. 1989. "Small Firm Entry in U.S. Manufacturing." *Economica* 56(2):255–265.

Acs, Z., and Audretsch, D.B. 1990. *Innovation and Small Firms*. Cambridge: MIT Press.

Acs, Z., and Audretsch, D.B. 1991. "Technological Regimes, Learning and Industry Turbulence." Berlin, unpublished manuscript.

Acs, Z., and Audretsch, D.B. 1991. "New Firm Survival and the Technological Regime." *Review of Economics and Statistics* 60, 441–50.

Aldrich, H., and Auster, A. 1987. "Selezione naturale e strategie d'impresa." *Sviluppo e Organizzazione* 103.

Beesley, M.E., and Hamilton, R.T. 1984. "Small Firms' Seedbed Role and the Concept of Turbulence." *Journal of Industrial Economics* 33:217–232.

Bond, R. 1975. "Mergers and Mobility Among the Largest Manufacturing Corporations." *Antitrust Bulletin* 20:505–519.

Cohen W.M., and Levin, R. 1989. "Empirical Studies of Innovation and Market Structure." In *Handbook of Industrial Organization*. R. Schmalensee and R. Willig, eds. Amsterdam: North Holland.

Collins, N.R., and Preston, L.E. 1961. "The Size Structure of the Large Industrial Firms." *American Economic Review* 51:986–1011.

Dosi, G. 1982. "Technological Paradigms and Technological Trajectories. A Suggested Interpretation of the Determinants and Directions of Technical Change." *Research Policy* 11, 147–162.

Dosi, G. 1984. *Technical Change and Industrial Transformation. The Theory and an Application to the Semiconductor Industry.* London: Macmillan.

Dosi, G. 1988. "The Microeconomic Sources and Effects of Innovation." *Journal of Economic Literature* 26, 1120–1171.

Dosi, G., Marsili, O., Orsenigo, L., and Salvatore, R. 1992. "Technological Regimes, Selection and Market Structure." Unpublished manuscript.

Dosi, G., and Salvatore, R. 1991. "The Structure of industrial Production and the Boundaries between Organizations and Markets." University of Rome, unpublished manuscript.

Dunne, T., Roberts, M.J., and Samuelson, L. 1989. "The Growth and Failure of U.S. Manufacturing Plants." *Quarterly Journal of Economics* 104:672–698.

Evans, D.S. 1987a. "The Relationship between Firm Growth, Size and Age: Estimates for 100 Manufacturing Industries." *Journal of Industrial Economics* 35:567–581.

Evans, D.S. 1987b. "Tests of Alternative Theories of Firm Growth." *Journal of Political Economy* 95:657–674.

Gort, M., and Klepper, S. 1982. "Time Paths in the Diffusion of Product Innovations." *The Economic Journal* 630–656.

Gort, M., and Konakayama, A. 1982. "A Model of Diffusion in the Production of an Innovation." *American Economic Review.*

Hall, B.H. 1987. "The Relationship between Firm Size and Firm Growth in the U.S. Manufacturing Sector." *Journal of Industrial Economics* 35:583–600.

Hannan, M.T., and Freeman, J. 1990. *Organizational Ecology.* Cambridge: Harvard University Press.

Jovanovic, B. 1982. "Selection and the Evolution of Industry." *Econometrica* 50:649–670.

Kaplan, A.D.H. 1964. *Big Enterprise in a Competitive System*. Washington, D.C.: The Brookings Institution.

Kessides, I.N. 1990. "The Persistence of Profits in U.S. Manufacturing Industries" in Mueller, D.C. (ed.), "*The Dynamics of Company Profits*, Cambridge, Cambridge University Press, pp. 59–75.

Lambson, V.E. 1991. "Industry Evolution with Sunk Costs and Uncertain Market Conditions." *International Journal of Industrial Organization* 9:171–196.

Levin, R., Klevorick, A., Nelson, R.R., and Winter, S. 1987. "Appropriating the Returns from Industrial Research and Development." *Brookings Papers on Economic Activity* 3.

Malerba, F. 1985a. "Demand Structure and Technological Change." *Research Policy* 14.

Malerba, F. 1985b. *The Semiconductor Business. The Economics of Rapid Growth and Decline.* London: Pinter.

Malerba, F., and Orsenigo, L. 1990. "Technological Regimes and Patterns of Innovation: A Theoretical and Empirical Investigation of the Italian Case." In *Evolving Industries and Market Structures. A.* Heertje, ed. Ann Arbor, MI: University of Michigan Press, pp. 283–306.

Malerba, F., and Orsenigo, L. 1992. "Schumpeterian Patterns of Innovation." Milan: Bocconi University, unpublished manuscript.

Malerba, F., and Orsenigo, L. 1993. "Technological Regimes and Firm Behaviour." *Industrial and Corporate Change* 2:45–72.

March, J.G. 1990. "Exploration and Exploitation in Organizational Learning." Stanford CA: Stanford University, unpublished manuscript.

Marengo, L. 1991. "Knowledge, Communication and Coordination in an Adaptive Model of the Firm." Rome, unpublished manuscript.

Mermelstein, D. 1969. "Large Industrial Corporations and Asset Shares." *American Economic Review* 59:531–541.

Mowery, D. 1983. "The Relationship between the Contractual and Intra-Firm Forms of Industrial Research in American Manufacturing, 1900–1940." *Explorations in Economic History* 20, 351–374.

Mueller, D. 1990. *The Persistence of Profits*. Cambridge, UK: Cambridge University Press.

Nelson, R.R. 1992. *National Systems of Innovation*. Oxford: Oxford University Press.

Nelson, R.R., and Winter, S. 1982. *An Evolutionary Theory of Economic Change*. Cambridge: The Belknap Press of Harvard University Press.

Odagiri, H., and Yamawaki, H. 1990. "The Persistence of Profits: International Comparison," in Mueller, D.C. (ed.), *The Dynamics of Company Profits*. Cambridge, Cambridge University Press, pp. 169–85.

Orsenigo, L. 1989. *The Emergence of Biotechnology*. London: Pinter.

Pavitt, K. 1984. "Sectoral Patterns of Technological Change: Towards a Taxonomy and a Theory." *Research Policy* 13(6):343–374.

Pavitt, K. 1990. "Some Foundations for the Theory of the Large Innovating Firm." Brighton, SPRU, University of Sussex, unpublished manuscript.

Rosenberg, N. 1982. *Inside the Black Box*. Cambridge, UK: Cambridge University Press.

Schumpeter, J. 1934. *The Theory of Economic Development.* Cambridge: Harvard UP.

Schumpeter, J. 1960. Capitalism, Socialism and Democracy. New York: Harper and Row.

Silverberg, G. 1987. "Technical Progress, Capital Accumulation and Effective Demand: A Self-Organisation Model." In *Economic Evolution and Structural* Adjustment. D. Batten et al., ed. Berlin: Springer Verlag.

Silverberg, G., Dosi, G., and Orsenigo, L. 1988. "Innovation, Diversity and Diffusion: A Self-Organisation Model." *Economic Journal* 98:1032–1054.

Sylos Labini, P. 1958. *Oligopoly and Technical Progress*. Cambridge: Harvard University Press.

Teece, D. 1986. "Profiting from Technological Innovation." *Research Policy* 15:285–306.

Teece, D., Pisano, G., and Shuen, A. 1990. "Firm capabilities, Resources and the Concept of Strategy." CCC Working Paper No. 90–8. Berkeley, CA: Center for Research in Management, University of California at Berkeley.

von Hippel, E. 1988. *The Sources of Innovation*. New York: Oxford University Press.

Winter, S. 1984. "Schumpeterian Competition in Alternative Technological Regimes." *Journal of Economic Behaviour and Organisation* 5(3–4):287–320.

8 THE ROLE OF FIRM DIFFERENCES IN AN EVOLUTIONARY THEORY OF TECHNICAL ADVANCE

Richard R. Nelson

Introduction

There is a curious disjunction between the treatment of firms and firm differences in the business management literature, and the treatment in much of economics. The former treats firms as complex organisms, but with management having considerable discretionary authority over broad firm policies. It is presumed that firms in roughly comparable situations often will differ in what they do, and that these differences will matter in terms of how they do. The question of what makes for good policies is what the business management field is all about.

In contrast, in most of economics firms are treated as simple entities; indeed until recently economists showed little interest in their internal structures. Management, as in the business management literature, is presumed to be able to determine what a firm does; if anything there is less attention given in the economics literature than in the management literature to internal constraints on what management can do. However, what management chooses to do is treated as strictly determined by the economic environment it is in. Given that environment management chooses the policies that will "maximize" firm profits, the "question" that is the center of concern in the business management field is assumed to be trivial to answer. Since it is, all firms in the same economic context are presumed to have the same policies—those that are best in that context—and to do the same thing.

On the one hand, it signals that scholars of technical advance can make little use of the theory of the firm contained in economic neoclassical theory. That theory of the firm completely represses the uncertainty, confusion, and surprise that often mark inventive efforts within firms, and it also represses the differences in opinions, bets, and efforts among firms that are the hallmark of technical advance. Scholars of technical advance have long recognized that at certain times some firms are simply much more effective innovators than others. Neoclassical firm theory offers no real starting point for understanding why.

On the other hand, it signals that there may be potentially fruitful intellectual alliances between scholars of technical advance and scholars of business management. It is widely recognized that understanding of technical advance can inform the business management literature. My point is different. It is that solid theoretical work in the firm management area may inform scholarship of technical advance. Indeed I think that is happening right now, and the purpose of this essay is to report on these developments.

Firms in Neoclassical and Evolutionary Theory

The view of firms in most of economics stems from the perception of what the economic problems and what competition is all about contained in standard economic theory. Since the formulation of general equilibrium theory almost a century ago, economists have been focused on how firms behave and the resulting allocation of resources, given technologies. The view of the economic problem is that of achieving the greatest possibly want satisfaction, given technologies. Partly reflecting this general orientation, but not the only formulation of firms' decision processes consistent with it, economists became wedded to a theory of firm behavior that posited that firms face a given and known choice set (constrained, among other things, by technology) and have no difficulty in choosing the action within those sets that is best for them, given their objectives (generally assumed to be as much profit as possible). Thus the economic problem amounts to, basically, getting the incentives (prices) right, not identifying the best thing to do, which was assumed to be no problem.

Scholars of technical advance by their very choice of subject reject both aspects of this formulation—that technologies are a given and the economic problem is to use them at maximum efficiency, and that the best things to be doing are obvious. Indeed most students of technical change follow Schumpeter in seeing technical advance as the most important economic problem over the long run, and in seeing the process of technical advance as an evolutionary one, with many new departures competing with each other and prevailing practice, with winners and losers determined in actual contest.

In our book, *An Evolutionary Theory of Economic Change*, Winter and I attempted to lay out a formal theory of economic activity, driven by industrial innovation, that was consistent with the Schumpeterean view. Our orientation was to understand technical advance, its sources, and its impacts at the level of an industry or an economy. However, we devoted considerable space presenting a "theory of the firm," which is consistent with, and motivates, a Schumpeterian or evolutionary theoretic view of economic process and economic change.

Our formulation then drew significantly on Simon, Cyert and March, and Penrose, as well as Schumpeter. With the vision of hindsight, it is clear that our writing then was handicapped by our insufficient knowledge of the writings of Chandler and other scholars of business organization and management. Since the time we wrote, there have been a number of theoretical papers on firm capabilities and behavior, many of them in the "business management" field that build from Chandler, and often our work, and that add significantly to the picture. Papers by Teece (1980, 1982, 1986); Rumelt (1984); Cohen and Levinthal (1989); Dosi et al. (1989); Prahalad and Hamel (1990); Pavitt (1987, 1992); Cantwell (1989, 1990); Kogut (1987); Clark and Fujimoto (1991), Henderson (1990); Burgelman and Rosenbloom (1989); and Langlois (1986, 1992); all present a similar or at least a conformable theoretical view, although with differences in stress. The recent paper by Teece et al. (1990) provides an overview of many of these works, and I believe correctly states that the common element is a focus on firm-specific dynamic capabilities.

This emerging theory of dynamic firm capabilities can be presented in different ways. Here it is convenient to focus on three different, if strongly related, features of a firm that must be recognized if one is to describe it adequately: its strategy, structure, and core capabilities. While each has a certain malleability, major changes in at least the latter two involve considerable cost. Thus they define a relatively stable firm character.

By strategy I mean, basically, what Chandler and contemporary scholars of management mean, as contrasted with game theorists. I mean a set of broad commitments made by a firm that define and rationalize its objectives and how it intends to pursue them. Some of this may be written down; some may not be but is in the management culture of the firm. Many economists would be wont to propose that the strategy represents a firm's solution of its profit maximization problem, but this seems misconceived to me. In the first place, the commitments contained in a strategy often are as much a matter of faith of top management and company tradition, as they are of calculation. Second, firm strategies seldom determine the details of firm actions, but usually at most the broad contours. Third, and of vital importance, there is no reason to argue a priori that these commitments are in fact optimal or even not self-destructive. If it is proposed that competition and selection force surviving strategies to be relatively profitable, this should be a theorem not an assumption.

My concept of structure also is Chandlerian (1966, 1990), as is the proposition that strategy tends to define a desired firm structure in a general way, but not the details. Structure involves how a firm is organized and governed, and how decisions actually are made and carried out, and thus largely determines what it actually does, given the broad strategy. A firm whose strategy calls for being a technological leader that does not have a sizeable R&D operation, or whose R&D director has little input into firm decision making, clearly has a structure out of tune with its strategy. However, the high-level strategy may be mute about links between its R&D lab and universities, whether to have a special biotech group, etc.

Change in strategy may require a change in management as well as a change in articulation; indeed, for the latter to be serious may require the former. However, structure, I would argue, is far more difficult to change effectively than is strategy. While changing formal organization, or at least the organization chart, is easy, and selloffs and buyups are possible, significantly changing the way a firm actually goes about making operating level decisions and carries them out is time consuming and costly to do. Rather, while it may not be too difficult to destroy an old structure or its effectiveness, it is a major task to get a new structure in shape and operating smoothly. Thus to the extent that a major change in strategy calls for a major change in structure, effecting the needed changes may take a long time.

The reason for changing structure often is to change, usually to augment, the things a firm is capable of doing well. This brings the discussion to the concept of core capabilities. Strategy and structure call forth and mold organizational capabilities, but what an organization can do well has something of a life of its own.

Winter and I have proposed that well-working firms can be understood in terms of a hierarchy of practiced organizational routines, which define lower order organizational skills and how these are coordinated, and higher order decision procedures for choosing what is to be done at lower levels. The notion of a hierarchy of organizational routines is the key building block under our concept of core organizational capabilities. At any time the practiced routines that are built into an organization define a set of things the organization is capable of doing confidently. If the lower order routines are not there for doing various tasks, or if they are but there is no practiced higher order routine for invoking them in the particular combination needed to accomplish a particular job, then the capability to do that job likely lies outside the organization's extant core capabilities.

The developing theory of dynamic firm capabilities I am discussing here starts from the premise that, in the industries of interest to the authors, firms are in a Schumpeterean or evolutionary context. Simply producing a given set of products with a given set of processes well will not enable a firm to survive for long. To be successful for any length of time, a firm must innovate. The capabilities on which this group of scholars focus are capabilities for innovation and to take economic advantage of innovation.

In industries where technological innovation is important, a firm needs a set of core capabilities in R&D. These capabilities will be defined and constrained by the skills, experience, and knowledge of the personnel in the R&D department, the nature of the extant teams and procedures for forming new ones, the character of the decision making processes, the links between R&D and production and marketing, etc. This means that at any time there will be certain kinds of R&D projects that a firm can carry out with some confidence and success, and a wide range of other projects that, while other firms might be able to do them, this particular firm cannot, with any real confidence.

R&D capabilities may be the lead ones in defining the dynamic capabilities of a firm. However, in a well-tuned firm, its production, procurement, marketing, and legal organizations must have built into them the capabilities to support and complement the new product and process technologies emanating from R&D. In Teece's terms (1986, 1982), the firm's capabilities must include control over or access to the complementary assets and activities needed to enable it to profit from innovation. In an environment of Schumpeterian competition, this means the capability to innovate and to make that innovation profitable, again and again.

If one thinks within the frame of evolutionary theory, it is nonsense to presume that a firm can calculate an actual "best" strategy, and the associated structure and core capabilities. A basic premise of evolutionary theory is that the world is too complicated for a firm to comprehend, in the sense that a firm understands its world in neoclassical theory. There are certain characteristics of a firm's strategy that management can have confidence will enhance the chances that it will develop the capabilities it needs to succeed. There are other characteristics that seem a prescription for failure. However, there is a lot of room in between, where a firm (or its management) simply has to lay its bets, knowing that is does not know how they will turn out.

Thus diversity of firms is just what one would expect under evolutionary theory. It is virtually inevitable that firms will choose somewhat different strategies. These, in turn, will lead to firms having different structures and different core capabilities, including their R&D capabilities. Inevitably firms will pursue somewhat different paths. Some will prove profitable, given what other firms are doing and the way markets evolve; other not. Firms that systematically lose money will have to change their strategy and structure, and develop new core capabilities, operate the ones they have more effectively, or drop out of the contest.

The Evolution of Technology

In real capitalist economies, in contrast with the neoclassical models, technical advance proceeds through an evolutionary process, with new products and processes competing with each other and with prevailing technology in real time, rather than solely in *ex ante* calculation. When we wrote our book, Winter and I found it convenient to model company R&D programs as generating results through a random draw. In fact, in the industries that I know well, there has tended to be a certain consistency in the R&D efforts of particular companies. This consistency reflects a basically stable company "strategy," and structure and core R&D and other dynamic capabilities it has put in place to carry it out. Where company strategies and associated capabilities differ significantly, their patterns of innovation are likely to differ significantly as well. Some of these strategies will prove better than others.

Thus to an extent the market is selecting strategies and companies, as well as new technologies. This suggests that in some circumstances strategic diversity may get extinguished.

There is something to this argument. A number of analysts, some working in the tradition of economic research, some in a business school research tradition, have suggested that there is natural industry life cycle. When an industry or a broad technology is new, a wide variety of approaches to technological innovation—strategies—are taken by different firms. As experience grows, certain of the approaches begin to look significantly better than others. Firms who have made the right bets do well. Those who have not need to switch over, or drop out. A number of studies have shown that as an industry or technology matures, there is a significant reduction in the number of firms, and in some cases the emergence of a "dominant design," with all surviving firms producing some variety of that tuned to the niche they have found.

One fascinating question is what happens in a relatively mature industry when a new and potentially superior technology comes into existence. The evidence suggests that it matters whether the new technology will conform with the core capabilities of extant firms or requires very different kinds of capabilities. Tushman and Anderson (1986) call these two kinds of developments *competence enhancing* and *competence destroying*. Under the latter circumstances, new firms are likely to be the innovators, and old firms often are unable to respond effectively. Tushman and Anderson note that a change in management, and presumably a major change in strategy, often is necessary if the old firm is to survive in the new environment. But it may not be sufficient. Structure and core capabilities are far more difficult to change than management and articulated strategies.

For a student of business management the question of what enables a firm to change directions effectively and be a viable competitor in the new regime is of central interest in its own right. For an economist what matters is that pharmaceutical R&D take advantage of the new possibilities opened by new biotechnology, and not whether the old pharmaceutical firms do it, or whether they fail, so long as new ones take up the torch. However, the fact that the leading edge companies in a field often change is a fascinating matter. It is consistent with the theory of focused and constrained core capabilities presented above.

The Evolution of Firm Organization

There has been far more study of the way technology advances than there has been of the way firm organization has evolved. By organization I mean what I think Chandler (1966) means by strategy and structure, those aspects of a firm that are wider and more durable than the particular technologies and other routines it employs at any moment, or even its extant core capabilities, and which in effect guide the internal evolution of these. Some writers clearly would like to give organizational change separate and equal billing with technical advance as a source of economic progress. I would like to argue here, however, that one needs to understand organizational change as usually a handmaiden to technological advance, and a not separate force behind economic progress.

If I understand him correctly, this would be Chandler's position. The new technology of the railroads required, for its effective implementation, the development of organizational capabilities far beyond that possessed by traditional owner-managed firms. Line and staff organizational form, along with the development of the position of hired manager, enabled the railroads to be effectively *governed*, to use Williamson's term. Later, new technologies that promised economies of scale and scope in manufacturing called for large firms operating in several different product fields, or market areas. The M form of managerial structure evolved to govern effectively this kind or business operation.

Over the long run what has mattered most has been organizational changes needed to enhance dynamic innovative capabilities. Leonard Reich (1985) and other writers have described how the organizational device of the industrial research and development laboratory came into existence to permit firms to shield a portion of their scientific and technical personnel from the pressures of day-to-day problem solving so that they could work on the development of new products and processes. This development was preconditioned by the rise of a new "technology" for product and process development, one employing the understandings and techniques of the sciences and engineering disciplines in a systematic way. One can read Chandler's (1966, 1990) account of the rise of other aspects of the modern corporation in terms of Teece's arguments about needed complementary assets or capabilities.

As I read the case-study evidence, devising and learning to use effectively a significantly new organizational form involves much the same kind of uncertainty, experimental groping, and learning by making mistakes and correcting them that marks technological invention and innovation. New modes of organization aren't simply "chosen" when circumstances make then appropriate, as neoclassical economists are wont to argue. They, like technologies, evolve in a manner that is foreseen only dimly. Even when a firm makes a conscious decision to change organization, it may take a long time before it is comfortable and effective in its new suit of clothes.

I suspect that the uncertainties about new organization are even greater than those surrounding technological innovations. This is especially so regarding an organization that molds effective dynamic innovative capabilities and the abilities to profit from innovation. At the present time there is little in the way of tested and proven theory (let me use the less pretentious word, knowledge) that enables confident prediction of the best way of organizing a particular activity, or what will be the consequences of adopting a different mode of organization. If the "rationally choosing" view of technological advance is misguided, the "rationally choosing" view of organizational change is even more so.

Just as important, it is common, not infrequently, for a particular mode of organization put in place for one reason to turn out to have advantages, or disadvantages, in arenas that were not considered at the time the original move was contemplated and made. It also is common, not infrequent, that there be considerable dispute about just what features of a firm's organization are responsible for certain successes or failures.

Thus, as I understand it, large Japanese firms adapted "lifetime employment" for their skilled workers in the early postwar era to try to deal with a problem of skill shortages and labor unrest. It is quite unclear how many Japanese managers foresaw advantages associated with worker loyalty and the ability of a firm to do in-house training without fear of losing the investment through worker defection. Just in time was, I understand, largely a response to scarce space, high inventory costs, and input shortages. It is not clear how many saw that it would facilitate quality control.

American companies looking at their Japanese competitors often have been uncertain about just why the Japanese are better in some respects and just what they can effectively transplant. They only will be able to learn by trying some things, seeing what happens, and having the good luck to see it right.

I want to put forth the argument that it is organizational differences, especially differences in abilities to generate and gain from innovation, rather than differences in command over particular technologies, that are the source of durable, not easily imitable, differences among firms. Particular technologies are much easier to understand, and imitate, than broader firm-dynamic capabilities.

On the Coevolution of Technology and Institutions

From one point of view it is technological advance that has been the key force that has driven economic growth over the past two centuries, with organizational change a handmaiden. From another perspective, we would not have got that technological advance without development of new ways of organization that can guide and support R&D, and enable firms to profit from these investments.

I have been concentrating on firm organization. However, it is clear that the organizational changes that have enabled nations to support the modern R&D system and the technological advance it generates go far beyond those of firm organization. Universities had to change. New scientific disciplines and societies had to come into being. In many cases new bodies of law were needed. Some technologies required major new public infrastructure for their effective development.

The coevolution of technology and institutions is a fascinating subject. Chandler, and a few other scholars, such as Hughes (1983) and Freeman (1982, 1989), have begun to address it. There clearly have been major national differences in how the institutions needed to support particular evolving technologies themselves evolved. Perhaps in the study of the coevolution of technology and institutions, we will begin to develop a serious theory of how national comparative advantage comes into being or is lost.

Acknowledgments

The author is indebted to the Sloan Foundation, through its funding of the Consortium on Competitiveness and Cooperation, and to the Conference on Fundamental Issues and Strategy, for whom a more extended version of this essay was written. Many people have commented helpfully on that earlier paper. I especially want to thank Alfred Chandler, Wesley Cohen, Rebecca Henderson, Richard Langlois, William Lazonick, Richard Rosebloom, Donald Sexton, David Teece, and Michael Tushman.

References

Abernathy, W.J., and Utterback, J.M. 1978. "Patterns of Industrial Innovation." *Technology Review.*

Armour, H., and Teece, D. 1978. "Organizational Structure and Economic Performance: A Test of the Multidivisonal Hypothesis." *Bell Journal of Economics.*

Burgelman, R., and Rosenbloom, R. 1989. "Technology Strategy: An Evolutionary Process Perspective." *Research on Technological Invention, Management, and Policy* 4.

Cantwell, J. 1989. *Technological Innovation and Multinational Corporations.* Oxford: Basil Blackwell.

Cantwell, J. 1990. "The Technological Competence Theory of International Production and its Implications." University of Reading Discussion paper #149, University of Reading, PA.

Chandler, A.D., Jr. 1966. *Strategy and Structure.* New York: Doubleday & Co. Anchor Books Edition.

Chandler, A. 1990. *Scale and Scope: The Dynamics of Industrial Capitalism.* Cambridge: Harvard University Press.

Clark, K., and Fujimoto, T. 1991. *Product Development Performance: Strategy Management and Organization in the World Auto Industry*. Cambridge: Harvard Business School Press.

Cohen, W., and Levinthal, D. 1989. "Innovation and Learning: the Two Faces of R & D." *Economic Journal.*

Cyert, R., and March, J. 1963. *A Behavioral Theory of the Firm.* Englewood Cliffs, NJ: Prentice Hall.

Dosi, G., Teece, D.J., and Winter, S. 1989. "Toward a Theory of Corporate Coherence: Preliminary Remarks." Unpublished paper, Center for Research in Management, University of California at Berkeley.

Florida, R., and Kenney, M. 1991. "Transplanted Organizations: The Transfer of Japanese Industrial Organization to the United States." *American Sociological Review.*

Freeman, C. 1982. *The Economics of Industrial Innovation.* London: Pinter.

Freeman, C. 1989. "The Nature of Innovation and the Evolution of the Production System." Xerox Unpublished manuscript.

Hays, R., Wheelwright, S., and Clark, K. 1988. *Dynamic Manufacturing: Creating the Learning Organization.* New York: Free Press.

Henderson, R. 1990. "Underinvestment and Incompetence as Responses to Radical Innovation: Evidence from the Photolithographic Alignment Equipment Industry." Cambridge: MIT Sloan School discussion paper.

Henderson, R., and Clark, K. 1990. "Architectural Innovation: The Reconfiguration of Existing Product Technologies and the Failure of Existing Firms." *Administrative Science Quarterly.*

Hounshell, D., and Smith, J. 1988. *Science and Corporate Strategy: Dupont R&D 1902–1980.* New York: Cambridge University Press.

Hughes, T. 1983. *Networks of Power: Electrical Supply Systems in the U.S., England, and Germany.* Baltimore, MO: Johns Hopkins Press.

Kogut, B. 1987. "Country Patterns in International Competition: Appropriability and Oligopolistic Agreement." In *Strategies in Global Competition.* N. Hood and J. Vahlae, eds. London: Croom-Helm.

Langlois, R. 1986. "Rationality, Institutions, and Evolution." In *Economics as a Process.* R. Langlois ed. New York: Cambridge University Press.

Langlois, R. 1992. "Transaction Cost Economics in Real Time." *Industrial and Corporate Change.*

Mansfield, E. 1989. "Technological Creativity: Japan and the United States." *Business Horizons* March/April.

Nelson, R., and Winter, S. 1982. *An Evolutionary Theory of Economic Change.* Cambridge: Harvard University Press.

Pavitt, K. 1987. "On the Nature of Technology." Inaugural lecture given at the University of Sussex, June 23, 1987.

Pavitt, K. 1992. "The Nature and Determinants of Innovation: A Major Factor in Firms' (and Countries') Competitiveness." Paper prepared for the conference "Fundamental Issues in Strategy: A Research Agenda for the 1990s."

Penrose, E. 1959. *The Theory of the Growth of the Firm.* London: Basil Blackwell.

Pisano, G. 1990. "The R&D Boundaries of the Firm." *Administrative Science Quarterly.*

Porter, M.E. 1990. *The Competitive Advantage of Nations.* New York: Free Press.

Prahalad, C.K., and Hamel, G. 1990. "The Core Competence of the Corporation." *Harvard Business Review*.

Reich, L. 1985. *The Making of American Industrial Research: Science and Business at G.E. and Bell*. New York: Cambridge University Press.

Rosenbloom, R., and Cusumano, M. 1987. "Technological Pioneering and Competitive Advantage: The Birth of the VCR Industry." *California Management Review*.

Rumelt, R.P. 1984. "Towards a Strategic Theory of the Firm." *Competitive Strategic Management*. Englewood Cliffs, NJ: Prentice-Hall.

Sachwald, F. 1990. "Which Theory of the Firm to Understand Competitiveness." Paris: Institut Francais des Relations Internationales.

Schumpeter, J. 1934. *The Theory of Economic Development*. Cambridge: Harvard University Press.

Schumpeter, J. 1942. *Capitalism, Socialism, and Democracy*. New York: Harper.

Teece, D. 1980. "Economics of Scope and the Scope of an Enterprise." *Journal of Economic Behavior and Organization*.

Teece, D. 1982. "Towards an Economic Theory of the Multiproduct Firm." *Journal of Economic Behavior and Organization*.

Teece, D. 1986. "Profiting from Technological Innovation." *Research Policy*.

Teece, D., Pisano, G., and Shuen, A. 1990. "Firm Capabilities, Resources, and the Concept of Strategy." CCC Working Paper 90–8, Center for Research on Management, University of California, Berkeley.

Tushman, M., and Anderson, P. 1986. "Technological Discontinuities and Organizational Environments." *Administrative Science Quarterly*.

Tushman, M., Newman, W.H., and Romanelli, E. 1986. "Convergence and Upheaval: Managing the Unsteady Pace of Organizational Evolution." *California Management Review*.

Womack, J., Jones, D., and Roos, D. 1991. *The Machine that Changed the World*. Cambridge: MIT Press.

III CRITIQUE AND NEW CHALLENGES

9 THE INTEGRATION OF THEORY AND HISTORY
Methodology and Ideology in Schumpeter's Economics

William Lazonick

Innovation as a Social Process

If one accepts Joseph A. Schumpeter's argument that innovation is the "fundamental phenomenon of economic development," then to understand the process of economic development requires that we study how and under what conditions innovation occurs. If one also accepts that an understanding of the process of economic development is of central concern to economics as a social science, then economists should possess the capability to study innovation (for an extended argument on which this essay draws, see Lazonick, 1991a).

How does one study innovation? I shall argue that the study of innovation, and thereby economic development, requires a methodology that integrates theory and history. I shall also argue that the study of innovation requires a rejection of individualist ideology—an ideology that assumes that individual incentives and actions lead to superior economic outcomes than collective incentives and actions.

From the perspective that I shall present, a critical task of both theoretical and historical analyses is to identify the collectivities responsible for innovation. If one takes Schumpeter's economics seriously—that is, if one seeks to relate his theoretical focus on innovation to the real world of economic development—then one must acquire a theoretical approach that can investigate the historical evolution of those collectivities that generate innovations. The economist who wants to study innovation and economic development must learn, through formal education and/or on-the-job training, to integrate theory and history.

Such a research agenda is not one for which the vast majority of today's "well-trained" economists are equipped. Their professional education emphasizes a static methodology that separates theory from reality and an individualist ideology that presumes that the relevant unit of analysis is the individual. For at least two generations the vast majority of economists, in the English-speaking world at least, have received a training that is antithetical to understanding how a successful economy actually works. In effect, through their professional formation and subsequent career demands and rewards, most economists have acquired a trained incapacity to study the most fundamental phenomenon of economics.

Why does the study of innovation require a methodology that integrates theory and history? Following Schumpeter, an innovation can be defined as a new combination of existing resources that results in products that are more desirable (higher quality) and/or more affordable (lower cost) than those products that had previously been available. A practitioner of static, individualistic theory could argue that the essence of innovation is an instantaneous flash of insight, and hence that innovation need not be studied as a *process*, let alone as a *social process*. A practitioner of static equilibrium theory might even argue that "subsequent" to the appearance of an innovation, other individuals instantaneously adopt the innovation, thus establishing a new equilibrium between supply and demand.

Of course, what an economist argues and what is in fact possible in the real world need not have anything to do with one another. In the real economic world, the essence of innovation is the transformation of inputs into outputs over an extended period of time, during which there is uncertainty whether the innovative strategy will be a success. Innovation must be studied as an evolutionary process in which strategic decision makers learn to manage the sources of uncertainty that they face in transforming innovative investments into higher quality/lower cost products than would otherwise exist [Lazonick, 1993a]. For purposes of both research and policy, economists need a theory of innovation. But the derivation of general theoretical principles of how innovation occurs requires the study of the actual process of innovation at different times and in different places.

The derivation of theoretical principles is only the beginning, not the end, of the intellectual task. By its very nature, each innovation is unique so that there can be no presumption that theoretical principles, once derived, will be sufficient to explain subsequent innovation. Theory must rather serve as a guide to the study of the reality of innovation, with hypothesis testing providing the basis on which to amend, elaborate, or even, if necessary, reject received theory. Put differently, the study of innovation requires a methodology that integrates theory and history.

Why does the study of innovation require the abandonment of individualist ideology? Innovation is a social process that requires the conscious involvement—or what I call the planned coordination (Lazonick, 1991a)—of many people with a variety of specialized skills and functions. Innovation requires collective organization because it is complex, cumulative, and continuous. Innovation is complex insofar as the knowledge that must be integrated and consolidated requires the participation in the innovation process of a specialized division of labor. Innovation is cumulative insofar as the attainment of certain types of knowledge is a prerequisite for acquiring other types of knowledge. Innovation is continuous insofar as a disruption in the accumulation of knowledge dissipates to some degree the knowledge that has already been accumulated.

The more complex, cumulative, and continuous an innovation, the more collective the innovation process is likely to be. Complexity means that many people must not only contribute their knowledge and skills to the innovation process, but also communicate with each other to integrate their individual contributions toward the common goal of achieving a higher quality product at a lower unit cost. Cumulativity means that the collective knowledge and skills that are built up at a point in time must form the foundations for the acquisition of new knowledge and skills at a later point in time. The collective entity that possesses collective knowledge and skills is in the best position to accumulate relevant knowledge. The collectivity can also contribute to the continuity of innovation by ensuring that individuals who possess important knowledge and skills continue to contribute their services to the innovation process.

The complex, cumulative, and continuous character of innovation makes the unit of analysis that one chooses to study of central importance to understanding how innovation actually occurs. The "correct" unit of analysis is the one in which the "key" decisions and actions that contribute to innovation are made. An important part of the intellectual task is to identify the "key" decisions and actions and to justify the reasons for designating them as "key." The correct unit of analysis may be, for example, an individual, a household, an enterprise, an industry, an industrial sector, a technological community, or a government. It is my contention that the more complex, cumulative, and continuous the innovation process, the more collective is the unit of analysis.

More collective organization does not automatically lead to more innovation, and different types of innovation require different types of collective organization. But to study innovation one must be willing to contemplate that individuals can work collectively in a planned and coordinated way to generate higher quality/lower cost products. One must abandon a commitment to individualist ideology. At the same time, one must acquire a dynamic integrative methodology in which theory serves as an intellectual tool for explaining a constantly changing real world rather than as an excuse for ignoring it. As Joseph Schumpeter (1947a, p. 9) put it toward the end of his essay, "Theoretical Problems of Economic Growth":

> The time may have come (that is not for me to judge) to co-ordinate and to organize [historical] work by means of comprehensive "programs" and to provide, for the use of the individual research worker, orderly schemata of possibilities and problems. It is here, and in its instrumental capacity, not as a master but as a servant of historical research, that theory may prove useful.

Schumpeter and Methodology

In *The Theory of Economic Development*, Joseph Schumpeter [1961, p. 60n] argued that "changes of technique and productive organization require special analysis," and he went on to say that "non-recognition of this is the most important single reason for what appears unsatisfactory to us in [neoclassical] economic theory." Schumpeter added that his own view of how to study the process of economic development "is more nearly parallel to that of Marx" than to that of contemporary neoclassical economists (he cited, in particular, the American economist, J.B. Clark). "For according to [Marx] there is an internal development and no mere adaptation of economic life to changing data." Schumpeter concluded by stating somewhat cryptically that his own "structure covers only a small part of Marx's ground."

Schumpeter published *The Theory of Economic Development* in German in 1911 and reiterated his approach to economic analysis in the opening chapters of his two-volume work *Business Cycles*, published 28 years later. In both works, Schumpeter's method reflects the Marxian influence. Marx constructed his labor theory of value to depict an exchange economy in equilibrium as a prelude to his theory of surplus value that sought to explain the process of capitalist development. In *The Theory of Economic*

Development, Schumpeter constructed his static model of resource allocation ("Circular Flow of Economic Life as Conditioned by Given Circumstances") as a prelude to his dynamic model of economic development ("Fundamental Phenomenon of Economic Development") to illustrate that economic development depends on a disruption of the tendencies toward an equilibration of supply and demand.

Schumpeter's circular flow—or "Equilibrium and the Theoretical Norm of Economic Quantities" to use the description of the static model in *Business Cycles* (Schumpeter, 1939)—is the Walrasian theory of the market economy that forms the microeconomic foundations of modern neoclassical economics. To this day, neoclassical economists have elaborated the theory of the circular flow as an end in itself. Indeed, they have tended to view what goes on within the circular flow as the full extent of relevant economic activity.

In focusing his analysis on the theory of economic development, Schumpeter shows what cannot be explained by the Walrasian system. Schumpeter's "Fundamental Phenomenon of Economic Development" is entrepreneurial activity that results in innovation, a concept that includes the introduction of a new process or product, entry into a new market, access to new supplies of inputs, and creation of a new organization, by which Schumpeter essentially meant building up or breaking down a barrier to entry (Schumpeter, 1961, p. 66). In *Business Cycles*, Schumpeter specifically included under the heading of innovation such things as "Taylorization of work, improved handling of materials, [and] the setting up of new business organizations such as department stores" (Schumpeter, 1939, p. 84).

Schumpeter's entrepreneur is a businessperson who is not caught up in the circular flow of economic life, but rather is able to create new profitable opportunities for the firm by the "setting up of a new production function [which] covers the case of a new commodity, as well as those of a new form of organization such as a merger, or the opening up of new markets, and so on." Innovation, according to Schumpeter, "dominates the picture of capitalistic life" by causing the "intrusion into the system of new production functions which incessantly shift existing cost curves" (Schumpeter, 1939, pp. 87, 91).

These *internal economies* (to use Alfred Marshall's term) form the basis for entrepreneurial profits, a return that Schumpeter viewed as resulting from entrepreneurial leadership in "carrying out New Combinations" of means of production [Schumpeter, 1961, p. 143; 1939, p. 88]. The determination of entrepreneurial profits, therefore, occurs outside the complex of interacting market forces that constitute the circular flow. With entrepreneurial innovation seen as the essence of economic development, Schumpeter's economics takes leave of the neoclassical theory of the market economy.

Schumpeter's theory of economic development contains, however, at best an incipient conception of the innovation process. Entrepreneurs "conceive and work out with varying promptness plans for innovations associated with varying (and ideally correct) anticipations of profits, and set about struggling with the obstacles incident to doing a new and unfamiliar thing" (Schumpeter, 1939, p. 130). The success or failure of the entrepreneurial strategy appears to depend solely on the energy and the ability of the entrepreneur.

This view is consistent with Schumpeter's earlier arguments in *The Theory of Economic Development*, in which he adopted Alfred Marshall's perspective on the rise and decline of firms. In *Principles of Economics*, Marshall (1961, p. 621) recited the aphorism "from shirtsleeves to shirtsleeves in three generations" to signify how the entrepreneurial vigor that constitutes the vital substance of the business enterprise is bound to decline with intergenerational succession. Those who inherit a successful business are not likely to have the energy and creative genius of the original entrepreneur, and therefore, as Marshall (1961, p. 323) argued, "a business firm grows and attains great strength, and afterward perhaps stagnates and decays." Schumpeter (1961, p. 156) quite literally clothed Marshall's notion of the rise and decline of firms in different garb, saying, "An American adage expresses it: three generations from overalls to overalls."

It was on the basis of this view of the rise and decline of firms that Marshall introduced into economic analysis the concept of the "Representative Firm"—a concept that then permitted him (as well as his followers) (see Lazonick, 1991a, ch. 5) to focus on the cost-minimizing adaptations of the firm in response to changing market forces rather than the innovative activities of the firm that could indeed shape market forces. In *Business Cycles*, Schumpeter (1939, p. 92n) referred to Marshall's "concept of the Representative Firm [as] one more of those devices used to hide the fundamental problem of economic change."

Writing in 1928 in the *Economic Journal* as part of a debate over increasing and decreasing returns in the Marshallian firm, Schumpeter (1928, p. 362) recognized that a historical transition had taken place between the 19th and 20th centuries from competitive capitalism to (as Schumpeter variously expressed it) "trustified," "organised," "regulated," or "managed" capitalism. Schumpeter (1928, p. 384) argued that in "trustified" capitalism, "innovation is . . . not any more embodied *typically* in new firms, but goes on, within the big units now existing, largely independently of individual persons."

In the 1930s, however, Schumpeter was still grappling with the issue of the type of enterprise that fostered innovation. In *Business Cycles*, Schumpeter (1939, pp. 94–95) made what he deemed to be the realistic assumption that all innovations are "embodied in New Firms founded for the purpose," a statement quite at odds with the view he had expressed a decade earlier. He went on to say that "everybody who looks around knows the type of [old] firm we are thinking of—living on the name, connections, quasi-rent, and reserves acquired in their youth, decorously dropping into the background, lingering in the fatally deepening dusk of respectable decay." Schumpeter (1939, p. 96) noted "that process of incessant rise and decay of firms and industries which is the central—though much neglected—fact about the capitalist machine."

In *Capitalism, Socialism, and Democracy*, first published in 1942, however, Schumpeter restored to the large corporation the leading role in what he now called the process of creative destruction. As a prime example of such an enterprise, he cited U.S. Steel, a somewhat ironic choice in the light of that company's history of "lingering in the fatally deepening dusk of respectable decay" (Schumpeter, 1950a, p. 82; on U.S. Steel, see McCraw and Reinhart, 1989). Schumpeter (1950a, pp. 118, 132) now admitted that "technological 'progress' tends, through systematization and rationalization of research and management, to become more effective and sure-footed" and becomes "the business of teams of trained specialists who turn out what is required and make it work in predictable ways."

By the last decade of his life, therefore, Schumpeter had apparently abandoned his earlier ideology that attributed innovation to the entrepreneurial individual. He had only a casual understanding of what (following Alfred Chandler, 1962) we would today call the strategy and structure of "big business," but he was well aware that innovation had become a highly collectivized process. In a 1949 paper entitled "Economic Theory and Entrepreneurial History" that was presented to the participants of the Research Center in Entrepreneurial History, Schumpeter [1949a, pp. 52–53] explicitly recognized the evolution of entrepreneurship into a cooperative activity, the organization of which varied across social environments and that might even be successfully carried out by the state:

> [As] has been often pointed out the entrepreneurial function need not be embodied in a physical person and in particular a single physical person. Every social environment has its own ways of filling the entrepreneurial function. For instance, the practice of farmers in [the United States] has been revolutionized again and again by the introduction of methods worked out in the Department

of Agriculture and by the Department of Agriculture's success in teaching these methods. It is another important point in our research program to find out how important this kind of activity has been in the past or is in the present. Again the entrepreneurial function may be and often is filled co-operatively. With the development of the largest-scale corporations this has evidently become of major importance: aptitudes that no single individual combines can thus be built into a corporate personality; on the other hand, the constituent physical personalities must inevitably to some extent, and very often to a serious extent, interfere with each other. In many cases, therefore, it is difficult or even impossible to name an individual who acts as an "entrepreneur" in a concern. (On the state as collective entrepreneur, see also Ferleger and Lazonick, 1993)

In his life's work as an economist, therefore, Schumpeter not only recognized the need for a theory of economic development, but also came to understand that such a theory would have to comprehend the ongoing role of collective entrepreneurship in the innovation process. Beginning his career as what he himself would have called a "pure theorist," Schumpeter ended up seeing the importance of historical analysis to elaborate his theoretical arguments and to establish their relevance. The analysis had to be historical because the forces for, and impacts of, innovation were subject to continuous change.

As Schumpeter (1950a, p. 82) argued in *Capitalism, Socialism, and Democracy*: "The essential point to grasp is that in dealing with capitalism we are dealing with an evolutionary process." He continued: "It may seem strange that anyone can fail to see so obvious a fact which moreover was long ago emphasized by Karl Marx." In Schumpeter's view, Marx was the pioneer among economists in integrating theory and history in the study of economic development. As Schumpeter (1950a, p. 44) put it in *Capitalism, Socialism, and Democracy*, there was "one thing of fundamental importance for the methodology of economics that [Marx] actually achieved."

Economists always have either themselves done work in economic history or else used the historical work of others. But the facts of economic history were assigned to a separate compartment. They entered theory, if at all, merely in the role of illustrations, or possibly of verifications of results. They mixed with it only mechanically. Now Marx's mixture is a chemical one; that is to say, he introduced them into the very argument that produces the results. He was the first economist of top rank to see and to teach systematically how economic theory may be turned into historical analysis and how the historical narrative may be turned into *histoire raisonnée.* (Schumpeter, 1950a, p. 44)

In *History of Economic Analysis*, written in the 1940s but published after his death, Schumpeter reinforced his understanding of the methodological implications of a theory of economic development by stating that if starting his work in economics afresh he were to be told that he could study only one of history, statistics, and theory, he would choose economic history.

> And this, on three grounds: First, the subject matter of economics is essentially a unique process in historic time. Nobody can hope to understand the economic phenomena of any, including the present, epoch who has not an adequate command of historical *facts* and an adequate amount of historical *sense* or of what may be described as *historical experience.*
>
> Second, the historical report cannot be purely economic but must inevitably reflect also "institutional" facts that are not purely economic: therefore it affords the best method for understanding how economic and noneconomic facts *are* related to one another and how the various social sciences *should* be related to one another.
>
> Third, it is, I believe, the fact that most of the fundamental errors currently committed in economic analysis are due to the lack of historical experience more often than to any other shortcoming of the economist's equipment. (Schumpeter, 1954, pp. 12–13, emphases in original)

What did Schumpeter mean by "historical experience"? Clearly, he did not see the study of economic history as simply the collection of historical data, nor did he view the study of economic history as the application of received theory to the analysis of historical facts. Rather, he saw the study of the historical process as the means by which one acquired the intellectual capability to study the process of change. Theory had to function "not as a master but as a servant of historical research." For "historical experience" to represent the most important analytical equipment of the economist, the historical research must reshape the theoretical framework that is indispensable for doing that research in the first place. To paraphrase his comments on Marx's method, "historical experience" required that economic theory be turned into historical analysis and that the historical narrative be turned into *histoire raisonnée.*

In the opening sentences of his essay, "The Creative Response in Economic History," Schumpeter (1947b, p. 149) called for intellectual communication between economic historians and economic theorists:

> Economic historians and economic theorists can make an interesting and socially valuable journey together, if they will. It would be an investigation into the sadly neglected area of economic change.

Schumpeter's notion of "historical experience" implies that the division of labor between the economic historian and economic theorist must be eliminated. To study the process of change, theory and history must be integrated in the mind of the economist.

Schumpeter and Ideology

By the 1940s, when Schumpeter articulated the importance of the integration of history and theory in economics, his own analysis emphasized the ways in which the social organization of the process of innovation was undermining capitalism as an economic and social system. By capitalism, Schumpeter meant a mode of economic organization in which the main agent of innovation was the individual entrepreneur. He argued that the entrepreneurial function "is losing its importance and is bound to lose it at an accelerating rate in the future even if the economic process itself of which entrepreneurship was the prime mover went on unabated." His contention was that "innovation itself is being reduced to a routine."

> Technological progress is increasingly becoming the business of teams of trained specialists who turn out what is required and make it work in predictable ways. The romance of earlier commercial adventure is rapidly wearing away, because so many more things can be strictly calculated that had of old to be visualized in a flash of genius. (Schumpeter, 1950a, p. 132; see also Solo, 1951)

The ideological implication of this transformation of the innovation process is clear. Economic development still continued apace but innovation—the driving force of economic development—had been collectivized.

If the social transformation of the innovation process meant that the entrepreneur was no longer the agent of the "fundamental phenomenon of economic development," it also rendered untenable perfect competition as an ideal mode of industrial organization. In *Capitalism, Socialism, and Democracy*, Schumpeter (1950a, p. 84) pointed out that, when innovation results in the concentration of industry into "a few big firms," the orthodox economist's notion that deviations from perfect competition result in economic inefficiency no longer holds. Schumpeter argued that "the problem that is usually being visualized [by economists] is how capitalism administers existing structures, whereas the relevant problem is how it creates and destroys them. As long as this is not recognized, the investigator does a meaningless job."

In his 1946 contribution to the *Encyclopedia Britannica*, Schumpeter provided a clear statement of this critique:

> The proposition that monopolists will sell smaller quantities of product at higher prices than will firms in conditions of perfect competition is true only under the proviso that other things—cost structures in particular—be strictly equal, and therefore has but little practical importance. Almost without exception, largest-scale concerns do alter the cost structure of their industry, by introducing new methods of production and in other ways that are beyond the reach of numerous

> competing concerns of medium size. Therefore it does not follow that their outputs are actually smaller and their prices actually higher than would be the outputs and prices with the methods within the reach of perfectly competitive business. (Schumpeter, 1946, p. 195)

In historical retrospect, by the 1940s Schumpeter's insights into the evolution of capitalism and his critique of neoclassical economics were long overdue. We now know that in the early 20th century a managerial revolution had occurred in a number of the most industrialized economies (Chandler, 1990). The characteristic feature of the managerial revolution was the planned coordination of a highly specialized division of labor in which salaried employees played key roles as both technical specialists and managerial generalists. The rise of planned coordination was typically, but not invariably, accompanied by the separation of legal asset ownership from strategic control over the disposition of these assets, with the strategic control in the hands of managerial generalists. As Chandler (1977) has argued for the case of the United States, the managerial revolution in American business occurred in the last half of the 19th century and the first decades of the 20th so that "by World War I, modern business enterprise had come of age" (Chandler, 1977, p. 455; see also Lazonick, 1991a, ch. 7).

So, too, by the second decade of this century a managerial revolution had occurred in Germany and Japan (Chandler, 1990; Morikawa, 1989; see also Morikawa, 1992). In Britain, by way of contrast, owner-managers failed to build managerial organizations, and the widespread separation of ownership from control took a few decades longer to occur (see Hannah, 1983; Elbaum and Lazonick, 1986; Lazonick, 1986; Chandler, 1990). As I have argued elsewhere (Lazonick, 1991a, ch. 1; Elbaum and Lazonick, 1986), the persistence of proprietary capitalism in Britain, far from unleashing a gale of entrepreneurial innovation, was a key factor in Britain's long-run economic decline. In Japan, however, where an early transition to managerial capitalism occurred, a central determinant of the post-World War II economic "miracle" in industries such as automobiles and electronics was an extension of the principles of managerial capitalism further down the organizational hierarchy to include male shop-floor workers as permanent members of the firm, and across legally distinct firms to create planned and coordinated enterprise groups.

It is because of this greater role for planned coordination in the Japanese model of business organization that I have labelled it *collective capitalism* (Lazonick, 1991a, ch. 1). Over the course of the 20th century, competitive advantage and industrial leadership has gone to those enterprises, industries, and economies that have engaged in more, not less, planned coordination of their economic activities. Hence American managerial capitalism won out over the highly individualistic British proprietary capitalism earlier in this century, and Japanese collective capitalism has won out over American managerial capitalism over the past few decades.

Fifty years ago, Schumpeter had the insight to see that this collectivization of economic activity was occurring not only or even primarily at the level of the state, but more fundamentally at the level of the "capitalist" enterprise. Surely, Schumpeter would have viewed the Japanese experience since World War II as further evidence of the 'march into socialism' of which he was already writing in the early 1940s (Schumpeter, 1950a), and which was the theme of his last piece of writing before his death in 1950 (Schumpeter, 1950b). In an age of collective capitalism, as in an age of managerial capitalism, individual entrepreneurship still counts for something. But for innovation to occur, the individual entrepreneur must build an organization that can develop and utilize productive resources in ways that have not been done before. As Schumpeter (1950a, p. 227, emphasis in original) put it in *Capitalism, Socialism, and Democracy*: "We shall see that gradual socialization *within the framework of capitalism* is not only possible but even the most obvious thing to expect."

Today, despite the even further collectivization of economic activity in the most successful industrial economies, we still call the advanced industrial economies "capitalist." Why? What in the 1990s is capitalist about the economies of, for example, the United States, Germany, and Japan? The obvious response is that they are economies that permit the private ownership of the means of production; that is, they permit the individual entrepreneur to invest in whatever line of business he or she wishes, provided it is legal. Indeed, the legal, cultural, and political structures of these economies do much to promote such entrepreneurship, as both an ideology and an economic activity. Yet, despite the continued importance of private entrepreneurship in these economies, the foundations of their long-run prosperity are, as Schumpeter recognized clearly during the last decade of his life, business organizations in which innovation is a collective process. To permit the collectivity to govern its actions generally requires the separation of ownership of the corporation's assets from control over the corporation's productive resources.

In the case of the United States, the separation of ownership from control was already an established fact by the early 1930s when Adolph Berle and Gardiner Means (1968) wrote *The Modern Corporation and Private Property* (for a retrospective on this landmark book, see McCraw, 1990). Berle and Means remained undecided about the economic consequences of the separation of ownership from control. On the one hand, control now rested with those who were in continuous contact with, and had intimate knowledge of, the activities of the corporation. On the other hand, there was concern that managers would become a self-perpetuating group of insiders immune to, and perhaps even in conflict with, the interests of the shareholders and society at large.

Berle and Means (whose work Schumpeter did not cite) did not possess a theory of innovation. Their intellectual effort was rather to document a central institutional transformation that had occurred in the American economy. They had no coherent perspective on this transformation as a phenomenon of economic development. If Berle and Means had embedded a theory of innovation in their work on the social transformation of the modern business enterprise, they might have placed more weight on the fact that the separation of ownership from control had put economic power in the hands of those with the knowledge of technology and organization to make the modern corporation an engine of continuous innovation. At the same time, they might have recognized that the ability and incentive of these professional managers to engage in continuous innovation derived from their participation in a collective organization that included middle and lower level managers, production workers, suppliers and distributors.

They might have also perceived that a problem of maintaining continuous innovation would arise when, as occurred increasingly from the 1950s, the professional managers who ran the corporations came to identify more with the interests of shareholders as portfolio investors than with the interests of the direct participants—employees, suppliers, and distributors—within their business organizations (for an elaboration, see Lazonick, 1992). Especially in the 1980s the advanced industrial economies experienced an onslaught of financial entrepreneurship and financial innovation that seriously undermined the productive capabilities of these economies. In effect, the actual and potential wealth of these nations was adversely affected by a reversion to entrepreneurial capitalism that preempted Schumpeter's "the march into socialism" as well as his "process of creative destruction."

The Schumpeterian Legacy

I have argued that any economist who takes seriously Schumpeter's economics, with its focus on the process of innovation, must recognize its methodological and ideological implications. The methodological implication is that economists must acquire the "historical experience" to integrate theory and history in their economic analysis. The ideological implication is that innovation, and hence economic development, is increasingly a collective process. That, since the time of Schumpeter's death, mainstream economists have clung to an ahistorical methodology and individualist ideology goes far to account for Schumpeter's relative lack of influence on Anglo-American economics in the post-World War II decades.

In the concluding paragraph of his 1949 address to the Research Center in Entrepreneurial History, Schumpeter (1949a, pp. 63–64) called for the integration of theory and history.

> New hypotheses and the marshalling of factual data, old and new, must proceed together . . . In the handling of old and new facts, the historian will gain from keeping in touch with theorists. Neither group should ever be distant from one another—but here the promise from collaboration is particularly great for both parties. As I have said before (see Schumpeter, 1947b), the study of economic change is an area of research where "economic historians and economic theorists can make an interesting and socially valuable journey together, if they will."

Elsewhere I have ventured an explanation of why mainstream economists and historians have not embarked on this "interesting and socially valuable journey together" (see Lazonick, 1991a,b). Let me summarize the main elements of the argument. Over the course of the 20th century prominent economists increasingly defined the subject matter of economics to be the optimal allocation of scarce resources rather than the process of economic development in which, as Schumpeter recognized, the constraints that create scarcity are constantly being overturned. Ignoring the requirements of the process of innovation for collective organization, orthodox economists argued that the optimal allocation of scarce resources required the maximum amount of mobility of factors of production from one use to another. They elaborated a theory of the market economy in which it was "perfect" markets that offered this maximum amount of mobility.

A system of perfect markets is by definition one in which individuals act autonomously of one another and collective organization does not exist. A belief in a system of perfect markets as a mechanism for optimal resource allocation is tantamount to a belief in the efficacy of individualism in economic life. By neglecting to construct a theory of economic development, mainstream economists not only avoided studying the collective realities of advanced industrial development but also were able to portray the optimal economic system as one populated by highly individualistic economic actors. Whether intended or not, by ignoring the process of economic development and focusing on static problems of resource allocation, mainstream economists have been able to portray the nature of economic activity in highly individualistic terms. Mainstream economics is first and foremost an ideology of individualism.

While economists were elaborating the theory of the market economy, the reality of successful economic development was undermining its basic premises about factor mobility and the triumph of individualism. Innovation requires collective organization, and the essence of collective organization is long-term relations among participants in the specialized division of labor (see Lazonick, 1991a, ch. 1–3). Intellectual prisoners of the ideology of individualism, mainstream economists have simply ignored this evolving reality.

The ahistorical methodology of mainstream economics derives from the way in which the ideology of individualism has been defended. Once mainstream economists had embarked on their flight from reality, they required some justification other than the historical record for the relevance of their theoretical approach. They found that justification by defining economics as a universal, self-contained science that would be independent of prevailing social institutions. They let the individual (or "household") be the unit of economic analysis because they saw any movement toward collective organization as creating a market "imperfection" in the form of a barrier to the optimal allocation of scarce resources. They saw no need to consider the possibility that such collective organization might be a necessary condition for innovation because they had already deemed the analysis of innovation to be outside the purview of economic analysis. Indeed, in analyzing the operation of "imperfect markets," economists make no attempt to break with ahistorical methodology. Rather they hold up perfect markets, and hence the ideology of individualism, as an economic ideal (the most prolific economist of this genre is Joseph Stiglitz; see, for example, Stiglitz, 1985, 1986).

Schumpeter himself did not sufficiently attack the irrelevance of the theory of the market economy inherent in the "circular flow." He tended to portray the underlying Walrasian vision as a purely "scientific" achievement, devoid of ideological content (see Schumpeter, 1949b, p. 274; 1951, ch. 2) Yet what Schumpeter (1951, p. 76) called Walras's "structure of purely economic relationships"—that is, a structure of market relationships—may or may not exist in reality and may or may not yield beneficial economic results. Such relationships are laden with ideological content, as has amply been borne out by the inability of Walrasian economists, especially since the time of Schumpeter, to recognize that their system cannot deal with the "fundamental phenomenon"—innovation.

Schumpeter's own emphasis on innovation and his recognition that innovation was increasingly becoming collectivized should lead economists to look for structures of economic relationships other than market-mediated ones. In pushing this research agenda forward, it has been the work of historians rather than economists that has led the way. Back in the 1950s, even as the mainstream of the economics profession was ignoring Schumpeter's call for the integration of theory and history, his call for the study of the historical process was leading to some outstanding results. The immediate academic source of intellectual advance was the Research Center in Entrepreneurial History, located at Harvard University for a decade beginning in 1948. The creator of the center was the economic and business historian, Arthur H. Cole. Schumpeter was a senior member of the center from 1949 until his death in early 1950. Most of the work of the center focused on the sociology and psychology of the entrepreneur—his social background, personality, and social status—rather than on the impact of entrepreneurial activity on economic outcomes (Aitken, 1965; Sass, 1986). But in launching the careers of both Alfred Chandler and David Landes, both of whom did their doctoral dissertations there, the center left an intellectual legacy that can help today's economists avoid (to repeat Schumpeter's words) "most of the fundamental errors currently committed in economic analysis" (Schumpeter, 1954, p. 13).

Chandler (1962, 1977, 1990) documented in detail the collectivization of economic activity within the industrial enterprise, a process that, as we have seen, Schumpeter had become increasingly aware of but on which the state of empirical knowledge had been at best anecdotal. Landes (1969) outlined the comparative impact of social institutions on national economic development, with a particular focus on the rise of the British economy and then its relative decline in the face of German industrial development.

As for the integration of history and theory, Chandler has stressed the importance of generalizing on the basis of the historical record, but has not himself used these generalizations well for the purposes of subsequent hypothesis testing (see Chandler, 1990; Lazonick, 1993b). Moreover, recent attempts by Chandler (1992) to link his work up with economic theory suffer from a lack of explicit attention to innovation as the driving force in the development process (for my own work in this area, see Lazonick, 1991a, 1993a). As for Landes, he has responded to my combined appreciation of his work and critique of its failure to influence economists by expressing strong doubts that the integration of theory and history is possible (Landes, 1991, pp. 19–20).

Nevertheless, as is evidenced by this volume as well as the proceedings of the biannual International Joseph A. Schumpeter Society (Hanusch, 1988; Heertje and Perlman, 1990; Scherer and Perlman, 1992), in recent years a number of economists have begun to push the Schumpeterian research agenda forward (see the seminal work by Nelson and Winter, 1982; the contributions of Scherer, 1984; Dosi et al., 1988; Best, 1990; Lazonick, 1991a; and the journal *Industrial and Corporate Change*). As suggested in this essay, that agenda must document the historical evolution of organizations as economic entities in different times and places, and must integrate this empirical research with a theory of innovation and development. To gain the "historical experience" of which Schumpeter spoke, economic theorists must become economic historians, and economic historians must become economic theorists, until the methodological divide between history and theory is brought to an end.

References

Aitken, H.G.J. (ed.). 1965. *Explorations in Enterprise*. Cambridge: Harvard University Press.

Berle, A., and Means, G.C. 1968. *The Modern Corporation and Private Property*, revised edition. New York: Harcourt, Brace & World.

Best, M. 1990. *The New Competition: Institutions of Industrial Restructuring*. Cambridge: Harvard University Press.

Chandler, Jr., A.D. 1962. *Strategy and Structure: Chapters in the History of the American Industrial Enterprise*. Cambridge: MIT Press.

Chandler, Jr., A.D. 1977. *The Visible Hand: The Managerial Revolution in American Business*. Cambridge: Harvard University Press.

Chandler, Jr., A.D. 1990. *Scale and Scope: The Dynamics of Industrial Capitalism*. Cambridge: Harvard University Press.

Chandler, Jr., A.D. 1992. Organizational Capabilities and the Theory of the Firm'. *Journal of Economic Perspectives*, 6, 79–100.

Dosi, G., C. Freeman, R. Nelson, and Soete, L. (eds.). 1988. *Technical Change and Economic Theory*, Pinter.

Elbaum, B., and Lazonick, W. (eds.). 1986. *The Decline of the British Economy*. Oxford, Oxford University Press.

Ferleger, Louis, and Lazonick, W. 1993. "The Managerial Revolution and the Developmental State: The Case of U.S. Agriculture." *Business and Economic History*, 22 (forthcoming).

Hannah, L. 1983. *The Rise of the Corporate Economy: The British Experience*, 2nd ed. Baltimore, MD: Johns Hopkins University Press.

Hanusch, Horst (ed.). 1988. *Evolutionary Economics: Applications of Schumpeter's Ideas*. Cambridge, UK: Cambridge University Press.

Heertje, A., and Perlman, M. (ed.). 1990. *Evolving Technology and Market*

Structure: Studies in Schumpeterian Economics. Ann Arbor, MI: University of Michigan Press.

Landes, D.S. 1969. *The Unbound Prometheus: Technological Change and Industrial Development in Western Europe from 1750 to the Present*. Cambridge, UK: Cambridge University Press.

Landes, D.S. 1991. "Introduction: On Technology and Growth." In *Favorites of Fortune: Technology, Growth and Economic Development since the Industrial Revolution*. P. Higonnet, D.S. Landes, and H. Rosovsky, eds. Cambridge: Harvard University Press.

Lazonick, W. 1986. "Strategy, Structure, and Management Development in the United States and Britain." In *Development of Managerial Enterprise*. K. Kobayashi and H. Morikawa, eds. Tokyo: University of Tokyo Press, pp. 101–146.

Lazonick, W. 1991a. *Business Organization and the Myth of the Market Economy*. Cambridge, UK: Cambridge University Press.

Lazonick, W. 1991b. "What Happened to the Theory of Economic Development?" In *Favorites of Fortune: Technology, Growth and Economic Development since the Industrial Revolution*. P. Higonnet, D.S. Landes, and H. Rosovsky, eds. Cambridge: Harvard University Press.

Lazonick, W. 1992. "Controlling the Market for Corporate Control: The Historical Significance of Managerial Capitalism." *Industrial and Corporate Change* 1:445–448.

Lazonick, W. 1993a. "Learning and the Dynamics of International Competitive Advantage." In *Learning and Technical Change*. R. Thomson, ed. New York St. Martin's Press.

Lazonick, W. 1993b. "Social Organization and Technological Leadership." In *Convergence of Productivity: Cross-National Studies and Historical Evidence*, W. Baumol, R. Nelson, and E. Wolff, eds. New York: Oxford University Press.

McCraw, T.K. 1990. "Berle and Means." *Reviews in American History* 18:578–596.

McCraw, T.K., and Reinhardt, F. 1989. "Losing to Win: U.S. Steel's Pricing, Investment Decisions, and Market Share, 1901–1938." *Journal of Economic History* 49:593–619.

Marshall, A. 1961. *Principles of Economics*, Vol. 1. 9th (variorum) ed. New York: Macmillan.

Morikawa, H. 1989. "The Increasing Power of Salaried Managers in Japan's Large Corporations." In *Managing Industrial Enterprise: Cases from Japan's Prewar Experience*. W.D. Wray, ed. Cambridge, MA: Council on East Asian Studies, pp. 27–51.

Morikawa, H. 1992. *Zaibatsu: The Rise and Fall of Family Enterprise Groups in Japan*. Tokyo: University of Tokyo Press.

Nelson, R.R., and Winter, S.G. 1982. *An Evolutionary Theory of Economic Change*. Cambridge: Harvard University Press.

Scherer, F.M. 1984. *Innovation and Growth: Schumpeterian Perspectives*. Cambridge: MIT Press.

Scherer, F.M., and Perlman, M. (eds.). 1992. *Entrepreneurship, Technological Innovation, and Economic Growth: Studies in the Schumpeterian Tradition*. Ann Arbor, MI. University of Michigan Press.

Schumpeter, J.A. 1928. "The Instability of Capitalism." *Economic Journal* 48:361–386.

Schumpeter, J.A. 1939. *Business Cycles*. New York: McGraw-Hill.

Schumpeter, J.A. 1946. "Capitalism." *Encyclopedia Britannica* 4:801–807.

Schumpeter, J.A. 1947a. "Theoretical Problems of Economic Growth." *Journal of Economic History* 7 (Suppl.) 1–9.

Schumpeter, J.A. 1947b. "The Creative Response in Economic History." *Journal of Economic History* 7:149–159.

Schumpeter, J.A. 1949a. "Economic Theory and Entrepreneurial History." In *Change and the Entrepreneur*. Research Center in Entrepreneurial History. Cambridge: Harvard University Press, pp. 63–84.

Schumpeter, J.A. 1949b. "Science and Ideology." *American Economic Review* 39:345–359.

Schumpeter, J.A. 1950a. *Capitalism, Socialism and Democracy*, New York: Harper.

Schumpeter, J.A. 1950b. "The March in Socialism." *American Economic Review* 40:446–456.

Schumpeter, J.A. 1951. *Ten Great Economists: From Marx to Keynes*, Oxford University Press.

Schumpeter, J.A. 1954. *History of Economic Analysis*, Oxford University Press.

Schumpeter, J.A. 1961. *The Theory of Economic Development*. New York: Oxford University Press.

Sass, S.A. 1986. *Entrepreneurial Historians and History: Leadership and Rationality in American Economic Historiography, 1940–1960*. New York: Garland.

Solo, C.S. 1951. "Innovation in the Capitalist Process: A Critique of the Schumpeterian Theory." *Quarterly Journal of Economics* 65:417–428.

Stiglitz, J.E. 1985. "Credit Markets and the Control of Capital." *Journal of Money, Credit, and Banking* 17:133–152.

Stiglitz, J.E. 1986. "Theory of Competition, Incentives, and Risk." In *New Developments in the Analysis of Market Structure*. J.E. Stiglitz and F. Mathewson, eds. Cambridge: MIT Press, pp. 399–446.

10 NEO-SCHUMPETERIANS AND ECONOMIC THEORY

Arnold Heertje

Introduction

This chapter deals with the contribution of the neo-Schumpeterians to economic theory. In fact, I shall present a cost-benefit analysis of the neo-Schumpeterian challenge to neoclassical economics. As the neo-Schumpeterians derive their inspiration from the works of J.A. Schumpeter, it seems appropriate and quite natural to start with a few observations on Schumpeter.

The relationship Schumpeter did bring to the fore between monopolization, the size of the firms, and innovation against the background of a changing capitalistic system from within has led to a still growing stream of publications and empirical research. For a long time Schumpeter remained in the shadow of Keynes, but in this last quarter of the present century their roles on the economic scene seem to be reversed. This development is linked both to the renewed attention for the supply side of the economic process and the possibility of rephrasing Schumpeter's often intuitive reasoning into nonlinear dynamic systems. But Schumpeter is a man of paradoxes. His discussion of the role of innovation in capitalism explains why his name is often mentioned with regard to the economic analysis of technical change. His treatment of innovation as an endogeneous process, triggered by entrepreneurs who implement new combinations in order to make profits, justifies this habit. On the other hand, technical change in the sense of the development of new knowledge and possibilities and the diffusion of knowledge are almost wholly absent from his exposition. The mutual relationship between development and application of new technology is outside the scope of his analysis. In fact, the circular character of invention, diffusion, innovation, and imitation escapes Schumpeter's attention. Schumpeter introduced the idea of creative destruction to describe the evolution of a capitalistic system, but he did not deal with the factors that might influence the creativity of innovators and entrepreneurs in a positive way. We cannot avoid the paradoxical conclusion that Schumpeter did not reflect enough on the factors that lie behind innovation, to understand and foresee the inclination of people, both as individuals and organizations, to remain creative and produce new technical insights, even if others tend to prefer the status quo and become victims of routine and a bureaucratic attitude.

In his book on economic development (Schumpeter, 1912), the creation of a new firm is a typical case of a new combination. In his book on business cycles (Schumpeter, 1939), written just a few years before *Capitalism, Socialism and Democracy* (Schumpeter, 1942), Schumpeter is even more outspoken about the role of new firms. New production functions are introduced into the system through new firms and as long as there are new ideas new firms will be founded. In *Capitalism, Socialism and Democracy* Schumpeter no longer refers to the establishment of new firms or to the entry of new entrepreneurs. In fact, he has lost sight of the relative importance of new, often small firms as sources of minor and sometimes major innovations, not to speak of their role in the process of invention. His slightly more integrated view of invention and innovation in *Capitalism, Socialism and Democracy* goes along with a change in view about the entrepreneurial function. The entrepreneur is no longer an outsider who sets up a new firm with a new product and new capital equipment. It is again paradoxical to conclude that one of the reasons for Schumpeter's prediction of the decay of capitalism lies in his overlooking the fact, which we have experienced again since the beginning of the 1980s, that, notwithstanding the existence and emergence of large, monopolistic, and often multinational firms, technical change presents the opportunity to create many new firms operating on a small scale, both in the industrial and service sector and in the formal and informal sector of the economy. If Schumpeter had been faithful to his original idea of considering the setting up of new firms as the important vehicle for innovation, he would on balance not have lost his confidence in the dynamics of capitalism.

From a theoretical point of view, Schumpeter is the economist of discontinuity. The evolutionary character of capitalism is discontinuous, due to the qualitative changes that are brought about by the new products, the new methods of production and transportation, the new markets, and the new organization. His emphasis on major innovations, by way of jumps and fundamental qualitative changes in economic life, does distinguish him from mainstream economists. Here also lies his striking difference from Keynes, who was able to prove the existence of equilibrium at low levels of unemployment. In his time the mathematical apparatus could take care of continuity both in microeconomics and macroeconomics. But the mathematical technique was not able to crack Schumpeter's vision.

On the whole Schumpeter appears to be more impressive for his historical knowledge, descriptive talent and elegance of expression, and above all his outspoken vision on the evolution of capitalism and the role of the entrepreneur as an innovator than for analytical insights, coherence, and consistent reasoning. This situation has not hampered the emergence of neo-Schumpeterians, who challenge neoclassical economics and who share a common interest in Schumpeter's writings and derive their inspiration from Schumpeter's evolutionary approach.

Neo-Schumpeterians

Neo-Schumpeterians have a tendency to consider themselves as a group or school, sharing common views and opposing in particular, the so-called neoclassical scheme. Well-known representatives, such as Nelson, Winter, Freeman, Dosi, Rosenberg, and Soete, refer to each other's work, of which they have a priori a higher opinion than research carried out by scholars outside the group. Their joint behavior is not without advantages. A lot of activity is going on, there is an almost fanatic urge to prove their case against "the enemy," and the emphasis on historical and empirical evidence brings about broader and deeper knowledge of facts. There can be no doubt that the whole profession could be much better informed about the economic role technology plays in our society if the other side would take notice of what neo-Schumpeterians are doing.

The neo-Schumpeterians confront the equilibrium approach of the neoclassicals, based on maximizing behavior of producers, consumers, and owners of the factors of production with an evolutionary framework of the dynamic process as the interaction of internal movements, activities, and decisions, and the environment of the firm, both being influenced and shaped by technical change, in particular. In doing so they underline the significance of discontinuous and qualitative changes, the role of restricted knowledge, information and fundamental uncertainty, increasing returns, external effects, and decision making. A typical feature also is the emphasis put on the process of diffusion of technology, both in the sense of knowledge and applications and the relationship with institutional changes in society at large. To describe these phenomena a specific wording, has been invented, such as technological paradigms, technological regimes, and technological trajectories.

Although the neo-Schumpeterian approach to economic reality is not without merit, some drawbacks have to be brought to the fore. The critical attitude of the neo-Schumpeterians has led to a clearer picture of the restricted significance of the neoclassical scheme and an impressive set of empirical results, but not to a consistent alternative theory. Instead of mathematical modelling, verbal exposition and description of economic phenomena is the overwhelming characteristic of the so-called new paradigm. It goes without saying that it is not an easy task to substitute the static neoclassical equilibrium analysis for a dynamic analysis of economic evolution, but this insight can only be a reason for modesty and a cooperative attitude, and not for self-applause and isolation.

The lack of theoretical sophistication has a further drawback. In the writings of the neo-Schumpeterians there is no clear borderline between the descriptive treatment of technical and social change, the behavior of the firm, and market structure and policy conclusions. Without realizing the difference between positive statements and value judgements, often an active technology policy is implied as a self-evident consequence of the description of historical and empirical developments and events. The following quotation (Nelson and Soete, 1988) is just one of the many possible illustrations: "the recognition that the creation of technological capabilities involves an evolutionary, endogeneous process of change, negotiated and mediated with society at large, implies that policies in the area of science and technology will not, nor should be limited to questions about the economic integration of technological change, but will include all aspects of the broader societal integration of such change." It is here that the complete avoidance of welfare economics as a building block in the sequence of analysis, theory of economic policy, and economic policy is felt more than anywhere else. Of course, the all too brief sketch I have presented is more clear cut than is compatible with the facts. Not only is description of the phenomena the first stage of new theoretical developments, but also bits of analysis can be found in the work of the neo-Schumpeterians. A clear example of advanced economic analysis by a neo-Schumpeterian is Silverberg's contribution on the mathematical approaches to self-organization and evolution (Silverberg, 1988). Furthermore there is already a move underway by some of them in the direction of more exchange of views with scholars such as Arrow and Stiglitz. However, it is still remarkable to note that almost all of the critical observations of the neo-Schumpeterians have been taken up by neoclassicals or mathematical economists who refine and improve economic theory, leaving the neo-Schumpeterians with the honor of asking for a breakthrough and the embarrassment of seeing the rest of the profession providing the always preliminary answers.

Economic Theory à la Schumpeter

Analysis inspired by Schumpeter and his followers has been carried out by many scholars, who also contribute to other domains of economic theory and who are for this reason open minded to all kind of challenges, not just the neo-Schumpeterian challenge. However, from the point of view of economic theory, the neo-Schumpeterian challenge is of major importance, due to both its empirical relevance and its scope.

Let us indicate a few theoretical developments that directly or indirectly go back to Schumpeter and his modern branch of representatives. In growth theory the recent revival of the endogeneous theory of economic growth and technical change is a well-balanced synthesis of a neoclassical approach and a Schumpeterian impact. Goodwin's work on chaotic economic dynamics is a wonderful example of a heroic attempt to solve with modern mathematical techniques problems set by Schumpeter, who happened to be one of Goodwin's teachers. Partly related to chaos theory is catastrophe theory, which is of help in unraveling the economics of discontinuity, again a theme with a strong Schumpeterian flavor. However, the problem solving and solution are provided by scholars, who are outside the sphere of what perhaps may be referred to as the neo-Schumpeterian circus. The analysis of learning processes, imperfect knowledge, incentives, and search behavior, claimed to be Schumpeterian themes, in fact, is still carried out by big shots such as Arrow, Laffont, and Stiglitz. The view of the market as a mechanism of discovery of new products, new methods of production, and new wants has been taken up by neo-Austrians, such as Kirzner in the footsteps of Hayek. A final typical case is the theory of international trade, in which neo-Schumpeterians, such as Dosi and Soete (1988), excel in a well-taken critical analysis of the theory, partly on the basis of empirical evidence and in a description of the factors that have to be included in a better theory, for example, of the relationship between technical change and international trade. In recent years most theoretical work in this direction has been done by Helpman and Krugman (1985), who not only list a number of factors but also theorize on their mutual relationship and prepare fresh econometric research in this area of economic theory. In a recently published contribution Grosman and Helpman studied the welfare implications of growth-enhancing trade and industrial policies for a small open economy, in which growth is due to endogeneous improvements in technology. (Grosman and Helpman, 1991; Siebert, 1991). Recently, Dosi, Pavitt, and Soete (1990) were able to build on their work in a volume on technical change and international trade, and Cimoli and Soete (1992) developed a generalized technology gap trade model.

Endogeneous growth theory in the hands of P.M. Romer (1986, 1990) has succeeded in dealing with increasing returns, connected with the use of knowledge in production, in a dynamic general equilibrium context. Technical change lies at the heart of endogeneous growth and results, to a large extent, from intentional actions taken by people who respond to market incentives. This refers, in particular, to the process whereby new knowledge is translated into goods with commercial value. The production of new knowledge, for example, through investment in human capital, plays an important role and is associated with external effects. Unbounded accumulation, nonrivalry, and incomplete appropriability of knowledge are essential features of the new theory of economic growth of which market power on the side of the entrepreneurs à la Schumpeter is an essential ingredient. Increasing returns of the use of knowledge can be handled in models with imperfect competition because the factors of production capital and labor will be paid less than their marginal product. Recently an endogeneous growth model has been constructed with both product improvements and uncertainty, in short growth through creative destruction from within (Aghion and Howitt, 1992). Each innovation consists of a new intermediate good that can be used to produce final output in a more efficient manner. Research firms derive their motivation from the prospect of monopoly rents. These rents are captured when a successful innovation is patented. Those rents will be destroyed by the next innovation.

The endogeneous growth theory is able to explain a pluriform pattern of growth rates over time and through space, starting from the individual behavior of economic agents. Within the framework of endogeneous growth theory, the relationship between technical change and institutional developments can also be incorporated. An interesting example is a model developed by Hartwick (1992) in the footsteps of Romer on endogeneous growth with public education. In other words, endogeneous growth theory is a clear answer to the challenge put forward both by Schumpeter and the neo-Schumpeterians. It comes, therefore, as no surprise that in a recent survey on endogeneous growth theory, the neo-Schumpeterians are referred to as scholars who develop "un cadre théorique non formalisé" (Amable and Guellec, 1992).

In his book on chaotic economic dynamics, Goodwin (1990) basically starts from Schumpeter, who in Goodwin's words formulated "economic evolution as technical progress in the shape of 'swarms' ". He develops a nonlinear model of a chaotic growth oscillator, the erratic movements of which are endogeneous, with the aim of incorporating in one system long and short waves. The final values of the first innovative swarm are the initial values of a second one and so forth. There can be no doubt that, Goodwin made a major contribution to the theory of economic dynamics the neo-Schumpeterians are seeking. Silverberg acknowledges this in his essay on modelling economic dynamics and technical change (Silverberg, 1988).

Several features of the neo-Schumpeterian approach are embodied in the very original work on technical change, carried out by Amendola and Gaffard (Amendola and Gaffard, 1988). In their model a decision to follow an innovative path appears as the most flexible choice, in the sense that it makes the greater range of future options available. Technical change then consists in the search for flexibility, considered as a qualitative change breaking a sequence and followed by a process of learning. The model of the role of technical change in the economy describes routine processes, which are the expression of an already established and fully developed technology, reflecting the skills of existing human resources and innovative processes, which are intermediate steps in the process of research and experimentation. The model enables the authors to describe the possible evolution of an economy under the influence of innovative choice, taken up as a discontinuity.

The economic analysis of discontinuity is one of the amazing developments in recent years of our discipline. No doubt the verbal description of the phenomenon has been laid down by Schumpeter and his followers. Almost 10 years ago H.W. Ursprung confronted the Schumpeterian entrepreneur who carries out innovations with catastrophe theory, a mathematical approach designed to cope with discontinuous phenomena (Ursprung, 1984). He points out that catastrophe models can exhibit discontinuous behavior on the basis of continuously changing-parameters. J. Barkley Rosser

Jr. has written the first treatise on the theory of economic discontinuities (Rosser, 1991). The books presents a splendid overview of the state of art and discusses Schumpeterian discontinuities against the background of the reswitching debate of capital theory. Both Ursprung and Barkley Rosser react to the neo-Schumpeterian challenge on discontinuity, as a major aspect of economic evolution, with attempts to apply new theoretical insights, which spring from advanced mathematical reasoning.

It would go too far to summarize in a few sentences the immense literature on the economics of information, fundamental and chaotic uncertainty, and learning by doing and using. Let us simply indicate that in recent books on industrial organization (Tirole, 1988) many of the new theoretical insights have been applied to the theory of the firm in a dynamic context. In other words, the evolutionary theme has been taken up and placed on a sound mathematical basis. Let me, by way of illustration, refer to Tirole's treatment of dynamic price competition and tacit collusion.

If a firm likes its competitor to charge high prices, it would like to convince its rival that it is likely to charge high prices itself. It has to build up a reputation of trust and friendly behavior. In a dynamic framework a firm can send costly signals in order to convey information. In a two-period price game a firm can charge in period 1 a price that exceeds the expected profit-maximizing price in order to pass on the information that it may charge a high price in period 1. This situation can be analyzed by means of a repeated price game with asymmetric information about marginal costs or demand, each firm sacrificing short-run profit by raising its price in order to build a reputation for higher prices. The element of uncertainty may be introduced by assuming that there is a small probability that the players express preferences that deviate from the pay-off matrix, based on maximizing behavior. Tirole introduces the evolutionary approach in this case by pointing out that this approach does not require any maximizing behavior at all. But, still it assumes that economic agents do not in the long run follow suboptimal rules. Actors who use rules that do relatively well against a variety of other rules, i.e., robust rules, will stay around. As Tirole rightly points out, the definition of a robust rule is a priori contingent on the set and probability distribution of mutations, and on the set of strategies the robust rule has to be compared with. In other words, a more sophisticated analysis is needed, for example, in terms of game theory, along the lines of the work done by Tirole, Laffont, Rubinstein, Fudenberg, Kreps, Stiglitz, and others. The illustration given is just one from an enormous rich collection of models, which takes into account Darwinian selection, signaling, screening, incentives, imperfect and incomplete information, network externalities, patent races, capacity constraints, process and product innovation, research and development, product selection, increasing returns to scale, reputation building, long-run relationships, and transaction costs. Again the conclusion must be that the neo-Schumpeterians did come up with interesting questions, but that the answers have been provided by others, who are permanently involved in a process of creative destruction.

As is well known Hayek emphasized the role of the discovery of knowledge in the process of economic development. Modern neo-Austrians, such as Kirzner, make it clear that Hayek not only referred to equilibrium prices as carriers of information for buyers and sellers, but also to market prices as "spontaneously generated flashing red lights *alerting* hitherto unwitting market participants to the possibility of pure entrepreneurial profit" (Kirzner, 1992, p. 151). In a wider context this leads to the distinction between the market as a static mechanism of allocation and the market as a method of discovery of new wants, new products, and methods of production. This also implies a shift from Pareto optimality as a criterion for the evaluation of situations to the notion of coordination in case of market processes. The analysis of the market as a mechanism of discovery fits in the neo-Schumpeterian approach, but it must be admitted that the neo-Austrians in the footsteps of Hayek devoted more energy and intellectual equipment to the issue than the neo-Schumpeterians. After a lengthy discussion of Nelson's argument on the market system, Thomsen draws the conclusion that Nelson did not fully grasp the nature of entrepreneurial competition as a discovery procedure and the role of prices in it (Thomsen, 1992, p. 95). Both streams of economic thought, however, share a common inclination to description instead of rigorous analysis.

The topics briefly discussed so far all point to the conclusion that neo-Schumpeterians have been productive in their criticism of the neoclassical scheme on the basis of an evolutionary approach, but that the questions they have raised have been addressed more or less successfully by many scholars, who often have close links with the neoclassical tradition.

Neo-Schumpeterians and Coase

It seems natural to expect that neo-Schumpeterians would rely heavily on several insights put forward by R.H. Coase (1988), in particular, his introduction of the role of transaction costs as an analytical device to understand the working and evolution of the economic system. In fact, Nelson and Winter (1982), in their widely read book on the evolutionary theory of economic change, devote some attention to the concept of transaction costs in passing, but they do not make use of it as a vehicle for an analytical approach. The wide variety of organizational structures within and between firms can be explained by means of a specification of transactions costs, as has been illustrated by the work of O.E. Williamson (1986). From the many contributions to *Technical Change and Economic Theory* (Dosi et al., 1988), only Lundvall confronts the economics of product innovations with Williamson's interpretation of the transaction costs. On the whole the neo-Schumpeterians neglect the work done by Coase, both on markets and firms as institutions, and on the economics of law. The modern development of new institutional economics seems, to a large extent, to be outside the scope of the neo-Schumpeterians.

This view can also be gathered from the exploration of equilibrium and evolution as connecting principles of economics by B.J. Loasby. He points out that the coordination of the growth of knowledge as an activity that involves fundamental uncertainty and—in my words—search behavior, depends on rational structures and procedures and systems that are "stable enough to give confidence to the people working within them to develop and try out new ideas" (Loasby, 1991, p. 101). This implies vague and tacit contracts, and organizational structures that make search behavior possible and effective. Here an extension of Coase's explanation for the existence of firms on the basis of transaction costs looks promising in order to explain the coordination between innovative individuals.

When Coase a few years ago made the point that his views have not been accepted and understood, he did not restrict himself to neoclassical economists, but did also include the neo-Schumpeterians. This again confirms our argument that the neo-Schumpeterians so far have not digested theoretical developments that are relevant from the point of view of their own reasoning.

Conclusions

No doubt the work of Schumpeter and the neo-Schumpeterians presents a major challenge to economic theory. Is it true that "the shift from mechanistic models to an evolutionary approach in economics is long overdue," as Freeman puts it (Freeman, 1992, p. 121)? In view of the apparent lack of theoretical sophistication of most but not all neo-Schumpeterians, a synthesis of the themes brought to the fore by the neo-Schumpeterians, and the work done by neoclassical and other economists, seems to be a more fruitful route.

There is no change or discontinuity without continuity, no disturbance without rest, no innovation without tradition and even stagnation, no chaos without order, no evolution without equilibrium. Markets and firms as established institutions are the backbone for the process of discovery of new technology and new methods of organization. The coordination of the development of new knowledge through search behavior not only presupposes the allocation of resources through choice behavior, but also demands a certain balance between structures that embody equilibrium and continuity and an informal framework of assumptions, conventions, and procedures that enable people to depart from the status quo, to introduce changes to innovate, and to provoke evolution.

In other words, broader theories are needed that take up the neo-Schumpeterian challenge by making use of modern mathematical techniques, such as chaos theory, the master equation, and nonlinear dynamic systems, on one hand, and fresh economic reasoning on technical change and welfare economics, on the other. I would not be surprised to see the present Schumpeterian mood to be part of mainstream economics before the end of this century.

References

Aghion, P., and Howitt, P. 1992. "A Model of Growth Through Creative Destruction," *Econometrica*, 323–352.

Amable, B., and Guellec, G. 1992. "Les Théories de la Croissance Endogène." *Revue d'Économie Politique*.

Amendola, M., and Gaffard, J.L. 1988. *The Innovative Choice*. New York: Oxford University Press.

Cimoli, M., and Soete, L. 1992. "A Generalized Technology Gap Trade Model." *Économie Appliquée*.

Coase, R.H. 1988. *The Firm, The Market and The Law*. Chicago and London.

Dosi, G., and Soete, L. 1988. "Technical Change and International Trade." In *Technical Change and Economic Theory*, pp. 401–431.

Dosi, G., Freeman, C., Nelson, R.R., Silverberg, G., and Soete, L. (eds). 1988. *Technical Change and Economic Theory*. London: University Press.

Dosi, G., Pavitt, K., and Soete, L. 1990. *The Economics of Technical Change and International Trade*. New York: Oxford University Press.

Freeman, C. 1992. *The Economics of Hope*. London: University Press.

Goodwin, R.M. 1990. *Chaotic Economic Dynamics*. Oxford: University Press, p. 56.

Grosman, G.M., and Helpman, E. 1991. "Growth and Welfare in a Small Open Economy." In *International Trade and Trade Policy*. E. Helpman and A. Razin, eds.: Cambridge: University Press.

Hartwick, J.M. 1992. "Endogeneous Growth with Public Education." *Economic Letters*, New York: University Press.

Helpman, E., and Krugman, P.R. 1985. Market Structure and Foreign Trade. Cambridge: University Press.

Kirzner, I.M. 1992. *The Meaning of Market Process*. London: University Press.

Loasby, B.J. 1991. *Equilibrium and Evolution*. Manchester: University Press.

Nelson, R.R., and Winter, S.G. 1982. *An Evolutionary Theory of Economic Change*. Cambridge: University Press.

Nelson, R.R., and Soete, L. 1988. "Policy Conclusions." In Dosi, G., Freeman, C., Nelson, R., Silfverberg, G., and Soete, L. *Technical Change and Economic Theory*. New York: University Press.

Romer, P.M. 1986. "Increasing Returns and Long-Run Growth." *Journal of Political Economy*.

Romer, P.M. 1990. "Endogeneous Technical Change." *Journal of Political Economy* 00:71–103.

Rosenberg, N. 1982. *Inside the Black Box, Technology and Economics*. Cambridge: University Press.

Rosser, J.B. 1991. *From Catastrophe to Chaos: A General Theory of Economic Discontinuities*. Boston: University Press.

Schumpeter, J.A. 1912. *Theorie der wirtschaflichen Entwicklung*. Leipzig: University Press.

Schumpeter, J.A. 1939. *Business Cycles*. New York: University Press.

Schumpeter, J.A. 1942. *Capitalism, Socialism and Democracy*. New York: University Press.

Siebert, M. 1991. "A Schumpeterian Model of Growth in the World Economy; Some Notes on a New Paradigm in International Economics." *Weltwirtschaftlichen Archiv*. University Press.

Silverberg, G. 1988. "Modelling Economic Dynamics and Technical Change: Mathematical Approaches to Self-organisation and Evolution." In Dosi, G., Freemanc, Nelson, R., Silrverbery, G. and Scole, L. *Technical Change and Economic Theory*.

Thomsen, E.F. 1992. *Prices and Knowledge*. London: University Press.

Tirole, J. 1988. *The Theory of Industrial Organization*. Cambridge: University Press.

Ursprung, H.W. 1984. "Schumpeterian Entrepreneurs and Catastrophe Theory or A New Chapter to the Foundation of Economic Analysis." *Journal of Economics*. University Press.

Weidlich, W., and Braun, M. 1992. "The Master Equation Approach to Nonlinear Economics." Journal of Evolutionary Economics University Press.

Williamson, O.E. 1986. *Economic Organization; Firms, Markets and Policy Controls*. Brighton: University Press.

11 RETHINKING ECONOMICS From GNP Growth to Ecological Sustainability

Peter Söderbaum

For a long time Gross National Product (GNP) growth has been regarded as the main idea of progress in Western societies. The GNP is seen as an indicator of the resources available for various purposes in a country. As an example Walter Heller, adviser to the president in the United States in the 1960s, made the judgement that "it will be hard enough to fight the wars on poverty, discrimination, and pollution even with vigorous economic growth" (Heller, 1972, p. 11). This idea of GNP as the main indicator, and of "economic growth" as a necessary part of progress, has been disseminated to all parts of the world. Countries are evaluated with respect to the level of GNP per capita and the rate of "economic growth." To facilitate measurements of this kind, systems of national accounting are now used in a large number of countries.

Mainstream neoclassical economists often warn against uncritical interpretations of the GNP as an indicator of welfare. This is true also of Walter Heller. Heller suggests that GNP mainly should be seen "(1) as a guide to fiscal and monetary policy for management of aggregate demand, and (2) as a measure of the availability of output to meet changing national priorities" (Heller, 1972, p. 13). The second function referred to has something to do with possibilities for welfare, according to Heller, but is not in itself a sufficient indicator of welfare. Also, with regard to the notion of modifying GNP in the hope of finding some other aggregate indicator of national or per capita welfare, Heller expresses considerable scepticism:

> Indeed, no *single* index of social welfare can be calculated, because we have nothing like the pricing system to solve the impossible problem of attaching weights to the various components, be they pollution, crime, health, discrimination or whatever. But to conclude that no *single* index can be constructed is not to undermine or discourage the efforts to develop a set of social indicators, not anchored in the GNP accounts, that will permit us to make better judgements on advances as well as failures in social performance." (Heller, 1972, p. 15)

While economists are aware of the limits to GNP as a welfare indicator, many actors on the public scene continue to refer to GNP as the main idea of progress. So, my criticism of neoclassical economists in this part is not that they are unaware of the problems but rather that they have done so little in terms of articulating other, alternative, ideas of progress in a modern society. The emphasis has rather been on explaining "economic growth" through various growth theories (e.g., Solow, 1957). This is done by relating the growth performance of specific countries to the size of the inputs of labor and capital. At some stage in this search process, it was suggested that economic growth could not be satisfactorily explained by changes in input quantities of labor and capital alone, but that some qualitative factors labelled *technical change* or *technical advance* were involved. Inputs related to natural resources or the environment were hardly taken seriously in these early attempts to explain economic growth.

Growth theory of the kind indicated is based on standard neoclassical economics, for example, the concept of production function, and various assumptions about independence between factor categories, about endogenous and exogenous factors, etc. It is, of course, possible to question these assumptions and to suggest some other approach to the explanation, or rather understanding, of GNP performance of various countries. Assuming that institutions are constant, for instance, is hardly realistic for studies that cover several decades. It is also possible to try to investigate the different components of "technological change." At some stage in such an attempt, it becomes fruitful to shift to some other conceptual framework than that of neoclassical economics. The concept of innovation may be used as a cornerstone and one may refer to a national system of innovation (NSI), where also institutional arrangements are considered as variables in the attempts to describe growth performance or an increase in labor productivity (Lundvall, 1992; Nelson, 1993).

Although the NSI approach, in my judgement, represents an important step forward and is worth pursuing, the focus in this essay will be on alternatives to "economic growth" (or labor productivity) as the indicator of welfare or progress in society. More precisely, ecological considerations will be at the heart of the analysis. In terms of national accounting of the conventional kind, distinctions could be made, as a first step, between those parts of GNP that, according to some nonmonetary performance indicators, are judged "environmentally sound" and those parts that are "environmentally detrimental." The NSI approach could perhaps be used in explaining or understanding innovations (in terms of products or processes) that represent improvements with respect to environmental performance when compared with competing products or processes.

Thus, in what follows environmental problems will be used as the point of departure, although the discussion claims to be relevant also to other areas of human concern. What I consider to be an oversimplification, for example, an overemphasis on monetary accounting, will be challenged at the micro and macro levels. Instead, the role of multidimensionality and of nonmonetary indicators will be emphasized. Moreover, it will be argued that exclusive reliance on neoclassical economics is not very promising if one wishes to open up new thinking in relation to environmental problems. Instead pluralism, in which institutional economics is seen as a complementary approach, is advocated.

Environmental Problems

Problems of environment and development have been the subject of two United Nations conferences, one in Stockholm 1972 and the other in Rio de Janeiro in 1992. Some local and regional problems that were known in 1972 have been handled with some success. Other problems known at the time of the first conference, such as acid rain, are more serious today. Also some new problem areas have been added in the period between the two conferences. The degradation of the ozone layer and possible climatic change are cases in point.

It is not possible here to go into detail about specific environmental problems. In broad and admittedly simplistic terms it can be argued, however, that the seriousness of the problems at a global level is related to the size of the human population and the life-styles of individuals (with related production and consumption activities) in various parts of the world. As indicated by Figure 1, human activities of production, consumption, etc. are embedded in a global ecosystem or biosphere, which essentially is

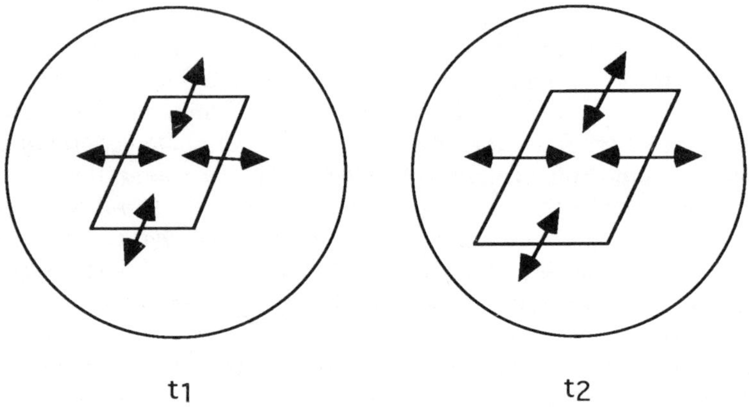

Figure 11.1. A simplified illustration of how the total human population on the planet and the load on ecosystems are expanding from one point in time t1 to another t2.

a finite system. Physical resources are extracted from this ecosystem, and waste as well as pollution are returned to the ecosystem. When it comes to this physical aspect, then, the global ecosystem has a "source" and a "sink" function in relation to the human subsystem with physical manmade capital etc. (Goodland, 1991, p. 16). These two functions are related, for instance, in the sense that a higher extraction of nonrenewable resources, such as oil and coal, will mean more pollution and waste, and thereby increased pressure on the assimilative capacity of the ecosystem.

By comparing the dates of the two conferences, one sees that the global environmental situation is in many respects more serious today than it was 20 years ago. This is indicated in Figure 1 by an increase in the inner surface that is assumed to be connected with the size of the human population times the average per capita load on the environment. The human population on this planet has increased and is presently at a level of 5.3 billion. The average load on the environment from those individuals has probably not decreased. Although no one-dimensional indicator is available, the scale of human activities seems to be increasing. If there is an ecological space on this planet that is limited and rather unchanging, the part of it occupied by humans is increasing in relation to other life forms. That nonhuman life forms are loosing ground is indicated, for instance, by estimates of losses in biodiversity. Some kinds of environmental degradation that are the result of human activities, like depletion of the ozone layer, may directly affect all kinds of life and ecosystems.

What can be done about environmental problems? According to the view indicated, the size of the human population is one part of the problem and the per capita load on the environment is another. The size of the population is clearly an important long-run issue. Possibilities of finding a stable population equilibrium in various parts of the world should be considered and the population in each area should be broadly adapted to the carrying capacity of that area. Within the scope of a specific assumed carrying capacity in an area, some trade-off may exist between population size and environmental load per capita. If the current situation is close to what the environment can assimilate, any increase in the size of the population has to be met by a correspondingly reduced pressure on a per capita basis. According to this reasoning, a reduction in the size of the population would mean that some increased per capita load on the environment and more detrimental life-styles would be possible.

However, since the carrying capacity of an ecosystem cannot be estimated easily ahead of time, one has to rely on a precautionary principle. To contribute to sustainable development at a national and global level, minimizing the load on the environment seems to be a more realistic objective. Each country can thus contribute to a betterment of the global situation. In Sweden, for example, where population is at a rather stable level, the main issue is one of reducing the average load on the environment on a per capita basis. Countries that are comparatively rich, at least in some conventional sense, have a special responsibility to reduce their claims on the assimilative capacity of the global ecosystem.

Returning for a moment to the issue of GNP growth, the relationship between growth in this sense and the load on the environment or environmental deterioration becomes crucial. In his early book, *The Costs of Economic Growth*, Ezra Mishan, a British economist, is critical about "growthmania" and what he calls "the no-choice myth," that is the idea that an economy cannot function satisfactorily without growth in GNP terms (Mishan, 1967). According to Mishan, an economy performing well in GNP terms may perform very poorly in other terms. There are "costs" of economic growth. For a given composition of GNP, similar to that experienced by industrial societies today, growth in GNP is as much a problem as a solution (Söderbaum, 1980), since it increases the extraction of natural resources and the flow of pollution and waste. Kenneth Boulding (1966) and many of his followers, such as Herman Daly and John Cobb (1989) and Robert Goodland (1991), refer to GNP as a measure of "throughput" in an economy. An increased throughput is not a very meaningful idea of progress. Reference to Kenneth Boulding's classic article, "The Economics of the Coming Spaceship Earth," is a good starting point for the reasoning that will follow:

> "... in the spaceman economy, throughput is by no means a desideratum, and is indeed to be regarded as something to be minimized rather than maximized. The essential measure of the success of the economy is not production and consumption at all, but the nature, extent, quality, and complexity of the total capital stock, including in this the state of the human bodies and minds included in the system. In the spaceman economy, what we are primarily concerned with is stock maintenance, and any technological change which results in the maintenance of a given total stock with a lessened throughput (that is, less production and consumption) is clearly a gain. This idea that both production and consumption are bad things rather than good things is very strange to economists, who have been obsessed with the income-flow concepts to the exclusion, almost, of capital stock concepts." (Boulding, 1966, pp. 9–10)

This statement by Boulding indicates that issues of paradigms in economics have to be raised. What are the alternatives to mainstream thinking?

Institutional Economics

The contemporary situation concerning schools of thought or paradigms in economics can be described in more ways than one. I will distinguish between Marxian economics, institutional economics, and neoclassical economics. Within each of these schools, there are some tensions. Among neoclassicals, for example, there are tensions between those who believe in a mixed economy and are less afraid of state regulation and Austrians, who all share a strong belief in market solutions.

Criticism of the neoclassical paradigm often evoke expectations of some other perspective that is similar in its logical structure, for instance, alternative ideas of what the consumer or business company is maximizing. Institutional economics—which can be traced back to American institutionalism in the 19th century, with Thorstein Veblen as one of the prominent figures—does not meet such expectations in all respects. Some heterogeneity prevails also on the institutional side, for instance, in the sense that institutionalists organized in the U.S.-based Association for Evolutionary Economics are not always pointing in the same direction as institutionalists in the European Association for Evolutionary Political Economy. It should, furthermore, be observed that the label *institutional* may not be the best today in discriminating against other approaches. It originally referred to a willingness to include and critically examine the institutional arrangements (organization, rules of the game, and power relationships) of a specific society rather than to regard these conditions as exogeneous and given. Public choice theory is an example of how this

Table 1. Two aspects of holism-reductionism

	Scope	
Degree of aggregation	*Narrow*	*Broad*
One dimensional	I	II
Multidimensional	III	IV

Neoclassical economics can be reductionist or holistic with respect to scope (cf. micro- versus macroeconomics) but tends to be reductionist with respect to approach, for example, degree of aggregation (cf. categories I and II). Institutional economics tends to be holistic in this latter sense (cf. categories III and IV).

interest in institutions is no longer limited to the group of scholars who, for historical reasons, refer to themselves as institutionalists.

Among European institutionalists of recent times, Gunnar Myrdal, winner of the Bank of Sweden's prize in memory of Alfred Nobel, is of particular importance in relation to this essay. Myrdal emphasized the political element in economic theory, and I will here suggest that this awareness about values and ideology in social research is a first characteristic of institutional economics.

A second characteristic of institutional research is interdisciplinarity and holism. The problems faced in our societies are not economic problems, sociological problems, or psychological problems but just problems, and they are all complex and require an open attitude to other disciplines and a willingness to learn and listen. Concerning the holistic ambitions of institutionalism, it should be noted that the terms *reductionism* and *holism* may be used in two different senses (Table 1). They may refer to scope and subject matter, where, for instance, microbiology tends to be reductionist and ecology or ecosystems analysis are holistic. Similarly, neoclassical microeconomics is reductionist as compared with macroeconomics. The same terms may, however, be used to refer to approach or method, where degree of aggregation may be the relevant variable. Highly aggregated, one-dimensional analysis is then an example of reductionism (e.g., monetary cost-benefit analysis, which can be called *monetary reductionism*), whereas multidimensional analysis is referred to as holistic. Institutional economics tends to be holistic in this latter sense, i.e., disaggregation and a search for patterns in multidimensional terms.

A third feature of institutional analysis is its evolutionary, i.e., historical and dynamic character. Institutionalists look for patterns in historical time

(Wilber et al., 1978). Patterns that are specific or unique are not necessarily of less interest than regularly occurring patterns. It is furthermore not regarded as particularly helpful to try to grasp all relevant factors in one mathematical formula, for instance, one equation for the welfare of all members of a society. Rather, open-ended models are preferred where simple calculations in monetary or other terms may enter as parts of a study, that is, represent partial analysis.

A fourth feature is a similarly open-minded attitude in relation to issues of methodology. *Methodological pluralism* (Caldwell, 1982) is a leading principle, with logical positivism regarded as one only of several possibilities. Other approaches, hermeneutics and action research, may serve a complementary purpose.

As the reader may understand, this open-ended view of institutionalism means that the approach has much in common with, and indeed may be difficult to distinguish from, some other perspectives that have been suggested as alternatives or complements to neoclassical economics. I will here refer to these other approaches as "relatives" of institutionalism. I am thinking of socioeconomics (cf. the Society for the Advancement of Socio-Economics), social economics (cf. *Review of Social Economy*), and humanistic economics (cf. the *Human Economy Newsletter*). Parts of ecological economics and interdisciplinary economics can be included among the relatives to institutionalism (cf. *Ecological Economics*, the *Journal of the International Society for Ecological Economics*, and the *Journal of Interdisciplinary Economics*, respectively.) It is clear, finally, that also some "mainly neoclassical" economists, such as Herbert Simon, with his early ideas about bounded rationality (Simon, 1945, 1983) and Amartya Sen's (1987) ideas on ethics and economics come close to the institutional family I am referring to.

The Political Element

As already indicated, Gunnar Myrdal emphasizes the political element in economic theory and analysis:

> Valuations are always with us. Disinterested research there has never been and can never be. Prior to answers there must be questions. There can be no view except from a viewpoint. In the questions raised and viewpoint chosen, valuations are implied. (Myrdal, 1978, pp. 778–779)

Against this background, I will suggest six statements (or sets of statements) concerning the schools of thought mentioned:

1. None of the schools are purely scientific. Each contains various valuational and ideological elements. For this reason Marxists and many institutionalists already speak about their approaches as *political economics*. But this label should rightly be used for all schools. Thus, for instance, socioeconomics represents one category (admittedly a bit heterogeneous) of political economy. (When the label *political economics* is sometimes used by mainstream economists, the focus is generally on subject matter that is seen as "political," for example, institutions, democracy, etc., and not on the ideological coloring of the analysis.)

2. The political element in all kinds of economics is one of the reasons why the idea of one and only one paradigm as being the "correct" one should be abandoned. There have always been and will always be competing schools of thought in economics. One school may gain ground considerably in relation to another between two points in time and schools may lose all their adherents. But the Kuhnian idea of "paradigm shift," that is, one school completely superceding the other, seems to be less relevant for economics and other social sciences than for natural sciences. This point has been made by Alan Randall (1986), a textbook writer in neoclassical environmental economics.

3. Competition between paradigms and, more generally, tensions between different perspectives, play an important and constructive role in research and education. It is fruitful to regard paradigms or perspectives as complementary in relation to some purposes and mutually exclusive in other cases. Therefore, a scholars preference for one school, such as institutional economics, need not imply that this person regards all as wrong with some other school such as neoclassical economics.

4. Our decisions as scholars to rely mainly on one paradigm rather than another are partly political decisions that reflect our personal beliefs and ideologies. Empirical tests along positivistic lines can play a role in challenging, for instance, the economic man idea of neoclassical economics. However, ethical reasoning about the social fruitfulness and dangers of various ideas concerning human motives and human behavior can be of equal importance (cf. Lutz, 1991).

5. Departments of economics are not only places of "scientific" research and education but also political propaganda centers. To the extent that one paradigm dominates the scene at a department (or at several departments of economics in a given country) to the exclusion of other paradigms, the specific ideology or political propaganda built into the paradigm will be more influential. If it—as part of teaching economics—is repeatedly assumed, for instance, that companies maximize monetary profits, then the teacher is obviously not doing much to open the mind of the student to

more holistic, multidimensional thinking or ethical reasoning. It can also be expected that those who are the students of economics at a certain time will later become the actors who are observed, for instance, in studies of a positivistic and alleged value-neutral kind. If these actors point to profits as the one and only goal of business activities, then the explanation may partly lie in the education previously received.

6. From the point of view of democracy, competition between paradigms at specific departments or in a country means a sounder situation than monopoly. Borrowing a bit from Caldwell's "methodological pluralism," "paradigmatic pluralism" can be suggested as a key concept (Söderbaum, 1989). As already indicated, such paradigmatic pluralism also contains some degree of ideological pluralism, using the word *ideology* in a broad sense.

Some of these ideas concerning economic theory in society can be brought together by applying the concepts of supply and demand at the level of economic ideas. It is possible to think of a market for economic theory or theories in a metaphorical sense (Söderbaum, 1991b). The reasons why some groups criticize neoclassical economics and call for a "new" economics, institutional economics, or ecological economics etc. are not purely scientific reasons (whatever that may mean). Conceptual and theoretical aspects are certainly involved but also valuational or political elements. In other words, there is a political and conceptual demand for alternatives to neoclassical theory. Similarly, there may be a considerable political and conceptual demand for parts of conventional economic theory. As already indicated, some actors in society, such as businessmen or politicians, may be very happy with the now dominant school of neoclassical economics because it rationalizes or legitimizes their present modes of thinking and patterns of behavior.

Neoclassical economists (just like institutional economists) at universities have their vested interests in a specific world view and may align themselves with various actors in society who somehow have established a similar world view. Coalitions or networks of a more or less conscious nature may be established (cf. the network idea of markets). This means, among other things, that success for a new paradigm, such as institutional economics (or ecological economics), will be as much a matter of public and political debate and acceptance as one of dialogue among economists and other scholars. For instance, advocates of institutional economics have to articulate a supply of economic theory and can then hope for some response, not only from their colleagues in the social sciences, but also from various groups in society who express a demand for the theory. Just as is the case with normal marketing activities in business, it is a good strategy to listen to the consumer. The suppliers of economic theory can learn from the consumers and modify the products accordingly. It is quite possible that many of the best ideas to reconsider economic theory come from public debate. In that sense, some essential inputs into economic theorizing, that is influence on the supply of social or economic theory, are not exclusively a product of scholarly work in economics departments.

Toward a New Microeconomic Foundation

Environmental problems and other problems have to be dealt with at a micro as well as a macro level. What happens at the macro level with ecosystems or natural resources (or with production and consumption activities) is a matter of the behavior and decisions of a large number of individuals in different roles. A microeconomic frame of reference seems, therefore, to be the obvious starting point for an analysis of these problems. The following components of such a theoretical framework are suggested:

1. The main idea behind economics and economic analysis is one of illuminating specific issues in relation to various categories of actors and interested parties with respect to perceived problems, alternatives of choice, impacts, valuational standpoints, and conflicts of interest. Emphasis is on contribution to public debate and analysis in a democratic society rather than on pointing out optimal solutions. Ideas of correct resource allocation connected with cost-benefit analysis, for instance, are rejected.
2. A more holistic and more complex idea of humans than that of neoclassical economics is recommended. Many roles, activities, and interests are relevant for the individual. The role of being a consumer, for instance, is only one of several possible roles. Neoclassical "economic man" assumptions are replaced by other assumptions.
3. Specific activities or sets of activities connected with individuals or organizations are seen as basic units of analysis. The conventional distinction between consumer and firm, and between production and consumption, is thereby somewhat downplayed.
4. Analysis focusing on specific (sets of) activities is carried out in multidimensional terms, where a distinction is made between monetary and nonmonetary dimensions and between measurement in terms of flows and positions (where position is broadly equivalent to "stocks" in the above citation from Boulding).
5. Articulation of many (rather than one) ideological, ethical, or

valuational standpoints. These valuational standpoints and ideas of progress should be relevant for the actors and interested parties taking part in public debate, negotiations, power games, etc. concerning the specific issue at hand. Conclusions from analysis are seen as conditional in relation to specific valuational standpoints.

6. An idea of decision making as pattern recognition or matching, rather than one-dimensional maximization. For instance, impact profiles of each alternative considered are matched against possible valuational standpoints (to arrive at conditional conclusions) or against the specific valuational or ideological profile of each decision maker, for instance, the politician as part of majority voting.

7. Analysis is often limited to subject matter, for example, the impacts of one land use versus another, but may also include a study of the values and behavior of the actors and interested parties involved, for instance, how they relate to their specific sociocultural, institutional, and physical context. As part of such an approach actors and networks are important units of analysis. Networks represents a way of looking at markets but also at other social relationships.

Some of these points will be further elaborated.

Political-Economic Man

Traditional economic man assumptions are specific. They may be useful for some purposes, for instance, when illustrating the importance of monetary budget constraints for humans as consumers. Even when considering the use of environmental charges as a policy option, economic man assumptions may contribute to understanding and explanation. But many of the assumptions are simplistic and not very realistic (e.g., the assumptions of perfect information and the idea that self-interest is the basis of each individual's maximization). For this reason an analysis that allows for complexity in some respects may prove fruitful.

Many are those who have criticized the reductionist view of human beings that neoclassical economists have used as the basis of their analysis. In his attempt to suggest some other economics, Friedrich Schumacher used the subtitle "Economics as if People Mattered" for his book *Small is Beautiful* (1973). More recently, Amitai Etzioni, has argued in favour of an "I & We paradigm" in *The Moral Dimension. Toward a New Economics* (1988). Etzioni argues that the fact that there is a strong ego in each

Table 2. Symbolic representation of "political economic man", a more holistic and integrated view of an individual's various roles, activities, and interests

Roles		*Activities*		*Interests*	
R1	"Identity"	A1	"Life-style"	I1	"Ideological orientation"
R2		A2		I2	
R3		A3		I3	
•		•		•	
•		•		•	
Rk		Ai		Im	

healthy individual is not enough reason to downplay or exclude the social and ethical aspects of human life. Each individual is part of many groups, "we-contexts", and such relationships involve a number of tensions and ethical issues. Similarly, Amartya Sen, a well-known and mainly neoclassical economist, has argued in favor of a return to an explicit consideration of ethics in economics (1987).

Some writers have referred to a "dual self" and others to a "multiple self" (Elster, 1986) to suggest that there are tensions between various motives and loyalties for each individual. An interest in alternatives to economic man assumptions is also indicated by terms such as Herbert Simon's *administrative man* (emphasizing limits to cognitive capacity, selective perception, search costs, etc.), *cooperative man* (suggesting that man is basically a social being), and "*thoughtful economic man*" (Meeks, 1991; pointing to our abilities to reason and reconsider previous positions, for instance, as part of public debate).

In table 2 it is assumed that for each individual there are a set of relevant roles R 1 to R k, a set of relevant activities, A 1 to A 1, and a set of relevant interests, I 1 to I m. The role R 1 is assumed to be connected with the activity (or set of activities) A 1 and with the interest (or set of interests) I 1. For the individual the total set of roles is somehow integrated parts of an "identity," whereas the total set of activities together form a "life-style," and the total set of interests an "ideological orientation," "valuational orientation," or even a "world view." Identity, life-style, and ideological orientation can then be seen as various aspects of an individual rather than separate categories.

This tendency of neoclassical economics to assume away human values and enjoyment connected with work activities has been criticized by Lester

Thurrow, himself (in my judgement) a "largely neoclassical" economist, as part of an assessment of international trade theory:

> Although it is true . . . that one can show that free trade maximizes consumption, free trade does not necessarily maximize producer's utility. If the French love to be a farmer or see farmers, it may be rational to protect French farmers with tariffs and quotas. What is lost in terms of extra consumption utility is more than gained in extra producer's utility. (Thurrow, 1984, p. 121)

Table 2 also suggests that there is an interdependence between various roles, actives, and interests. Consumer behaviour is influenced by other behavior and vice versa. Consumption activities cannot be isolated from other human activities. Various personality variables, such as identity, life-style and ideological orientation, are of interest in understanding total behavior and partial behavior. The individual strives for some congruence and balance between roles, activities, and interests, and sometimes experiences such a balance but incongruencies and tensions are as much a characteristic of the human experience.

The political economic man suggested also opens up an interest in environmental and other nonprofit organizations. Individuals and organizations no longer exclusively strive for income in monetary terms and a "larger part of the cake," but may also work according to specific ideas of progress in society. Ideology, that is, ideas about means-ends relationships in a broad sense, becomes important. Individuals or actors sharing a similar ideology (such as ecological sustainability) may work together in more or less coordinated and more or less formal networks. Neoclassical public choice theory is built on the simplistic idea of one individual–one interest, for example, the farmer is only a farmer. Allowing for more roles, activities, and interests than one opens up ideological debate and competition in society as another force shaping the future. If actors belonging to a number of different professional categories move ideologically towards ecological sustainability, then the pessimistic prediction of public choice theory (Olson, 1965, 1982) concerning the environment (a large group with very diffused interests is difficult to organize) may prove wrong (Söderbaum, 1991a, 1992).

It is clear that the model of man suggested is complex rather than simple. It is an open-ended rather than closed model in terms of understanding and explanation, and it is open ended rather than closed with respect to valuational or ethical standpoints. In this sense the model breaks with a tradition of rather closed models often formulated in mathematical terms and closed ideas about ethics or valuational rules. I believe that this move, which is compatible with institutional economics as previously defined, represents an important step forward.

Table 3. A four-field classification scheme for variables in economic analysis

	Flow (referring to a period of time)	*Position (referring to a point in time)*
Monetary	I	II
Nonmonetary	III	IV

Analysis and Valuation of Activities

Activities may be private or public. They may be seen as producer activities (production) or consumer activities (consumption), or perhaps some third category of activities. Analysis and valuation may focus on ongoing activities or future activities (projects) being considered as alternatives of choice.

The two aspects, analysis and valuation are of course related. A specific analysis, for instance, estimates of the monetary profitability of an activity, assumes a specific valuational standpoint as the relevant one. In this essay, our interest is not limited to monetary profitability or other monetary analysis. Our valuational standpoint also embraces nonmonetary performance, for instance, ideas about ecological sustainability. This, in turn, calls for a broader analysis than that of estimating present values, internal rate of returns, payoffs, and the like.

The analytic aspect can be discussed in relation to two tables. In Table 3, a distinction is made between impacts that are measured in monetary and nonmonetary terms. Another distinction is made between flows, that is measurement that relates to periods of time and positions, that is, measurement expressed for points in time. Monetary flows (cf. category I in table 3) can be exemplified by GNP. This concept is expressed in monetary terms and refers to a specific period of time, usually a year. The balance sheet of a particular business company at a particular point in time, that is, the end of an accounting period, exemplifies a monetary position (cf. category II). On the nonmonetary side, the growth of a forest in cubic metres in a year is a flow variable (cf. category III), whereas the the stock of wood or timber at a particular point in time is a stock or positional variable (category IV).

Economic analysis is as much an analysis in nonmonetary as in monetary terms. Both nonmonetary flows and positions are relevant. If the objective is to perform well in relation to the environment, however, a focus on changes in nonmonetary positional terms becomes crucial. Are natural resources and ecosystems being degraded from one point in time

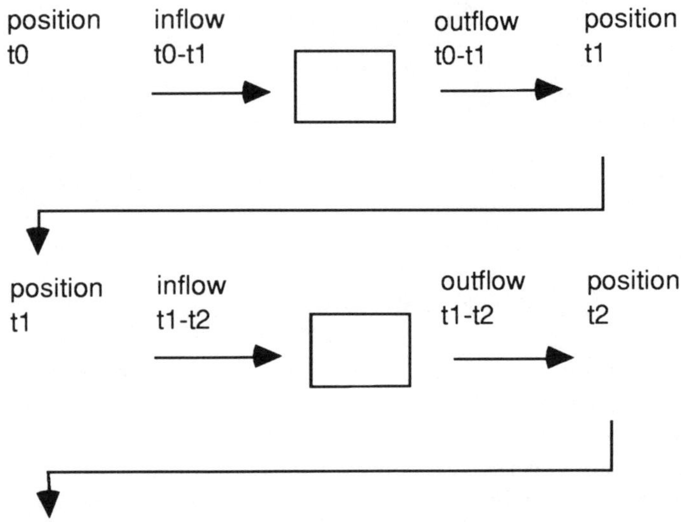

Figure 11.2. Frame of reference for analysis of specific activities in flow and positional terms.

to another? Or are the nonmonetary resource positions improving in some respects?

Pollution is generally measured in flow terms, for example, the discharge of some heavy metal, such as mercury, from a pulp factory into a nearby lake. Reducing the discharges on a yearly basis will always improve the situation as compared with an unchanged level of discharges. But the fact that the level of discharges is reduced to some extent does not necessarily bring forward an improvement in positional terms. The yearly reductions have to be of a certain size for an improvement to occur in the state of the environment.

In Figure 2, the black box refers to a specific activity, such as grain production at a specific farm. For a given time period, the activity can be described by some inflows (or inputs) and some outflows (or outputs). Productivity measures generally focus on some desired outflow (harvest of wheat) in relation to some inflow, such as hectars of land used in wheat production. But, generally, there are many kinds of inflows and many kinds of outflows, and therefore a large number of efficiency or productivity ratios can be constructed.

Figure 2 also indicates that there are a large number of possibly relevant, positive or negative, changes in positional terms between the beginning of a period, t0, and the end of that same period, t1. The end position at t1 becomes the starting position for the period t1–t2. A many-sided idea of efficiency or performance of a given activity then emerges from the analysis suggested in Table 3 and Figure 2. Measuring many inputs (consumption of nonrenewable raw materials, labor time, amount of fertilizer, pesticides, etc.) and many outputs (for instance, kilograms of wheat, leakage of nutrients and pesticides) will mean a better understanding of the activity or process than a more reductionist strategy. The same is true of a many-sided set of indicators for positional changes.

The choice of indicators in flow terms or in positional terms is of course a matter of valuational standpoint and judgments of relevance. Many actors do not want to know about the negative aspects of their activities. Others realize that a reductionist view of efficiency (for instance, money profitability or labor productivity) may involve a long-run degradation in other terms. The judgements of relevance of an actor are related to the sociocultural context, including specific institutional arrangements. As part of a dynamic perspective, specific actors and interest groups use their power and resources to influence the rules of the game in what is seen by them as a favorable direction (Dietz, 1992).

On the meaning of Sustainability

Ideologies expressed in monetary terms, such as GNP growth at the macro level, profitability at the level of firms, and maximum income for individuals (to allow for a large amount of "freedom" in consumption), are well established in large parts of the world. Values and thinking habits of this kind are reinforced by institutional frameworks and are legitimized by neoclassical economics. Other ideologies, such as ecological sustainability, however, are not so well articulated and need further elaboration. The Brundtland commission (World Commission, 1987), for example, defined *sustainability* in a rather unclear way, which permitted various kinds of interpretations. There was some focus on natural resources and equality in relation to future generations but also on economic growth as a way of satisfying the needs of current generations.

Some neoclassical economists tend to speak of sustainable development and interpret this concept in monetary terms. Kal-Göran Mäler, for example, argues as follows:

> The economic development in a specified area (region, nation, the globe) is sustainable if the total stock of resources—human capital, physical reproducible

> capital, environmental resources, exhaustible resources—does not decrease over time.
>
> The basic idea behind this definition is the notion of substitutability between resources. If physical or human capital can be substituted for an environmental resource, then the environmental resource can be exploited in such a way that it is severely reduced if, and only if, the investment in the stock of human and physical capital is such that the total resource base is not reduced. The exploitation of oil reserves may therefore be part of sustainable development, but only if investments in alternative energy sources and in energy conservation are made in such a way that the welfare of future generations is not threatened by the exhaustion of the reserves. For example, the cutting down of forests in order to increase export earnings is consistent with sustainable development only if the whole or parts of the proceeds are invested in other export earning or import reducing activities in order to maintain the welfare of future generations. (Mäler, 1990, p. 240; see also Mäler in Bojö et al., 1990, pp. 13–14)

Mäler's arguments follow traditional neoclassical lines, which can be traced back to Barnett and Morse's (1963) empirical study in 1963 on the substitutability of natural resources. Barnett and Morse found no signs of increased resource scarcity and concluded optimistically that technological development and the price mechanism would be as helpful in the future as they had been in the past. The idea of substitutability in the version suggested by Mäler means essentially that various resources and impacts can be traded against each other in monetary terms. The monetary value of the stock of all resources at future points in time is the main indicator, and nonrenewable resources can be exploited and exhausted if the consequent monetary reduction is compensated for by an increase in the value of some other resource.

The idea of monetary compensation is certainly an attractive one. It legitimizes current exploitation of nonrenewable resources. So, the demand for this kind of theory and ideology may be considerable. The fuzzy aspect of the theory and the difficulties in making it operational in terms of measuring the total stock of all resources meaningfully in monetary terms, or in assessing whether some specific resource degradation has been compensated for by some value increase of the stock, may be regarded as an extra advantage of the theory.

The main weaknesses of the neoclassical approach, as indicated here, relate directly to the previous discussion of the environmental problems faced. Addressing multidimensional problems with a one-dimensional strategy is already somewhat questionable. Ideas of trading and compensation do not fit well with a situation where irreversibility is the normal case rather than an exception. How does one put a price on the use of the

Table 4. A taxonomy of activities

Activities	*Private*	*Public*
Ongoing, individual	I	II
Ongoing, collective	III	IV
New, individual	V	VI
New, collective	VII	VIII

limited assimilative capacity of ecosystems? Or more generally, at what prices should the trading of impacts take place? Reference is made to "correct" prices and "true" costs, and it is sometimes added that all costs should be reflected in the prices (according to the "polluter pays principle"). But current incentive systems are not built on such principles, and ideas of "correct" prices for irreversible degradation of the natural resource base seem a bit impractical, to say the least. In terms of Table 3, the idea of progress proposed by Mäler represents a move from monetary flows (cf. GNP growth) to monetary stocks or positions, that is, from III to IV. Ideologically this is only a modification of the previous view. Contrary to the ideology suggested by Mäler, I prefer a move to an ethics or ideology expressed in nonmonetary terms and a nonmonetary analysis along the lines suggested in Table 3 and Figure 2. As already indicated, such an analysis can focus on ongoing activities that may be either individual or collective, and either private or public (Table 4). Analysis may also be connected with "new" activities, that is, proposals for activities (e.g., changes in life-style, a move from conventional to "ecological" farming practices, or investment projects in industry). Again, such new activities may be either individual or collective, private or public.

Such activities can be scrutinized with respect to immediate nonmonetary impacts and with respect to linkages to other activities that again may perform well or badly in nonmonetary terms. At a broader level, systems of activities, such as transportation systems, energy systems, and so on, have to be evaluated. Present (ongoing) activities can be compared with some considered partly or wholly different set of activities. Disaggregated approaches to evaluation and decision making; such as environmental impact statements (EIS) or positional analysis (Söderbaum, 1987), are here recommended as opposed to aggregated approaches (conventional cost-benefit analysis).

Analysis has to be guided by some values, however. Ideas of sustainability expressed in terms of ethics can be useful. For instance, degradation of the natural resource base within the area where the activity takes place, for instance, a municipality should be avoided, as should degradation of the natural base outside the affected area. In situations with risk for significant negative impacts, a precautionary principle should be obeyed, etc. Focus on the natural resource base in nonmonetary terms is, of course, a way to consider the options of future generations. Making nonmonetary impacts from activities in a specific area A upon activities and living conditions outside A visible is a similar objective.

Strategies for Sustainability

In discussing policy, textbooks in neoclassical environmental economics (e.g., Pearce and Turner, 1990; Tietenberg, 1992) tend to focus on measures at the level of governments. Market intervention of some kind is one possibility, whereas "command-and-control" instruments are another. Generally, the former group of instrument is advocated, whereas the second group is supposed to remind us of planned economies. The authors tend to forget that intervention in markets, such as environmental charges, is also state intervention and that the differences between the two sets of instruments are a matter of degree.

Contrary to the view indicated, it seems, much more fruitful to argue that environmental policy starts at the level of the individual. All roles, activities, and interests of the individual are potentially relevant (cf. Table 2). His or her identity, life-style, and ideological orientation influence the outcome in terms of environmental performance. The possibilities for desired changes have to do with the individual's awareness of environmental problems, knowledge or information about possible impacts, value orientation, world view, and so on (cf. Clark, 1989). Consequently, education and research are as important as, or even more fundamental than, state regulation for the necessary changes to occur. Unfortunately, neoclassical economists tend to regard knowledge and information as perfect and values as given. But if the problem has to do with the dominant world view and ideology in the West, then this part of the issue also has to be considered as a problem.

Not only may individuals have an environmental policy or environmental orientation, the same is true of various collectives other than the state or nation. Specific businesses may have their own environmental policies and may go together to improve their reputation and good will for success in the marketplace or for other reasons. An environmental profile may be suggested by brand names and various systems of environmental control.

Control and intervention is thus not something that exclusively is connected with national or local governments. Specific ecological monitoring systems can be designed for all levels from the individual via organizations, such as businesses, to nations and the global situation (Spellerberg, 1991). At some stage, nonmonetary accounting systems may have a role that is much more important than the now dominating monetary systems, and thinking about economics in nonmonetary resource terms may become as natural as the now dominant reductionist monetary economics.

Feedback from such accounting and other control systems represents opportunities for learning to perform better in environmental and other nonmonetary terms. Self-reliance may prove to be a strategy that outcompetes the current internationalization trend for many commodities (Sachs, 1976, 1984). Rather than maximizing the monetary net value of energy and transportation systems, the transportation work in ton-kilometres has to be totally reduced on a per capita basis. Focusing systematically on both the monetary and nonmonetary impacts is thus suggested as a key to a sustainable future. Such information will make various agents and actors aware of the problems and facilitate the implementation of measures of various kinds (including market intervention according to neoclassical preferences) to protect ecosystems and the human environment. Political economic man and political economic woman have to become conscious about the problems faced and about the possibilities to improve systematically rather than degrade nonmonetary resource positions.

References

Barnett, H.J., and Morse, C. 1963. "Scarcity and Growth: The Economics of Natural Resources Availability." Baltimore, MD: John Hopkins.

Bojö, J., Mäler, K.G., and Unemo, L. 1990. *Environment and Development. An Economic approach*. Dordrecht: Kluwer.

Boulding, K.E. 1966. *The Economics of the Coming Spaceship Earth*. In *Environmental Quality in a Growing Economy*. J. Henry, ed. Baltimore: John Hopkins, pp. 3–14.

Caldwell, B. 1982. *Beyond Positivism. Economic Methodology in the Twentieth Century*. London: Basil Blackwell.

Clark, M.E. 1989. *Ariadne's Thread. The Search for New Modes of Thinking*. New York: St. Martin's Press.

Daly, H.E., and J.B. Cobb, Jr. 1989. *For the Common Good. Redirecting the Economy Toward Community, the Environment and a Sustainable Future*. Boston: Beacon Press.

Dietz, F.J., and J. van der Straaten 1992. Rethinking Environmental Economics:

Missing Links between Economic Theory and Environmental Policy. *Journal of Economic Issues* 26(1): 27–51.

Elster, J. (ed.). 1986. *The Multiple Self*. Cambridge, UK: Cambridge University Press.

Etzioni, A. 1988. *The Moral Dimension. Toward a New Economics*. New York: Free Press.

Goodland, R. 1991. "The Case that the World has Reached Limits. More Precisely that Current Throughput Growth in the Global Economy Cannot be Sustained." In: *Environmentally Sustainable Economic Development: Building on Brundtland*. G. Robert, H. Daly, S. EI Serafy, and B. von Droste, eds. Paris: UNESCO, pp. 15–27.

Heller, W.W. 1972. "Coming to Terms with Growth and the Environment." In: *Energy, Economic Growth, and the Environment*. S.H. Schurr, ed. Baltimore: John Hopkins, pp. 3–29.

Lundvall, B.Å. (ed.). 1992. *National Systems of Innovation—Toward a Theory of Innovation and Interactive Learning*. London: Pinter.

Lutz, M.A. 1991. "Emphasizing the Social. Social Economics and Socio-Economics." *Review of Social Economy* 38(3):303–320.

Mäler, K.G. 1990. "Sustainable Development." In *Sustainable Development, Science and Policy. Bergen 8–12 May. The Conference Report*. Oslo: Norwegian Research Council for Science and the Humanities.

Meeks, G. (ed.). 1991. *Thoughtful Economic Man. Essays on Rationality, Moral Rules & Benevolence*. Cambridge, UK: Cambridge University Press.

Mishan, E.J. 1967. *The Costs of Economic Growth*. Harmondsworth: Penguin Books.

Myrdal, G. 1978. "Institutional Economics." Journal of Economic Issues, 12(4): 771–783.

Nelson, R.R. (ed.). 1993. *National Innovation Systems*. Oxford: Oxford University Press.

Olson, M. 1965. *The Logic of Collective Action. Public Goods and the Theory of Groups*. Cambridge: Harvard University Press.

Olson, M. 1982. *The Rise and Decline of Nations. Economic Growth, Stagflation, and Social Rigidities*. New Haven: Yale University Press.

Pearce, D.W., and Turner, R.K. 1990. *Economics of Natural Resources and the Environment*. Hempstead: Harvester Wheatsheaf.

Randall, A. 1986. "Institutional and Neoclassical Approaches to Environmental Policy." In *Agriculture and the Environment*. T.T. Phiggs, P.R. Crosson, and K.A. Price, eds. The National Center for Food and Agricultural Policy. Annual Policy Review, 1986. Washington D.C.: Resources for the Future, pp. 205–224.

Sachs, I. 1976. "Environment and Styles of Development." In *Outer Limits and Human Needs*. W.H. Matthews, ed. Uppsala: Dag Hammarskjöld Foundation.

Sachs, I. 1984. *The Strategies of Eco-Development*. Ceres. FAO Review on Agriculture and Development, Vol. 17, pp. 17–21.

Schumacher, E.F. 1973. *Small is Beautiful. Economics as if People Mattered*. New York: Harper & Row.

Sen, A. 1987. *On Ethics and Economics*. Oxford: Basic Blackwell.

Simon, H. 1945. *Administrative Behaviour*. New York: Free Press.

Simon, H. 1983. *Reason in Human Affairs*. London: Basic Blackwell.

Solow, R.M. 1957. "Technical Change and the Aggregate Production Function." *Review of Economics and Statistics* 39(40):312–320.

Söderbaum, P. 1980. "Towards a Reconciliation of Economics and Ecology." *European Review of Agricultural Economics* 7(1):55–77.

Söderbaum, P. 1987. "Environmental Management. A Non-Traditional Approach." *Journal of Economic Issues* 21(1):139–165.

Söderbaum, P. 1989. "Paradigms and Environmental Economics." In A. Dubgaard and A. Hjortshöj Nielsen, eds. *Economic aspects of Environmental Regulation in Agriculture* Kiel: Wissenschaftsverlag Vauk, pp. 309–324.

Söderbaum, P. 1991a. "Environmental and Agricultural Issues: What is the Alternative to Public Choice Theory?" In *Issues in Contemporary Economics. Vol. 3. Policy and Development*. P. Dasgupta, ed. Proceedings of the Ninth World Congress of the International Economic Association, Athens, Greece. London: Macmillan, pp. 24–42.

Söderbaum, P. 1991b. "Supply and Demand of Economic Theory." *Methodus Bulletin of the International Network of Economic Method* 5(1):124–128.

Söderbaum, P. 1992. "Neoclassical and Institutional Approaches to Development and the Environment." *Ecological Economics* 5(2):127–144.

Spellerberg, I.F. 1991. *Monitoring Ecological Change*. Cambridge, UK: Cambridge University Press.

Tietenberg, T. 1992. *Environmental and Natural Resource Economics*, 3rd ed. New York: Harper Collins.

Thurrow, L. 1984. *Dangerous Currents*. New York: Vintage Books.

Wilber, C.K., and Harison, R.S. 1978. "The Methodological Basis of Institutional Economics: Pattern Model, Story Telling and Holism." *Journal of Economic Issues* 12(1):61–89.

World Commission on Environment and Development. 1987. *Our Common Future*. Oxford: Oxford University Press.

12 INNOVATIONS, MARKETS AND INSTITUTIONS
An Historical Approach

Lars Magnusson
Göran Marklund

In recent economic history there has been a strong tendency to downplay the importance of the industrialization process as a radical break with the past. Thus even the notion of an "industrial revolution" has been put to question by many scholars such that industrialization as a continuous process has tended to replace the older picture of discontinuity and radical change. For example, newly estimated indicators for the growth achievement of Britain during industrialization seem to suggest that growth was much more sluggish and its effects much less dramatic than once perceived (Crafts, 1985; Williamson, 1987). Further, the discussion concerning the existence of a certain "proto-industrial" stage before the emergence of the real industrial revolution has also tended to stress the longevity of the process. Hence from this discussion has emerged a host of regional studies that suggest industrialization mainly carried further processes of growth and change rooted in older cultural, social, and demographic conditions (Kriedte et al., 1983; Berg et al., 1987; Isacson and Magnusson, 1987; Hudson, 1992). Lastly, in much of the recent "flexible specialization" debate, which has emphasized the vitality of a "craft alternative" to large-scale industrialization (for example, in Piore and Sabel, 1984; Sable and Zeitlin, 1984), there is also stress on the gradual and slow emergence of industrial economies, the emergence of large-scale industry, and the factory as a stylized manifestion of the process of organizational change during this period.

Without doubt this emphasis on industrialization as a gradual and less dramatic process of change has advantages in relation to some of the old simplistic "big spurt" interpretations of industrialization that used to be so common. Thus it is clear that the industrial revolution, to a large extent, really was an uneven process drawn out in time and influenced by regional and other patterns of social contexts and environments. However, it is possible that this recent revision of the industrialization process has gone too much to one extreme. First, as in the model put forward by Piore, Sabel, and Zeitlin, the notion of industrialization as a dynamic process of change affecting both the micro and macro levels has tended to disappear almost totally. According to their view not only can a "craft alternative" be seen as an existing viable alternative to large-scale industrialization over time, they also argue that large-scale forms of industrial production did not win out because of an embodied higher efficiency or productive capacity. Rather, to the extent that this transformation came about, it was caused by forces from "outside": cultural, ideological, political, or preferences on the market that were treated as exogenous. Second, with the justified aim of denouncing previous technological bias in the general explanations of the industrialization process, the "revisionist" view has tended to neglect technology, organizational change, and the role of innovations as important forces behind this process of change. Rather, as we have seen, cultural, regional, and social factors have been put in the forefront of the analysis.

It is our aim here to argue that the industrial revolution and industrialization still must be regarded as processes of dynamic change that during the 19th and 20th century transformed especially the Western socities in a fundamental way. Without doubt they led to dramatic changes in the way products were produced, sold, and consumed, and thus also to the social and institutional nexus within which these activities have been taking place since that time. We also argue that this process of change must be linked to the behavior of individuals acting on bounded rationality within a competitive framework. Thus above all we need a theory of economic change that can link such behavior on the micro level to macro processes of growth, technical change, and innovation. In the rest of this paper we will argue that the neoclassical interpretation of industrial growth and transformation as well as the factors that shape this process are unable to provide a framework for such a discussion. Rather, we believe that an institutional and Neo-Schumpeterian interpretation provides a much more realistic point of departure. In this paper we will discuss the implications of this view for the historical question we raised regarding the transition to industrial structures and their dynamic transformations during the 19th and 20th century.

Neo-classical Growth Theory

Without doubt most of the neoclassical theories of growth—from Marshall and Cassel to Harrod and Solow—point to the importance of innovations and technology (Heertje, 1977). However, traditional, neoclassical economic theory has without doubt, severe limits when applied to the analysis of innovations, as well as technological development as a whole. Obviously, this is due to the very hard core of the neoclassical theory.

First, with regard to technological development, it is very limiting for a theory, like the neoclassical one, to start out from a rationality assumption implying that the actors maximize some kind of preference functions. The obvious problem with this assumption is that if lacking the actual, if existing, preference function, it is really very hard to use this assumption in any real analytical situation. In addition, a fundamental problem is denying neoclassical theory that institutional and other nonmarket variables are active analytical categories molding the behavior of the actors.

Second, a very severe limitation inherent in the neoclassical theory is the fundamentally static character of the theoretical structure. When analyzing a dynamic phenomenon such as industrial change, including technological and organizational innovations, this fact takes away much of the analytical power of the theory. It is clearly the case that the dynamic competition mechanisms works quite differently than the static mechanisms. While in the static situation the price mechanism is very important, questions of technical and organizational change become most important with a longer time horizon. This fact makes the so—called radical uncertainty, characterizing longer term decisions, a very demanding problem for economic agents. For short-term purposes it can sometimes be appropriate, as in neoclassical theory, to start the analysis with the assumption of reasonably equal agents competing on reasonably equal grounds. This, however, is not at all appropriate when analyzing dynamic processes. Instead, it is more appropriate to see temporary monopoly situations as a natural point of departure, as in approaches founded on Schumpeter's view of capitalist development (Schumpeter, 1934).

In order to gain such monopoly positions, strategical factors such as property rights over technological innovations, internal organizational efficiency, control over markets, and market processes, etc., play crucial roles for entrepreneurs who seek to expand their businesses. Our aim here, in addition to providing a theoretical framework for discussing this problem, is to give some stylized historical illustrations emphasizing this important point.

Firms and Innovations

Economic historians, who are always occupied with dynamic processes in some sense, have of course always been concerned with the explanations behind the coming into existence industry as well as of industrial change and development. As the importance of technical change in such processes has long been recognized, it should come as no surprise that technological factors have come to play a crucial role in many economic historical explanations of capitalist development. However, these explanations have never really come to grips with the inner logic of either dynamic processes as such nor the role of technology in such processes, as they have been poorly equipped theoretically for such elaborations and have been hardly helped, or probably have even been mislead, by the neoclassical view of technology and technical change. The recognition of the importance of technical development in dynamic processes has, however, lead economic historians to try to explain technical change as such. Two important examples of economic historical explanations of technical change and the causes of technological development shall be examined here. Both could be said to be fundamentally neoclassical, or compatible with neoclassical theory. The first is the demand-pull theory, whose most familiar proponent is J. Schmookler (1966). Another influential writer taking a similar view is D. Landes (1976). A third major theory is the property rights approach of Douglass C. North (1981, 1990), who tried to ameliorate neoclassical theory by complementing it with an analysis of institutional and structural change.

Landes explained the technical development in Western Europe primarily by reference to growth of the market. However, we find this explanation much too simple and thus we feel it explains in the real sense of this word, very little. Implicit in such an explanation is, according to Dosi (1989, p. 9) ". . . . that there generally exists a possibility of knowing a priori (before the invention process takes place) the direction in which the market is 'pulling' the inventing activity of producers, and furthermore that an important part of the 'signalling process' operates through movements in relative prices and quantities." The demand-pull argument cannot explain the why and when in technological change, and a fundamental reason for this is the almost complete neglect of institutional relationships with bearing upon economic and technological factors. There is first a completely unrealistic theory of the firm and the way it handles questions of technical change. Second, it involves a severe neglect of the inner logic of technology and innovation activities. Third, it disregards many of the institutional structures influencing technical change, such as government policy, culture, unions, and other such organizations. Instead, it seems as if demand-pull theories "explain" technological development in hindsight and not by identifying the inner logic of such developments or the key variables in the institutional setting concerning specific technological change. The result is a black-box view of technical change as well as of the internal logic of firms. The credibility that, despite this, is lended to this explanation is probably due primarily to two factors: First, it is compatible with the production function view in neoclassical theory. According to this view a change in demand should change relative prices, and thus the cost structure for the firms, which in consequence could be seen as an incentive to innovate. However, one could say that this is only one example of a not seldom repeated tendency in economics to prefer the map to empirical "facts." Second, seen from the perspective of hindsight, it is easy to ascribe demand as a central force. This is because the focus is on technical change that has actually taken place, and thus, by definition, all technical "improvements" have found their demands. Thus, the demand-pull explanation has an air of "technological anachronism" over.

In the property rights approach of Douglass C. North, institutional factors are taken into account seriously, and this is clearly a step in the right direction. This approach focuses explicitly on the incentives to innovate. This is done by viewing institutional factors, such as the state, as merely "structure" or rule-makers in the game, and it is primarily as rule-markers they influence innovative activities. However, while the recognition of institutional factors as creators of incentive structures in the sense given here is important, it is not the whole story of the role of institutions. One important departure from this view is the recognition that institutions are not merely constraints on a fundamental economic mechanism, which is basically "effective," but that they take part in the actual shaping of the mechanism itself (Hodgson, 1988, ch. 6). It should be necessary to take account of such factors as the cultural and social shaping and molding of behaviors. Likewise, it is not possible to analyze technical change and the effects of different incentive structures without a proper understanding of firms as organizations as well as of the special character of technology and technological activity.

In our view a institutional theory about innovations and technical change should start with the assumption that innovations are implemented and diffused differently depending on within which economic-institutional forms of organization they are taking place. Also the speed of these processes should be influenced by the same factors. Such forms of organization also contribute to the determination of the boundaries within which choices of technology may take place. It is important to recognize that influential factors in this case are such things as culturally molded ideas and habits, ideologies, etc. These forms of organizations could be viewed on different levels of aggregation. When viewed on a national level, we talk about different national innovation systems.

However, we share the basic recognition of North that property rights, or rather factors governing private appropriability, are central to an understanding of technical change as well as broader processes of economic growth. It is this part of our approach to innovations that we will discuss here. A fundamental flaw in neoclassical theory is the lack of a realistic theory of the firm. While the firm is a key actor in capitalist economies, a proper understanding of its behavior is necessary for real comprehension of such processes. When analyzing dynamics the most fundamental shortcoming of neoclassical theory is the basically static view of the firm and its actions. To comprehend these matters, we have to be equipped with an understanding of the firm as a dynamic "organism." This includes comprehension of both the firm's relations to a dynamic environment and its own inner dynamic.

There still have some distance to travel to reach "complete" evolutionary theory of the firm, but we would like to propose that the Nelson and Winter's (NW) approach (1982) be taken as the point of departure for this goal. In NW, as of course in neoclassical theory, it is taken for granted that the firm's basic aim is profit. However, the economy is dynamic and not static in character. Dynamic processes in the economy are inherently uncertain with regard to outcome. This makes it virtually impossible for the firm to approach decision making with the intention of maximizing some static function. The problem of uncertainty is even more obvious when considering decisions regarding technical change. In these cases the uncertainty is "radical" in the sense that even the variables of the problem could not be specified with any certainty in advance, let alone the parameters of these uncertain variables (Hodgson, 1988, p. 203).

In NW the firms' behavior contains different kinds of "routines," such that certain routines are "search routines," governing the change and modifications of the "operational" characteristics of the firm. The basic reason for the firms' reliance on routines is the fundamental uncertainty characterizing the firms' decisions. NW sees the routines as having the same function for the firm as do genes for biological organisms. However, apart from these routines, NW also acknowledges "stochastic" elements in decision making, as well as in explaining the outcome of these decisions.

This way of viewing the behavior of the firm has certain important implications for dynamic change in firms, whether questions of technology or organizational matters. The routines make these firm decisions partly "bounded" by the existing structure and techniques within the firm. Hence, there are no clear boundaries between different activities within a firm. This is clearly and importantly a fundamental difference from neoclassical theory, where there is a sharp line drawn between the presently used technique in a firm and decisions regarding the technique to be in the future. Moreover, organizational matters do not hardly find a place in any "pure" variation of neoclassical theory.

The NW view of the capitalistic firm is basically Schumpeterian in character, which, implies a focus on the incentives behind innovations. These are seen as fundamentally determined by the opportunities, or more exactly, the subjective perceptions of such opportunities, to gain profits that are temporarily monopolistic. A theoretical approach, which takes the NW analysis further regarding dynamical change, is that of Giovanni Dosi. While sharing the NW view of the firm, Dosi goes further in emphasizing the importance of private appropriability in innovative work. According to Dosi, private appropriability and technological opportunities are the two most fundamental conditions for innovative activity of capitalistic firms (Dosi, 1984, p. 88). However, while Dosi applied this view explicitly to technical change, we propose a broader approach in which organizational matters are also incorporated in the dynamics of firms.

Here we confine the analysis to the incentives in innovative activities, broadly understood. We want to illuminate questions of private appropriation of profit opportunities produced by innovations. To do this, however, we have to take a somewhat closer look at knowledge or information, which is actually the output of innovations, as a special kind of product and commodity in the economy.

It should be clear that innovative activity is a "prototypical economic activity" in that it is a process of production, which ". . . .requires the commitment of resources to the production of information" (Rosegger, 1985, p. 8). However, the product of this process, that is, information, is anything but typical of the "normal" exchanging of commodities in the economy and ". . . cannot be the object of pure exchange" (Hodgson, 1988, p. 163). Instead, there is an inherent tendency of innovations to become "public goods." Basically, the problem with the innovation as a product is one of readily defining it in "physical" terms and thereby rendering the immediate appropriation and control of the object possible.

While transactions of physical commodities in the economy usually are well organized in an often almost "routinized" manner, this is not the case with knowledge. In "normal" transactions property rights to a commodity become protected by law immediately after the transaction has taken place, but because of the inherent volatility of information, this cannot be the case with knowledge. While the ways of appropriating profits are basically different between the two types of commodities, a fundamental feature is common between them: It takes some kind of private appropriation of the commodities to be able to make any profits, but while this process is quite straightforward and direct in the first case, it poses special problems in the second. Thus, a fundamental feature of knowledge is the inherent difficulty in appropriating property rights to this information.

Fundamentally, the dynamic competition in the economy is a struggle to appropriate "extranormal" profits or "temporary" monopoly profits. One important way to do this is through innovation. However, since one competes to be the first to innovate, it becomes, after the innovation has come into effect, a competition for the 'extranormal" profit margin generated by the innovation. Due to the special character of innovations as a commodity, this competition can never reach a final and complete solution, which is, at least in some sense, the case with the private appropriation of "other" commodities. Instead, this competition in itself undermines the very basis for the struggle, that is, the "extranormal" profit margin produced by the innovation. This is due to the fact that it is impossible for anybody, over time, to appropriate the full benefits of the innovation. As time passes the information content of the innovation will, despite every effort to the contrary, be revealed and diffused to ever more competitors. Moreover, the new and "better" innovations will eventually undermine the value of the first one. In addition to these processes, there are others, that could take part in this "value-undermining" process, such as broader structural changes in the economy, for example, changes in consumers' tastes. We can conclude here that central to the firms' striving for profits should be appropriation/control of the information content of innovations, which thus should be seen as an important determinant of firm behavior.

The purpose of the rest of this paper is to point out some of the implications of the—admittedly very sketchy—foregoing theoretical discussion for understanding the historical process of industrialization. We argue that the pace and actual shape, to a large degree, is determined by the logic of an economic dynamic of the kind outlined above. It is this institutional and dynamic approach we want to apply to the historical record of industrial development in Western Europe since the coming of the industrial revolution.

The Contest for Control

Two decades ago Stephen Marglin (1974) reopened a debate on a classic topic in economic history that at this point in time seemed to suffer from inertia, namely, the causes behind the emergence of factories and centralized production as a consequence and part of the process of the industrial revolution. Thus, posing the question of why a strictly regulated division of labor was introduced within the large output sector, as well as in factories, in many parts of Western Europe just before the emergence of mechanized factories, he emphasized the role of control over the labor force as a main factor. By dividing labor into a number of minuscule operations, the manufacturer was able (1) to pace his workers and increase his exploitation of them and (2) to control the special entrepreneurial skill of combining different resources, work processes, and marketing of the product; for example, putting the product together from potential or actual small-scale competitors (perhaps working with embezzled materials stolen from the manufacturer).

Before Marglin's intervention and the debate that followed, most interpretations of the causes behind the rise of the factory and centralized production had either been of the kind of technological "muscle and engine" explanations emphasizing the introduction of steam technology leading to the rise of indivisibilities, or emphasis of the role of demand in creating a necessity for enlarged units of production. The problem with the first of these is that it is clear from the historical record of industrialization that in many cases that introduction of factorylike production (for example, in textiles on the metal industry) preceded the introduction of machinery to any greater extent, and many of the new machines (for example, the spinning jenny) could be combined with decentralized forms of organization very well, and in some cases led to increased small-scale production. The problem with the market interpretation, on the other hand, was that it did not specify the mechanism that led entrepreneurs to introduce centralized production when demand increased. Why not enlarge the circle of independent producers and continue business on an output basis instead (Magnusson, 1990, 1994; Berg, 1987; Landes, 1986; Hudson, 1992)?

In the debate following Marglin, an approach such as Oliver Williamson's transaction—cost analysis (the centralized firm as a means to economize on transaction costs)—as well as other institutional approaches emphasizing the role of control over resources, skills, and knowledge, market channels, innovation processes, etc.—was offered in order to understand industrialization and the rise of centralized production. Williamson's emphasis on the importance of transaction costs seems apparently to provide a solution to the dilemma of the increasing demand interpretation: how transaction costs within a putting out system increase dramatically when demand rises. However, according to the present authors this view only gives a partial explanation of the rise of factory production and does so in too general terms. Obviously the notion of "asset specificity" that Williamson brings is of crucial importance and determines the kind of organizational step taken by an entrepreneur. However, in addition to other important theoretical problems with Williamson's interpretation, must be added the understanding of actual content of the concept of "asset specificity." This concept has to be specified concretely in any given context in order to achieve a realistic view of the real historical process (Williamson, 1985; Hodgson, 1988).

However, the stress put in the recent discussion on the role of control and asset specificity for the emergence of the factory and centralized organizational forms as part of the industrialization process can very easily be adapted to the kind of theoretical framework that we described earlier. According to this point of view, the industrialization process must be regarded as a competitive struggle for control over firm-specific assets (knowledge and skills referring to markets, innovation processes, etc.). In order to yield such firm-specific assets, new organizational modes are introduced that rely on different degrees of centralization. Moreover, insights from such an approach can help us to detect and specify the general links between a more narrow form of organizing the labor process (conventionally defined as the rise of the factory) and a wider form of concentration process, including such assets as we have already spoken of. By further linking this to a Neo-Schumpeterian theory of innovation it might be possible to see how control, in a broad sense (including the introduction of new products, new ways to market goods or organize production)—within a competitive framework—is necessary to reap the Marshallian quasirents that are so crucial for understanding the role of innovative behavior stressed by this approach. Thus we also have a mechanism working on the micro level that is directly connected to the actual behavior of the economic agents.

Thus, according to such an approach we must pay attention to the role of control over certain assets as part and parcel of the industrialization process. The importance of this must be seen in relation to the problems that seem to have dogged preindustrial forms of industry almost everywhere. First, it is clear that the existence of different forms of embezzlement practices were an important part of the introduction of the factory in which the worker's labor could be more easily supervised and controlled. Such practices seem to have been extremely widespread in most putting out forms of industry in Western Europe during the 18th and 19th centuries from the textiles to metal industries. In many cases such customary practices included the actual selling of finished goods by output workers who had made them with materials stolen from their entrepreneurs. In many small communities such "selling on the side" provided serious competition for the manufacturers (Magnusson, 1990). Thus the introduction of a factory—and also, the introduction of a miniscule division of labor, as in Adam Smith's pin-manufacturing example, as Marglin pointed out—was also a way to increase control over the marketing of products.

Secondly, as pointed out by many historians, the undeveloped character of the commercial arrangements was as important a restrictive factor during this period as the lack of sufficient credit institutions. Thus, it became necessary for many small entrepreneurs to develop their own selling organizations; that is, to integrate the selling and productive functions of a firm. The access to certain product markets or markets for the selling of the finished product was in many cases crucial for the success of firm-specific growth. However, at the same time the introduction of their own selling and buying organizations surely led to important organizational changes for the firms: A certain "bigness" was certainly needed to introduce such selling departments and it is also probable that a closer contact with the market created a need for greater speed and flexibility, something that could hardly be provided within an output framework (Chandler, 1977; Magnusson, 1994).

Thirdly, it is clear from many of the examples of successful firm growth that the introduction of innovations in a broad sense was of crucial importance to a business' capacity to grow and develop. However, within the decentralized milieu of most preindustrial production, the private rate of return of innovating activities seems to have been rather low. As long as there was almost free access to knowledge and the general skills of manufacturing a certain set of items, it was almost impossible for a certain craftsman or manufacturer to reap profit from his innovation. Without doubt such feeble property rights over innovations had serious repercussions for growth in general, and more specifically for the climate of as innovation such. Thus, an important aspect of the rise of more centralized production during the transition to industrialization was the attempt to increase control over innovation processes. Within a factory, which to at least some extent relied on a certain division of labor, the generalized knowledge of how to produce a certain good could be made into an asset controlled by the manager or owner. In many expanding industries the appropriation of such a monopoly was crucial in order to expand their markets and to reap an extra surplus that the firm could use for subsequent growth. Innovation, in this sense, includes the introduction of new production methods, new products, new ways to organize selling activities, etc.

In order to understand the dynamic features of the industrialization process a view of the importance of the contest for control—linked to a neo-Schumpeterian theory of the role of innovation for sucessful firm-based growth—is surely necessary. Without doubt the rise of the factory in the early stages of industrialization can only be understood in such a context.

A Technology of Mass Production

Another much debated topic in economic history is the radical transformation of the leading industrial capitalist economies during the second half of the 19th century. This period witnessed the breakthrough of mass production and mass distribution as well as a marked tendency to growth in firm size and monopolistic collaboration of different kinds. This change also partly included the birth of new administrative forms of control and management in industrial enterprises. These implied primarily creating hierarchies and division in the internal structure of firms as well as vertical integration (Chandler, 1980). Another important feature of this process was the crucial role played by technological factors in the transformation of industry. Fairly rapid and radical as this development was, this period could be labeled the second industrial revolution. Economic historians have long been debating the causes of this profound change in the structure of industry during this period. Some have emphasized demand factors (Landes, 1976) and others technological ones, etc. According to Chandler (1977, 1990), the main reason for introducing the large firm was to introduce vertical integration. Thus, organizational change was part and parcel of—and really made possible—the modern large-scale firm. This is also stressed by Oliver Williamson in his work on the importance of transaction costs in the rise of the modern firm and vertical integration (Williamson, 1990). Hence, it is also possible to stress the importance of control over firm-specific assets as the basic competitive mechanism in play. As such we would like to see this as the fundamental force behind the behavior of firms. But, without explaining the important innovations as such during this period, we will take for a fact the fundamental impact of the "major" innovations in the late 19th century. These innovations were both of a process and of an organizational kind. Thus, to some extent the second industrial revolution carried further a logic—the contest for control/appropriation over markets, innovation processes, technically skilled labor, etc.—that was an important aspect of the rise of the factory in the first place. Fundamental consequences of the further development of these previous processes were increased markets and profit opportunities, which, in turn, raised the pace of innovative activities.

The most important technological foundation for the many process innovations was probably the enormous progress made in the ability to produce steel relatively cheaply and in good quality. This technological "steel revolution" made possible, together with the use of steam power, the transportation revolution. Highly interrelated with the process innovations were the main organizational innovations of the period, the changeable parts, the assembly line, and the hierarchization of management as well as the verticalization of firms. This latter kind of innovation could in a way be said to follow on the innovations of the former kind as these innovations opened up unprecedented possibilities for mass distribution and thus mass production. Thus, there should be no doubt about the fundamental role played by innovations, of a process, product, or organizational kind, in the second industrial revolution. However, establishing this does not lead us very far in understanding the fundamental forces in motion in this process. To achieve this we have to turn to the basic behavioral features of the principal economic agents in this process, that is, the industrial enterprises.

In this analysis we will see the different "major" innovations mentioned above as, in a way, constituting the "limits", of both a technological and organizational kind, for profits and profit seeking, and thus for the behavior of firms and the competitive struggle between them. From this point of departure we will see that the above-mentioned strive for control over firm-specific assets in order to reduce transaction costs or appropriate profits from technical or organizational innovations as the fundamental driving force in the development of industry during the second industrial revolution. Seen from this perspective, the "major" innovations of the time could be regarded as, through competition, "forcing" production on a large scale to minimize production costs, which was done by integrating resources, and thereby reducing transaction costs. In turn, this meant large investments in plants and machines, that is, the "optimal plant size" grew considerably, and competition forced the actual achievement of this plant size by the capitalistic firms. However, the competition mechanisms had wider implications than this mainly because the large-scale dimensions of enterprises make them, through competition, much more sensitive to production costs of various kinds, on the one hand, and output-market realities on the other. Accordingly, there are strong incentives to lower costs by way of seizing control of all sources of transaction costs, be it financial sources, input goods, or output markets. Thus, this desire of firms resulted not only in vertical integration on the input side, but also in efforts to control output markets. Thus, this process of struggle for control could be seen basically as a struggle for the Marshallian quasirents made possible by technological progress. Seen from a Schumpeterian perspective, the competitive struggle concerned the appropriation of the "temporary" monopoly profits produced by the above-mentioned "major" innovations, including new forms of organization.

However, relatively soon competition reached its limits. While, being a competitive struggle insofar as cost-minimizing measures were taken, whether rationalizations or minimization of transaction costs by way of integration, a right-out competition in output markets would have been disastrous for many enterprises. Such competition would have led to a tendency for price and production costs to coincide, which would have left huge investments unpaid, which, in turn, would have forced some firms out of business. However, as the size of enterprises involved in this competition had grown, and thus the in actual numbers were relatively small, it had become possible to come to terms with such disastrous competition through collaboration with regard to output markets. This, we suggest, is what basically took place during the second industrial revolution, and as such it is a fundamental feature of modern capitalism. Concerning the Schumpeterian theory, this means that the first line in this competitive struggle for appropriation of "temporary" monopoly profits caused by innovations basically worked its way through the economic system. However, the other tendency, the ultimate dispersion of these profit margins, was effectively stopped or much delayed by noncompetitive, collaborative actions taken by the actors involved.

Much simplified as is this overview of the "forces" involved in the process, it should only be pointed out that the actual paths taken to seize control over financial capital, input markets, output markets, etc. differed between countries, industries, etc. However, we believe that the underlying forces were basically the same everywhere and that they ultimately made their way regardless of differing environmental factors. It is clear that they led to fundamental changes in the way production and selling were arranged.

Control and Appropriation in the Postwar Economy

The postwar period has brought an unprecedented growth of wealth to the industrial capitalist world and could be labeled the third industrial revolution. For industry this period has been characterized by a general, and continued, growth in the size of firms, a steady growth of the internationalization of markets, a much larger role of technology in firms' activities, together with an ever growing "scientification" of technological knowledge and a generally growing importance of government involvement, direct and indirect, in economic life, including industry.

Again, technical progress, in a wide sense of the term, that is, including change in industrial organization, could be seen as a prime mover in development (Dosi, 1984, p. 4). The postwar period has witnessed a large number of technological innovations of major as well as of minor kinds. Prominent technological areas in the postwar period have been electronics and chemistry, etc. The technology used has in most industries become ever more dependent on scientific knowledge. Accordingly, the need for sophisticated technological knowledge as a device for profit appropriation has grown considerably during the period. Thus, firm-specific assets in the form of such technological knowledge and skills have become a primary competition device in almost every industry. This is why most enterprise, above some minimum size have some kind of R&D function. Technological knowledge or information has, in fact, in many industries become the most important firm asset. Consequently, the technological knowledge and skills in firms have in many cases become the most important "capital investment." While the importance of technological knowledge certainly is all but a new feature of capitalism, the generality and degree of importance this has come to play during the postwar period surely is something new. In other words, it could be said that the relative importance of transaction costs involved in appropriating technological knowledge and skills has risen considerably for industrial enterprises during the postwar period.

The continued tendency of firm-size growth can still be partly explained in terms of transaction costs. Here we would like to emphasize two forces behind this tendency: first, the steadily growing output and input markets, as concerns machinery and financial capital, due to the continued internationalization of economic flows during the postwar period: second, the continually growing need for sophisticated technological knowledge and skills, which in many cases demanded huge financial resources. Thus, the greater internationalization of the industrial competitive arena has, through competitive mechanisms, "forced" ever greater savings of transaction costs, which in many cases mean integration, or control, of the sources of such costs. The technological development has, generally speaking, caused transaction costs for technological knowledge to rise to the extent that it is practically impossible to "buy" such knowledge in its entirety in any marketlike way. Instead, the ever-growing need for technological knowledge and skills has, through competition, "forced" industrial enterprises to integrate ever greater resources of this "human" or informational kind. Clearly, this should have put pressure on firms to grow in order to be able to free resources for this growing "overhead" in the enterprise. At the same time the relative "effectiveness" of this "overhead" should have made a decisive difference between firms and thus should have caused differences in relative growth between them. Thus, from one angle it could be concluded that the competitive "force" behind big R&D departments is actually that the technological knowledge stored and produced in such departments is a competitive "necessity" for the appropriation of part of the "temporary" monopoly profits generated by "major" innovations.

Another important feature of postwar capitalism is the much larger government involvement in industrial matters than previously seen. The role of government in industrial economies and societies at large has constantly been growing in general and in many different areas. However, the governmental role in industry has a momentum of its own, and this has been especially the case during the postwar years. In this period the role of government has changed from being merely indirect to one of direct influence on industrial behavior: From a role of merely a "rule-maker," with an often unintended influence on industry, the government has become a more important actor in these systems, primarily by way of its explicit policy measures to influence industrial performance, but also through the growing importance of the unintended effects of its policy on the performance of industry. While this is a general tendency, it should also be recognized that there are major differences between countries with regard to the ways governments actually interact with and influence industry. While it should be recognized that this development has been gradual since the late 19th century, we argue that the direct and conscious government involvement in industry, to a very large degree, is a postwar phenomenon for most industrialized countries.

A special feature of this more general development is the growing importance of government involvement, directly and indirectly, in innovative activities performed by private firms. It should be clear that, with regard to private appropriation and property rights in innovations this development indicates something qualitatively new. The government has, of course, always had a central role in creating and deciding the property rights structure, but mostly as merely a "rule-maker" and a "judge" between private firms and private interests. In this role the government policy could influence industry and industrial behavior mostly in an indirect fashion, presumably working its way by and through the "market forces." However, the change to more direct public involvement in industry and innovative activities has brought about a clear change in the role of government in this respect. Now, the government influence on property rights structures has direct implications for industry and industrial behavior in manner that is different than before. This is the case whether or not the measures actually taken in this respect are intended and explicit.

From this it should be clear that government and government policy should be an important factor in explaining the evolving appropriation patterns in postwar capitalism. Our suggestion, following Dosi, is that more or less direct government involvement in innovative activities affects the incentives facing the agents in three important and related ways: (1) by affecting the degree of private appropriability of the benefits of innovation, (2) by affecting the cost and profitability of innovation, and (3) by affecting the intensity of competitive threats (Dosi, 1988, p. 139), which, in certain cases, should be very important in shaping "... the strategies and the managerial outlooks ..." of firms (Dosi, 1988, p. 141). It should be clear that these means of influencing innovative incentives are closely interrelated. This is because the important question for the innovator, that is, the firm, is what the profit opportunities are, and all these factors influence these opportunities, although in different ways. It is actually through the influence on profit opportunities that these factors shape the behavior of agents. We suggest that government policy towards industry, especially inasmuch as this influences appropriation patterns, should be a major factor in explaining the ways different national innovation systems work. Thus, government interaction with big industry should be one key variable explaining the performance of different national systems.

We believe that the generally growing role of government in industrial activities could be partly explained by the internationalization of markets and the general growth of firms. Because these two interrelated developments have brought with them government understanding of the considerable importance of big enterprises in national economies and the understanding that these enterprises have to compete in an international arena, to a great extent, by virtue of technological knowledge. Thus, there has developed what could be called a technological competition between countries, or national innovation systems, and the role of government has steadily grown in this arena.

Conclusions

On this – sketchy historical illustration we have tried to show the relevance of applying an institutional and Neo-Schumpeterian approach to the industrialization process. Thus we have particulary emphasized the role of innovation as a main factor in the successive development of the main stages of industrial change—the first, second, and third industrial revolution. However, at the same time we have stressed the importance of the capitalistic struggle for control over input assets, such as innovations, market channels, etc., as a dynamic logic affecting the actual behavior of the principal agents—the firms. Thus, as we argued, they were able to reap a quasirent that served as an incentive for others to take part in the competitive struggle. In this paper we have thus stressed the importance of a dynamic that links the behavior of agents on the micro level to technological change, markets, the rise of new organizational forms, etc. on the macro level.

References

Berg, M. 1987. "Will the Real Bosses Please Stand Up: Marglin and Landes on the Origins of Capitalist Hierarchy." *Warwick Economic Research Papers*, 305.

Berg, M., Hudson, P., and Sonenscher, M. (eds.). 1984. *Manufacture in Town and Country Before the Factory*. Cambridge: Cambridge University Press.

Chandler, A. 1977. *The Visible Hand*. Cambridge: Harvard University Press.

Chandler, A., and Daems, H. (eds). 1980. *Managerial Hierarchies*. Cambridge: Cambridge University Press.

Chandler, A. 1990. Scale and Scope. Cambridge: Cambridge University Press.

Crafts, N. 1985. *British Economic Growth During the Industrial Revolution*. Oxford: Oxford University Press.

Dosi, G. 1984. *Technical Change and Industrial Transformation*. London: MacMillan.

Dosi, G. 1988. "Institutions and Markets in a Dynamic World." *The Manchester School* 56:2.

Heertje, A. 1977. *Economics and Technical Change*. London: Weidenfeld & Nicholson.

Hodgson, G. 1988. *Economics and Institutions*. Cambridge, UK: Polity Press.

Hudson, P. 1992. *The Industrial Revolution*. London: Edward Arnold.

Isacson, M., and Magnusson, L. 1987. *Proto-Industrialisation in Scandinavia*. Leamington Spa: Berg.

Kriedte, P., Medick, H., and Schlumbohm, J. 1983. *Industrialisation before Industrialisation*. Cambridge, UK: Cambridge University Press.

Landes, D. 1976. *The Unbound Prometheus*. Cambridge: Cambridge University Press.

Landes, D. 1986. "What Do Bosses Really Do." *Journal of Economic History* 46:3.

Magnusson, L. 1990. "From Verlag to Factory: Embezzlement, Theft, Secret Trading and the Contest for Control." In Gustafsson, B. (ed.). *Power and Economic Institutions. Reinterpretations in Economic History*. London: Edward Elgar, pp. 195–222.

Magnusson, L. 1994. *The Contest for Control: Metal Industries in Transition 1800–1920*. Oxford: Berg Publishers.

Marglin, S. 1974. "What Do Bosses Do?" *Review of Radical Political Economy* 6:2.

Nelson, R., and Winter, S. 1982. *An Evolutionary Theory of Economic Change*. Cambridge: Belknap.

North, D.C. 1981. *Structure and Change in Economic History*. New York: Norton.

North, D.C. 1990. *Institutions, Institutional Change and Economic Performance*. Cambridge: Cambridge University Press.

Piore, M., and Sabel, C. 1984. *The Second Industrial Divide*. New York: Basic Backs.

Rosegger, G. 1985. *The Economics of Production and Innovation*. Oxford: Oxford University Press.

Sabel, C., Zeitilin, J. 1984. "Historical Alternatives to Mass Production: Politics, Markets and Technology in Nineteenth Century Industrialisation." *Past & Present*, 108.

Schmookler, J. 1966. *Invention and Economic Growth*. Cambridge: Cambridge University Press.

Schumpeter, J.A. 1934. *The Theory of Economic Development*. Cambridge: Cambridge University Press.

Williamson, J.G. 1987. "Debating the British Industrial Revolution." *Explorations in Economic History* 24.

Williamson, O. 1985. *The Economic Institutions of Capitalism: Firms, Markets, Relational Contracting*. New York: The Free Press.

Contributing Authors

Kurt Dopfer
Institute of Economics
Sandrainstrasse 21
CH-9010 St. Gallen
Switzerland

Giovanni Dosi, Franco Malerba, and Luigi Orsenigo
ASSI
Corso di Porta Romana 57
20122 Milano Italy

Gunnar Eliasson
IUI Box 5501
114 85 Stockholm
Sweden

Arnold Heertje
Laegieskampweg 17
1412 ER Naardan
The Netherlands

Michael Hutter
Lehretuhl fur Theorie der Wirtschaft
Wirtschaftswissanschaftliche Fakultät
5810 Witten-Rudinghausen
Germany

Richard Langlois and Michael Ewerett Department of Economics
The College of Liberal Arts and Sciences

Box U-63 Room 328
341 Mansfield Road
Storrs, CT 06269-1063
USA

William Lazonick
12 Newport Road
Cambridge MA 02140
USA

Lare Magnusson
Department of Economic History
Box 513
751 20 Uppsala
Sweden

Göran Marklund
Department of Economic History
Box 513
751 20 Uppsala
Sweden

Richard Nelson
Columbia University
School of International and Public Affairs
Public Policy Research Centre
420 West 118th Street
New York, NY 10027
USA

Yngve Ramstad
University of Rhode Island
College of Arts and Sciences
Economics Department
Kingston, RI 02881
USA

Peter Söderbaum
Department of Economics
The Swedish University of Agricultural Science
Box 7013
750 07 Uppsala
Sweden

Index